RECOVERING
SELF-EVIDENT TRUTHS

RECOVERING
SELF-EVIDENT TRUTHS

Catholic Perspectives on American Law

Edited by

MICHAEL A. SCAPERLANDA

and

TERESA STANTON COLLETT

The Catholic University of America Press
Washington, D.C.

The paper used in this publication meets the minimum requirements of American
National Standards for Information Science—Permanence of Paper for Printed
Library materials, ANSI Z39.48-1984.
∞

LIBRARY OF CONGRESS CATALOGING-IN-PUBLICATION DATA
Recovering self-evident truths : Catholic perspectives on American law /
edited by Michael A. Scaperlanda and Teresa Stanton Collett.
p. cm.
Includes bibliographical references and index.
ISBN-13: 978-0-8132-1482-5 (pbk. : alk. paper)
ISBN-10: 0-8132-1482-3 (pbk. : alk. paper)
1. Law—United States. 2. Religion and law—United States.
3. Christianity and justice—Catholic Church. 4. Catholic Church—Influence.
I. Scaperlanda, Michael A. II. Collett, Teresa S., 1956– III. Title.
KF358.R43 2007
349.73—dc22
2006014951

In Memory of Our Beloved Friend and Colleague

David Orgon Coolidge (1956–2002)

CONTENTS

FOREWORD

The blow the Second World War dealt to humane ideals and values was so great that when it ended world leaders and their peoples were ready to declare: "This shall never happen again." In the new start that was made then, a fundamental legal structure was decided upon on the basis of "responsibility before God."[1] It stated the connection of law and politics with the great imperatives of biblical facts.

Sixty years later the hopes of that postwar moment seem to have evaporated in face of a moral crisis of humanity, a crisis taking new and desperate forms. In the aftermath of the Enlightenment, an erosion of religious faith has precipitated the separation of law and politics from metaphysical concepts in the liberal democracies. In these democracies, which have become the world political norm, religion is kept outside rational discourse. Arguably, this is not what the founders of the United States Constitution had in mind; nor probably did they envisage the taking over of ultimate political power by the Supreme Court.

According to the justices, the rule of law today requires, at most, only that the courts allow some space in which religion can operate as worship. There is less and less space for moral reasoning, and prescriptions for a fulfilled human existence are kept out of discourse on law and public policy. Contemporary legal thought, born of modernist and postmodernist philosophies, is at odds with much Catholic teaching.

To this situation, the present volume brings a challenge that is healthy both for the state of law in the United States and for Catholic jurists. It is important that these reflections are often rooted in the teaching of Pope John Paul II, who put radical questions to many assumptions of current secular legal thought and practice and delineated the boundaries of authentic Catholic legal scholarship. This legal theory is deepened and anchored by the exposition of a Chris-

---

1. Joseph Cardinal Ratzinger, *Truth and Tolerance: Christian Belief and World Religions,* trans. Henry Taylor (San Francisco: Ignatius Press, 2004), 140.

tian anthropology. The nature of the human person is basic to Catholic perspectives on American law and the place of religious faith in public discourse.
Law and spirit, conscience and positive legislation, belong together. A Catholic anthropology elicits the values of freedom, solidarity, subsidiarity, and the
common good, which should equip Catholic legal thought for a dialogue with
secular disciplines and secular culture by opening up a space of truth in what
is common to all.

The contributions in this volume turn to the task of working out how principles derived from Catholic teaching apply to concrete situations of contemporary American culture. Applications of principles are always more open to
debate and less certain than the pure enunciations of those principles, and it
is likely that these contributions will be critiqued in turn by those who believe
the principles should yield different results. And yet for all their lack of certainty and openness to development, such applications are an invaluable contribution to the project of inculturating Gospel values into particular concrete expressions. Without such attempts at determining proper applications, even the
most robust and fully developed principles are a dead letter.

These selections do not pretend to present a comprehensive Catholic approach to the full universe of legal issues. Rather the authors employ diverse
methods to advance legal scholarship by reflecting on current issues in light of
various aspects of the Catholic intellectual tradition. The reader will find Catholic teaching used to critique current legal doctrine, to propose new avenues
of reflection, to shine light on neglected implications of legal doctrines, and to
raise new questions in legal debates.

Some authors offer practical advice to lawyers in light of Catholic teaching,
while others trace current legal doctrines back to Catholic theological roots in
order to better explain seeming inconsistencies. Principles derived from Catholic teaching are used as starting points, as measuring lines, as correctives to
distorted notions in law and policy debates. Section three takes these principles into the sphere of particularly American political and legal theory, with
one contribution offering a critique and praising, in some measure, the foundations of political liberalism. A second contribution revisits one of the most
important legal debates in the twentieth century, over the proper role of morality in the law. With these foundations, the last section turns to more particular
legal problems.

Most notable is the breadth of topics covered in the final section. Rather
than focus on contributions from only one area of the law, as is most common

in legal anthologies, we hear from scholars working in a wide variety of areas of legal specialization. Like a well-rounded curriculum, this collection offers reflections from scholars working on problems presented in the law of torts, contracts, criminal defense, property, immigration law, labor law, family law, and international human rights. This breadth reflects a key aspect of Catholicism—its universality and centrality to all areas of human life. It should be noted that this volume has very little to say about the highly contentious issues usually presented under the heading of the "culture wars." While those subjects are exceptionally important to a well-ordered society, the Catholic legal tradition has the potential to be vastly more creative and productive of a fully rounded just social order, as these scholars demonstrate.

What emerges from these chapters is akin to a snapshot in time, demonstrating how a community of scholars, each working in his or her own sphere, is attempting to work out the implications of a set of principles that is too often neglected in legal scholarship. Or, better still, what emerges is an effort to craft a set of notes that might be used to compose a symphony, one that expresses a society in tune with the fullest truth of the dignity of the human person.

Very few of the Constitution's framers who confidently pledged their lives and sacred honor to a defense of the "self-evident truths" that define our nation's ideals were Catholics. The entry of large numbers of Catholics into the legal profession in the United States is a relatively recent phenomenon. Much has been made of the fact that a majority of Justices on the United States Supreme Court are now Catholic, and Catholics are well represented in all branches of government, at both the state and the national level. What remains to be seen is whether the entry of Catholics in such numbers will mute their potentially distinctive contributions. The present volume offers hope that a vital and engaged Catholic community of legal scholars will meet the challenge passed onto us by the framers and hand on an enriched legacy of reflections on those self-evident truths to future generations.

The book ends with the demanding question (directed primarily to Catholic readers) of whether there can be an effective contribution to American jurisprudence from a Catholic perspective until there is again clarity about Catholic ways of living and thinking, and, as Pope John Paul II says, "faith becomes culture," in which to nurture that perspective.

Francis Cardinal George, O.M.I.
Archbishop of Chicago

ACKNOWLEDGMENTS

The insight, critique, support, and cooperation of many individuals and institutions have brought this book to its completion. We wish to express our sincere gratitude to the authors contributing to this volume. Without their wide-ranging expertise and their patience, this project would not have been possible. We are grateful to the many other individuals who were sounding boards, providing advice and critique to various parts of the project. They include Helen Alvaré, Gerry Bradley, John Breen, Patrick Brennan, Barry Carter, Sam Casey, Bob Cochran, John Duncan, Elizabeth Duncan, Scott Fitzgibbon, George Garvey, Dan Gibbons, David Gregory, Kevin Johnson, Randy Lee, Nora O'Callaghan, Francesco Parisi, Patrick Quirk, Steve Safranek, Bill Saunders, Mike Schutt, Thomas Schweitzer, and Bill Wagner. Nine law students were instrumental in doing unheralded behind-the-scenes work in various phases of this project's development: Donna Benke, Jeannie Bernardy, Jeb Boatman, Erik Grayless, Fr. Jim Goins, Caroline McClimon, Stacie Nicholson, David Prentice, and Steven Steffey. And Dawn Tomlins provided invaluable service in making sure the manuscript was in order.

We are deeply grateful to the Our Sunday Visitor Institute for providing financial support allowing us to convene a conference where the ideas and structure of this book came together. We are also grateful to Bob Destro and the Catholic University of America Columbus School of Law for hosting the conference. We thank Archbishops Beltran of Oklahoma City and Fiorenza of Galveston-Houston for their support. We also acknowledge the support of our respective institutions, the University of Oklahoma and the University of St. Thomas (Minnesota) (and also South Texas College of Law), as well as the support of Gene and Elaine Edwards through their generous gift to the University of Oklahoma. We would like to thank David McGonagle and Theresa Walker at the Catholic University of America Press for their editorial assistance and advice during the course of this project.

On a personal plane, our spouses, María Ruiz Scaperlanda and Bob Collett, and our children, Christopher, Anamaría, Rebekah, and Michelle Scaperlanda and Rob, Christi, and Laura Collett, supported us throughout this project.

Parts of this book appeared in print, sometimes in very different form, in a number of places. We wish to thank the various publishers for permission to use previously published material here. Cardinal Dulles's essay appeared in the Acton Institute's Occasional Papers series as "Truth as the Ground for Freedom: A Theme from John Paul II." Thomas Kohler's contribution appeared as "Labor Law and Labor Relations: Comparative and Historical Perspectives," *Pontificiae Academiae Scientiarum Socialium Acta* (Proceedings of the Second Plenary Session of the Pontifical Academy of the Social Sciences) 2 (1998): 305. A version of Amelia Uelmen's essay appeared as "Toward a Trinitarian Theory of Products Liability," *Journal of Catholic Social Thought* 1 (2004): 603. Richard Garnett's chapter appeared as "Sectarian Reflections on Lawyers' Ethics and Death Row Volunteers," *Notre Dame Law Review* 77 (2002): 795. John Coughlin's essay appeared as "Natural Law, Marriage, and the Thought of Karol Wojtyla," *Fordham Urban Law Journal* 28 (2001): 1771. Michael Scaperlanda's essay originally appeared as "Immigration Justice: Beyond Liberal Egalitarian and Communitarian Perspectives," *Review of Social Economy* 57 (1999): 523. A different version appeared as "Immigration Justice: A Catholic Christian Perspective," *Journal of Catholic Social Thought* 1 (2004): 535. Mary Ann Glendon's essay appeared as "Foundations of Human Rights: The Unfinished Business," *American Journal of Jurisprudence* 44 (1999): 1.

RECOVERING
SELF-EVIDENT TRUTHS

INTRODUCTION

༺✿༻

MICHAEL A. SCAPERLANDA and
TERESA STANTON COLLETT

We hold these truths to be self-evident, that all men are created equal, that they are endowed by their Creator with certain unalienable Rights, that among these are Life, Liberty and the pursuit of Happiness.—

That to secure these rights, Governments are instituted among Men, deriving their just powers from the consent of the governed.

As the dark clouds of division threatened to pull the United States apart limb by limb, Abraham Lincoln dared to speak of America's great vocation. In a speech given during his ill-fated senatorial race in 1858, Lincoln attacked the Supreme Court's crimped understanding of the Declaration of Independence as it had been expressed in the infamous *Dred Scott* case. Where the Court saw a document of political expediency that claimed rights mainly for the British colonials who had suffered under King George's tyranny and few others, Lincoln saw universal possibilities in the Declaration's understanding that all persons "are created equal" and have unalienable rights. He said, "I think the authors of that notable instrument intended to include *all*. . . . They did not mean to assert the obvious untruth, that all were then actually enjoying equality. . . . They meant simply to declare the *right,* so that the *enforcement* of it might follow as fast as circumstances should permit."[1] To Lincoln, the Declaration and its principles were a gift to be shared with the world:

1. Abraham Lincoln, "Speech at Springfield, Ill. (June 26, 1857)," in *The Collected Works of Abraham Lincoln,* ed. Roy P. Basler, vol. 2 (New Brunswick: Rutgers University Press, 1953), 398, 405–6.

"They meant to set up a standard maxim for free society, which should be familiar to all, and revered by all; constantly looked to, constantly labored for, and even though never perfectly attained, constantly approximated, and thereby constantly spreading and deepening its influence, and augmenting the happiness and value of life to all people of all colors everywhere."[2]

Every generation must take ownership of these principles. In the aftermath of the bloody battle at Gettysburg, President Lincoln called his generation to create "a new birth of freedom" so that "this nation under God" and its "government of the people, by the people, for the people shall not perish from the earth."[3] More recently, another public figure opined that "the continuing success of American democracy depends on the degree to which each new generation, native-born and immigrant, makes its own the moral truths on which the Founding Fathers staked the future of [the] Republic. Their commitment to build a free society with liberty and justice for all must be constantly renewed if the United States is to fulfill the destiny to which the Founders pledged their 'lives . . . fortunes . . . and sacred honor.'"[4]

Every generation in every democracy since Aristotle has faced the moral question he posed: "How ought we to live together?" How to live together and flourish in a pluralistic society in which agreement on the source and fact of "self-evident truth" can no longer be assumed presents an even trickier question. This is the great challenge facing the United States today. More specifically, for our purposes, how can "law" be used as a tool to facilitate our ongoing experiment in representative self-governance in a country that seems to have lost its shared moral foundations? This volume presents a timely and engaging collection of essays exploring "catholic" and "Catholic" perspectives on American law—catholic in their claims of universal truths accessible to all through reason and experience, and Catholic in their grounding in the teachings of the Roman Catholic Church. What emerges is a model of human freedom and flourishing that has its foundation in the transcendent vocation of every human person.

Legal systems are meant to order relationships among human persons;

---

2. Ibid. at 406.

3. Abraham Lincoln, "Gettysburg Address (November 19, 1863)," in *Collected Works*, vol. 7, 23.

4. Pope John Paul II, "Address of John Paul II to H.E. Mrs. Corine (Lindy) Claiborne Boggs: New Ambassador of the United States of America to the Holy See—16 December 1997," online at http://www.vatican.va/holy_father/john_paul_ii/speeches/1997/december/documents/hf_jp-ii_spe_19971216_ambassador-usa_en.html, 1997.

they are not designed to bring order to the angelic realm or the animal kingdom. Our law operates on beings who are matter and spirit, intellect and will, rational yet driven by passion, determined partly by the forces of nature and nurture yet ultimately free to make fundamental moral choices for which they can be held accountable. The Declaration of Independence itself reflects several assumptions about the nature of the human person. Broadly speaking, it assumes that (a) the human race did not bring itself into existence but was created by some transcendent Being, variously referred to as "Nature's God," "Creator," and "Supreme Judge"; (b) the human person has an unalienable and equal right to be free; (c) freedom is exercised in community; (d) freedom must be ordered by government and law; and (e) these truths are self-evident.

As the new nation crawled out of its infancy, these self-evident truths remained in the fore. The Constitution was adopted by and for a community of persons with the purpose of securing the "Blessings of Liberty." The Constitution itself places textual and structural limits on government, facilitating authentic freedom by creating room for civil society to work and flourish. As Madison explained in Federalist 51, "[i]n framing a government which is to be administered by men over men, the great difficulty lies in this: you must first enable the government to control the governed; and in the next place oblige it to control itself." As to the transcendent, Washington believed that "[o]f all the dispositions and habits, which lead to political prosperity, Religion and Morality are indispensable supports." He also warned the young country that "reason and experience both forbid us to expect that national morality can prevail in exclusion of religious principle."[5] John Adams expressed it this way: "The safety and prosperity of nations ultimately and essentially depend on the protection and the blessing of Almighty God, and the national acknowledgment of this truth is . . . a duty whose natural influence is favorable to the promotion of that morality and piety without which social happiness can not exist, nor the blessings of a free government enjoyed."[6]

Two hundred thirty-one years after the signing of the Declaration, the American polity continues, by near acclamation, to acknowledge these self-evident truths, except the one that provides the foundation for all the rest. A

5. George Washington, "Farewell Address (Sept. 17, 1796)," in *The Writings of George Washington from the Original Manuscript Sources* (1745-1789), vol. 35, ed. John C. Fitzpatrick (Washington, D.C.: Government Printing Office, 1940), 214, 224.

6. James D. Richardson, *A Compilation of the Messages and Papers of the Presidents 1789–1908* (New York: Bureau of National Literature, 1908), 284–86 (quoting John Adams).

desire for liberty and equality lie at the core of our identity as a people. And, even as the autonomous self is exalted in some quarters, we still recognize that freedom is exercised in community and must be ordered by law.

That we did not create ourselves but came into being by an act of a Creator is the only self-evident truth mentioned by the framers to come under serious attack in modern America. There are two parts to this self-evident truth: (1) we did not bring ourselves into existence, or, to put it another way, a human person was not the first cause of the human race; and (2) we came into existence by the act of Another and not by some freak accident. The first proposition cannot seriously be questioned, although our society often ignores it as we organize our personal and public lives as if we were our own creators. The second proposition is under full-scale assault by those who would sweep the public square clean of any meaningful religious sense, confining that undeniable aspect of the human personality to the private sphere.

As we journey into the twenty-first century, we the people of the United States desire to promote ordered liberty in a pluralistic society that treats all persons as equals. Liberty and equality can travel as companions only so far before tensions arise and some criterion of judgment is necessary to mediate between the conflicting claims of liberty and equality. Ordered liberty also presents itself to us as a paradox, with the competing claims of the individual, the collective, and the common good demanding a criterion for judgment and a tribunal to exercise wisdom and justice in mediating between conflicting demands.

To properly order liberty, the founding generation sought to tie freedom to objective truth as the criterion for judgment. Not naive utopians, they knew that our grasp on objective truth is fallible, that we at times will lack prudence in acting upon that truth, and that passion and self-interest would corrupt our public life together, so they devised a system of checks and balances and multiple points of accountability to diminish the impulse toward tyranny. But they also knew that if this new republic was to flourish, the citizenry's moral and religious understanding must inform the public life of the nation. In other words, many in that generation believed religion-based understandings of moral truth to be *essential* to the nation's health. The first and most profound of these truths is that the human person has unalienable rights given by a Creator. Or, to put it another way, states are bound by a higher authority to respect these unalienable rights, and when a state exercises its power in contravention of these rights, it can be judged by an objective standard and held accountable for its abusive actions. Reflecting on the injustice of slavery, Jefferson "tremble[ed]" reflecting "that God is just," he asked: "[C]an the liberties of a nation be thought secure, when we have removed their only firm basis, a conviction in the mind of the people that these liberties are the gift of God? That they are not to be violated but with his wrath? . . . The Almighty has no attribute which can take side with" slaveholders.[7]

A strong current flows through our society threatening to pull us from our moorings in this self-evident truth, dis-integrating the person by reducing her (at least in public persona) to her material needs and desires by marginalizing or trivializing the transcendent, the spiritual, the sacred, and, among postmodernists, even the rational. This current tells us that "[j]ustice is a human construction"[8] and that liberty and equality can be maintained, even advanced, without an acknowledgement that these rights are gifts given to the human person by Another. This strong current untethers freedom from its anchor—objective truth—by relegating the religious sense and religious truth to the private sphere. It argues not only that religious morality and sentiment are irrelevant to public life but also that the intrusion of religion into public life is unconstitutional. Some, like United States Supreme Court Justices John Paul Stevens and Harry Blackmun, go so far as to argue that the Establishment Clause is violated by the enactment of laws motivated by "theological and sectarian" interests.[9]

What are the consequences for the public order of rejecting truth as a criterion for judgment? Richard Rorty and Pope John Paul II reside at opposite ends of the spectrum regarding truth. Rorty trades the possibility of universal and objective truth for a freedom lived within contingent and relative re-

7. Thomas Jefferson, "Notes on the State of Virginia," ch. XVIII (1787), available at http://xroads.virginia.edu/~hyper/jefferson/ch18.html. Madison, writing more generally, said: "Before any man can be considered as a member of Civil Society, he must be considered as a subject of the Governor of the Universe: and if a member of Civil Society, do it with a saving of his allegiance to the Universal Sovereign." James Madison, "Memorial and Remonstrance against Religious Assessments" (1785), available at http://www.law.ou.edu/hist/remon.html. Madison ended the Memorial and Remonstrance "praying, as we are in duty bound, that the Supreme Lawgiver of the Universe" (id.).

8. E.g., Michael Walzer, *Spheres of Justice: A Defense of Pluralism and Equality* (New York: Basic Books, 1983).

9. E.g., *Planned Parenthood of Southeastern Pennsylvania v. Casey*, 505 US 833, 932 (1992) (Blackmun, J., concurring in part, concurring in judgment in part, and dissenting in part). See also *Webster v. Reproductive Services*, 492 US 490, 566–67 (1989) (Stevens, J., concurring in part, dissenting in part) (Establishment Clause violation occurs when a law lacks an "identifiable secular purpose.").

ality, while John Paul II insists that freedom must be tied to the truth Rorty so fervently denies. But on one critical issue they are in agreement. They both understand that without objective truth, there are no universal criteria for forming a morally just society. Rorty puts the issue starkly: without objective truth, we "cannot give a criterion for wrongness," and, therefore, we must give "up the idea that liberalism could be justified, and Nazi or Marxist enemies of liberalism refuted by . . . argument."[10] The pope agrees:

> If there is no transcendent truth, in obedience to which man achieves his full identity, then there is no sure principle for guaranteeing just relations between people. Their self-interest as a class, group or nation would inevitably set them in opposition to one another. If one does not acknowledge transcendent truth, then the force of power takes over, and each person tends to make full use of the means at his disposal in order to impose his own interests or his own opinion. . . . Thus the root of modern totalitarianism is to be found in the denial of the transcendent dignity of the human person who, as the visible image of the invisible God, is therefore by his very nature the subject of rights which no one may violate—no individual, group, class, nation, or State.[11]

Therefore, for John Paul II but not for Rorty, "the inseparable connection between truth and freedom . . . is extremely significant for the life of persons in the socioeconomic and sociopolitical spheres."[12]

If liberty is to be safeguarded against the threat of tyranny and the community and its members are to flourish, freedom must be ordered toward objective truth about the nature of the human person. But there is just one small problem: in a pluralistic nontheocratic democracy, multiple voices claim to speak on behalf of objective truth. Which voices should we privilege, if any? Secular liberalism answers that we should not publicly privilege any "private conception" of the good and the true above the rest. Ronald Dworkin captures this view: "[G]overnment does not treat [people] as equals if it prefers one conception [of the good] to another."[13] But is liberal neutrality really neutral? Can this supposed neutrality really form a neutral basis for a pluralistic society that equally recognizes and values competing conceptions of life and its origin, purpose, and destination? As many secular liberal theorists, including Joseph Carens and James Dwyer, recognize, the answer is unequivocally no.

10. Richard Rorty, *Contingency, Irony, and Solidarity* (Cambridge: Cambridge University Press, 1989), 75, 53.

11. Pope John Paul II, *Centesimus annus* ¶ 44 (1991).

12. Pope John Paul II, *Veritatis splendor* ¶ 99 (1993).

13. Ronald Dworkin, *A Matter of Principle* (Cambridge: Harvard University Press, 1985), 191.

Carens concludes that "[t]he ideal of cultural neutrality is an illusion."[14] Dwyer goes further, explaining that the "principle of state neutrality is not itself ideologically neutral. . . . [O]n the higher-order normative questions of whether the state *should* be strictly secular in this way, it reflects a partisan liberal position."[15]

The "neutral" position is flawed. It cannot make explicit a truth claim about the nature of the human person without violating its principle of neutrality. But without an understanding of the human person rooted in truth, it has no basis for asserting that the human person has unalienable rights. Therefore, the state must assume the role of licensing various freedoms as power fills the vacuum and determines the shape and substance of ordered liberty without the aid of an external objective criterion. The non-neutral "neutral" position does, in fact, make an implicit assumption about ultimate reality. By rejecting the relevance of transcendent or universal truth claims for public discourse, the "neutral" position reduces humanity to its biological common denominator, thereby favoring the material aspects of existence, marginalizing the public significance of both the natural law and the great spiritual questions of meaning and purpose. Additionally, while claiming to be the champion of pluralism, the "neutral" position can, in actuality, tolerate only a very weak form of pluralism. Since the "neutral" society cannot privilege any conception of the good over any other without betraying its supposed neutrality, it requires its members to subordinate any strong public commitment to truth in favor of a neutral dialogue or conversation. In

14. Joseph Carens, *Culture, Citizenship, and Community: A Contextual Exploration of Justice as Evenhandedness* (Oxford: Oxford University Press, 2000), 53.

15. James Dwyer, *Religious Schools v. Children's Rights* (Ithaca, NY: Cornell University Press, 1998), 82. Jacques Maritain once said that "[i]t has been frequently noted that bourgeois liberalism with its ambition to ground everything in the unchecked initiative of the individual, conceived as a little God, and the absolute liberty of property, business and pleasure, inevitably ends in statism." Jacques Maritain, *The Person and the Common Good* (Notre Dame, IN: Notre Dame University Press, 1966), 91–92. Dwyer's vision of the liberal state unmasks the totalitarian possibilities of this predicted statism. To protect the ability of children to make future choices about their life's direction and goals unencumbered by the baggage associated with more traditional Christianity, Dwyer argues that parents and educators are merely agents licensed by the state to raise and educate children and that the "child-rearing privilege [should be] limited in its scope to actions and decisions not inconsistent with children's temporal interests." Dwyer, *Religious Schools v. Children's Rights*, 64. See also Michael Scaperlanda, "Producing Trousered Apes in Dwyer's Totalitarian State," *Texas Review of Law and Politics* 7 (2002): 175 (reviewing Dwyer's second book, *Vouchers within Reason: A Child-Centered Approach to Education Reform* (Ithaca, NY: Cornell University Press, 2001)).

the name of plurality and neutrality, the Jew, Muslim, Buddhist, Hindu, or Christian who organizes his life around the principles of his faith is asked to set aside the core of his being as the price for participating in this exercise in pluralism. Instead of robust pluralism, superficial multiculturalism emerges. What is the alternative to this flawed attempt at neutrality?

An open, pluralistic, and democratic society should not fear difference and diversity. It should allow people to engage the ongoing public conversation from the core of their being. Joseph Carens put its well:

> [O]ne model of deliberative democracy requires that people abstract themselves from their identities. But there is an alternative model of democracy that simply requires that people listen and engage each other. To treat other people with respect—which is a requirement of deliberative democracy—does not necessarily require that one suspend one's own commitments or distance oneself from one's own identity. Indeed, conversations are often most fruitful when people speak from their deepest selves.[16]

This book is offered in the spirit of strong pluralism, which accepts the many voices of those seated around the banquet table of our society. The two-thousand-year-old Catholic intellectual tradition, which produced "the first modern Western legal system,"[17] has retained its spiritual and intellectual vibrancy and can therefore offer compelling insights into the most serious issues facing the United States today. Rooted in faith and reason, revelation and natural law, these insights transcend the current ideological battle lines drawn by the left and the right. The essays in this volume are drawn from this tradition and are unapologetically Christian. The arguments presented, therefore, should be more readily accessible to Catholics and other Christians than to those outside of this faith system. This is simply a product of an authentic pluralism. These Catholic perspectives are also catholic; they are universal in nature and accessible at some level by all. In addition to its theological insights, Catholicism has a strong philosophical tradition rooted in the reasoning capacity of the human animal. And, although there is interplay between theology and philosophy, with one informing the other, each remains rooted within its own discipline. In its account of the human encounter with reality, Catholicism proposes certain truths about the human person, human flourishing, and human community. Because these truths are made evident by our basic human needs (the deepest longings of the human

---

16. Carens, *Culture, Citizenship, and Community,* 143.

17. Harold Berman, *Law and Revolution: The Formation of the Western Legal Tradition* (Cambridge: Harvard University Press, 1983), 44.

heart), these insights from Catholicism are discernible even by those who do not share the Catholic faith tradition.

Kevin P. Lee's opening chapter recognizes and addresses the current obstacles and opportunities facing those wanting "to renew American democracy by renewing Catholic thinking about law and legal systems."[18] Acknowledging a plurality of authentically Catholic approaches, Lee uses the teachings of Pope John Paul II to suggest four distinctive traits of this project. First, law and legal study must be situated within and be seen as an integral part of the broader realm of humanistic studies. Second, the Catholic legal scholar must retain a dogged commitment to truth with a capital "T." Third and fourth, Catholic legal theory will be rooted in the natural law while recognizing that natural law is the first grace; in other words, it recognizes the role of reason and the "primacy of faith."[19]

Part I of the book consists of two essays, one by Lorenzo Albacete and the other by Benedict M. Ashley, exploring Catholic moral anthropology, which provide the foundation for all of the other essays. At first blush, the reader might wonder why a book about American law would contain essays in moral anthropology. The answer is quite simple. Law is one means by which the relations among human beings are ordered. To determine how to use the tool of law properly to govern human relations, the governing authority needs a working hypothesis about the nature of its subject—the human person. Madison saw this clearly when he opined that "government itself" is "the greatest of all reflections of human nature," positing that "[i]f men were angels, no government would be necessary."[20] As the framers of our Constitution knew well, a society cannot avoid the question of what is the human person. Because law operates on human beings, "[e]very system of law [must] reflect certain foundational assumptions about what it means to be human."[21] Quite simply, this is a public question, and, explicitly or implicitly, there will always be a public answer.

To a large extent, our society, with its story of "neutrality" among competing conceptions of the true and the good, has created a myth that this question is the property solely of the private domain and that it is largely a

---

18. See chapter 1, infra.

19. See chapter 1, infra. See also Russell Hittinger, *The First Grace: Rediscovering the Natural Law in a Post-Christian World* (Wilmington, DE: ISI Books, 2003).

20. The Federalist Papers, No. 51.

21. John Coughlin, "Law and Theology: Reflections on What it Means to be Human from a Franciscan Perspective," *St. John's Law Review* 74 (2000): 609, 610.

matter of human construction. The well-known mystery passage from the joint opinion in *Planned Parenthood v. Casey* epitomizes this account: "At the heart of liberty is the right to define one's own concept of existence, of meaning, of the universe, and of the mystery of human life."[22] But, in fact, Hitler's National Socialism, Lenin's Communism, and our representative democracy were each built on very *public* understandings of "existence, of meaning, of the universe, and of the mystery of human life." The mystery passage itself and the political philosophy from which it derives reflect (and attempt to impose) a *public* moral anthropology that views the human person as radically autonomous and contingent.

A Catholic Christian understanding of human nature, by comparison, includes the understandings that the human person is created in God's image and likeness; that the person was given freedom by God, which is to be respected by other human beings; that freedom is the right to do what we ought; that the person is made for community (with both God and other human beings); that human nature became corrupt, alienating human beings from God and each other by the actions of our first parents (what we call "original sin"); and that all things (including human nature) are reconciled and perfected through the person of Jesus Christ. By laying out a Christian anthropology in chapters 2 and 3, we make explicit our answer to this essential inquiry about the nature of the human person upon which our perspectives on American law are based.

Before examining Catholic perspectives on particular areas of American law, we pause to take a necessary intermediate step. Part II of the book draws from Catholic anthropology four values: freedom, solidarity, subsidiarity, and the common good, which will be important in understanding the later essays. Liberty resides at the core of American self-understanding. But, what is liberty? In chapter 4, Avery Cardinal Dulles addresses the nature of liberty, arguing that authentic freedom must be grounded in the truth about the human person. In chapter 5, Robert Vischer addresses the concepts of solidarity and subsidiarity, "the two pillars of Catholic social teaching," by placing these complementary concepts in dialogue with a culture that appears to value "consumerism as a collective ideal."[23] Catholic thought rejects the idea that communal goods are merely the aggregated preferences of self-interested

---

22. *Planned Parenthood of Southeastern Pennsylvania v. Casey*, 505 US 833, 851 (1992).
23. See chapter 5, infra.

individuals within the society. In chapter 6, Robert John Araujo develops the Catholic understanding of the common good.

Catholic thought, which provides the foundation for our perspectives on American law, is in continuous dialogue with secular disciplines and secular culture, drawing from them whatever is true and good while seeking to remind those disciplines and cultures of the transcendent nature and vocation of the human person. Political theory is a particularly relevant discipline to our discussion on American law in that it provides many of the background norms underlying the American legal system. The chapters in Part III illustrate two different aspects of Catholic thought in dialogue with political theory. In chapter 7, Christopher Wolfe examines the terrain common to both the Catholic thinker and the liberal political theorist while noting the seemingly inevitable boundary line where they must part company. In chapter 8, Robert P. George reenters the Fuller-Hart debate, bringing it up to date, by exploring the importance of the rule of law to political morality.

With the foundation laid, Part IV considers the implications of authoritative teachings of the Roman Catholic Church for the questions confronting the American legal system on a daily basis. While the possibilities were endless, the editors have chosen to address labor law, contract law, property law, torts/products liability, criminal law, family law, and transnational legal concerns. Modern Catholic Social Thought began in 1891 when Pope Leo XIII addressed the issue of labor in his encyclical letter *Rerum novarum*. We, therefore, start at the same place, with Thomas C. Kohler's chapter. The next four subjects, addressed in James Gordley's, Vincent D. Rougeau's, Amelia J. Uelmen's, and Richard W. Garnett's chapters, are essential to a basic understanding of the legal duties and correlative rights in any free and open society; they are also all basic areas of study in the law school curriculum. The sixth, family law, much contested in the current legal landscape, is discussed by John J. Coughlin. Catholic anthropology, which understands the family as the most vital cell—the primary community—in society and in the development of the human person, provides a powerful alternative to systems that view family in purely instrumental terms. Finally, the book would not be complete without looking at our national border and beyond, and Michael A. Scaperlanda explores our obligations to the broader human community and the duty of all nations to recognize self-evident truth. Mary Ann Glendon's chapter brings us back to the essential question for America at this moment in our history—upon what foundation do we build a regime of human rights?—recognizing that this is also the central question for the global community. We could have included chapters on administrative, agricultural, antitrust, aviation, bankruptcy, civil rights, communications, education, entertainment, environmental, estates and trusts, health care, poverty, regulated industries, securities regulation, and any number of other areas of law. It is our hope that Catholic scholars who specialize in these areas will continue to contribute Catholic perspectives on these subjects in various forums.

These essays provide the reader an understanding of human freedom, responsibility, and law that is explicitly or implicitly Catholic, yet expressed in terms of principled truths to which many non-Catholic readers can assent. Three brief points will clarify our use of the word "Catholic."

First, all of the essayists have attempted to incorporate authoritative and authentic teachings of the Church in their reflections; therefore, readers who wish to see the reflections on American law by those who "dissent" from Church teaching will have to look elsewhere.

Second, Roman Catholic teaching does not propose one type of political, philosophical, economic, or legal system. Instead, it encourages those involved in forming culture to create political, economic, and legal structures in ways consistent with the truth about the human person, which takes us back to the anthropological question. Other Catholic scholars, attempting to apply the authoritative teachings of the Church to the same problems, might address them in very different ways. In fact, it is our hope that this volume will help spur debate and dialogue among Catholic legal scholars within their specific subject areas as they attempt to use prudential judgment in addressing the needs of American law and culture.

Third, by using the word "Catholic," we are not attempting to suggest that the line of reasoning is exclusively Catholic; to the contrary, we are hoping that our readers will recognize it as catholic in the fullest sense. After Michael A. Scaperlanda published an article presenting a Catholic perspective on immigration and welfare reform, he received a very warm letter from one of the nation's preeminent legal scholars. The only note of criticism in the letter was an expression of regret that Scaperlanda had called his position "Catholic" because it also happened, according to the letter writer, to reflect the Lutheran position to which the letter writer ascribed. It is our hope that we will find many fellow travelers from all faiths and creeds, even among those who profess no belief in a transcendent Creator, who see something good and valuable in our perspectives. We use the word "Catholic" here not as a means of exclusion but as "fair disclosure" for the purpose of explicitly articulating the foundation of this project.

On a number of occasions at the end of the twentieth century and the dawn of the twenty-first, Pope John Paul II took up Lincoln's mantle and reminded the United States of its great vocation in the world:

The Founding Fathers of the United States asserted their claim to freedom and independence on the basis of certain "self-evident" truths about the human person: truths which could be discerned in human nature, built into it by "nature's God." Thus they meant to bring into being, not just an independent territory, but a great experiment in what George Washington called "ordered liberty": an experiment in which men and women would enjoy equality of rights and opportunities in the pursuit of happiness and in service to the common good.[24]

Because of our successes and despite our failures, "many other nations and peoples look to [us] as the principal model and pattern for their own advancement in democracy."[25] But the pope is adamant that our public life must be animated by and grounded in the "unchanging principles of the natural law" embedded in our founding documents and "whose permanent truth and validity can be known by reason."[26] And he insists that our

deepest identity and truest character as a nation is revealed in the position [taken] towards the human person. *The ultimate test of [our] greatness is the way [we] treat every human being, but especially the weakest and most defenseless ones.* . . . All the great causes that are [ours] today will have meaning only to the extent that [we] guarantee the right to life and protect the human person:

- feeding the poor and welcoming refugees;
- reinforcing the social fabric of this nation;
- promoting the true advancement of women;
- securing the rights of minorities . . .

This is the dignity of America, the reason she exists, the condition of her survival—yes, the ultimate test of her greatness.[27]

24. Pope John Paul II, "Address of John Paul II to H.E. Mrs. Corine (Lindy) Claiborne Boggs," 36–37.

25. Pope John Paul II, "Departing Remarks from New York Visit (October 8, 1995)," available at www.catholic-forum.com/saints/pope0264iw.htm.

26. Ibid.

27. Pope John Paul II, "Departing Remarks from Detroit (September 19, 1987)," available at www.priestsforlife.org/magisterium/87-09-19popejohnpaulusa.htm.

Can our society recover and build upon the self-evident truths proclaimed by our predecessors more than 225 years ago? The road before us will not be easy. We close the book with Russell Shaw's bucket of cold water thrown on us as a reality check on the current state of our predominately secular culture and the advanced state of Catholic assimilation into that culture. Shaw argues that in order for Catholic perspectives on American law to gain traction, a viable subculture—a "healthy community, possessing a strong and self-confident sense of its identity"—of Catholics must be formed in order to take the first steps toward "regain[ing] the critical mass to be a culture-forming agent in America." It is our sincere hope and prayer that this volume may play some small role in the creation of such a community.

THE FOUNDATIONS OF CATHOLIC LEGAL THEORY

A Primer

KEVIN P. LEE

Catholic lawyers and legal educators have found a renewed interest in the Catholic intellectual tradition. They are hoping to find a distinctively Catholic voice that is both capable of addressing some of the problems faced by contemporary society and broadly persuasive to appeal to diverse audiences of lawyers, judges, policymakers, legal scholars, and political theorists. New law schools have been founded with explicitly Catholic missions,[1] and new journals stressing explicitly Catholic themes are appearing.[2] These are hopeful developments, but ones that should not be viewed glibly or triumphantly.

The desire to recapture the best that the Catholic intellectual tradition has to offer to contemporary society is met with complex and largely unresolved issues that have led to the diversity of approaches that exist today. A number of questions center on whether and how the Catholic intellectual tradition

---

1. Two law schools with explicitly Catholic missions have been founded in the last six years: Ave Maria School of Law (2000) and University of St. Thomas School of Law (2001).

2. In addition to the law reviews at the newly founded Catholic laws schools, Villanova University has founded the *Journal of Catholic Social Thought*, which has been a forum for Catholic legal scholars.

is compatible with modern liberal democracy and free market capitalism.[3] Some argue that the moral values of the Catholic tradition are compatible with liberal democracy and indeed were a part of the background assumptions of the founders of the nation.[4] Others view the Christian faith as intrinsically distant from any earthly politics, and the Christian as a pilgrim in an alien and sometimes hostile land.[5] So, despite clear objectives and a strong sense of purpose, Catholics are not united in a single approach to the project of renewing Catholic legal scholarship. This volume reflects a variety of perspectives that are united today under the flag of being Catholic treatments of law and legal theory, and yet these approaches to law and legal theory remain strikingly diverse.

The essays in this volume touch on a wide variety of subjects ranging from moral anthropology to jurisprudence to particular prescriptions for various areas of substantive law. And a variety of philosophical and theological perspectives are put forth. An initial essay, for example, draws from the moral anthropology developed in the personalist philosophy[6] of Pope John Paul II, while later essays cite to the so-called New Natural Law theory of John Finnis (who views moral anthropology to be less relevant to the law).[7] Yet all of these essays, despite their sometimes contradictory views of law and the Church's teaching, claim to be presenting an authentically Catholic view. All of this diversity and the richness of these perspectives might leave a sharp reader wondering whether there is a distinctive Catholic perspective at all, and, if so, hoping for a sustained treatment of that conception, whatever it might be.

This essay seeks to bring some order to the scene by introducing the boundary concepts of a Catholic approach to law and legal theory based on the teachings of Pope John Paul II, whose life and thought make his writings especially suited to the task. One of the most important challenges to the project of renewing Catholic legal thought is coming to a clear understanding of the theological significance of culture and the possibility of the

---

3. For a sampling of this debate see Doug Bandow and David L. Schindler, *Wealth, Poverty and Human Destiny* (Wilmington, DE: ISI Books, 2003).

4. See, e.g., Richard John Neuhaus, "Proposing Democracy Anew," *First Things* 98 (Dec. 1999): 68–88.

5. See, e.g., David Schindler, *Heart of the World, Center of the Church* (Grand Rapids, MI: Eerdmans, 1996).

6. See chapter 2, infra.

7. See chapter 8, infra.

compatibility of Catholic thought with the cultures of modernity.[8] Of particular concern is developing a clear understanding of the role of culture in moral formation and the unique place of the legal system in shaping culture.[9] The theme of the Church in modern culture was a formative one for the thought of Pope John Paul II throughout his life. He came to philosophic and political consciousness as a young seminarian, taking his lessons in an underground seminary in Nazi-occupied Poland.[10] He was a parish priest, a professor of philosophical ethics, and later archbishop of Krakow under a repressive Soviet regime. His pontificate faced its greatest challenges in the Cold War and the chaotic aftermath of the collapse of the Soviet empire.[11] This continued confrontation with modern totalitarian regimes gave shape to his call for Catholic intellectuals to develop "a coherent critique of the culture of modernity, rather than a simple accommodation to it."[12] John Paul II's mission, summarized by George Weigel in his splendid biography, *Witness to Hope,* was to develop a vision of a Church that is evangelically assertive and culture transforming.[13] My thesis here is that the pontiff's vision for the Church in modern culture provides the context for thinking coherently about what it means today to be Catholic and engaged in legal scholarship that is both evangelical and transformative.

This essay draws from three of John Paul's pontifical documents—the encyclical letters *Fides et ratio*[14] and *Veritatis splendor,*[15] and the Apostolic Constitution on Higher Education, *Ex corde ecclesiae.*[16] *Fides et ratio* presents a bold new proposal for the renewal of Christian philosophy as well as political and legal philosophy. John Paul II's program for the renewal of Catholic phi-

8. For a broad discussion of these issues, see Tracey Rowland, *Culture and the Thomist Tradition* (New York: Routledge Press, 2003).

9. For a discussion of some natural law thinkers' resistance to considering the role of culture in moral formation, see Rowland, *Culture and the Thomist Tradition,* 136–58.

10. George Weigel, *Witness to Hope* (New York: Harper Collins, 1999).

11. Ibid., 582–88.

12. For a broad discussion of these issues, see Rowland, *Culture and the Thomist Tradition,* 19.

13. Weigel, *Witness to Hope,* 846–47.

14. Pope John Paul II, *On the Relationship between Faith and Reason (Fides et Ratio)* (Boston: Pauline Books and Media, 1998).

15. Pope John Paul II, *The Splendor of Truth (Veritatis Splendor)* (Boston: Pauline Books and Media, 1993).

16. Pope John Paul II, *On Catholic Universities (Ex Corde Ecclesiae)* (Washington, DC: United States Catholic Conference, 1990).

losophy holds potential for contributing to the contemporary understanding of the cultural meaning of law and legal theory. *Veritatis splendor* develops a clear vision of the limits of an acceptable Catholic moral theory. It suggests modes for understanding the limits of decency in any legal system and the nature of the common good that a polity should seek. *Ex corde ecclesiae* contains a wealth of magisterial teaching on the nature of knowledge and learning, the objectives of Catholic scholarship, and the relation of Catholic thought to the modern world. These documents present a sound footing to answer some basic questions that are at play in the other essays in this volume.

IS THERE A CATHOLIC APPROACH TO LAW AND LEGAL THEORY?

The authors of the essays in this book argue, in various ways, for a Catholic approach to law and legal theory, but this is a difficult claim to make in the legal academy today because the dominant perspective is disinterested and even hostile to religious thought. So powerful is the dominant view that even some Catholic legal educators publicly wonder whether it makes any sense at all to speak of a Catholic law of torts or contracts.[17] It is clear that Catholics hold a marginalized position in today's legal academy, and it is clear that those who seek to renew Catholic legal scholarship must come to grips with this fact. The reason for this dissonance with Catholicism is that contemporary legal theories are born of modern and postmodern philosophy, both of which are at odds in different ways with core teachings of the Church. It is therefore useful to understand how the dominant view of law, politics, and religion challenges the project of renewing Catholic legal scholarship.

The Dominant Perspective: The Modern Political Problematic

The dominant perspective is set out in Franklin I. Gamwell's book, *The Meaning of Religious Freedom*, which presents a useful account of what he calls the "modern political problematic."[18] He notes that a shared claim among the variety of political theories that dominates today's academy is the

---

17. See Ferdinand N. Dutile, "A Catholic University Maybe, but a Catholic Law School?" in *The Challenge and the Promise of a Catholic University*, ed. Theodore M. Hesburgh (Notre Dame, IN: University of Notre Dame Press, 1994).

18. Franklin I. Gamwell, *The Meaning of Religious Freedom* (Albany: State University of New York Press, 1995), 1.

belief that liberal democracy "legitimates an indeterminate plurality of re-ligions."[19] That is to say that any religious view that a member of the politi-cal community might hold will be accommodated to the greatest possible extent commensurate with public health, safety, and the rights of others.[20] The rationale for this belief is founded somewhat differently among modern and postmodern political theorists, but most agree with some version of the claim that religions are personal affectations that cannot be opened to ratio-nal public discourse. Therefore, since religious claims cannot be publicly as-sessed, they ought not to be the basis for law or public policy.[21]

The term "religion" is used broadly in this context to include not only ex-plicitly theistic beliefs, but any "metaphysical" claims about human nature, or the meaning of human existence or the conditions for a fulfilled human life.[22] Although many definitions of metaphysics are put forward by philoso-phers, for the purposes of this essay, metaphysics refers to statements about what is ultimately real.[23] Metaphysics deals with the nature of reality and the place of the human being in it. And metaphysical claims about human be-ings are comprehensive in the sense that they apply universally (to all per-sons) and include all aspects of the human being.

One aspect of the dominant view has to do with making legal systems rational. This concern with rationalizing law developed from nineteenth-century sociology, which came to view law as progressing toward a certain sort of rationality. Gamwell explains that most advocates of the indetermi-nate pluralism view of liberal democracy agree with the sociologist Max We-ber, who argued that the rationalization of law and legal theory requires that law and politics be separated from "metaphysical" conceptions that grant le-gal rights based on metaphysical status.[24] One camp views law as a social sci-ence that progresses through empirical observations and technological in-novation. A prime example of this sort of theory is the economic analysis of law, or "law and economics," movement in the form developed by Richard Posner, who describes his approach as "opposed to metaphysical and 'right answers' moral realism and so to natural-law theory whether metaphysical or nonmetaphysical."[25] (So, Posner objects to natural law theories, citing We-

19. Ibid., 5.

21. Ibid., 48–49.

23. Ibid., 235n4.

20. Ibid., 6.

22. Ibid., 232–35.

24. Ibid., 49.

25. Richard A. Posner, *The Problematics of Moral and Legal Theory* (Cambridge: Harvard University Press, 1999), 12.

ber with approval.)[26] This, then, is the challenge for those who seek a renewal of Catholic legal scholarship: most legal scholars today will balk at any religiously motivated scholarship, particularly any prescriptions that are related to a view of what constitutes a fulfilled human existence, as being regressive for political discourse on law and public policy.

Another aspect of the desire to be independent of any comprehensive account of the meaning and fulfillment of a human life has to do with the belief that religious tolerance requires acceptance of a broad array of beliefs about what it means to be a human being.[27] When Justice Kennedy wrote in *Planned Parenthood v. Casey*[28] of a right of people to define for themselves their "own concept of existence, of meaning, of the universe, and the mystery of life,"[29] he expressed his belief that members of the political community ought to be free to develop their own metaphysical beliefs about human nature and fulfillment because to hold otherwise would infringe upon the contemporary commitment to an open pluralist liberal democracy. He means that people should be free to explore the meaning of their own lives without coercive interference by the state.

The overall effect of these desires to keep the state free from metaphysical beliefs about what is ultimately good and meaningful for human beings has led to theoretical perspectives that fail to see the rationality of moral discourse. That is to say, for a wide range of policymakers and political scientists, moral reasoning is an oxymoron. They view morality as subjective, nonrational, and arbitrary. Proper rationality is scientific, technical, and theoretical. Accordingly, moral reasoning has been excluded from most legal scholarship.

The hegemony of the scientific conception of rationality is well described by Karl Otto Apel in an insightful article titled "Types of Rationality Today."[30] Apel contends that since the sorts of instrumental reasoning involved in sci-

26. Ibid., 13.

27. See, e.g., Owen Flanagan, *Varieties of Moral Personality* (Cambridge: Harvard University Press, 1991), which contains a useful discussion of how recent developments in psychology present challenges to both the liberal view and various classical and contemporary alternative proposals.

28. *Planned Parenthood of Southeastern Pennsylvania v. Casey*, 505 US 833 (1992).

29. *Casey* at 851.

30. Karl Otto Apel, "Types of Rationality Today: The Continuum of Reason between Science and Ethics," in *La Rationalité Aujourd'hui* (Ottawa: University of Ottawa Press, 1979), 307–50.

ence and technology have proven to be so successful in extending human knowledge and power, other forms of reasoning (philosophical, hermeneutical, and so on) are ignored or even driven from the field.[31] In attempting to be scientific, social sciences have rejected forms of rationality that integrate moral meaning and the facts of human existence.[32] Metaphysical speculation is rejected in favor of means-to-ends pragmatism.[33] Science considers other sorts of rationality to be in competition with scientific explanation and so dismisses alternative forms of rationality as being "pre-rational" or obscurantist.[34] What results is the hegemony in our culture of a particular form of value-free rationality that holds practical efficiency to prevail in the public realm. The private subjective consciousness is the only proper place for decisions about self-identity because such choices are nonrational.

Many respected scholars have noted, however, that this amoral form of political liberalism has problems of its own and is now viewed by some analysts with a jaundiced eye. Jean Bethke Elshtain, for example, has noted that it is common for people to speak of a growing sense of the cheapening of human life; of growing violence, anger, and suspicion; of predatory pressures (sexual, economic, legal, social) upon the young; of the rushing pace of life that leaves little time to be a committed worker, a caring parent, and a good citizen.[35] Commentators and analysts look to a loss of civic responsibility and a hardened sense of greedy entitlement.[36] They speak of a breakdown of basic institutions—of neighborhoods, churches, schools, and families.[37] Elshtain argues that the once powerful overlapping relations of local ties and social unions have been eroded by waves of rights-based individualism and covetous bourgeois consumerism, both of which are the common coin of the dismal, violent, and anti-civic culture that has resulted in the absence of re-

---

31. Ibid., 309–10.

32. For a discussion of the fact/value dichotomy see Kevin Lee, "The Collapse of the Fact/Value Dichotomy: A Brief for Catholic Legal Scholars," *Journal of Catholic Social Thought* 1 (2004): 685–706.

33. Apel, "Types of Rationality Today," 308.

34. Ibid., 309.

35. For a discussion of the decline of American society see Jean Bethke Elshtain, "Catholic Social Thought, the City, and Liberal America," in *Catholicism, Liberalism, and Communitarianism: The Catholic Intellectual Tradition and the Moral Foundations of Democracy*, ed. Kenneth L. Grasso, Gerard V. Bradley, and Robert P. Hunt (New York: Rowman and Littlefield, 1995), 97–113.

36. Ibid., 98.

37. Ibid., 99.

ligious thought in the public sphere. Elshtain has termed this contemporary view "ultraliberalism"[38] to distinguish it from more moderate forms of classical liberalism. The rebirth of interest in the Catholic intellectual tradition arises in no small part from a hopeful appraisal of what the Church has to say about our contemporary malaise. There is a growing sense that something has gone wrong in American culture and a growing belief that Christian thought might provide a palliative if not curative perspective.

Catholic Culture and Legal Scholarship

Given the hardened dominance of the ultraliberal perspective, the challenge for Catholic legal scholars is to renew American democracy by renewing Catholic thinking about law and legal systems. What is needed is a Catholic critique of modern culture and the modern *Zeitgeist*. Such a critique was the objective of Pope John Paul II throughout his intellectual life, and the Catholic legal scholar can find much of value in his writings. Although he did not write extensively on the topic, John Paul II made a few important observations about the nature of legal systems and the nature of democracy, which he held to be "possible only in a State ruled by law, and on the basis of a correct conception of the human person."[39]

In his writing, John Paul II conceives of law as being closely linked to humanistic studies that seek to know the purpose and meaning of human existence. In order to understand his conception of law it is useful first to consider the insightful comments on the nature of human knowledge and understanding contained in *Ex corde ecclesiae,* where John Paul II teaches that it is the nature of a Catholic university to be "an academic community which, in a rigorous and critical fashion, assists in the protection and advancement of human dignity and of a cultural heritage through research, teaching and various services offered to the local, national and international communities."[40] In the document, he makes it clear that a Catholic university should be viewed as a place where research is performed with the firm conviction that human knowledge is an integrated whole. Although different disciplines may seek knowledge with different starting assumptions and different methodologies, human knowledge is fundamentally an integral whole

---

38. Ibid., 100.

39. Pope John Paul II, *On the Hundredth Anniversary of Rerum Novarum (Centesimus Annus)* (Boston: Pauline Books and Media, 1991), 46.

40. Pope John Paul II, *On Catholic Universities (Ex Corde Ecclesiae),* (¶ 12) 12.

rooted in the human search for a meaningful existence. Therefore, he explains, that research done in a Catholic educational institution should include (a) the search for an integration of knowledge, (b) a dialogue between faith and reason, (c) an ethical concern, and (d) a theological perspective.[41] These four principles assure that the sweep of knowledge will be integrated in seeking answers to the great questions about human existence.

That knowledge is an integrated whole has been taught by most Catholic philosophers and theologians. Josef Pieper, for example, describes philosophy—by which he means the classical notion of philosophy, the love of wisdom—as "reflect[ion] on the totality of things we encounter, in view of their ultimate reasons; and philosophy, thus understood, is a meaningful, even necessary endeavor, with which man, the spiritual being, cannot dispense."[42] Pieper views the integrity of knowledge as indispensable to the human spirit because humans seek the true meaning of their own lives and of things in the world. In this sense "the philosophical quest [is] an existential experience centered in the core of the human mind, a spontaneous, urgent, inescapable stirring of the person's innermost life."[43] The same can be said of theology. Both are attempts to understand an elementary experience of meaning that gives unity and integrity to human knowledge.[44] Thus, John Paul teaches that philosophy and theology aid scholars in other disciplines "in a constant effort to determine the relative place and meaning of the world that is enlightened by Gospel, and therefore by a faith in Christ, the Logos, at the center of creation and of human history."[45]

This integrated view of human learning and knowledge includes law within its ambit. John Paul II wrote that every legal system is an outworking of a culture's multiple attempts to gain basic insights into questions about the meaning and purpose of human life, of deep-centered struggles within the human heart and mind to grasp at the meaning of one's own existence.[46] In this view, legal systems are not separate from culture and philosophy, but draw their vitality and authority from their relation to philosophy and other

---

41. Ibid.

42. Josef Pieper, *In Defense of Philosophy* (San Francisco: Ignatius Press, 1995), 12.

43. Ibid., 24.

44. A similar account of knowledge and meaning is given in Luigi Giussani, *The Religious Sense* (Montreal: McGill-Queens University Press, 1997).

45. Pope John Paul II, *On Catholic Universities (Ex Corde Ecclesiae)*, (¶ 16) 15–16.

46. Citations are to Pope John Paul II, *On the Relationship between Faith and Reason (Fides et Ratio)*, (¶ 69) 87–88.

cultural forms that seek to know the meaning and purpose of human existence. Legal systems grasp for inspiration from the answers that a culture had developed in philosophy (but also in history, art, music, and literature) to the most basic mysteries of human life: what is the purpose of human life?[47] Thus legal systems are founded on many dense layers of shared meaning and value, and in this way every system of law reflects some basic assumptions about what it means to be fully human.[48]

Taken together, these scattered comments suggest an approach for thinking about the nature of a genuinely Catholic approach to law. It must be an integrative approach, one that permits law to be viewed not as an autonomous discipline, but as a humanistic activity rooted in philosophy, theology, literature, art, music, and myriad other human strivings that probe the meaning of human existence. Such humanistic endeavors provide the context in which the legal system derives its authority and the basic guiding principles. Conclusions about what is most important in human life, what is the most that human beings can hope to achieve by living together in a polity, what are the most praiseworthy uses of power and authority, and other such value judgments are derived from human self-understanding, embedded in richly textured social significations.

This is a hopeful place to begin a renewal of Catholic legal thought because it is a view of law that already has many supporters in the contemporary secular university. For example, that there are complex interactions between individual persons, cultural systems, and norms was also observed by the influential sociologist Robert Bellah, who claims that the variables studied by the social sciences are not interpreted in isolation, but require a social context to be meaningful. He claims that "it is only in the context of society as a whole, with its possibilities, its limitations, and its aspirations, that particular [social] variables can be understood."[49] According to Bellah, it is because social sciences make assumptions about the nature of the human person, the nature of society, and the nature of the relation between them that it is essential for social scientists to become self-conscious of their assumptions. This means that for Bellah those who would study law as a social sci-

---

47. Ibid. (¶¶ 1–6) 1–16.

48. See, e.g., John J. Coughlin, "Law and Theology: Reflections on What It Means to Be a Human from a Franciscan Perspective," *St. Johns Law Review* 74 (2000): 609–10 (discussing John Paul II's view that canon law should reflect an "integrated concept of the person").

49. Robert Bellah, *Habits of the Heart* (New York: Harper and Row, 1985), 300.

ence (using the law and economics approach, for example), must realize that they too are drawing on controversial views of the meaning of human existence.

Among legal scholars, James Boyd White and Robert Cover, both involved in the law and literature field, contend that there is a reflexive cultural/hermeneutical structure to legal systems. White's *The Legal Imagination*,[50] a casebook that includes excerpts from Western and non-Western literary sources, encourages the law student to expand his or her understanding of the relationships among law, language, and culture. In a later book, *Justice in Translation*,[51] White argues that the practice of law is a practice of translation—of translating the narratives told by clients into a language and narrative acceptable for the court. He contends that law is "a culture of argument" that creates a world of meaning.[52] In a similar vein, the late Robert Cover argues in his influential article "*Nomos* and Narrative"[53] that the narratives that inform a community about right and wrong are much broader than moral norms or legal precepts. He writes, "Once understood in the context of narratives that give meaning, law becomes not merely a system of rules to be observed, but a world in which we live."[54] Again, these literary lawyers agree with the basic insight that John Paul II advances about law, which links the legal system to deeply shared beliefs about the meaning and purpose of human existence known through multiple humanistic endeavors within a culture.

It is an important caveat, however, that while Catholic scholars can share in the literary and humanistic views of some in the secular university, there are limits to that agreement. They can agree that there exists a legitimate plurality in the methodologies of inquiry and scholarship, reflecting different sensibilities and cultures,[55] but this does not mean denying that through rev-

---

50. James Boyd White, *The Legal Imagination* (Boston: Little, Brown, 1973).

51. James Boyd White, *Justice as Translation* (Chicago: University of Chicago Press, 1990).

52. White writes, "For me it is more valuable to think of law in a third way, as a culture—as a 'culture of argument'—or, what is much the same thing, as a set of ways of making sense of things and acting in the world." Ibid., xiii.

53. Robert Cover, *Narrative, Violence and the Law*, ed. Martha Minow, Michael Ryan, and Austin Surat (Ann Arbor, MI: University of Michigan Press, 1995), 95–172.

54. Robert Cover, "*Nomos* and Narrative," in *Narrative, Violence, and the Law*, 95–172.

55. This point is made by Dave Ruel Foster, "The implications of *Fides et Ratio* for Catholic Universities," in *The Two Wings of Catholic Thought: Essays on Fides et Ratio*, ed. Dave R. Foster and Joseph W. Koterski (Washington, DC: The Catholic University of America Press, 2003), 124–25.

elation, Catholics can know the eternal and universal truth about the nature and fulfillment of the human being. This is an issue that John Paul II addressed in some detail, particularly in *Fides et ratio*, where he describes contemporary philosophy as having "abandoned the search for truth in itself and made [its] sole aim the attainment of objective certainty or a pragmatic sense of utility."[56] He has cautioned Catholic philosophers against following contemporary philosophy in embracing all viewpoints.

John Paul teaches that "at the present time in particular, the search for ultimate truth seems often neglected."[57] The philosopher today "is expected to rest content with more modest tasks such as the simple interpretation of facts or enquires into restricted fields of human knowing or its structures."[58] This has been a disaster for philosophy and the overall culture. John Paul II explained the effects of this narrowing of philosophy in the following passage:

> Sundered from that truth, individuals are at the mercy of caprice, and their state as persons ends up being judged by pragmatic criteria based essentially upon experimental data, in the mistaken belief that technology must dominate all. It has happened before that reason, rather than voicing the human orientation toward truth, has wilted under the weight of so much knowledge and little by little lost the capacity to lift its gaze to the heights, not daring to rise to the truth of being. Abandoning the investigation of being, modern philosophical research has concentrated instead upon human knowing. Rather than make use of the human capacity to know the truth, modern philosophy has preferred to accentuate the ways in which this capacity is limited and conditioned.[59]

In this rich passage, John Paul suggests that modern philosophy's twin focus on epistemology and the dichotomy between facts and moral values, which were asserted by modern philosophers such as David Hume, Immanuel Kant, and Rudolph Carnap, caused human reason to become "wilted" and philosophical reflection to have "lost its gaze to the heights." It has forced reason to be confined narrowly to scientific and technical reasoning, which views instrumental satisfaction of immediate objectives to be the highest expression of rationality. Against the crisis of modern philosophy, John Paul II calls on Catholic philosophers to ask "radical questions"[60] and to shun the "false modesty"[61] of views that claim to be humble in their neutrality, while asserting false comprehensive

---

56. Pope John Paul II, *On the Relationship between Faith and Reason (Fides et Ratio)*, (¶ 47), 64.

57. Ibid., (¶ 5) 13.   58. Ibid., (¶ 55) 73.

59. Ibid., (¶ 5) 14.   60. Ibid., (¶ 5) 15.

61. Ibid., (¶¶ 5, 56) 15, 75.

claims about human nature and the nature of reality. Catholics should boldly assert the truth known in and through the Holy Trinity.

This commitment to truth distinguishes Catholic culture from postmodern and some hermeneutical perspectives that as mentioned above have influenced modern legal theories, particularly in the law and literature movement. While thinkers such as White and Cover might reason from the legitimate premise that law is culturally derived to conclude that law is arbitrary and "all about power," a Catholic approach will hold fast to the truth that is known through revelation and reason working together. This difference between the literary view and the Catholic perspective should not, however, exclude Catholic philosophy and culture from being a legitimate source of insight for law.

There is an important opportunity here for the project of Catholic renewal. Since the dominant perspective of indeterminate religious pluralism has sought to give voice to marginalized perspectives, and given the long history of oppression of Catholics in the United States,[62] it would appear that there is a legitimate claim that the Catholic perspective is badly marginalized and underrepresented in today's legal education. Understanding exactly how the Catholic intellectual tradition is related to the law of torts, for example, or the way the contemporary legal system sometimes supports and sometimes oppresses the goals and objectives unique to the Catholic faith is, it would seem, at least as legitimate and academically rigorous as understanding how the law is experienced by and sometimes oppresses women, minorities, the poor, and persons of differing sexual practices. Even at this superficial level, a Catholic perspective on the law of torts would seem to be as legitimate as tort law from a feminist perspective or critical race theory or gender studies or queer theory approach. Since these other specific identities have been given privileged voices in American law schools, it is not clear why Catholics should not be welcomed as well, particularly at institutions that derive substantial benefits from their Catholic identification.

To summarize, the project of renewing Catholic legal scholarship rejects the hegemony of scientific/technical rationality in our times. At its core, a Catholic view of legal scholarship intends to hold law and institutions up to moral scrutiny with some confidence that to do so is a rational pursuit that serves purposes that are not merely strategic. Moreover, a renewal of Catholic approaches to law denies that moral autonomy is purely private and ar-

---

62. For a description of Catholic oppression, see Philip Hamburger, *Separation of Church and State* (Cambridge: Harvard University Press, 2002).

bitrary. It asserts that moral identity, the sort of self-understanding that Justice Kennedy seeks to encourage in *Casey* by asserting a right to define the meaning of one's own life, relies on complex social and cultural interactions. Coming to one's own concept of the meaning and the mystery of life is not possible without complex processes of social development. We come to understand the meaning of moral behavior in terms of interactions with others, and we come to understand the fulfillment of persons in terms of webs of social explanation. Thus, the moral meaning of life is highly contextual. Moral ideals and concepts cannot be understood apart from the webs of social signification in which they are found. The "epistemic priority of the Trinity"[63] in Catholic culture and the Catholic intellectual heritage are proper sources for Catholics to express the moral meaning of human life and human fulfillment and to critique the legal and political institutions of contemporary society.

WHAT IS THE CHARACTER OF
CATHOLIC LEGAL THEORY?

If there is a Catholic approach to law and legal theory, derived from Catholic conceptions of the meaning and purpose of human existence worked out in the richness of Catholic culture, then what is its distinctive character? There can be little doubt about this. Catholic culture and tradition have held natural law views of jurisprudence and moral theory to be normative.[64]

Roughly speaking, a natural law theory holds that human actions can and should be guided by precepts that are knowable and true for all persons regardless of their race, sex, religion, or cultural heritage.[65] Natural law theories have existed at least since the Stoic philosophers[66] of ancient Greece, but the

---

63. I borrow this expression from Bruce D. Marshall, in Bruce D. Marshall and Daniel W. Hardy, eds., *Trinity and Truth* (Cambridge: Cambridge University Press, 2003).

64. According to the *Catechism of the Catholic Church*, the natural law "shows man the way to follow so as to practice the good and attain his end." *Catechism of the Catholic Church* (New York: Bantam, Doubleday, Dell Publishing Group, 1995), (¶ 1955) 527.

65. Paragraph 1957 of the *Catechism* states:

Application of the natural law varies greatly; it can demand reflection that takes account of various conditions of life according to places, times, and circumstances. Nevertheless, in the diversity of cultures, the natural law remains as a rule that binds men among themselves and imposes on them, beyond the inevitable differences, common principles.

Ibid., (¶ 1957) 527.

66. See Alexander Passerin d'Entrèves, *Natural Law: An Introduction to Legal Philosophy* (New Brunswick, NJ: Transaction Publishers, 1994), 16.

highest theoretical expression of the pre-Christian form was attained in ancient Rome in the thought of Cicero,[67] who followed the Stoics in identifying
the precepts of natural law with dictates of reason. For Cicero, reason shows
the human mind what is eternally true and required by the gods—what the
laws of man cannot alter.

When the Catholic intellectual tradition adopted natural law, two passages of Scripture were particularly important to Christian understanding of the
significance of the natural law tradition: the first is St. Paul's epistle to the Romans 2:14–15, which states:

For when the Gentiles, who do not have the law by nature observe the prescriptions of
the law, they are a law for themselves even though they do not have the law.

They show that the demands of the law are written in their hearts, while their conscience also bears witness and their conflicting thoughts accuse or even defend them.

The second passage, which was very important for the thought of both St. Augustine and St. Thomas Aquinas, is Exodus 3:13–14, in which God reveals His
name to Moses, which in the Latin of the Vulgate was rendered *Ego sum qui
sum* [I am who am]. The medieval historian and philosopher Etienne Gilson
observed that

St. Thomas Aquinas, referring expressly to this text of Exodus, will declare that among
all divine names there is one that is eminently proper to God, name *Qui est* [Who is]
because this *Qui est* signifies nothing other than being itself. . . . There is but one God
and this God is Being, that is the corner-stone of all Christian philosophy, and it was
not Plato, it was not even Aristotle, it was Moses who put it in position.[68]

By the time the Christian writers encountered this enigmatic passage, there
was a substantial body of Greek and Roman philosophy that sought to understand the nature of Being or first causes, which since the time of Aristotle had
been known as metaphysics.

Catholic natural law theory has been concerned with understanding the
meaning of human existence before the God who revealed Himself to be the
Supreme Being. Catholic natural law theory puts a heavy emphasis on the
ultimate end, purpose, or goal of human life because it is concerned with
the place of the finite human being before the infinite being of God. Philosophers usually call a theory that seeks to understand morality by thinking

67. Ibid., 27.
68. Etienne Gilson, *The Spirit of Medieval Philosophy* (New York: Charles Scribner's Sons,
1991), 51.

about end, goal, purpose, or fulfillment of human existence a theory of teleological ethics. And when such a teleology is founded in a conception of the
nature of ultimate being or reality as such (in the Catholic case, what a human being is in relation to God, who is the source and sustainer of all that
is), then the ethical system can be characterized as being metaphysically teleological. A distinctive feature of Catholic thought is the assertion that there
exists a metaphysically teleological purpose for human life.[69]

The fulfillment of human existence recognized by Catholic natural law
theory is God, since our human desire to see God is synonymous with the
desire to live a happy and fulfilled life.[70] This means that for Catholics, the
moral good is in complete conformity with beatitude. As Pope John Paul II
explains, "Acting is morally good when the choices of freedom are in conformity with man's true good and thus express the voluntary ordering of the
person towards his ultimate end; God, the supreme good in whom man finds
his full and perfect happiness."[71] We need God's loving embrace and freely given grace to attain complete fulfillment and happiness in the afterlife.
The best that we can hope for in earthly life is to achieve the moral rectitude

---

69. Modern philosophy led some Catholic philosophers to badly misread St. Thomas
Aquinas, interpreting him as asserting that the nature is autonomous from the divine. This is
an anachronistic reading of Aquinas—a matter of reading him through modern philosophy.
When Aquinas is read carefully and in the context of his times, it is clear that he was totally Augustinian on this point. And when one reads Aquinas as both theologian and philosopher, he appears to have held the view that nothing can be fully understood outside of grace
or faith. So, for Aquinas, nature never exists apart from God's love for us. For a discussion
of the origins and development of the anachronistic reading of Thomism, see Servais Pinckaers, *The Sources of Christian Ethics* (Washington, D.C.: The Catholic University of America
Press, 1993).

70. This foundational commitment of Catholic moral thought is summarized by Romanus Cessario in the following passage:

The theological virtues of hope and charity enable the believer to realize the fulfillment of
this end in grace and glory. Philosophers may conclude that one ought to reverence a higher
power that transcends the confines of the created order, but only divine grace freely bestowed
by Christ enables one to know and love the God of Abraham, Isaac and Jacob. This refection
attributed to Blaise Pascal still holds true. Furthermore, divine grace is bestowed without regard for the person's human stature. When the dying Christ promises the Good Thief, "Today you will be with me in Paradise" (Lk 23:43), the New Testament makes it abundantly
clear that Paradise remains open even to the most miserable among men and women.

Romanus Cessario, *Introduction to Moral Theology* (Washington, DC: The Catholic University of America Press, 2001), 334–35.

71. Pope John Paul II, *The Splendor of Truth (Veritatis Splendor),* (¶ 72) 91.

(conformity to the moral law) that is necessary for the attainment of earthly happiness.[72]

A distinctive feature of Catholic natural law theories has been the belief that moral law is "self-evident." It is known through that part of conscience that St. Thomas calls *synderesis*.[73] Some contemporary natural law theorists argue that it is by virtue of the self-evident character of moral law that it can be applied universally. All persons, regardless of class, race, gender, or culture have access to what is universally known by humans qua humans. It is because there is a universal human nature that there can be self-evident truths. This view of self-evidence, however, should be taken with some caution, however, because St. Thomas also affirmed that although all persons have the ability to know the moral law, all do not know it equally. There are two reasons for the inequality: original sin and ignorance. Human reason may be distorted by sin so as to fail to judge properly how the principles should be applied in particular cases.[74] Also, not all people are capable of careful application of the principles in particular cases. Moral perfection takes a certain virtuosity or wisdom.[75]

Again, an important caveat: the claim of self-evidence must not be read as justifying oppression. John Paul II was emphatic about this. He taught: "Christian truth is not of this kind. Since it is not an ideology, the Christian faith does not presume to imprison changing socio-political realities in a ridged schema, and it recognizes that human life is realized in history in conditions that are diverse and imperfect."[76] Moreover, it should be noted that John Paul teaches that "the Church has no philosophy of her own, nor does she canonize any one particular philosophy in preference to others,"[77] and even goes so far as to affirm that his endorsement of St. Thomas as a guide for studying theology does not mean "to take a position on properly philosophical questions nor to demand adherence to particular theses."[78] And, when he speaks of the need in the modern age for "a philosophy of genuinely metaphysical range," he does not mean to prescribe "a specific school or a particular historical current of thought."[79] Instead, he "is convinced that it is

---

72. Thomas Aquinas, *Summa Theologica* Ia.IIae.4.4.

73. Ibid., Ia.IIae.94.1R2; I.79.12.   74. Ibid., Ia.IIae.99.2.

75. Ibid., Ia.IIae.100.1.

76. Pope John Paul II, *On the Hundredth Anniversary of Rerum Novarum (Centesimus Annus)*, 46.

77. Pope John Paul II, *The Splendor of Truth (Veritatis splendor)*, (¶ 49) 66.

78. Ibid., (¶ 78) 98.   79. Ibid., (¶ 83) 104.

the path to be taken in order to move beyond the crisis pervading large sections of philosophy at the present moment, and thus correct mistaken modes of behavior now widespread in our society."[80]

Another caveat has to do with a proper understanding of human freedom and its relation to human nature. There is some confusion about the nature of human freedom today that is related to different conceptions of Catholic moral theories in the modern world.[81] The difference centers on controversies that arose after the collapse of broad philosophical respectability of medieval metaphysical theory.[82] One approach suggested that moral theory can be done without appeal to metaphysics at all. This view of moral theory holds that morality is mostly about making the right choices. It focuses on duties and rules. Elements of this can be seen in the casuistry that developed in the wake of the Reformation.[83] Some Catholic thinkers still advance non-metaphysical approaches to their ethical theories,[84] despite John Paul II's clear call to return to virtue ethics and metaphysically teleological approaches to human flourishing that seek to develop a rich understanding of what is meant by the "moral good"[85] rather than what is right or required.

This is not to say that John Paul II recommended a return to medieval thought. While it is clear that John Paul II continued many aspects of the medieval view of natural law, it is also clear that he audaciously proposed a new approach that maintains the primacy of faith, while calling for a renewal of philosophy. John Paul II maintained that Catholic moral thinking proceeds from revealed truth about human nature, which exists prior to human

---

80. Ibid., (¶ 83) 105.

81. See Alistair MacIntyre, *After Virtue* (South Bend: University of Notre Dame Press, 1984), wherein MacIntyre argues that the concepts of virtue and moral agency became incompatible structurally in Enlightenment ethics.

82. See MacIntyre, *After Virtue;* Anthony Lisska, *Aquinas's Theory of Natural Law: An Analytic Reconstruction* (Oxford: Oxford University Press, 1996); William F. Frankena, *Ethics* (Englewood Cliffs, NJ: Prentice-Hall, 1973).

83. For a discussion of the development of casuistry, see Cessario, *Introduction to Moral Theology,* Appendix.

84. Pinckaers identifies two versions of deontology in Catholic thought: one views law as an expression of God's will and reason. It is the idea of freedom overlaid with obligation. The other views morality as being centered on "duty, linked to obligations but connoting a greater interiority." Servais Pinckaers, *The Sources of Christian Ethics,* 4–5.

85. Two works, G. E. M. Anscombe, "Modern Moral Philosophy," *Philosophy* 33/44 (Jan. 1958), and MacIntyre, *After Virtue,* have helped to generate renewed interest in virtue ethic over the past thirty years.

thinking,[86] and thus "The theological virtues [faith, hope and charity] are the foundation of Christian moral activity; they animate it and give it its special character."[87] While recognizing the need for the principles of natural law in the moral life, John Paul II also recognized the need for a well-formed conscience to rightly apply the natural law to concrete situations. He taught that reason, shaped by the virtue of prudence, formed in the light of the Lord's Cross,[88] makes possible right moral choice in complex situations.

John Paul II also developed a view of human autonomy that is critical of non-teleological approaches because they distort the Catholic view of human freedom. The non-teleological conception of human autonomy views freedom as an absence of coercion, and law is viewed as coercive. *Veritatis splendor* is critical of this view because in such theories freedom becomes an absolute: choice becomes an end in itself, and maximal choosing is viewed as identical to the highest good.[89] Instead, *Veritatis splendor* develops a conception of freedom as a gift of divine grace. Because of noetic effects of original sin, the realization of human freedom is impossible without God's gift of forgiveness and reconciliation.[90] Freedom is, in this sense, freedom to become

86. See Joseph Ratzinger, "Some Reflections on Subjectivity, Christology, and the Church," in *Proclaiming the Truth of Jesus Christ, Papers from the Vallonbrosa Meeting* (Washington, DC: United States Catholic Conference, 2000).

87. *Catechism of the Catholic Church*, (¶ 1813) 498.

88. The relevant passages from the *Catechism* are as follows:

1783 Conscience must be informed and moral judgment enlightened. A well-formed conscience is upright and truthful. It formulates its judgments according to reason, in conformity with the true good willed by the wisdom of the Creator. The education of conscience is indispensable for human beings who are subjected to negative influences and tempted by sin to prefer their own judgment and reject authoritative teachings.

1784 The education of the conscience is a life-long task. From the earliest years, it awakens the child to the knowledge and practice of the interior law recognized by conscience. Prudent education teaches virtue; it prevents or cures fear, selfishness and pride, resentment arising from guilt, and feelings of compliancy, born of human weakness and faults. The education of the conscience guarantees freedom and engenders peace of heart.

1785 In the formation of conscience, the Word of God is the light for our path, we must assimilate it in faith in prayer and put it into practice. We must also examine our conscience before the Lord's Cross. We are assisted by the gifts of the Holy Spirit, aided by the witness or advice of others and guided by the authoritative teaching of the Church.

Ibid., (¶ 1783–85) 492.

89. Pope John Paul II, *The Splendor of Truth (Veritatis Splendor)*, (¶¶ 54–61) 72–79.

90. Weigel, *Witness to Hope*, 744.

what human persons ought to become. It is freedom for excellence. That is to say that for Catholic moral theory, human freedom means more than the absence of coercion by the state (as modern political theories will hold). As Servais Pinckaers puts it:

The natural root of freedom develops in us principally through a sense of the true and the good, or uprightness and love, and through a desire of knowledge and happiness. Or again, by what the ancients called *semina virtutum*, the seeds of virtue, which give rise to these natural dispositions—that sense of justice, or courage, truth, friendship, and generosity—which cause us to give spontaneous praise to acts so conformed and to condemn their absence, at least in a general way. Such dispositions project a certain ideal of life, which gives direction to our desires and forms and influences our moral judgments.[91]

Human nature, known to believers through faith and worked out through many cultural forms and formulations, is the horizon from which freedom can be discerned. John Paul II taught that "[o]nly within this horizon of truth will people understand their freedom in its fullness and their call to know and love God as the supreme realization of their true self."[92] In the supreme gift of Jesus Christ, God has offered human beings a truly liberating freedom.

To summarize, then, a Catholic approach to law will be a natural law theory. It will be concerned with understanding human nature before the God who is Supreme Being. It will hold to the belief that there are some truths, at least general ones, that are self-evident because there is a universal nature to human beings. But it must not be an ideology that is inflexible or expects equal measures of human perfection from all persons, regardless of their cultural and sociopolitical horizon. And it must not be a natural law theory that judges human freedom apart from human nature. Only by fulfilling human nature is a person truly free. The mere absence of coercion by the state is not freeing to the human mind, body, or spirit. These broad principles provide boundaries for what John Paul II believed to be a proper Catholic view of law and legal theory.

CONCLUSION

This essay suggests that the writings of Pope John Paul II, which propose a new vision for the Church in the modern world, provide the context for

---

91. Pinckaers, *The Sources of Christian Ethics*, 357–58.

92. Pope John Paul II, *On the Relationship between Faith and Reason (Fides et Ratio)*, (§ 107) 129–30.

thinking coherently about what it means today to be Catholic and engaged in evangelical and transformative Catholic legal scholarship. The renewal of Catholic legal scholarship waits on certain unresolved issues concerning the compatibility of Catholic thought with the culture of modernity. The modern view of separation of law and religion has left the contemporary legal academy questioning whether there can be anything like a Catholic legal scholarship, and if so what its distinctive character should be.

The boundary concepts of a Catholic approach to law and legal theory introduced here suggest that the project of renewing Catholic legal scholarship waits on developing the means to counter the scientific/technical rationality that dominates modern culture. Since a core task for Catholic legal scholarship should be to evaluate the morality of laws and legal institutions, Catholics need a conceptualization of the nature of rationality that can persuasively show that moral evaluation is a rational pursuit. John Paul II encouraged Catholic scholars to confront the hegemony of modern scientific rationality by confidently drawing from Catholic culture and the Catholic intellectual heritage to express the moral meaning of human life and human fulfillment. Evaluating laws and the legal system from within the distinctly Catholic conceptions of human nature and human fulfillment, firmly rooted in the Trinity, should be the goal of Catholic legal scholarship. John Paul II taught that distinctively Catholic legal scholarship is committed to natural law. It is concerned with understanding and promoting the common good, and the conception of the good is founded in a comprehensive conception of human nature before the God who is Supreme Being. Also, such a natural law theory must be committed to the belief that a fulfilled human nature is the necessary and sufficient condition for a person to be truly free.

These observations about John Paul II's teaching show the boundaries of authentic Catholic legal scholarship. These boundaries can help to clarify the scope and range of distinctive voices that are united in seeking the means to persuade policymakers and legal theorists of the relevancy of Catholic thought for the problems of contemporary culture. If the project of renewal of the Catholic intellectual tradition is to succeed, gaining clarity about the nature of the project must be an ongoing exercise. It is the hope of opening space for multiple approaches and multiple voices that inspires the need for clarity about what is genuinely faithful to the Church and her teaching.

PART I

THE NATURE OF THE
HUMAN PERSON

[2]

A THEOLOGICAL ANTHROPOLOGY
OF THE HUMAN PERSON

LORENZO ALBACETE

The teaching of Pope John Paul II has been tied recently to American law by no less a figure than Supreme Court Justice Clarence Thomas in his "Frances Boyer Lecture" to the American Enterprise Institute on February 13, 2001. Justice Thomas decried a politicization of the interpretation of law that stands in the way of tolerance for divergent viewpoints, seeking to destroy with vilification what it cannot overcome with reasonable argument. When this happens, he said, "the rule of law surrenders to the rule of fear." To those contemplating silence in the face of such vilification, Justice Thomas commended the cry of Pope John Paul II, "Be not afraid." These are the words, he said, of a man who has traveled all over the world "challenging tyrants and murderers of all sorts," bringing this message—"be not afraid"—"to people living under Communist tyranny in Poland, in Czechoslovakia, in Nicaragua and in China. . . . He preached it to Africans facing death from marauding tribes and murderous disease. . . . And he preached it to us, warning us how easy it is to be trapped in a 'culture of death' even in our comfortable and luxurious country."[1]

But how not to be afraid in a world where the defense of authentic freedom and the inalienable rights of the human person are asserted against

1. Clarence Thomas, "Be Not Afraid," lecture, Francis Boyer Lecture, American Enterprise Institute for Public Policy Research, Washington, D.C., 13 Feb. 2001. http://www.aei.org/boyer/thomas.htm.

powerful opposition? What is the basis for Pope John Paul II's appeal? Towards what does he point us when he tells us not to be afraid?

In a sense, he points us to "self-evident truths." It is to self-evident truths that the founders of our country appealed to justify their decision to defend their liberty and assert their rights. It was with certainty about these self-evident truths that they presented their argument to "the opinions of mankind." In a sense, there was but one certain self-evident truth, namely, that the value of the human person was to be the norm of all political and social life, a value that originates in the will of the Creator of the universe, and, as such, had to be respected by all human authorities.

This is also the case with Pope John Paul II. "Be not afraid" is an appeal to a self-evident truth, namely, the infinite value of the human person, an infinite value engraved in the very structure of human personhood itself, in its deepest level, at the very origin of its existence. This self-evident truth, this evidence, is sustained by the link between each human person and his or her infinite destiny, a link that constitutes the very creation of man. In other words, the human person is the link between creation and the origin of all that exists, between creatures and their Creator. Pope John Paul II teaches that man is the "priest of all creation," that is, the mediator, the point of intersection between the cosmos and its transcendent origin and destiny. The human person is the point at which creation becomes conscious and free and thus able to offer to God a "canticle of praise" by developing the resources of creation as an "offering of praise," a *sacrificium laudis*. But, to repeat, in John Paul II's anthropology, the infinite value of the human person is a self-evident truth upon which all other truths about the human person, human society, and the cosmos depend.

What I propose to do in this essay is to review the way in which John Paul II argues that the infinite value of human personhood is a self-evident truth. The Pope sees in the Second Vatican Council's Pastoral Constitution on the Church in the Modern World (*GS: Gaudium et spes*), paragraph twenty-four, a perfect declaration of that self-evident truth, which is the basis for his anthropology. In this paragraph, the council declares that the human being is the only creature on earth that God willed for its own sake, that is, that its value comes from itself—so to speak—from its sheer existence, and it cannot and should not be measured by anything else.[2] As Jesus said, the Sabbath—

---

2. Second Vatican Ecumenical Council, *Pastoral Constitution of the Church in the Modern World (Gaudium et spes)*, ¶ 24 (1965):

and the Law—was given for the sake of man. Man was not created for the sake of the Law. This, the Holy Father would say, shows that the infinite dignity of human personhood is a self-evident truth, coinciding with the very creation of man by God.

But how does one go about discovering this self-evident truth, recognizing it, encountering it? Every year the Church celebrates the season of Lent. It begins on Ash Wednesday with the traditional, sobering reminder, "Remember Man that you are dust, and to dust you shall return." And just in case we forget, the Church sprinkles ashes over us, reminiscent of the ashes that we will become. Now, I am aware that cultural prejudices have led the Church to allow other versions of the reminder, lest we continue to sink into the depression lurking in the mind of each citizen of our psychologically haunted society, but I am a Hispanic Catholic, and we don't like those other formulas. Ash Wednesday is one of those few days all of us feel like going to church, and if we do go, we expect the real thing, the reminder of death, and not some sort of watered down inspiration to live better lives. We want to be able to say what is a typical expression in our language: *No somos nada.* Actually, the allowed substitute formula, "repent and believe in the gospel," means the same thing, because Christian repentance is a real dying with Christ, and faith the beginning of a totally new existence, but those words have been "deprived of their meaning," as Walker Percy said. They have been evacuated of their full meaning, devalued as currency for communication, they now mean

---

God, Who has fatherly concern for everyone, has willed that all men should constitute one family and treat one another in a spirit of brotherhood. For having been created in the image of God, Who "from once man has created the whole human race and made them live all over the face of the earth" (Acts 17:26), all men are called to one and the same goal, namely God Himself.

For this reason, love for God and neighbor is the first and greatest commandment. Sacred Scripture, however, teaches us that the love of God cannot be separated from the love of neighbor: "If there is any other commandment, it is summed up in this saying: Thou shalt love thy neighbor as thyself. . . . Love therefore is the fulfillment of the Law" (Rom. 13:9–10); cf. 1 John 4:20). To men growing daily more dependent on one another, and to a world becoming more unified every day, this truth proves to be of paramount importance.

Indeed, the Lord Jesus, when He prayed to the Father, "that all may be one . . . as we are one" (John 17:21–22) opened up vistas closed to human reason, for He implied a certain likeness between the union of the divine Persons, and the unity of God's sons in truth and charity. *This likeness reveals that man, who is the only creature which God willed for itself, cannot fully find himself except through a sincere gift of himself.*

Ibid.; emphasis added.

much less. It is hard, though, to devalue the words, "Remember, Man, that you are dust, and to dust you shall return." And, in any case, there are those ashes to make it all quite concrete.

I propose that we can make these words the point of departure of John Paul II's theological anthropology. Let me anticipate a point to which we shall return. I have been using the term "theological anthropology" to designate a view of the meaning of human personhood grasped by the Christian faithful in acceptance of God's Revelation in Jesus Christ. On the one hand, this distinguishes it from all other views—all other "anthropologies" or all other understandings of the human person—guided by other points of view: philosophical, psychological, sociological, or biological, for example. On the other hand, it is John Paul's claim that these other views are only partial views and that the full truth of the human person can be grasped only in and through the mystery of Jesus Christ. This is, of course, also the teaching of *Gaudium et spes* in its famous twenty-second chapter, which contains what can be called the summary of all of Pope John Paul II's teaching.[3]

In this view, all anthropology is a derivative of Christology, and is thus theological. It is not simply that Christology "adds" information to the other anthropological views; it is that the deepest meaning of all the discoveries made by all other anthropologies can be fully grasped only in the mystery of Jesus Christ. That is, all anthropological discoveries—unveiled by philosophical or scientific analysis—all of them point to what is fully revealed only in and through Jesus Christ. Without Jesus Christ we simply cannot know what man is; we cannot understand fully the reason for that self-evident truth discovered in the human heart. For this reason, "Remember Man that you are dust and to dust you shall return" is a proclamation of the mystery of Christ, equivalent indeed to the call to repentance and faith.

I have said that this Ash Wednesday proclamation could be seen as the

3. Ibid., ¶ 22 (1965). Paragraph 22 begins:

In reality it is only in the mystery of the Word made flesh that the mystery of man truly becomes clear. For Adam, the first man, was a type of him who was to come, Christ the Lord. Christ, the new Adam, in the very revelation of the Mystery of the Father and of his love, fully reveals man to himself and brings to light his most high calling. . . . He who is the "image of the invisible God" (Col. 1:15), is himself the perfect man who has restored in the children of Adam that likeness to God which had been disfigured ever since the first sin. Human nature, by the very fact that it was assumed, not absorbed, in him, has been raised in us to a dignity beyond compare. For, by his incarnation, he, the son of God, has in a certain way united himself with each man.

point of departure of Pope John Paul II's anthropology. The most complete and systematic presentation of his anthropology as Christological is found in the so-called Catechesis on Human Love, a meditation on theological anthropology, which he read to the thousands assembled at the weekly Wednesday public audience for a period of almost five years, from 1979 to 1984, interrupted only by special feasts, events, trips, and an assassination attempt![4]

"Remember Man that you are dust, and to dust you shall return." Those words are found in Genesis 3:19, and they are addressed to man after the fall as a summary of the consequences of sin. In particular, they immediately follow the description of the difficulties and suffering that accompany man as he works the resources of creation in order to remain alive. That they are found in the Book of Genesis means that they are quite essential to the pope's anthropology, since its basis is precisely a reflection on the creation and fall narratives found in Genesis. John Paul II sees these narratives as expressing the most fundamental experiences in human selfhood, that is, the experience of being a person, of being "someone" and not just "some thing." John Paul is quite clear that he is looking for an anthropology based on this human experience. An anthropology based on experience is of course one of the most important characteristics of modern thought, pursued mostly as an alternative to—and even in contradiction to—a traditional metaphysical anthropology. But the philosophical agenda, so to speak, of Pope John Paul II has been precisely to rescue the modern notion of experience by incorporating it into the results of a realist metaphysics. Convinced that this is possible, John Paul is not afraid to make the experience of personhood the basis for his anthropology, philosophical as well as theological. That is, the pope is convinced that an adequate analysis of the experience of personhood will rescue it from the pitfalls of subjectivism and relativism.

His purpose is to develop what he calls an "adequate anthropology," and this is defined as an anthropology based on the "essentially human" experience in contrast to an anthropology falling into the errors of reductionism.[5] That is to say, as long as no aspect or dimension of the experience of being a human person is ignored, suppressed, or reduced to another one, there is

---

4. Pope John Paul II, *The Theology of the Body: Human Love in the Divine Plan* (Boston: Pauline Books and Media, 1997). Actually, most of this work was intended for publication before Karol Wojtyla was elected pope, and it was intended as a work of theological anthropology. It has since been published as *The Theology of the Body*, and one could think of it as the theological compliment to *The Acting Person*.

5. Ibid., 58.

nothing to fear from an anthropology based on the experience of being a person, the experience of subjectivity. The pope argues that instead of a reductionism, which offers us only a partial perspective on the human person, what is needed is the principle of reduction determining the methodology proper to an adequate anthropology.

This is a very precise terminology, and it is important to see how the pope himself defines these terms, because other authors may use them differently. For this essay, it is enough to point out that the methodology that follows the principle of reduction is precisely that which, analyzing the human experience of subjectivity or personhood, searches for those self-evident truths written by the Creator in the very structure of personhood and experienced each time the human being acts as a person, that is, as a free, responsible "someone" who is unique and unrepeatable, the true author of free acts, and not just as a sample of universal abstract principles or the planned or unplanned course of evolution and history. Indeed, using John Paul II as an example, it could be said that an important Catholic contribution to American culture is to reassert and explain the notion of self-evident truths that can serve as the basis for unity in a multicultural, pluralistic nation. Later essays, of course, will develop the implications of this for American law.

The creation and fall accounts in the Book of Genesis are a most appropriate source for this study because they express in mythological terms the most profound experiences of the human person "in the dimensions of the mystery of creation, and, at the same time, in the perspective of the mystery of redemption."[6] The pope uses the term "mythological" in the way it is understood in contemporary studies in the phenomenology of religion, that is, not as hiding the truth, not as a flight into the imagination, not as fantasy, not as an underdeveloped way of accounting for reality, but as a privileged mode of communication for what is otherwise incommunicable. The myth is not the opposite of a historical account as we understand it today; the myth is a narrative that communicates the deepest experiences of human interiority. The myth is the articulation of that which cannot be articulated, the expression of the inexpressible, namely, the link between time and eternity, between the finite and the infinite.

The true myth is thus not an escape from reality, but the introduction to reality's deepest level. All meaningful human action and communication

---

6. Ibid., 25.

(that is, truly revelatory of human interiority, of the experience of selfhood) take place in the context of an experience of ultimate meaning that is inexpressible. Ultimate meaning is the horizon within which human life is lived in time and space. This horizon is the boundary between time and eternity, and myth takes us from one into the other. There are myths of creation taking us back to the beginnings, to the origins of our existence as humans, found by looking not back in time, but deeper into time, so to speak, deeper into the experience of time to that "beginning" beyond which is a dizzying abyss that we cannot grasp. Eschatological myths describe the boundary of the abyss that lies at the end of our existence within time and space. Myths thus express like no other language our experiences of "coming from" and "going toward" that frame the mystery of personhood. Myth, if you will, is the privileged language of the self-evident. That is why it gives us unique access to those primordial or original experiences upon which the adequate anthropology must be based.

Pope John Paul II's concept of "original experiences" is the key to understanding what a "self-evident truth" is. The original experiences are the experiences of the self-in-action. Not in just any action, but in those actions through which the self expresses its own sense of value, through which it shows its awareness of its own worth. The original experiences are thus ethical experiences. They are experiences of total commitment, as when we say, "unless I do this (or if I do this) I will no longer be myself." The original experience is precisely that experience of uniqueness and unrepeatability that defines the human person. The human person acts as a person by reliving or projecting the experience of uniqueness and unrepeatability, an experience lived through a particular existential context. The argument is that the truth about personhood, the truth about man, is expressed by action motivated by this "experience lived through" particular circumstances. The category of "experience lived through" is, he says, necessary for an adequate anthropology.[7]

In contrast to the phenomenology of Max Scheler, the pope holds that the person is not merely the subjective unity of these experiences. Instead, at the heart of these experiences, there is a free decision that has been made, a free stand taken in response to the impact of reality mediated by the concrete circumstances. For this reason, the object of an adequate anthropological anal-

7. Ibid., 52.

ysis is not exactly the "experience" itself, as if it were purely a passive thing; rather it is the human action itself. It is the act that unveils man as the protagonist of his life, as its creative protagonist of the human drama. The original experience is this experience of creativity that the human person is capable of and is free to realize. In terms of the Declaration of Independence, the self-evident truths are revealed by the action itself; they are revealed in the decision to risk it all in the pursuit of independence. It is this decision, this stand, this commitment of all or nothing that reveals the self-evident truths; they are not the conclusions of an abstract philosophical analysis. This is why the signers can say at the end of the document, "And for the support of this declaration, with a firm reliance on Divine Providence we mutually pledge to each other our lives, our fortunes and our sacred honor." Notice the experience of a link to infinity that emerges as part of this original experience, the experience of the infinite value of the human person, the experience of the transcendence of the person.

The Wednesday Catechesis is built around four of these original experiences found in the creation accounts of the Book of Genesis, analyzed according to the phenomenological principle of reduction, taking into account that what we are looking for is the sense of self-worth demonstrated by Adam and Eve as they respond to the reality of their existence in the world, and later, before each other. The original experiences identified are those of original solitude, original unity, original nakedness, and original innocence or, better, holiness. In this study, these are experiences of the human body.

One might think that the body is emphasized because the pope is constructing an adequate anthropology that would serve as the basis for the teaching of the Church on love and sexuality, but this is not true. The pope argues repeatedly that an adequate anthropology cannot be built by studying purely spiritual experiences. All of our original experiences are mediated through the body because they are precisely the experience of how we stand in or relate to the world around us. Indeed, the conclusion of his analysis of these experiences is the discovery of our awareness of what he calls the "nuptial meaning of the body." This is, in fact, the test of the adequacy of all anthropological proposals, namely their ability to grasp and express the nuptial meaning of the body.

The nuptial meaning of the body expresses the experience of the human body as the visible expression of the truth that the human person cannot exist as an isolated individual. Human personhood is in fact a capacity for, and a call to, a communion of mutual self-surrender between persons, a communion of love. This capacity and call to communion is what distinguishes the human person from the animals. It is in this capacity and call that we discover what it means to be created in the "image of God." Amazingly, it is the human experience of bodiliness, of our material dimension, that reveals that we are called to personal fulfillment by engaging in a relationship with the mystery of God at the origin and destiny of our existence. Self-evident truths, therefore, are not abstract principles. They are always incarnate; that is, they are expressed in our relation with the material world, with material creation.

Self-evident truths are found in our engagement with the created universe as we try to find a "home" in it, that is, a way of living our capacity for interpersonal communion based on the total gift of self to another. Of course, what is going on here is the Holy Father's conviction that if we dig deep enough into our original experiences, into the "fundamental needs of the human heart" (as Father Luigi Giussani calls them—indeed the word "heart" is also used by the pope to indicate the source of these original experiences)—we will discover that the human person is, above all, a cry for Another, a call to a communion of love that embraces the mystery of God himself, discovered in the heart of the other person, to whom we freely and totally give ourselves through a mutual, unconditional acceptance and affirmation. Only an anthropology that reaches this awesome conclusion is an adequate anthropology.

But from where does the Holy Father derive this confidence that an adequate anthropology can unveil the call to communion as the self-evident truth upon which we can build our lives by building a civilization where our social, economic, and political structures reflect that relation with the resources of creation discovered in the experience of the nuptial meaning of the body? From where are we as Catholics to derive the confidence that the deepest truth about the human person, his or her call to communion, is a self-evident truth that we can point out to our fellow citizens in this pluralistic, multicultural society as the basis for a legal system that respects all the implications of the infinite dignity of each human being? The answer is paragraph twenty-two of *Gaudium et spes*. We will find this confidence through our faith in the mystery of Christ—not as an abstract affirmation of our intellects—but as an experience of encounter with the One that is the "center of history and the cosmos," the very Truth of all of creation in a human body.[8]

8. Second Vatican Ecumenical Council, *Gaudium et spes*, ¶ 22 (1965) (emphasis added).

Pope John Paul II offers his adequate anthropology of self-evident truths not only to Christians, but to all human beings. But he can do this only because he is a Christian. So too will it be with us. We offer our Catholic perspective on American law not only to Catholics, but to all because we are Catholics, because we have encountered Christ as the truth about our deepest self in the life of the Catholic Church, the full manifestation on earth of that communion to which all human beings are called, for which they were created. Indeed, predestined in Christ before the creation of the world, convinced of this predestination, convinced that creation is in fact this predestination, we are confident that each human being, living in a human world—a network of human relations already wrapped into Christ by the grace of his death and resurrection—will find in his or her heart what the pope calls a real, if distant, "echo" of this self-evident truth.

In the second cycle of his theological anthropology, still working within the symbolic and primordial world of myths and symbols, the Holy Father explores the mystery of sin as it impacts each one of the original human experiences. Obviously, no anthropology is adequate if it ignores the fact that human beings do not have the strength by themselves to live in accordance with the original desires of the heart. That is why the Holy Father says we can find those desires only as a "distant echo" of our creation for the communion of love in Christ.[9]

In terms of the original experiences, Genesis's account of the fall, Pope John Paul II argues, shows that the need for another expressed in original solitude becomes an aversion to otherness and the desire to re-create the world to overcome this fear through power and manipulation. Original unity is lost as a result, and we feel the need to be protected from others with whom we have no choice to unite for certain purposes. Indeed, in many instances our perception of the other as other is in fact lost, and all we see is a reflection of our interests, the "looking with lust" in Jesus' condemnation of adultery.[10] Original nakedness is replaced by shame and distrust of the body as an apt vehicle of communication, making it instead an object for domination. Original innocence is replaced by guilt and the efforts to escape it by claiming to be the ultimate arbiters of what is right or wrong. All of this can be summarized as the total loss of the perception of the nuptial meaning of the body, the radical alienation between man and the rest of the universe.

9. Pope John Paul II, *The Theology of the Body,* 204.
10. Ibid., 147.

This is what the pope calls the "man of concupiscence" disclosed by the account of the fall in Genesis.[11]

It is important to underline that as expressing the conditions of the experience of personhood, that is, the state of our ability to experience ourselves and others as unique and unrepeatable, as the free agents of our own creativity, both of these states of life—the *original* and the *fallen* state—designate the interior state not only of individuals, but of the cultures through which the person expresses his defining experiences. Culture comes from "cultivate," and culture is the way we cultivate our lives as persons. A distortion at the very deepest levels of interiority, touching the very experience of selfhood, fragmenting and wounding our experience of being an "I" before a "you," will spread throughout the entire world of man, to all human relations with the universe, and, through man's inseparable tie to all of creation (remember the absolute importance of the body!), to the material universe itself.

Faith in the mystery of Christ and the redemption proclaimed by it, the alteration in the deepest levels of human experience of the self and the world brought about by Christ's incarnation, death, and resurrection, convinces the pope that the man of concupiscence does not exist. Otherwise sin would have proven stronger than our predestination in Christ. Absolutely nothing can be stronger than the bond that unites us to the Incarnate Son of the Father: no sin, no death can destroy our orientation to communion with Him. It is true that original man does not exist anymore and can be described only in terms of the myths of creation, but our roots in that mysterious original state have not been totally destroyed by sin. Because of the predestination of each person to communion with Christ, we saw that it is possible to appeal to the experiences of all human beings with the confidence that they might be led to grasp that distant echo of the original state present in those self-evident truths. We can do this in spite of the consequences of original sin. One way we contribute to our society's efforts to construct a civilization in accordance with those self-evident truths—a just civilization—is precisely to insist that sin and corruption do not define man, that we need not surrender to despair or cynicism about the possibility of building a just world because there is in each human being still a trace of that call to be a person in communion with Christ, who has in fact entered the theater of human history, the network of human relations that constitutes the world of man.

11. Ibid.

Christ is present in our relations with one another, with nature, with all of creation, and with infinity itself. That, and only that, is why the Holy Father can say, "Be not afraid!" Be not afraid even to lose your life in the struggle for justice, for peace, for true liberty. Be not afraid because everything truly human in you is preserved by the Risen Christ and cannot be destroyed. Do not let the masters of suspicion—says the pope—and accusers of the human heart tell us that we are all corrupt through and through, that our noblest ideals are but illusions to prevent us from confronting the truth.

The myths that express the deepest ideals and hopes of humankind, the eschatological myths, must also be incorporated into this adequate anthropology. But where do they come from, if they are not the fruit of human self-delusion? The myths about creation came from those original experiences, those self-evident truths found in the heart in spite of sin. But these are not enough to sustain our hope. Just as there are original experiences in the heart, there must also be eschatological experiences sustaining the certainty, the self-evidence of our hopes. Somehow, man must be able now to experience his radical future beyond death. And this is also possible for all human beings, Christian or not, because of the fact, the real event in this world, of the resurrection of Christ and his continuing presence in this world as the Risen One. Indeed, real man, "historical man," as the pope calls him, is neither the man of origins nor eschatological man. Historical man lives already caught in the interplay between those two horizons: the beginning and the world to come that is already here in the Risen Christ. That is why the "eschatological experience" is also present in all human hearts. What is this experience like?

In terms reminding us of the famous polarities that frame human existence in history according to Balthasar, the eschatological experience is somehow the experience of life according to our hearts' fundamental desires, which are now polarized so that they appear irreconcilable, namely: the relation between matter and spirit, between individual and community, and between male and female. On this side of eternity we will always experience the tension between these polarities. But in our experience of the presence of Christ we can also begin to experience how these will be reconciled, how they will be the basis of our eschatological communion of love in which no fundamental desire or self-evident truth is eliminated, for each one is absolutely necessary for our continuing existence as human beings. This too has great consequences for our contributions to our society based on our perspective of what is taking place in the legal world, in the world of politics and economics, of work and leisure, of science and technology, of sexuality, gender, and love.

Law, of course, mediates the polarity between individual and community. Our perspective, based on the mystery of Christ, allows us to recognize that these polarities constitute historical human life, and therefore legislation should never seek to reduce one into the other, for example, individual into community or community into individual. The interests of the human spirit—the religious sense, that is—cannot be set aside in favor of, say, economic progress. But, economic progress, and especially the care of the poor, cannot be set aside to favor expressions of the religious quest. Finally, and so important today in legislation concerning marriage, family, reproduction, and sexual orientation, the difference between men and women should not be obliterated, nor the rights of either one denied. Laws should protect the experiences of fatherhood and motherhood as appropriate to male and female, respectively, and should defend the integrity of marriage as the basis for family and society. Both the rights of individuals and communities should be promoted without seeking to force a harmony that we are unable to construct by ourselves, but can only anticipate imperfectly as a result of our union with Christ.

Without this union, without the presence of the Risen Christ in the world for two thousand years now—Jesus Christ, present as our true ideal without limits sustaining our efforts to build a civilization of love—without this Presence, there would be only one self-evident truth: "Remember Man that you are dust, and to dust you shall return." That in spite of being dust we can still hope to attain what our hearts desire, the eternity sought by all life, is the greatest contribution our perspective on reality can offer to American law and everything else. Indeed, it is all really a matter of not being afraid.

A PHILOSOPHICAL ANTHROPOLOGY
OF THE HUMAN PERSON

Can We Know the Nature
of Human Persons?

BENEDICT M. ASHLEY, O.P.

Some persons today deny that human persons have a human nature. Others claim that a "human being" or an "individual of the human species" is not necessarily a human "person." They sometimes argue that terms like "human person" and "human nature" are merely "social constructs" whose definition depends entirely on the particular "culture" in which they are used. Hence, it is useless, some say, to try to distinguish between "nature" and "culture," or, as it is often phrased, "nature versus nurture."

People in different cultures certainly do have different notions about what makes one really a human person, and as a result these cultures behave in very different ways. This very fact, however, betrays what is common to the human species, namely, that humans are the only animals that do not live simply by instinct or conditioned learning but by *inventing a culture,* a notion obviously manifested by the thousands of human languages still in use. The fact that every human culture depends on a humanly invented language is proof enough that the human species has a common nature that is species-specific. Thus, our common human nature is marked by at least two forms of behavior not found in other animals: the ability (1) to invent a culture and (2) to express and transmit that culture through language.[1]

Therefore, although it is often not easy to determine whether a particular element of human behavior is "natural," and, although human nature is so complex that we will never be able to define it exhaustively, there is no doubt that a general account can be given of it that holds for all members of the human species throughout history. Indeed, to speak of a "human species" can only mean that we have at least a general notion of the nature that defines that species. In common usage, therefore, we should take the term human "person" to mean simply any member of the human species.

In this essay, I endeavor to develop a general understanding of the "human person" using tools provided in nature rather than introducing concepts of the transcendent derived from religious revelation (at least not until the end of my essay) because the latter requires special knowledge that not everyone recognizes. Even within the natural order, however, a distinction is often made today between what we can know about human persons by "science" and what we can know by "philosophy." Yet this distinction is itself problematic and was not introduced until the Enlightenment of the eighteenth century.[2] For the great ancient and medieval thinkers about human nature "philosophy" meant any kind of purely natural systematic thought, so that what we now call "science" was also part of "philosophy." These thinkers employed three branches of philosophy to explore human nature: "natural philosophy" (what today we would call "natural science" or simply "science") to deal with the material or bodily aspect of human nature, "ethics" to deal with free human behavior, and "metaphysics" to deal with the spiritual aspects of the human person.

To untangle this confusion, I will use the term "science" as it is now used to include both what we today call "science" and whatever in the philosophical tradition refers like modern science directly to the study of our material world known to us by sense observation and governed by natural laws. The

1. The popular notion that animal languages are essentially the same as human language or that animals can be taught to speak a human language is false; see Thomas A. Sebeok and Robert Rosenthal, *The Clever Hans Phenomenon: Communication with Horses, Whales, Apes, and People* (New York: New York Academy of Sciences, 1981).

2. This is usually attributed to Christian Wolff (1679–1754) a follower of Descartes and Leibniz; see Richard J. Blackwell, "The Structure of Wolffian Philosophy," *Modern Schoolman* 38 (1960): 203–18.

term "ethics" I will use for human free decisions that are not determined by natural laws, although they are governed by the "natural moral law" and involve not just the explanation of facts but the weighing of what we speak of as "values." The term "philosophy" I will use only for what everyone regards (if they are willing to admit the validity of such a discipline) as philosophy par excellence—namely, "metaphysics," which deals with the whole range of beings, material and immaterial. Thus to deal with the human person in its spiritual aspects is to think metaphysically, that is, "philosophically," but this is valid only if it has first been proven that in fact there is an immaterial aspect to human nature, since many scientists deny this. Certainly we cannot know whether this is the case except from the material effects of such immaterial causes, and we can only know something of what spiritual beings are like by analogy from the material things we directly experience. Therefore, we turn first to the scientific exploration of human nature.

THE SCIENTIFIC EXPLORATION
OF HUMAN NATURE

The first or scientific phase of our inquiry must make use of what physics, chemistry, and the life sciences show us about human nature. We must, however, avoid the materialist, reductionist, and idealist presuppositions that too often influence the theories of modern scientists. Hence scientific study of human nature must begin with a study of human behavior because "as a thing acts so it is," and there is no way to arrive at an understanding of nature except through its activities that are sensibly observable. Yet it is essential not to prejudice this research by the *behavioristic* assumption made by B. F. Skinner and other psychologists that the human person is a "black box" about which we can know nothing except how we stimulate it and how it responds. That assumption results from the influence of the idealist philosophy of Immanuel Kant that Skinner and his disciples uncritically accepted.[3]

Biology tells us a great deal about the natural structure and function of the human organism and how it differs from that of other animals. Our anatomical structure must be understood not just statically but in terms of the unified functions of its differentiated parts. From the moment of the formation of the one-celled zygote from the union of the nuclei of a sperm and an

---

3. Kant held that we cannot know the nature of the human self or of things outside the mind but only sense impressions on which the mind imposes its own logical categories.

ovum, the nucleus of the zygote contains the information needed to construct a mature human body. While the genome contains the blueprint or information for this construction, it is the organism as a whole that is able to use this information to do the actual work of organic construction to full human physical maturity and to maintain it during its lifespan. This genome thus both defines the organism as a member of the human species and also gives to it unique characteristics that distinguish it from every other member of the species.[4]

It would take volumes to describe human nature in all the physical aspects that science has discovered, and yet we are far from exhausting the subject. Embryological development takes place by repeated divisions of the original one-celled human organism such that each new cell also contains the complete genome, yet in different cells different genes are deactivated in a gradual process that differentiates sets of cells to form the different organs of the body, each having special functions within the whole.

Within the first month of embryological development the embryo develops a central nervous system, and by the end of the month the primitive brain is evident.[5] The brain is clearly the primary organ of the body, unifying all the other life processes, and is far more complex and unified in its operation than the brains of other animals. If deprived of energy from the blood and the lungs, it dies, and with it the whole organism dies in a few minutes. The sense organs—the sense of touch in the skin and muscles, the eyes, the ears, the nose, and the tongue—differentiate but remain connected together by the brain. From the brain go out nervous impulses that activate the muscles of the body and the skeleton to make it possible for the human body to move about in its environment.

Thus, the human organism begins to be able to operate not only from the information in the genome but also from learned information stored in the brain. These learned activities further promote the brain's maturation. The rest of the organs of the body, the digestive system, the lungs, and the circulatory and hormonal systems are needed to supply the brain and the loco-

---

4. In the human species a clone or identical twin is not strictly natural but is due to some developmental defect perhaps resulting from a genetic defect or simply some other embryological accident. The preference of nature is to produce individual diversity within the species since this has at least an advantage for survival of some individuals in special circumstances.

5. For more details see Benedict M. Ashley and Albert Moraczewski, "Cloning, Aquinas, and the Embryonic Person," *National Catholic Bioethics Quarterly* 1, no. 2 (2001): 189–202.

motor system with energy. Thus, the human brain is the physical core of the human person, which the rest of the body serves by supplying it with information and the energy it needs to function and govern the body.

Each of these various levels of bodily structure and function has a certain autonomy. For example, as we now know from open-heart surgery, the brain can be kept alive artificially, as can the heart even when the patient is brain-dead. Persons, however, are still living as long as their brains are alive. When the brain is dead, any life remaining in the other organs, even if artificially sustained, is no longer the life of the organism as such and hence not human, personal life.[6]

Besides its work of unifying the action of the other organs and moving the body by stimulating the muscles of the body, what does the brain do? It is primarily the organ of the *internal* senses, as distinguished from the external senses of touch, sight, sound, and the rest. By observing the behavior of animals and humans, we can distinguish four processes that distinguish this internal activity of the brain.[7] First, the brain *synthesizes* the information coming from the five external senses, since it is evident that all animals, including ourselves, recognize that the same object contacts us through several senses. I perceive a dog, just as a dog perceives a dog, as a single entity that I see, hear, smell, touch. Second, the brain has the power of *memory,* which retains such information and is often able to recall it and place it in chronological order of reception. Third, it has the power of *imagination,* by which we separate an image from its original situation, and can also modify it and combine it with other images. Fourth, the brain endows an image with the power negatively or positively to stimulate our reaction to it, that is, it gives it "value" as something we like or dislike, the *cogitative* or *evaluative* sense.

Most animals evidently have these four internal senses, but in them the fourth or evaluative sense is often highly determined from birth as an "instinct." In higher animals, however, instincts are more general, thus permitting them to learn from experience and to be more flexible and adaptive in their behavior. Hence, we humans are not born knowing our way home like migratory birds or with the ability to build a hive we have never seen be-

---

6. Some are questioning brain-death as an adequate criterion, but see James L. Bernat, "A Defense of the Whole-Brain Concept of Death," *Hastings Center Report* 28, no. 2 (1998): 14–26.

7. The distinction of these four internal senses was accepted by Aquinas and by Aristotle and seems consistent with modern psychology. See Thomas Aquinas, *Summa Theologiae,* I:q.78.aa.3–4; Aristotle, *De Anima* III.

fore like a bee. Yet we do have some instincts, but all these are greatly refined through learned habits. The baby instinctively clings to its mother and sucks her breast. Later this simple instinct will be modified to form various eating habits adapted to different cultures.

It is through this evaluative sense that we experience physical pleasure or pain and we call such positive and negative experiences "feelings" or "emotions." They arise because we recognize, either instinctively or through learning experiences, that an object is of value or disvalue for the satisfaction of one of our basic biological drives. Because the basic functions of a living organism are to take in energy (nutrition), to grow or develop, and to reproduce, humans too have these three fundamental drives, and our internal senses help us to recognize which objects can satisfy these drives and which objects frustrate them and hence imperil our survival. These drives, as such, are unconscious, but they become conscious as emotions or feelings when they are stimulated by sense images and then cause physiological changes in the body that become conscious through our external senses. For example, the drive for food is not itself conscious, but when, at the right time, I see something appetizing as judged by the evaluative sense, my digestive system is stimulated. I sense this effect in my body as "I'm hungry," and experience a feeling or emotion.[8]

The drive to reproduce, biologically necessary for the preservation of the species, but not, like the drive for nutrition, necessary for the survival of the individual, is basically instinctual. Yet, like the nutrition drive, the sexual drive can be modified and refined in various ways through learning. Thus, humans are in a general way instinctually heterosexual in their sex drives, but mature heterosexuality requires development through normal experience of human, especially family, relationships, and developmental factors may lead to various other sexual tendencies that frustrate that drive's natural orientation toward reproduction.[9]

That animals also have a second type of biological drive is also evident from their competition for mates and their struggles to obtain food against

8. Aquinas treats the drives or "appetites" in *Summa Theologiae*, I:q.81 in general and their acts in great detail in I-II qq. 22–48. This is based on Aristotle's *Rhetoric*, which in turn was based on the extensive Greek experience of how "emotions" operate in political persuasion.

9. This of course is a highly controversial topic, and research on the subject is inadequate because it is discouraged by the gay movement. In my opinion, however, the position of John F. Harvey, *The Truth about Homosexuality* (San Francisco: Ignatius Press, 1996), is essentially correct.

many obstacles or to escape from enemies and other dangers. These can be called the *aggressive* drives, although they are also exhibited in an animal's refusal to escape pain and hostile forces if this endurance is necessary to achieve the satisfaction of its pleasure needs. Such aggressive or endurance feelings and emotions are even more complex than those of pain and pleasure because they presuppose the latter. Thus, the emotions felt in battle combine a longing for peace and its pleasures with an aggressive daring and a patient endurance. All affectivity or emotion can be reduced to eleven basic kinds of feeling. When we sense an object as pleasant, we feel (1) an initial pleasure; (2) a drive to attain it by moving toward it; (3) enjoyment when we get it. But if it begins to slip away, we are (4) displeased; (5) fearful or anxious about being deprived of it; (6) sad and grieving at having lost it. If, on the other hand, we perceive something pleasant that we desire to obtain but also see that its attainment will involve painful obstacles, we experience (7) courage to overcome and win what we desire; (8) the excitement of attack against the obstacle; and (9) anger if it resists our attack. Then if we lose in the battle, we escape and feel (10) discouragement as we run away, and finally we feel (11) despair when the battle is over and we have lost. All human emotional states at the physical level are one of these eleven or a combination of them.

To express their sensations and feelings and communicate with others, animals have language, but it consists either in signs that stand for sensible things, or in signals that attack or warn other animals. Human language contains such signs, but differs essentially from animal language in two ways. First, though our words are derived from sensible objects just like those of animals, they can also represent *abstract ideas*. The clearest example of this is to be found in mathematics. The mathematician's idea of "3" was derived from seeing three sensible objects, such as counting three fingers. Yet the 3 he uses in the equation $3 + 4 = 7$ completely omits the concrete qualities, places, or times that are included in any sensible image. It is true in arithmetic that $3 + 4 = 7$, but it is not true in anything sensed or imaged. For example, 3 fingers + 4 toes does not equal either 7 fingers or 7 toes. Thus the whole of mathematics, and hence most of modern science, which uses so much mathematics, illustrates that human thought is capable of abstraction. Indeed, even such a notion as "human person" has this abstract character because, if it is to apply to all human beings, that notion must eliminate all individual characteristics.

A second, and perhaps even clearer, evidence that human language differs from animal language is found in the *syntactical* use of words, by which they are formed into sentences and larger units of expression. The *relation* of a predicate to its subject found in every sentence and of phrases to each other represented by such words as "the," "and," "therefore," "because," by which complex sentences are composed even in children's speaking, are not relations found between physical objects or their images. The concept of "because" is a product of human thinking. It is not a sign of anything in the real world.

Some have tried to identify human thought with the language it expresses, but this is contradicted by the fact that although there are a great variety of human languages, they can all be translated into each other. In such translations, much of the imagery with its affective connotations has to be eliminated, but what remains and makes communication effective is the abstract concepts common to diverse languages. The English word "one" and the Latin word *unum* carry with them somewhat different connotations, images, and feeling tones, but both are essentially translated by the Arabic numeral 1. Thus, conscious thought as we experience it introspectively and its expression in language are not identical, as we see in every conversation when people struggle to make themselves clear to each other.

Moreover, and it is this that explains our cultural inventiveness, abstract thought makes *freedom of choice* possible, that is, the ability to see the various means that could be used to achieve some end or goal that we desire. The more an animal acts by instinct, the less free it can be in its actions and the more deterministic are its observed behaviors. Abstract thought can perceive the *relation* of any available means to the end sought and thus the advantages and disadvantages of trying a particular means. Although sometimes only one means is available or one is much more effective than another, usually there is a balance between advantages and disadvantages of the several available means to a goal. This leaves us *free to choose.* If we could not choose freely, cultural inventiveness would be impossible.

Therefore, describing human nature through observable behavior without depending on private introspection that as such is not publicly available, we can still say that what is most specific to human organisms is that they converse and communicate in language that involves abstract signs. When we center on this plain fact, a great deal of what we know about human biology, anatomical structure and function, human culture, and its history begins to make sense. There is a remarkable difference between the human hand with its thumb opposable to the other fingers and the paws of most animals, even the "hands" of the great apes. The human hand is "the instrument of instruments" that makes possible for us to make and use a complicated technology. Animals can have simple tools, as when a chimpanzee cracks open a nut with a stone, but they are of the simplest sort. Humans, in contrast, have invented the computer, and even the people of the caves of Lascaux were already able to paint remarkable pictures of animals. The upright stature of humans frees their hands for such work. The naked, sensitive human skin, the position of human eyes for three-dimensional vision, and, indeed, every item of human anatomy and physiology work together to enable the human animal to speak in abstract language and to invent tools and the diverse cultures they make possible. In short, the human body is appropriate to the human mind. It makes little difference how one explains scientifically the origin of this body through evolution, whether according to Darwin's theory or some other theory; the fact remains that ours is a human body adapted to abstract thought in a very effective manner.

We come then by a purely scientific approach based on observation and abstract analysis of our observations to the question of how it is possible for the human, who is a network of interacting neurons carrying information from one point in the brain to another, to form abstract ideas.[10] Scientists today generally assume that somehow, as we know more and more about the brain, we will be able to explain this in the usual manner. Hence, some think that eventually we will be able to produce computers that think even more effectively than humans. Such scientists suppose that to deny this possibility is to undermine the very concept of scientific thought. This exhibits an unwarranted assumption, a prejudice derived not from science itself or its actual successes but from the attempts of certain "philosophers" to deal with this question. Some of these philosophers have argued that nothing is real but matter, and others have argued that nothing we know exists outside our minds. There is no need to restrict scientific thinking to either of these dead-end paths of materialism or idealism.

The way out of this dilemma is to grant that we have derived all of our abstract concepts somehow from concrete images in the internal senses in the brain that were themselves originally derived from the external senses' contact with material objects. Abstract thinking, however, permits us to recognize in our material world that what we directly observe is the *effect* of causes

---

10. See the noted physicist Roger Penrose, *The Emperor's New Mind: Concerning Computers, Minds, and the Laws of Physics* (New York: Viking-Penguin, 1990), for discussion of this question.

that sometimes we can observe but whose existence we quite often have logically to *infer* from these effects.[11] The whole of modern science depends on the validity of such inferences, because, for example, we use this type of reasoning to establish Newton's laws and Einstein's refinement of them on which modern physics, and hence modern biology, depend. Such reasoning from effect to cause then necessarily leads to the conclusion that modern science, limited as it is to material, sensible things, cannot give an *ultimate* explanation of the effects it observes. Every series of effects and secondary causes science may discover ultimately leads to some ultimate cause or causes that are not material causes. If they were material they would not be ultimate because material things are always changing, and these changes take place only if caused. Thus, modern science sets its own limits by proving that the universe it studies is not completely self-explanatory but must depend on an uncaused cause or causes that cannot be material.[12]

This conclusion established at the very foundations of physics, that the material universe cannot be scientifically explained unless we also grant that it has immaterial causes, has a special application to the human person. We have seen that human persons, notably scientists, can think abstractly. It is certainly true that without a material brain and our external and internal senses, we would have no concrete sense data from which to form abstract concepts. Yet just as it is impossible for a material universe to exist and change without an immaterial first cause, so also is it impossible for the brain (or any material system, such as a computer) to form abstract concepts or to be self-conscious. Whatever information exists in matter is also quantified and qualified and located in time and place so as to be individuated; but as we have seen this is not the case with abstract thoughts. Moreover, be-

11. David Hume was right in saying that the relation of cause and effect is not, as such, observable by our senses, but could not explain how we can give valid scientific explanations in terms of cause and effect. His error resulted from a failure to understand the difference between sense knowledge and our intelligence, which, although it depends for all our knowledge on the senses, is able to analyze the data they provide so as to sort out existential dependencies from merely chance sequences of events. Kant was forced into idealism by Hume's false arguments.

12. Such a proof of the existence of a First Immaterial Cause of the world does not depend on the "ontological" a priori proof of St. Anselm, nor on the "cosmological argument" in the a priori form in which Kant presented it. St. Thomas Aquinas had shown the error of any such a priori approach to the problem. What I refer to here is an a posteriori argument from observed change in the world, common to all the explanations that modern science gives to phenomena, but carried to their ultimate conclusion, which modern science fails to do.

cause matter is quantified, spread out, it cannot be "all together," yet human self-consciousness is precisely the ability to know oneself as a whole, not part by part. Hence, animals can be conscious of objects, even of their own bodies, but not of themselves as thinking bodies. I know that I know, and, if I like, I can know that I know that I know. This self-reflexion excludes material extension. This is why human intelligence will always be able to think of a problem that no computer can solve until by the same human intelligence we invent a better computer to solve it.[13]

Thus, the human power to think abstractly, exhibited especially in modern science, to invent wonderful machines to assist us to think, and above all our power to communicate with each other shows that, like the universe as a whole, the human body has a spiritual principle necessary to explain its behavior. This is manifest in our freedom of choice by which we transcend the determinism of the material world and can explore, understand, and control it.

THE ETHICAL AND TECHNOLOGICAL
EXPLORATION OF HUMAN NATURE

The fact that humans can make free choices not determined by natural laws implies not only that we have theoretical knowledge of facts and their causal explanation as in science, but that human persons also have *practical* knowledge that guides free decisions though it does not finally determine them. Furthermore, it implies that in addition to intelligence, human persons have the power of *will*, which, enlightened by practical knowledge, finally determines definite choices and causes them to be executed by the other human powers. For example, we can choose to go to the beach, the country, or the city for vacation, and this choice actually moves us to those places. Thus, what is most specific to human persons is that they have, and other animals do not have, the powers of abstract intelligence and free will.

Practical knowledge that guides free choice is of two kinds. First, we make decisions about how we are to live, and sometimes we give guidance to oth-

13. Another approach to this question is to point out that the famous theorems of Kurt Gödel proved mathematically show that no formal logical system can solve all the problems that our reason can raise and perhaps solve, nor can it prove its own self-consistency without reference to some other system. Since computer programs are such formal logical systems, this shows that no matter how comprehensively such a program is constructed, the human mind can make a more comprehensive one. Moreover, the self-consistency and hence the validity of any computer program will always depend on human experience to verify it.

ers on how they are to live. This is the *ethical* aspect of human nature.[14] To speak of the "nature" of anything is to speak of how it behaves, and anything either behaves in such a way as to preserve and complete itself or self-destructs. Indeed, human persons naturally seek to live and to satisfy their basic, natural needs. Their intelligence guides them in how this can be realistically achieved, and their free will enables them to make actual and effective decisions. We can, however, either through ignorance of our real needs, powers of fulfillment, or the circumstances in which we act, make serious mistakes in this matter. Or, because we are free, we can ignore what we know about all this and yield to emotions that we realize are destructive. Thus, it is no small problem to understand our needs and their relative importance in the total fulfillment of our natures. Just as science observes the facts of the world and develops theories to explain them, so the discipline of *ethics* is a study of the factors in human free choices of behavior as means to human fulfillment or "happiness."

Yet the general knowledge of what is ethical or moral is insufficient to actually attain happiness unless all the human powers subject to our conscious and free control are trained to act together both in making decisions and in carrying them out. Hence, human persons have to acquire moral skills or *virtues* that enable them to consistently make and carry out good decisions in changing circumstances.[15] They learn this first in the reproductive unit, the family, which depends on the fidelity of the couple to each other and to their offspring. The family, however, is insufficient to supply all human needs, material or intellectual. Consequently, human persons are citizens of a larger community and require civic virtues of obedience to law, mutual cooperation, and responsible government for the common good.

A second type of freedom possessed by human persons is the freedom of technological invention and the control over our bodies and the material world. It is precisely because we have used this power that our culture has become so artificial that we sometimes forget that all of these innovations and culture itself are based on our unique nature, and so some have come to doubt that we

14. For a concise statement of Thomistic ethics see the chapters on the logic and principles of ethics in B. M. Ashley and Kevin D. O'Rourke, O.P., *Health Care Ethics: A Theological Analysis,* 4th ed., rev. (Washington, D.C.: Georgetown University Press, 1997).

15. On this now much discussed topic see Jean Porter, *The Recovery of Virtue: The Relevance of Aquinas for Christian Ethics* (Louisville, KY: Westminster John Knox, 1990), and Linda Trinkaus Zagzebski, *Virtues of the Mind: An Inquiry into the Nature of Virtue and the Ethical Foundations of Knowledge* (Cambridge: Cambridge University Press, 1996).

have a human nature.[16] Much more needs to be said, but must be passed over here, about this ethical and technological side of the human person. Yet one important point must be made. Because we are intelligent and free persons who strive together to advance in understanding the truth about ourselves and about our world, the ethical goal of both the individual person and the community is not economic prosperity, military power, or the pursuit of physical pleasure, as some suppose. The goal of human persons is "meaning," that is, truth about themselves, each other, and the world.[17] Moreover, because nothing is so interesting in our material universe as human persons, the goal of human life is mutual understanding and sharing of that understanding in love.

At first sight modern politics seems little concerned with "contemplation" until we notice how big a topic in political debates is the question of "free speech," whose ultimate value is defended on the grounds that it will eventually lead to more complete understanding and consensus on practical and theoretical truths. Even the separation of politics and religion is limited by a democratic consensus on a "public philosophy," and "freedom of conscience" is defended on the grounds that persons in their search for ultimate meaning in life have a right to transcend popular opinion. Moreover, decisions about education and the advance of science are increasingly the subject of such political debates.

THE METAPHYSICAL EXPLORATION
OF HUMAN NATURE

Although science establishes that the material world ultimately depends on an immaterial First Cause and other immaterial causes such as the human soul, it is unable to study what these immaterial realities are like because it relies exclusively on sense observation of material facts. Similarly, although ethics can show that human happiness, individual and communal, consists supremely in the exploration of the mystery of spiritual persons, it cannot turn to science for enlightenment on these subjects. Hence, we need the discipline of metaphysics, or philosophy par excellence, to explore human spir-

16. Martin Heidegger made popular this topic of the modern dominance of technology and the "Forgetfulness of Being" that it has produced. See Michael E. Zimmerman, *Heidegger's Confrontation with Modernity: Technology, Politics, Art* (Bloomington: Indiana University Press, 1990), and Benedict M. Ashley, "Truth and Technology," *American Catholic Philosophical Association Proceedings: The Importance of Truth* 68 (1993): 27–40.

17. This is what Aristotle in the *Nicomachean Ethics*, Bk. X, 6–9, and Thomas Aquinas, *Summa Theologiae* I-II, qq. 1–5, meant by "contemplation" as constituting true human happiness.

ituality and our relation to our Creator. The method of metaphysics can be only interdisciplinary and analogical. That is, the metaphysician argues from what has been learned in science, mathematics, and ethics, as well as from human historical experience, as from effects to causes. What we can know of spiritual things we know by analogy from their material effects.

Metaphysics thus enables us to attain a certain understanding of God as spiritual first Cause and his relation to his creatures—to the whole universe and in particular to created persons. We come to realize that it is at least highly probable that we are not the only intelligent, created persons in our universe. There must also be a host of intelligences far more perfect than is our kind of intelligence, which depends on a brain and a body. We cannot directly know this community of pure spirits, but their presence is evident in the wonderful order and evolutionary development of our cosmos, as well as in the inspiration felt by the human geniuses that have led the invention of human cultures.[18]

God himself has to be understood by us through the analogy of the best creatures that we directly know, the saints, heroes, and sages of human culture, and through what science reveals to us about the wonderful diversity and order of our material universe in its temporal and spatial vastness.

As we contemplate these wonders, however, we more and more realize their mystery: how far they exceed what we now know of them. Even more plainly, we have to recognize that this beautiful universe, our beautiful earth, and the glory of our human community are in fact somehow mysteriously frustrated. Therefore, we must recognize that the miseries of our human community, the devastation we have wrought on our earth, are not God's fault since he is infinitely wise and good, but can only be the fault of free creatures. Faced with this tragic mystery, therefore, we as persons must turn to God in prayer for help. Those who have done so will find that God has answered our prayer by his providential intervention in cosmic and human history by revealing himself to his prophets, of whom the greatest is his own Son, who showed God's love for us by exposing himself to our malicious misuse of human freedom, even to killing him on a cross. His resurrection provides to faith the fundamental answer to our human quest in all its perspectives, scientific, ethical, and philosophical.[19]

18. See Mortimer J. Adler, *The Angels and Us* (New York: Macmillan, Collier Books, 1988).

19. For this transition from reason to faith see Benedict M. Ashley, *Choosing a Worldview and Value System: An Ecumenical Apologetics* (Staten Island, NY: Alba House, 2000).

PART II

THE PERSON IN COMMUNITY

[4]

TRUTH AS THE GROUND OF FREEDOM

A Theme from John Paul II

AVERY CARDINAL DULLES, S.J.

For Lord Acton, according to Gertrude Himmelfarb, liberty is no mere social arrangement recommended by convenience but is on the contrary "the highest ideal of man, the reflection of his divinity."[1] Another great historian of the concept of freedom, Mortimer Adler, writes that "there is perhaps no philosophical idea which has had so much impact on political action."[2] For centuries, he points out, the world has been divided by rival conceptions of freedom. Whether liberty consists in doing what one likes or in doing what one ought makes an overriding difference in practice. A great rift exists between those who absolutize freedom of indifference and those who hold that true freedom can only be freedom in the truth.

The rootedness of freedom in the truth was a constant and central theme in the writings of John Paul II. Already in 1964, as a young bishop at Vatican II, Karol Wojtyla, as he was then called, criticized the draft of the declaration on religious freedom because it did not sufficiently emphasize the connection between freedom and truth. "For freedom on the one hand is for the sake of truth and on the other hand it cannot be perfected except by means of

1. Gertrude Himmelfarb, *Lord Acton: A Study in Conscience and Politics* (Chicago: University of Chicago Press, 1952), 241.

2. Mortimer J. Adler, *Freedom: A Study of the Development of the Concept in the English and American Traditions of Philosophy* (Albany, NY: Magi Books, 1968), 5.

truth. Hence the words of our Lord, which speak so clearly to everyone: 'The truth will make you free' (John 8:32). There is no freedom without truth."[3] In his first encyclical, *Redemptor hominis* (1979), John Paul II again quoted the words of Christ, "You will know the truth, and the truth will make you free." He added: "These words contain both a fundamental requirement and a warning: The requirement of an honest relationship with regard to truth as a condition for authentic freedom, and the warning to avoid every kind of illusory freedom, every superficial unilateral freedom, every freedom that fails to enter into the whole truth about man and the world."[4] In a later encyclical, *Veritatis splendor* (1993), the pope rejected a series of ethical systems that propose novel criteria for the moral evaluation of human action.[5] Despite their variety, he declared, these systems are at one in minimizing or even denying the dependence of freedom upon truth. This dependence, he says, finds its clearest and most authoritative expression in the words of Christ, "You will know the truth, and the truth will make you free."[6]

Pope John Paul II's philosophy of freedom runs counter to the value-free concept so prevalent in contemporary culture, perhaps especially in the United States. Many people today would say that freedom and truth are wholly separable, since anyone is free to affirm the truth and abide by it, to ignore the truth, or even to deny it and act against it. If freedom were bound by the truth, they ask, how could it be freedom? In the course of his discussion of freedom and law in *Veritatis splendor*, the pope proposes his answer to questions such as these.

THE CONCEPT OF FREEDOM

Before considering this answer, we would do well, I believe, to take a close look at the meaning of the term "freedom," which has different implications at the natural and the personal levels. At the lower level, that of nature, freedom means the absence of physical constraint. A balloon rises freely when nothing obstructs it; a stone falls freely when nothing impedes it. A dog is free if it is let off the leash so that it can follow its impulses. To be free, in this

---

3. Karol Wojtyla, "Intervention of September 25, 1964," in *Acta synodalia Concilii Vaticani II, Period III*, vol. 2, 530–32, at 531.

4. Pope John Paul II, *Redemptor hominis*, ¶ 12 (1979).

5. John Paul II deals with "The Church and the Discernment of Certain Tendencies in Present-Day Moral Theology" in his encyclical *Veritatis splendor*, chapter 2, ¶¶ 28–83 (1993).

6. Pope John Paul II, *Veritatis splendor*, ¶ 34 (1993).

sense, is to act according to an inner inclination. To be unfree is to have that inclination frustrated.

At the higher level, distinctive to persons, freedom demands, in addition, the absence of psychological compulsion. My freedom as a person is limited to the extent that instinct or passion compels me to act in certain ways—for example, to flee from danger or flinch with pain. If my motives could never transcend my individual self-interest or the collective self-interest of my group, I could never be truly free. I could always be manipulated and compelled to act in specific ways by fear of punishment or hope of reward. Just as animals can be drawn by dangling a carrot or banana in front of their noses, so a child can be induced to behave in certain ways by the prospect of gratification or the fear of pain. Unable to escape from the determinism of instinct or appetite, we could be forced to act by threats and promises.

One of the benefits of training and discipline is to enhance our zone of inner freedom. By education and exercise we develop the motivation and character that enables us to resist physical and especially psychological pressures. Some learn to go for long periods without sleep, to abstain from food, or to endure intense physical pain without abandoning their resolve. Such persons have greater freedom than others. They have a larger zone of inner self-determination.

In determining my own course of action, I cannot dispense with motives. If choices were completely arbitrary, freedom would be meaningless and, in the last analysis, impossible. Every act of freedom has two poles—negative and positive. Negatively, it means *freedom from* inner or outer coercion; positively, it means *freedom for* some good known to the mind. Freedom *from* would by itself be useless because it could never find an object to be chosen; freedom *for* would be impossible unless one were uncoerced.[7]

In my free actions I pursue what I apprehend as good and worthy of being chosen, but the choice is not forced upon me. I consent to the attraction because my reason approves of it. In acting freely I experience myself as the source of my own activity and as responsible for the results. My actions recoil to some degree on myself, and so make me to be what I am. Thus, the freedom to determine one's activity is, at the same time, self-determination.

The late pope explains this at some length in his major work, *The Acting*

---

7. For an extended discussion of positive and negative liberty from a liberal perspective see Isaiah Berlin, "Two Concepts of Liberty," in his *Five Essays on Liberty* (Oxford: Oxford University Press, 2002), 166–217.

Person, and in various philosophical essays written before he became pope.[8] In *Veritatis splendor* John Paul II quotes Saint Gregory of Nyssa on the royal dignity that pertains to those who have this kind of dominion over themselves. "The soul shows its royal and exalted character . . . in that it is free and self-governed, swayed autonomously by its own will. Of whom else can this be said, save a king?"[9] According to the pope, freedom does not attain this royal dignity until it rises to the level of making choices that perfect the dynamism of the human spirit toward the divine, following motives that solicit its free adherence. To this effect the pope quotes from Vatican II: "God willed to leave them [human beings] 'in the hands of their own counsel' (cf. Sir. 15:14), so that they would seek their Creator of their own accord and would freely arrive at full and blessed perfection by cleaving to God."[10]

As I have said, we possess this freedom only when we go beyond individual and collective selfishness and reach out to that which reason perceives as objectively good and true. Our freedom is not diminished, but expanded and fulfilled, when we employ it to bring about a true good. This, again, is the teaching of Vatican II:

Human dignity requires one to act through conscious and free choice, as motivated and prompted personally from within, and not through blind impulse or merely external pressure. People achieve such dignity when they free themselves from all subservience to their feelings, and in a free choice of the good, pursue their own end by effectively and assiduously marshaling the appropriate means.[11]

Because the moral law, as known by reason, does not constrain us, it leaves us physically and psychologically free either to obey or to violate it. If we reject the true good, we inevitably yield to the passions and instincts of our lower nature and thereby undermine our authentic freedom. To act freely against the truth is to erode freedom itself. Michael Polanyi, the great philosopher of science, speaks in much the same terms as John Paul II. He writes: "While compulsion by force or by neurotic obsession excludes responsibility, compulsion

---

8. Karol Wojtyla, *The Acting Person* (Dordrecht, Holland: D. Reidel, 1979), esp. 106–86; Karol Wojtyla, "The Personal Structure of Self-Determination," chap. 13 in *Person and Community: Selected Essays,* ed. Theresa Sandok, O.S.M. (New York: P. Lang, 1993), 187–95.

9. Gregory of Nyssa, *De hominis opificio.* Cf. Pope John Paul II, *Veritatis splendor,* ¶ 38 (1993).

10. Second Vatican Ecumenical Council, Pastoral Constitution of the Church in the Modern World (*Gaudium et spes*), ¶ 17 (1965); Pope John Paul II, *Veritatis splendor,* ¶ 38 (1993).

11. Second Vatican Ecumenical Council, *Gaudium et spes,* ¶ 17 (1965); Pope John Paul II, *Veritatis splendor,* ¶ 42 (1993).

by universal intent establishes responsibility. . . . *The freedom of the subjective person to do as he pleases is overruled by the freedom of the responsible person to act as he must.*"[12]

Liberty, according to Lord Acton, is "not the power of doing what we like, but the right of being able to do what we ought."[13] As this definition indicates, Acton is concerned not so much with the philosophical as with the political definition of freedom. Those who have a constitutional right to do as they ought are politically free, and if they are not physically or psychologically impeded from following the moral imperative, they are also free in the philosophical sense of the word.

FREEDOM AND SELF-GIVING

In a paper on *The Personal Structure of Self-Determination,* from which I have already drawn some ideas, John Paul II makes a further inference, based on the relational character of the person. Every person, he maintains, is both a being willed by God for itself and at the same time a being turned toward others. To be isolated from others is a form of self-imprisonment. We become most truly human in the measure that we go out of ourselves and give ourselves for the sake of others. This "law of the gift," as the pope calls it, is inscribed deep in the dynamic structure of the person as fashioned in the image of the divine.[14] He confirms this insight by quoting from Vatican II: "The human being, who is the only creature on earth that God willed for itself, cannot attain its full identity except through a disinterested gift of self."[15] The citizen serves the common good out of a free commitment or devotion. Those who love God serve Him freely, and if they refuse that service they undermine the freedom that God has given them. Those who obey the commandments out of fear are not fully free, but they fall into even deeper slavery if they disobey God to gratify their own impulses. The truly free person is one who does what is good out of love for goodness itself.

Thinkers who consider the law of God to be a hindrance to human freedom have been misled into regarding obedience as a form of heteronomy or

12. Michael Polanyi, *Personal Knowledge* (New York: Harper Torchbooks, 1964), 309; italics in original.

13. John Lord Acton, "The Roman Question," *The Rambler* 2nd new series 2 (January 1860): 137–54, at 146.

14. Wojtyla, *Person and Community,* 194.

15. Second Vatican Ecumenical Council, *Gaudium et spes,* ¶ 24 (1965).

self-alienation, as though God were a hostile power imposing terms on humanity as a defeated enemy. In fact, God's law proceeds only from benevolence toward creatures whom God loves. The moral law is intended to safeguard human dignity. Human freedom and divine law conspire to the same end. In this connection John Paul II speaks of "theonomy." Rational knowledge enables us to participate in the light of eternal wisdom, which is expressed in the divine law. In obeying God's law I incline myself before His divine majesty and at the same time follow my deepest vocation as a creature. In the pope's own words,

> Law must therefore be considered an expression of divine wisdom: by submitting to the law, freedom submits to the truth of creation. Consequently one must acknowledge in the freedom of the human person the image and the nearness of God, who is present in all (cf. Eph. 4:6). But one must likewise acknowledge the majesty of the God of the universe and revere the holiness of the law of God, who is infinitely transcendent: *Deus semper maior.*[16]

The supreme exemplars of freedom, for John Paul II, are the martyrs. They are the heroic persons who are so committed to the known good that they stand up under pressures that would overcome the willpower of most others. Given the choice between denying their principles and losing their lives, they freely lay down their lives and thereby give witness to the truth. Jesus, who freely laid down His life for our sake, sets the pattern for martyrs. The martyrs represent an achievement of freedom beyond the capacities of the great majority of men and women. They inspire us by their example to rise above the more limited measure of freedom that we can claim for ourselves. For the theology of freedom it is important to recognize that the freedom with which we are born is frail and limited. John Paul II compares it to a seed that must be cultivated. Some degree of freedom is an essential part of the reflection of God that is constitutive of human nature, but our freedom is incomplete. Wounded as we are by original sin, we often prefer limited and ephemeral goods to those that are pure and abiding. We are even tempted to assert our freedom against our Creator, as if freedom could exist without regard for truth. God's redemptive action in Christ helps to liberate us from this illusion. As Paul writes in Galatians 5:1, "For freedom Christ has set us free."[17] Since Christ Himself is the truth (John 14:6), it is also correct to say that the truth sets us free (cf. John 8:32).

---

16. Pope John Paul II, *Veritatis splendor,* ¶ 34 (1993).
17. Ibid., ¶ 86.

FREEDOM AND GRACE

It is partly in revealing the law that God liberates his people. Already in the Old Testament, God brought the tribes of Israel out of bondage and united them to Himself through the Sinai Covenant, which contained the basic precepts of the moral law. That covenant was perfected by the new law of the gospel, which Scripture describes as an interior law "written not with ink but with the Spirit of the living God, not on tablets of stone but on tablets of human hearts" (2 Cor. 3:3).[18] As a new and interior law, the gospel teaches us both by enlightening our minds and by instilling a love and affection for the truth. The divinely given attraction toward the true goal of human existence, which is none other than God Himself, does not impede our freedom of choice, since it inclines us toward the very thing that right reason would select. The inner instinct of grace heals our rebellious wills and inclines us to do as God wills. In so doing it removes an obstacle to freedom—our innate tendency to pursue the immediate and apparent good rather than the ultimate and true good. It brings us closer to the final condition of the blessed in heaven, who cannot do other than love God, but who do so freely because they see how lovable God is.

FREEDOM AND CONSCIENCE

In speaking of the interior law of the gospel imprinted by God on the human heart, I am inevitably raising the question of conscience, which is a subject of considerable confusion in our day. John Paul II remarks that the idea of conscience has been deformed by modern thinkers who have lost the sense of the transcendent and are in some cases atheistic. These thinkers often depict conscience as a supreme and infallible tribunal that dispenses us from considerations of law and truth, putting in their place purely subjective and individualist criteria such as sincerity, authenticity, and being at peace with oneself.[19] In opposition to this trend John Paul II shows in *Veritatis splendor* that conscience is an act of intelligence that adheres to objective norms. The freedom of conscience is secured by its conformity to truth. The classical biblical text on conscience, quoted by John Paul II, is Romans 2:14–16: "When Gentiles who have not the law do by nature what the law re-

---

18. Quoted in Pope John Paul II, *Veritatis splendor,* ¶ 45 (1993), with additional references to Jeremiah and Paul.

19. Ibid., ¶ 32.

quires, they are a law unto themselves, even though they do not have the law. They show that what the law requires is written on their hearts, while their conscience also bears witness and their conflicting thoughts accuse or perhaps excuse them."[20]

The meaning of this dense and complex passage is clarified by a paragraph from Vatican II that John Paul II also quotes: "In the depths of his own conscience man detects a law which he does not impose on himself, but which holds him to obedience. Always summoning him to love good and avoid evil, the voice of conscience can when necessary speak to his heart more specifically: 'Do this, shun that.' For man has in his heart a law written by God. To obey it is the very dignity of man; according to it he will be judged."[21]

According to these authoritative texts, conscience is not a purely subjective and autonomous principle; it is in no way opposed to the truth of God's law, which is its ground. Its judgments always presuppose the first principle of practical reason, the obligation to do good and avoid evil. Paul, as we have seen, describes conscience as an unwritten law inscribed by God on the human heart. Saint Bonaventure spells out this relationship more explicitly. In a text quoted by John Paul II he writes: "Conscience is like God's herald and messenger; it does not command things on its own authority, but commands them as coming from God's authority, like a herald when he proclaims the edict of a king. This is why conscience has a binding force."[22]

In the history of Catholic theology, John Henry Newman is outstanding for having clarified the relationship between conscience and God. Conscience, he writes in his *Letter to the Duke of Norfolk,* is the voice of God in the nature and heart of man.[23] In his *Grammar of Assent* Newman speaks of conscience as "our great internal teacher of religion."[24] It "teaches us not only that God is but what He is; it provides for the mind a real image of Him, as a medium of worship."[25] Newman then goes on to explain how it

20. Ibid., ¶ 57.

21. Second Vatican Ecumenical Council, *Gaudium et spes,* ¶ 16 (1965); quoted in Pope John Paul II, *Veritatis splendor,* ¶ 54 (1993); cf. Rom 2:14–6.

22. Bonaventure, In II Libr Sent., dist. 39, a. 1, q. 3, concl.; cf. Pope John Paul II, *Veritatis splendor,* ¶ 58 (1993).

23. John Henry Newman, "Letter to the Duke of Norfolk," in *Newman and Gladstone: The Vatican Decrees,* ed. Alvan S. Ryan (Notre Dame, IN: University of Notre Dame Press, 1962), 128.

24. John Henry Newman, *Grammar of Assent* (Garden City: Doubleday Image, 1955), 304.

25. Ibid.

discloses God as lawgiver, judge, and rewarder. In a justly famous paragraph he declares: "Conscience is the aboriginal Vicar of Christ, a prophet in its informations, a monarch in its peremptoriness, a priest in its blessings and anathemas."[26] Newman contrasts this true and traditional conception of conscience with what he calls its modern counterfeit. While some philosophers attack the very concept of conscience as a primitive and irrational force, the popular mind, in advocating the rights of conscience, really seeks to assert human self-will, without any thought of God at all. Conscience thus becomes "a license to take up any or no religion." For Newman, on the contrary, conscience is a stern monitor and is essentially bound up with the acknowledgment of God. "Conscience has its rights because it has duties."[27] Building on passages such as these, John Paul II is able to show that, far from being a power to make one's decisions autonomously and creatively, conscience binds us to the law of God, to whom conscience is responsible. He then goes on to remark that conscience is neither adequate nor infallible as a source of moral guidance. Because it attests to a higher intelligence and will to which it is subject, it arouses a concern or anxiety to find out what course of action is here and now required of the individual to do good and avoid evil.

Conscience impels one to seek authoritative direction. Newman eloquently points out the providential role of the Church in supplying this need. In his *Letter to the Duke of Norfolk* he writes:

All sciences, except the science of Religion, have their certainty in themselves; as far as they are sciences, they consist of necessary conclusions from undeniable premises, or of phenomena manipulated into general truths by an irresistible deduction. But the sense of right and wrong, which is the first element in religion, is so delicate, so fitful, so easily puzzled, obscured, perverted, so subtle in its argumentative methods, so impressible by education, so biased by pride and passion, so unsteady in its flight, that, in the struggle for existence amid the various exercises and triumphs of the human intellect, this sense is at once the highest of all teachers; yet the least luminous; and the Church, the Pope, the Hierarchy are, in the Divine purpose, the supply of an urgent demand.[28]

Conscience, therefore, is in no way opposed to the use of external sources of traditional and revealed wisdom. It seeks help from authority in forming its judgments. Far from being an exception to the general rule that freedom is oriented toward objective truth, the experience of conscientious decision making

26. Newman, "Letter to the Duke of Norfolk," 129.
27. Ibid., 130.
28. Ibid., 132–33.

confirms the rule that, as the pope expresses it, the freedom of conscience is never freedom *from* the truth but always and only freedom *in* the truth.[29]

FREEDOM AND VOCATION

I have tried thus far to establish that freedom is meaningless and self-destructive if it is not used in the service of what is truly good. A freedom that dispenses itself from concern with truth could only be a false and illusory freedom, but it does not follow that the whole course of our life is prescribed in advance by an objective order of truth that excludes any originality and creativity on our part. In most situations we are faced with a choice between several competing goods. Just as I am free to order peas or carrots at dinner, or to wear a plain or striped shirt, so, on a larger scale, I am at liberty to choose any occupation, profession, or walk of life that is honorable in itself and consonant with my abilities and temperament. It would be a mistake to imagine that there would be only one acceptable course of action. Without prescribing everything in advance, God invites us to make creative decisions, in consonance with the moral law.

In this connection one must consider the idea of vocation. God may invite us, without compelling us, to do more than duty requires. In his meditation on the call of the rich young man at the beginning of *Veritatis splendor* John Paul II points out the distinction between obedience to the commandments, which is required for salvation, and a particular vocation, which may enable an individual to attain more perfect freedom. Many spiritual writers hold that the rich young man, whom Jesus urged to give away his goods to the poor, was not strictly required to perform this generous act. He could presumably have saved his soul by continuing to observe the commandments, as he had been doing for years. Ordinarily, at least, the vocation to the life of the evangelical counsels does not come as a command but as a gracious invitation. Although we cannot achieve perfect freedom without accepting the highest possibilities opened up to us by God's grace, we are morally free to do all that God does not forbid.

29. Pope John Paul II, *Veritatis splendor*, ¶ 64 (1993).

THE FREE SOCIETY

Up to this point I have focused on the freedom of the individual. In the final section of this chapter I turn to the free society. It is more difficult to see how a society can be directed by truth unless the convictions of many of the members are overridden, in which case the society can hardly be called free. John Paul II, acutely conscious of this problem, offers some important considerations that I shall attempt to summarize.

The free society rests on the supposition that the members are endowed with inalienable rights. If the rights of individuals were conferred by the state or by the society, they could be removed by human power, and the way would be open to tyranny. As the authors of our Declaration of Independence recognized, the Creator Himself has given human beings an inalienable right to life, liberty, and the pursuit of happiness, though, of course, the exercise of these rights has to be regulated with regard to the common good. Alluding to the biblical and patristic doctrine that human beings are made in the image of God, the pope contends that the human person, as the visible image of the invisible God, is by nature the subject of rights that no individual, group, class, nation, or state may violate. Where the transcendent source of human dignity is denied, the way lies open for totalitarianism and other forms of despotism, in which naked power takes over, so that the interests of a particular person or group are imposed on the rest of society.[30]

As the pope goes on to explain, authentic democracy is possible only on the basis of a rule of law and a correct conception of the human person. "If there is no ultimate truth to guide and direct political activity, then ideas and convictions can easily be manipulated for reasons of power. . . . In a world without truth, freedom loses its foundation and man is exposed to the violence of passion and to manipulation, both open and hidden."[31] But an objection still arises. People are not free unless they can determine their own form of government and participate in the making of their own laws. Thus, it would seem that if they are not at liberty to deny the transcendent truth, they are not really free. On a purely political definition of freedom, we may concede that people are free to institute slavery or to adopt a totalitarian form of government, but in so doing they damage or destroy their own freedom. An abiding freedom requires a consensus based on transcendent truth. Just

30. Pope John Paul II, *Centesimus annus*, ¶ 44 (1991).
31. Ibid., ¶ 46.

as individuals forfeit their own freedom when they try to liberate themselves from moral norms, so the society surrenders its freedom if it fails to respect the personal dignity of its members.

The concept of public consensus is not always rightly understood. According to a widely prevalent view, it is simply a majority opinion, which may be based on fashion or emotion, or an ideology, based on the self-interest of a class. John Courtney Murray, in his masterful work, *We Hold These Truths*, explains that according to the classical tradition of political thought, consensus is a very different thing: it is a doctrine or judgment that commands public agreement because of the merits of the arguments in its favor.[32]

Public consensus, according to Murray, transcends sheer experience and expediency; it is basically a moral conception. Those who articulate it are the ones whom Thomas Aquinas called the "wise" *(sapientes)*[33] and whom George Washington called "the wise and honest."[34] The ability to discern what laws and policies best safeguard the dignity and rights of the citizens depends upon a careful inquiry in which intelligence is tutored by experience and reflection and guided by an instinct for the right and the good. The reason of the wise and the good is a responsible reason, concerned with fidelity to moral principle, and matured through familiarity with the complexities of the developing human situation. The consensus, therefore, must be articulated by those who excel in practical wisdom, but to be a real consensus it must also be accepted by the people. At the basis of the American experiment in ordered liberty, Murray explains, there are truths. "We the People" hold these truths and, showing "a decent respect for the opinions of mankind," declare them in public documents.[35] The American consensus consists not only in the general principles expressed in the Declaration of Independence but also in the more specific provisions of the Constitution and the Bill of Rights.

32. John Courtney Murray, *We Hold These Truths: Catholic Reflections on the American Proposition* (New York: Sheed and Ward, 1960), chap. 4, 97–123, at 105.

33. Thomas Aquinas, in *Summa theologiae*, 1–2. qu. 100, art. 1c, points out that to judge matters that require extensive consideration of different circumstances is the task of the wise, who then have the task of teaching the rest of the community.

34. Murray, *We Hold These Truths*, 111. Murray gives no specific reference. Presumably he is thinking of Washington's statement in his speech to the Constitutional Convention at Philadelphia in 1787, "Let us raise a standard to which the wise and honest can repair; the rest is in the hands of God." Caroline T. Harnsberger, ed., *A Treasury of Presidential Quotations* (Chicago: Follett, 1964), 300.

35. Murray, *We Hold These Truths*, 106.

These provisions likewise embody truths, formulated by the wise and accepted by the people at large.

In the atmosphere of contemporary pluralism, there is a tendency to overlook the inviolable connection between freedom and truth, as though freedom implies a right to construct one's own moral universe without accountability to any higher agency. Václav Havel speaks in this connection of a deep moral crisis in the post-totalitarian society: "A person who has been seduced by the consumer value system, whose identity is dissolved in an amalgam of the accouterments of mass civilization, and who has no roots in the order of being, no sense of responsibility for anything higher than his or her own personal survival, is a *demoralized* person. The system depends on this demoralization, deepens it, is in fact a projection of it into society."[36]

Pope John Paul II, from a similar perspective, speaks of a "crisis of truth."[37] All around us, says the pope, the saving power of the truth is contested, and freedom alone, uprooted from any objectivity, is left to decide for itself what is good and what is evil.[38] As he writes in *Centesimus annus*:

Nowadays there is a tendency to claim that agnosticism and skeptical relativism are the philosophy and the basic attitude which correspond to democratic forms of political life. Those who are convinced that they know the truth and firmly adhere to it are considered unreliable from a democratic point of view, since they do not accept that truth is determined by the majority or that it is subject to variation according to different political trends.[39]

Democracy, Murray insisted, is more than a political experiment. It is a spiritual and moral enterprise, depending for its success upon the virtue of the citizens.[40] Political freedom is endangered if the institutions no longer serve the ends of virtue and if the people fail to discipline themselves. The crisis of society, therefore, is simply that of the individual writ large. Just as the freedom of the individual cannot stand without personal adherence to truth, so the free society cannot flourish without a virtuous citizenry, disposed to live out their identity as children of God and as brothers and sisters in a common humanity. The general consensus must be nourished not by disordered passion but by an inner sense of responsibility to a higher law,

---

36. Václav Havel, *Living in Truth* (London: Faber and Faber, 1987), 62.
37. Pope John Paul II, *Veritatis splendor*, ¶¶ 32, 53 (1993).
38. Ibid., ¶¶ 84, 129.
39. Pope John Paul II, *Centesimus annus*, ¶¶ 46, 18 (1991).
40. Murray, *We Hold These Truths*, 36–37.

interpreted by the wise and honest. Because so many of us live according to purely pragmatic standards of pleasure, wealth, and power, we are in danger of losing the moral and spiritual foundations on which our freedom rests.

The contemporary crisis of freedom, therefore, is at root a crisis of truth. Lord Acton perceived this more than a century ago. John Courtney Murray reached similar conclusions on the basis of his study of the American political tradition. In our own day, John Paul II clearly demonstrated the inseparable connection between freedom and truth. In the course of his long career, he eloquently and forcefully proclaimed the principles that must underlie every free society, including the American experiment of ordered liberty.

LAW AND VIRTUE

Murray's observations on the American experiment prompt some concluding reflections on the interrelationship between law and virtue. The founding fathers of the nation agreed with the French political philosopher Montesquieu that in a republic the dominant spirit of the laws must be virtue. Echoing this thesis, our fourth president, James Madison, declared: "To suppose any form of government will secure liberty or happiness without any virtue in the people is a chimerical idea."[41]

Civic virtue, of course, is not a substitute for law. Even if all citizens were paragons of virtue, laws would be needed to coordinate social relationships. We justly pride ourselves on having a government of laws that prevents tyranny and capriciousness. But it is possible to put too much stock in law, as though it made virtue unnecessary. Alexis de Tocqueville, a keen observer of the American scene, said that the Europeans of his day gave too much attention to laws and too little to mores. In the United States, he contended, customs and religious beliefs pervaded social life so thoroughly that the laws could be less onerous.[42]

Where virtue prevails, laws will be framed with a view to the common good, not private self-interest. The laws, perceived as agreeing with the norms of justice, will carry moral authority. A virtuous people will feel obliged in conscience to observe them. But if laws are framed to satisfy the interests of particular groups, they will lose their moral authority, and citizens will feel

---

41. James Madison, "Speech of June 20, 1788," in Jonathan Elliott, ed., *The Debates in the Several State Conventions,* vol. 3 (Philadelphia: Lippincott, 1836), 537.

42. Alexis de Tocqueville, *Democracy in America,* vol. 1 (New York: A. A. Knopf, 1991), 322.

entitled to disobey, provided they do not get caught. Vice and criminality will proliferate.

Civilization depends on habits of the heart. It requires citizens who can trust one another to be honest, considerate, and truthful. When trust evaporates, the law has to assume a coercive function, compelling people to obey against their will. Elaborate mechanisms of surveillance, prosecution, and punishment must be erected. An army of auditors, detectives, police, attorneys, trial judges, and prison guards strives in vain to secure the order that responsible freedom would spontaneously achieve. The free society gradually deteriorates, transforming itself into a police state.

In our litigious society, thirst for gain almost eclipses the passion for justice. Friends and family members readily take each other to court. Malpractice suits and the mounting cost of insurance are forcing doctors and other professionals to abandon their practice. The courts are congested with heavy backlogs. We build more and larger prisons, which prove only to be schools of crime.

Virtue, to be sure, cannot be legislated. But a proper concern for the law imparts a sense of the importance of moral convictions and communal spirit for the health of society. In our American tradition, great reliance has been placed on private institutions that directly inculcate virtue. Families, schools, and churches are among the primary agencies for transmitting sound moral values.

The family, as the nucleus where life is born and where coming generations are formed, is today under severe pressure. It needs to be protected so that children can be raised in a stable and healthy environment. Broken homes and dysfunctional families are breeding grounds of crime.

Schools extend the pedagogical function of the family. To the degree that public education fails to instill moral convictions and behavior, this task will fall more heavily on private institutions, especially those conducted under religious auspices. Schools of this character fill the void left by value-free institutions that limit their instruction to factual information and technical skills.

Religious institutions are of inestimable importance for transmitting moral probity. Perceiving this, John Adams declared: "Our Constitution was made only for a moral and religious people. It is wholly inadequate for the government of any other."[43] George Washington said much the same: "Reason and

---

43. John Adams, "Letter to Officers of the First Brigade, 11 October 1798," in *The Works of John Adams*, vol. 9 (Boston: Little, Brown, 1854), 229.

experience both forbid us to expect that national morality can prevail to the exclusion of religious principle."[44] The government in this country cannot establish any given religion by law, but it can protect and support religion, just as it can support the family, private education, and various voluntary associations as aids to civic virtue.

Law and spirit belong together. They are as inseparable as body and soul. Law, at least civil law, is a human achievement, but the spirit, if it is to be upright, depends chiefly upon the grace of God, who can transform our hearts and fill them with his love. Prayer and worship, therefore, are not irrelevant to the good society. They orient us to the transcendent ground of all freedom and truth.

44. George Washington, "Farewell Address," in *Writings*, ed. John H. Rhodehamel (New York: Library of America, 1997), 962–77, at 971.

[5]

SOLIDARITY, SUBSIDIARITY,
AND THE CONSUMERIST IMPETUS OF
AMERICAN LAW

ROBERT K. VISCHER

Catholic social teaching is, by design, ill-suited to abstract formulation. It can be understood only through exploration in the context of pressing social problems, as underscored by the Church's consistent and deliberate recitation of relevant real-world circumstances in tandem with invocations of the theoretical principles on which the social teaching is based. At the same time, the value of the Church's teaching emanates from its grounding in truths that are not cabined by the contingent nature of modern epistemological understanding. The Church offers lessons to particular participants in a particular scene of the human drama because the content of its lessons speaks to all participants in the human drama, everywhere and in every age. This context-driven elucidation of unmistakably transcendent truths is no simple endeavor, but it is the path by which Catholicism speaks to the temporal order.

Nowhere is this attribute reflected more clearly than in discussions of the two pillars of Catholic social teaching—solidarity and subsidiarity. In simple terms, solidarity represents the "commitment to the good of one's neighbor,"[1] and subsidiarity represents the conviction that "needs are best understood

Thanks to David Gregory, Susan Stabile, and Brian Tamanaha for helpful comments on earlier drafts of this chapter.

1. Pope John Paul II, *Sollicitudo rei socialis,* ⁋ 38 (1987).

and satisfied by people who are closest to them."[2] Unhinged either from real-world context or from the anthropological presumptions that the doctrines embody, however, both can become unhelpfully malleable, empty vessels waiting to be filled by a whole range of preexisting agendas.

In many respects, both doctrines have already been routinely captured and unfurled as ideological flags in battles that pit them not as complementary elements of a comprehensive vision of the human person in society, but as mutually exclusive directives regarding the social order. Solidarity has long been in fashion across the spectrum of progressive causes, religious or not, especially those centered on the empowerment of traditionally marginalized populations. Subsidiarity, at least on the American legal scene,[3] is routinely invoked by those who are suspicious of centralized power, most notably by the purveyors of "compassionate conservatism." Too often, both doctrines have been vulnerable to an emptying out of their theological content as they are molded to suit the political expediency of the respective causes, regardless of whether the factual contexts in which they are invoked support the overarching vision of the human person from which they spring.

My hope is that the import of Catholic social thought for American law can be understood in a more fulsome, robust way if we reconnect the doctrines of solidarity and subsidiarity to each other, bringing the resulting anthropological insight to bear on the sharply conflicting anthropological presumptions reflected in the current direction of American law. Rather than prop up one doctrine or the other as superfluous support for positions that are already fleshed out in terms that do not even purport to depend on the Christian moral anthropology for their coherence, I seek to anchor the inquiry in the premises of that anthropology, as expressed jointly and interdependently through solidarity and subsidiarity.

In American law, the triumphant norms of consumerism are ascending to the status of nonnegotiable, absolute values, to be enforced through the coercive power of the collective. Subsidiarity and solidarity, taken together, offer an effective rejoinder to this trend. Allowing these doctrines to speak transcendent truth to a web of elevated, but historically contingent, values and priorities provides rich insight not only into the ongoing power of Catholic social teach-

2. Pope John Paul II, *Centesimus annus*, ¶ 48 (1991).

3. Subsidiarity is also used as an organizing principle for the European Union, standing for the notion that power should be exercised at the lowest level of government authority equipped to address a given problem effectively.

ing, but also into the fundamentally flawed anthropological presumptions embodied in the unfettered consumer autonomy emerging under American law.

CONSUMERISM AS A COLLECTIVE IDEAL

Throughout the Cold War, articulating the real-world implications of Catholic social teaching was a relatively simple task. With the West championing the individual to the exclusion of meaningful conceptions of community, while the Soviet bloc championed the collective without regard for the inherent dignity of the individual, subsidiarity and solidarity became the dual pillars on which the Church's alternative vision of man in relation to society was built:

Intimately linked to the foundation, which is man's dignity, are the principle of solidarity and the principle of subsidiarity. By virtue of the first, man with his brothers is obliged to contribute to the common good of society at all its levels. Hence the Church's doctrine is opposed to all the forms of social or political individualism. By virtue of the second, neither the State nor any society must ever substitute itself for the initiative and responsibility of individuals and of intermediate communities at the level on which they can function, nor must they take away the room necessary for their freedom. Hence the Church's social doctrine is opposed to all forms of collectivism.[4]

The human person was not to be treated instrumentally, either as a pawn in the state's pursuit of some utopian vision of society that was premised on the disempowerment of nongovernment bodies, or conversely, as an atomistic market actor, composed only of the sum total of her material desires and consumer preferences. Thus, it was no secret that the Church adopted "a critical attitude towards both liberal capitalism and Marxist collectivism,"[5] labeling individualism and collectivism the "twin rocks of shipwreck."[6] As the Church navigated the East-West ideological split, the substantive import of its social teachings was clear: championing the dignity of the individual to the collectivist Soviets, and championing a sense of communal obligation to the individualist West.

With communism's retreat from the geopolitical stage, things have become less clearly demarcated. Individualism has triumphed, for the most

---

4. Congregation for the Doctrine of the Faith, "Instructio de libertate christiana et liberatione," ¶ 73 (1986).

5. Pope John Paul II, *Sollicitudo rei socialis,* ¶ 21 (1987).

6. Pope Pius XI, *Quadragesimo anno,* ¶ 46 (1931).

part, but its triumph, in turn, gives rise to new and more subtle forms of collectivism. Catholic social teaching makes clear that its focus has never been simply the geopolitical battle between forces of individualism and collectivism. Rather, the perils of both extremes are wrapped up with human nature, and one tendency is prone to meld into the other. The dynamic has not escaped the Church's attention, as it has previously expressed caution regarding liberation movements that have risen up against the inequities fostered by individualist ideologies, but that have, in turn, "led to new forms of servitude, being inspired by concepts which ignored the transcendental vocation of the human person," and "have sometimes been directed toward collectivist goals, which have then given rise to injustices just as grave as the ones they were meant to eliminate."[7]

The story is somewhat different in American law. Far from embracing collectivism as a rejection of individualism, much of American law embodies such an extreme brand of consumer-driven individualism that it gives rise to a relatively new form of social order: the pursuit of consumer autonomy as a collective ideal. Individualist norms of morality have long held sway in the United States, especially when it comes to the individual as consumer. As the Church has recognized, that Enlightenment conception of freedom tends to posit a human subject "whose finality is the satisfaction of his own interests in the enjoyment of earthly goods."[8] Increasingly, consumer freedom is being elevated as a nonnegotiable absolute value and enforced through the coercive power of the legal system. In particular, the state has taken upon itself the responsibility to compel providers to honor the individual's decisions in matters of consumption, regardless of how morally problematic those decisions might be from the provider's perspective. Examples of this trend abound, and are especially obvious in areas that are viewed as essential "public goods" in modern American life, such as health care, education, and law.

In the health care arena, reproductive and religious freedoms came into direct conflict recently in California, and reproductive freedom emerged victorious. The state legislature passed a law requiring employers who provide prescription drug coverage to their employees to cover contraceptives. The law included a religious exemption, but this was drawn narrowly, defining "religious employer" as employers whose purpose is to inculcate religious

7. Congregation for the Doctrine of the Faith, "Instructio de libertate christiana et liberatione," ¶ 13 (1986).
8. Ibid.

values, who primarily employ persons of the employer's same faith, and who primarily serve people of the employer's same faith.[9] In other words, any religious organization who took seriously the Gospel's call to service fell outside the exemption, including Catholic Charities, which challenged the statute as an encroachment on its religious liberty. The California Supreme Court rejected the challenge, employing stark individualist reasoning in the process. The law, the Court held, did not threaten the Catholic Church's internal governance, but simply "implicates the relationship between a nonprofit public benefit corporation and its employees, most of whom do not belong to the Catholic Church."[10] After all, "[o]nly those who join a church impliedly consent to its religious governance on matters of faith and discipline."[11]

In these terms, reproductive freedom is not simply about negative liberty—that is, it does not consist of the individual consumer's entitlement to use birth control free from government interference. Rather, it is a distinctly positive liberty—the individual consumer can compel her employer to pay for her birth control, even if the act of payment violates the employer's most fundamental beliefs. It is not only that the individual cannot be bound by the Catholic Church's teachings unless she freely consents to do so, but further that the individual cannot be inconvenienced by the Church's teaching unless she consents to do so. The individual's conception of the good does not just coexist with the intermediate body's conception of the good; the individual's conception, backed up by state power, trumps the intermediate body's contrary conception. The individual preference has become the collective norm.

The consumerist trend in reproductive access is by no means without challenge. Many state legislatures have passed "conscience clauses" ensuring that health care providers are not held liable or fired because of their refusal to participate in morally controversial procedures such as abortion. But even the terms of these debates reflect the degree to which the individual consumer has already been elevated. In Wisconsin, for example, the governor promised to veto his state's conscience clause, offering the bizarre explanation that "you're moving into very dangerous precedent where doctors make moral decisions on what medical care they'll provide."[12] In other states, the battle

9. Calif. Health & Safety Code § 1367.25 (also requiring nonprofit status).

10. *Catholic Charities v. Superior Court*, 85 P3d 67, 77 (Cal 2004).

11. Ibid.

12. Stacy Forster, "Women's Health Debate Intensifies," *Milw. Journal-Sentinel*, 21 April 2004, 1B.

lines have shifted to the previously unfathomable questions of whether hospitals and pharmacists should be legally required to provide the "morning-
after" emergency contraception pill.[13] These new points of contention, whatever their outcome, reflect the degree to which consumer preferences are the
driving force behind the creation and expansion of collective legal norms.

Educational providers, by comparison, appear to enjoy substantially unfettered institutional autonomy in pursuing their missions through the shaping
of a distinct educational environment. Certainly American law is no stranger
to the imposition of collective educational ideals, but historically these have
been motivated by animus against a particular group (Catholics, most notably),[14] rather than the abstract elevation of the individual student's purported well-being. But this may be changing as well, and the change may be imposed through a path actually intended to enhance educational freedom.

To some, the school choice movement represents the hope of meaningful
educational freedom, as families would be equipped through school vouchers to attend private schools that they otherwise would be unable to afford
financially. Such a vision of school choice is expressly embodied in Catholic social thought, which reminds us of the centrality of the family in educational decisions and reminds the state that it "cannot without injustice merely tolerate so-called private schools" because "[s]uch schools render a public
service and therefore have a right to financial assistance."[15]

Adherence to this vision is far from universal, of course, and to many, the
school choice movement represents the most promising path toward state
regulation of private schools. In a market where school vouchers are prevalent, a school will be hard-pressed to keep its tuition levels competitive without the subsidy of voucher money. At a minimum, religious schools whose
missions compel them to maintain educational access among a variety of
economic classes will need to accept vouchers in order to remain viable in
the market. And with the vouchers will come, almost invariably, government
regulation.

13. See Marilyn Gardner, "Pharmacists' Moral Beliefs vs. Women's Legal Rights," *Christian Science Monitor* (26 April 2004): 11; Brietta Clark, "When Free Exercise Exemptions Undermine Religious Liberty and the Liberty of Conscience: A Case Study of the Catholic Hospital Conflict," *Oregon Law Review* 82 (2003): 625.

14. See Kyle Duncan, "Secularism's Laws: State Blaine Amendments and Religious Persecution," *Fordham Law Review* 72 (2003): 493.

15. Congregation for the Doctrine of the Faith, "Instructio de libertate christiana et liberatione," ¶ 94 (1986).

For our purposes, it is important to recognize that proposed regulations for voucher schools are justified based on the purported best interest of the student. This is a collectivist twist on the consumerist ideology, for the child as consumer is not able to realize or articulate, much less act on, her own best interests. As a result, the state takes on the role of identifying and protecting the student's best interests on her behalf, albeit on a collective scale. As one academic commentator explains, "states must attach to vouchers whatever regulatory strings are needed to ensure that children in all private schools receive a good secular education," and if this means that "some parents cannot use their children's schooling to proclaim the 'good news,' because in the state's judgment the parents' news is not so good, then so be it."[16]

Many proposed regulations, some of which already have been adopted in voucher districts, seem relatively innocuous, but by no means unobjectionable, such as mandating certain curricular requirements, requiring teachers to be state-certified, ensuring that religious instruction or services are not mandatory for voucher students, and prohibiting the use of religious criteria in the admission of students. Others are more problematic, most notably the power to censor the transmission of more controversial religious teachings. Whatever our view of a particular regulation's reasonableness, the content is not as significant as the underlying notion that the state is equipped to define and pursue collectively the student consumer's interests, even at the expense of the educational providers' institutional autonomy and the efficacy of parents' child-forming decisions.

The law's elevation of the consumer extends to the legal profession itself. Lawyers are trained to function as amoral technicians, agents who provide access to the law. The access is, for the most part, to remain unfettered by the lawyer's personal affiliations, motivations, or worldviews. In providing such access, the lawyer is constrained by the law, but not by any perceived need to reconcile her own conscience or personal values with the client or the client's cause. As the Model Code of Professional Responsibility provides, clients are "entitled to . . . seek any lawful objective through legally permissible means."[17] The lawyer, then, aims not to inject her own vision of the good into the representation, but simply to pursue the client's vision of the good through the maximization of the client's legal rights. One prominent legal

16. James G. Dwyer, "School Vouchers: Inviting the Public into the Religious Square," *William and Mary Law Review* 42 (2001): 963, 992, 1005.

17. Model Code of Professional Responsibility EC 7-1 (1969).

ethics scholar nicely captures the paradigm's essence: "For access to the law to be filtered unequally through the disparate moral views of each individual's lawyer does not appear to be justifiable."[18]

The consumerist mindset is collectivized through the profession-wide embrace of role-differentiated morality, under which "behavior that is potentially criticizable on moral grounds is blocked from such criticism by an appeal to the existence of the actor's role which, it is claimed, makes the moral difference."[19] When a client asks a lawyer to provide representation in pursuit of an objective that clashes with the lawyer's own vision of the good, the lawyer's good gives way to the client's good, as reflected in the Model Rules of Professional Conduct, which remind lawyers that representation of a client does not constitute an endorsement of the client's morality.[20] And if the means or ends of the representation threaten to cause harm to third parties, the lawyer's role warrants deference to the client's views on the acceptability of that harm, as stated expressly in the Model Rules.[21] By effectively depriving the lawyer of her moral agency, the legal system ensures that the client's preferences are honored within the bounds of the law, no matter how morally problematic they might be.

The collectivist ramifications of role-differentiated morality were seen in Tennessee, where a Catholic lawyer tried to turn down a court appointment to represent a minor seeking an abortion without her parents' consent. The state ethics board advised that the lawyer's religiously derived objection was not a legitimate ground on which to justify his replacement, and that he was ethically obligated to proceed with the case.[22] Under most circumstances, a lawyer can refuse a given representation—most commonly for a prospective

18. Stephen Pepper, "The Lawyer's Amoral Ethical Role: A Defense, a Problem, and Some Possibilities," *American Bar Foundation Research Journal* (1986): 613.

19. Richard Wasserstrom, "Roles and Morality," in *The Good Lawyer: Lawyers' Roles and Lawyers' Ethics,* ed. David Luban (Totowa, NJ: Rowman and Allanheld, 1983), 25, 28.

20. Model Rules of Professional Conduct R. 1.2(b) (2003) ("A lawyer's representation of a client, including representation by appointment, does not constitute an endorsement of the client's political, economic, social or moral views or activities.").

21. Ibid., cmt. 2 (explaining that "lawyers usually defer to the client regarding such questions as . . . concern for third persons who might be adversely affected").

22. See Board of Professional Responsibility of the Superior Court of Tennessee, Formal Opinion 96-F-140 (1996) (requiring Catholic lawyer to proceed with a court appointment in such a case despite his religiously grounded objection); see also Teresa Stanton Collett, "Professional versus Moral Duty: Accepting Appointments in Unjust Civil Cases," *Wake Forest Law Review* 32 (1997): 635 (discussing case).

client's inability to pay, but for moral considerations as well, or for no reason at all. However, once the attorney-client relationship is established, the collective norms of the profession suggest that the lawyer functions more as a mere conduit for the client's values than as a partner in a rich moral dialogue with another human. This is in keeping with the consumerist paradigm, which tends to view the individual as a bundle of preferences to be satisfied on the open market, not as a human person capable of meaningful moral reflection and growth.

In strictly legal terms, the elevation of consumer autonomy as a nonnegotiable collective mandate is difficult to counter. After all, its democratic legitimacy is largely unimpeachable. The California contraceptives statute, for example, was enacted by a popularly elected legislature, and its interpretation by the state courts was defensible under the United States Supreme Court's binding interpretation of the Free Exercise Clause.[23] More fundamentally, anyone seeking to narrow our conception of individual freedom will find an uphill battle in our legal culture, which is rightfully skeptical of such efforts. Building our legal system around a robust conception of individual liberty has served the country well, as it has allowed us to escape much of the oppression and instrumentalism that has afflicted other experiments in government. How, exactly, does one challenge the oncoming legal enshrinement of consumerism without denigrating the legal standing of the individual? It is precisely at this point of the inquiry that Catholic social teaching speaks directly to American law.

BUILDING A COUNTER-CONSUMERIST CULTURE

The law's preoccupation with consumer autonomy is no surprise to students of Catholic social teaching, for as early as 1931, Pope Pius XI observed that "following upon the overthrow and near extinction of that rich social life which was once highly developed through associations of various kinds, there remain virtually only individuals and the State."[24] Decades later, Pope John Paul II diagnosed the sort of hyper-individualism found in the West as a "blind submission to pure consumerism,"[25] and warned that "[t]rue devel-

23. See *Employment Div. v. Smith,* 494 US 872 (1990) (holding that free exercise rights do not excuse compliance with neutral, generally applicable laws).

24. Pope Pius XI, *Quadragesimo anno,* ¶ 78 (1931).

25. Pope John Paul II, *Sollicitudo rei socialis,* ¶ 28 (1987).

opment" could not consist simply in the "greater availability of goods and services," but must include "due consideration for the social, cultural and spiritual dimensions of the human being."[26]

The danger posed by the recent trend of American law is especially pressing, though, in that it effectively blocks the path by which to escape the consumerist delusion, as identified by Pope John Paul II. He explained that, because "an economic system does not possess criteria for correctly distinguishing new and higher forms of satisfying human needs from artificial new needs which hinder the formation of a mature personality," among society's urgent needs are "the formation of a strong sense of responsibility among producers," and "the necessary intervention by public authorities."[27] In the American legal system, public authorities have intervened in the provision of certain goods, but their intervention has more deeply entrenched the consumerist paradigm by effectively forbidding market actors from showing moral responsibility for the services they provide. Once again, the prescience of the pontiff's social diagnosis looms large, for by removing an individual's moral agency based on her role as a satisfier of consumer preferences, "[m]an is thus reduced to a series of social relationships, and the concept of the person as the autonomous subject of moral decision disappears, the very subject whose decisions build the social order."[28]

Before unpacking the lessons that solidarity and subsidiarity have to offer American law, it bears emphasis that these lessons are indivisible from the broader framework of Catholic social thought. Try as they might, modern secularists have not been able to maintain either doctrine's vibrancy without taking account of the theologically informed anthropological presumptions from which both doctrines arise.

The effect of solidarity's decontextualization is especially drastic, as it becomes a largely empty feel-good slogan for a whole range of random and ungrounded, if often noble, social causes.[29] Richard Rorty's work typifies the efforts of secular intellectuals to provide solidarity with meaningful content that does not depend on truth claims about the nature of man. Rorty tries to construct a theory under which we are able to achieve a sense of solidar-

---

26. Ibid., ¶ 9.

27. Pope John Paul II, *Centesimus annus*, ¶ 36 (1991).

28. Ibid., ¶ 13.

29. See Giles Gunn, *Beyond Solidarity: Pragmatism and Difference in a Globalized World* (Chicago: University of Chicago Press, 2001), 31 (listing various causes that have relied explicitly on the concept of solidarity).

ity with our fellow humans despite the contingent qualities of history, culture, language, and all other sources of meaning. His effort is hindered by the seemingly inescapable tension between an individual's inherently self-serving behavior and solidarity's call to consider and act on others' interests. He concedes that we must "drop the demand for a theory which unifies the public and private," and "treat the demands of self-creation and of human solidarity as equally valid, yet forever incommensurable."[30] As such, the quest for human solidarity entails "an endless, proliferating realization of Freedom, rather than a convergence toward an already existing Truth."[31]

Crucially, this means that, in Rorty's view, solidarity is something to be created, rather than recognized.[32] Given our unavoidably self-centered worldview, though, the only possible way to make this happen is for us to "try to notice our similarities with" those who have been marginalized.[33] In other words, Rorty "is obliged to turn solidarity into the attempt to expand our sense of 'we' to include as many 'others' as possible," and by doing so he "shrinks solidarity into little more than a form of goodwill."[34] To Rorty and others who want to mine the concept of solidarity for its social justice potential without being saddled with its truth claims, we exhibit solidarity when we envision "the other" as resembling ourselves. Notice, however, that this is a solidarity of sentiment, mustering up our feelings of familiarity, and has nothing to do with the inherent value or dignity of the human person, calling to be recognized. Notice also that this solidarity, with its foundation in freedom, unfettered even by the possible existence of truth, will attempt nothing beyond the facilitation of the other's autonomy—it makes no claims as to the good beyond autonomy itself.

So what does Catholic social thought's vision of solidarity add to this thin, but seemingly harmless, form of goodwill? Put simply, it adds a worldview emanating from the Incarnation. Absent the Gospel's story of God dwelling in man, it is more difficult to articulate a compelling basis for valuing others as we value ourselves. Left to our own devices, we cannot relate to the other without incorporating the other into ourselves (which can give rise to collectivism), defining ourselves in opposition to the other (which can give rise to tribalism or nationalism), or forgoing the attempt at relationship altogether

30. Richard Rorty, *Contingency, Irony, and Solidarity* (Cambridge: Cambridge University Press, 1989), xv.

31. Ibid., xvi.

32. Ibid., 196.

33. Ibid.

34. See Gunn, *Beyond Solidarity*, xii.

(which can give rise to individualism). Without being able to see every person as infinitely valuable on their own terms, the fallback tendency is to see human difference as divergence to be rooted out, which is the backdrop of the twentieth century. The opposite extreme, however, which sees difference as the defining value of humanity, is too thin an account to overcome the paralyzing tension between human nature's self-furthering instincts and the perceived obligation to help others.

We need the Incarnation as the foundation for a conception of solidarity as robust as the vision cast by the Church as it recommitted itself to engaging the modern era: "The joys and the hopes, the griefs and anxieties of the mean of this age, especially those who are poor or in any way afflicted, these are the joys and hopes, the griefs and anxieties of the followers of Christ."[35]

Reflecting the whole of the Church's social teaching, solidarity is grounded in the day-to-day rhythms of human existence. It does not beckon individuals to give themselves "to an abstract ideal or to a false utopia," but "to another person or to other persons."[36] At the same time, solidarity reflects the transcendence of the human spirit, for the individual's giving of herself goes "ultimately to God, who is the author of his being and who alone can fully accept his gift."[37]

In sharp contrast to Rorty's conception, solidarity is not contingent on our ability to identify similarities between us and the other, but rather "binds us to make ourselves the neighbor of every person without exception, and of actively helping him when he comes across our path."[38] Far from being selective in its reach, solidarity is all-encompassing in scope and depth, for the other is "not only a human being with his or her own rights and a fundamental equality with everyone else, but . . . the living image of God the Father, redeemed by the blood of Jesus Christ and placed under the permanent action of the Holy Spirit."[39] As a result, every person must "be loved, even if an enemy, with the same love with which the Lord loves him or her; and for that person's sake one must be ready for sacrifice, even the ultimate one: to lay down one's life for the brethren."[40]

---

35. Pope Paul VI, *Gaudium et spes*, ¶ 1 (1965).
36. Pope John Paul II, *Centesimus annus*, ¶ 41 (1991).
37. Ibid.
38. Pope Paul VI, *Gaudium et spes*, ¶ 27 (1965).
39. Pope John Paul II, *Sollicitudo rei socialis*, ¶ 40 (1987).
40. Ibid., ¶ 40.

Solidarity's implications for American law are formidable, for "[a] society is alienated if its forms of social organization, production and consumption make it more difficult to offer this gift of self and to establish this solidarity between people."[41] Our commitment to others must not be instrumentalist,[42] nor can it be a question of individual duty, for solidarity "is an imperative which obliges each and every man and woman, as well as societies and nations."[43] At its core, then, solidarity "is not a feeling of vague compassion or shallow distress" at others' misfortunes, but rather "a firm and persevering determination to commit oneself to the common good; that is to say to the good of all and of each individual, because we are all really responsible for all."[44] What is needed is "a commitment to the good of one's neighbor with the readiness, in the gospel sense, to 'lose oneself' for the sake of the other instead of exploiting him, and to 'serve him' instead of oppressing him for one's advantage."[45]

Especially significant from the perspective of American law is the fact that solidarity entails the pursuit of truth, not just the maximization of autonomy. The freedom made possible by solidarity is not "achieved in total self-sufficiency and an absence of relationships," but only "where reciprocal bonds, governed by truth and justice, link people to one another."[46] In recognizing the inherent dignity and value of others, we are called not to use individual consent as validation of any market transaction, but to oppose "whatever violates the integrity of the human person."[47] Solidarity, like the entire web of Catholic social thought, defines freedom in terms that are largely absent from American legal culture: "Freedom is not the liberty to do anything whatsoever," but rather is aimed at doing good, and the good, under this worldview, can be articulated only as a claim of truth.[48]

If solidarity embodies Catholic social teaching's substantive vision of the human person in relationship with others, subsidiarity provides the framework through which that vision can best be pursued. Subsidiarity springs

41. Pope John Paul II, *Centesimus annus,* ¶ 41 (1991).

42. Pope John Paul II, *Sollicitudo rei socialis,* ¶ 39 (1987).

43. Ibid., ¶ 32.   44. Ibid., ¶ 38.

45. Ibid.

46. Congregation for the Doctrine of the Faith, "Instructio de libertate christiana et liberatione," ¶ 26 (1986).

47. Pope Paul VI, *Gaudium et spes,* ¶ 27 (1965).

48. Congregation for the Doctrine of the Faith, "Instructio de libertate christiana et liberatione," ¶ 26 (1986).

from the Church's recognition that man cannot be adequately understood simply by his market function or political status, even though under the modern worldview "it seems as though he exists only as a producer and consumer of goods, or as an object of State administration."[49] Instead, the human person "is realized in various intermediary groups, beginning with the family and including economic, social, political and cultural groups which stem from human nature itself and have their own autonomy, always with a view to the common good."[50] The civil society, which these institutions compose, operates not through power, as does political society, but through "affinities, voluntary alliances and natural forms of solidarity."[51]

The importance of the free, meaningful, and efficacious operation of these institutions presents the "most weighty principle" of subsidiarity:

> Just as it is gravely wrong to take from individuals what they can accomplish by their own initiative and industry and give it to the community, so also it is an injustice and at the same time a grave evil and disturbance of right order to assign to a greater and higher association what lesser and subordinate organizations can do. For every social activity ought of its very nature to furnish help to the members of the body social, and never destroy or absorb them.[52]

This fundamental ordering "must be respected" because "needs are best understood and satisfied by people who are closest to them and who act as neighbours to those in need," a perception that derives, in turn, from the fact that "certain kinds of demands often call for a response which is not simply material but which is capable of perceiving the deeper human need."[53]

Subsidiarity's call for localized and personalized responses to human need, if removed from the broader context of Catholic social teaching, becomes either a one-dimensional tagline for political conservatism or an inconsequential throwback to a hopelessly outdated decentralized way of life. In the political sense, subsidiarity becomes an intellectual cover theory for across-the-board devolution of government power with little concern for the common good, as though Catholicism opposes all forms of collective action.[54] In

---

49. Pope John Paul II, *Centesimus annus*, ¶ 49 (1991).

50. Ibid., ¶ 13.

51. Pontifical Council for the Family, "The Family and Human Rights," ¶ 64 (1999).

52. Pope Pius XI, *Quadragesimo anno*, ¶ 79 (1931).

53. Pope John Paul II, *Centesimus annus*, ¶ 48 (1991).

54. See Robert K. Vischer, "Subsidiarity as a Principle of Governance: Beyond Devolution," *Indiana Law Review* 35 (2001): 103.

the communitarian sense, subsidiarity becomes completely uncontroversial, and is seen through a Tocquevillean gloss as a harmless but noble endorsement of neighbors helping one another, as though Catholicism is stuck in an era of community barn raisings and potluck dinners.

In reality, subsidiarity in the twenty-first century is a much more radical proposition than either its conservative or its communitarian purveyors imagine. In an era when the modern liberal state seeks either to marginalize intermediate associations or to remake them in the state's own image, subsidiarity stands out as a subversive wrench in the collective enthronement of consumerism. Casting social action as the responsibility of those who are in the closest proximity to a given problem reconfigures the modern citizen as a proactive moral agent, not simply as a reactive subject of higher authority. Contrary to its more conservative interpretations, subsidiarity does not foreclose a role for centralized authority, for often local problems are not susceptible to effective remedy without society's collectively channeled attention. But subsidiarity does reframe our image of the modern state, envisioning it as a resource for localized empowerment and coordination, rather than as the arbiter and provider of the social good. Indeed, defending non-state actors as legitimate sources for the identification and pursuit of the social good makes up the crux of subsidiarity's radicalism and lies at the heart of Catholic social teaching's prophetic message to modern liberalism.

This message melds both doctrines: Catholic social teaching speaks truth to the power of the liberal state by bearing witness to solidarity's vision of the human person, realized within subsidiarity's framework for the ordering of society. In the context of a free market economy, the practice of solidarity requires that service providers honor the dignity of the consumer, which is not coextensive with the autonomy of the consumer. Solidarity, then, can be realized only to the extent that service providers are empowered to meet needs in ways that diverge from, or even defy, the overarching norms of the collective—that is, solidarity is not possible absent a legal system that accepts the premise of subsidiarity.

The trend in American law defies the foundational premises of both solidarity and subsidiarity. By harnessing consumerist norms to the coercive power of the state, modern liberalism has set out on a course that not only rejects any collective attempt to cultivate the common good, but trumps any effort by service providers to pursue the common good through their own relationships with the consumer. By requiring Catholic Charities, for example, to provide contraceptives to its employees or else cease offering prescription drug coverage altogether, the state forces the organization to defy its own conception of the good by either facilitating sin or foregoing the obligation to provide for those within its care. We are left with a purely individualist sense of morality, as actors are permitted to concern themselves only with their own morally laden choices of consumption, not with their morally laden choices of provision.

This contradicts Catholic social teaching's relentless call to contribute to the common good and better the collective conditions of human life,[55] a call that is directed toward injustice arising from an individual's omissions as much as from her affirmative acts. As we are reminded, "[f]eed the man dying of hunger, because if you have not fed him, you have killed him."[56] Providers are called to bear witness to the true nature of the human person, even through their relationships with the consumer; abandoning that witness under the guise of facilitating individual autonomy does not signal a necessary truce among warring conceptions of the good, but a state-imposed surrender of any claims to truth that transcend individual preference. As an increasingly evident presumption of our legal system, the trump of consumer autonomy threatens to relegate Catholic social teaching to practical obsolescence in the lived reality of many Americans.

PROSPECTS FOR ENGAGEMENT

While the anthropological insights of Catholic social teaching are becoming more difficult to pursue for those who are constrained by the dictates of a legal system increasingly wedded to consumerism as a nonnegotiable value, this trend should not be construed as the defeatist epilogue of the Church's formative relationship with American society. As evidenced by Pope John Paul II's prophetic role in the collapse of communism, the Church's social teaching is at its most vibrant and vital when the cultural powers have purported to reject its most fundamental tenets. After all, the path by which to speak truth to power tends to be clearer and more direct when the disconnect between truth and power is stark. This does not make the moral quandaries in which many service providers find themselves any less tragic, but it

---

55. Pope Paul VI, *Gaudium et spes*, ¶ 30 (1965).
56. Ibid., ¶ 69.

does bring into focus the primary points of impact through which the call of Catholic social teaching will continue to bear witness against the atomizing wave of legally mandated consumerism.

First, proponents of Catholic social teaching will need to continue engaging the political arena, for that is where many of the consumer culture's most morally oppressive initiatives emerge. But the aim of the engagement warrants careful thought. If Catholics seek to capture the legislative apparatus in order to define and pursue, on a collective level, an anthropologically informed conception of the good, are they employing the same morally oppressive measures to which they now object? By way of obvious illustration, those who support Catholic Charities' resistance to the state's efforts to compel the provision of contraceptives would no doubt express some misgivings were the organization to embark on an effort to convince legislators to prohibit any employer from providing coverage for contraceptives. The misgivings would be well-placed, for replacing one state-imposed vision of the morally contested good with another does not advance the cause of Catholic social teaching in the long run. Such top-down articulations of the common good not only stand in tension with subsidiarity's premise, but also turn the cultivation of the common good into a zero-sum contest of raw power. As we have seen in California, such contests do not necessarily hold out hope for the realization of the social teaching's basic premises.

Catholic social teaching is more likely to retain its prophetic quality if we instead envision it against the background of the marketplace of ideas that American pluralism, at its best, represents. Instead of focusing efforts on our elected officials, Catholics will be better served targeting the hearts and minds of our fellow citizens. There is still an advocacy role to be played in the legislative arena, make no mistake, but the advocacy will support claims to robust conceptions of autonomy, not just among individual consumers, but among individuals and communities who participate in all segments of the American market economy. If we foster a political culture that values alternative conceptions of the good, even widely divergent conceptions of the good, we will have created bulwarks to defend meaningful moral decision making in the marketplace, which will prove invaluable when the pendulum of public opinion invariably swings against any recognizable conception of morality. As the old adage suggests, the Catholic Church does not impose, it proposes, and any political agenda born out of the Church's social teaching should reflect that fact, not only out of recognition of the dignity of those with whom we disagree, but also because the continued relevance of the social teaching depends on it.

Second, proponents of Catholic social teaching need to mount a defense of their freedom of moral agency that is steeped in the language of legal rights. Given that many of the legal debates over individual rights result in outcomes that diverge from objective conceptions of morality, Catholics tend to be skeptical of much of the "rights talk" that goes on in contemporary American legal culture. Some of this skepticism is certainly understandable, but it is a mistake to disregard the conversation entirely. In particular, Catholics must be especially cautious about turning their backs on theories that create and maintain spheres of autonomy from state intervention. As reflected in recent Catholic scholarship regarding parental rights,[57] a robust conception of constitutional freedom need not be expressed as merely the market preferences of individual consumers. Subsidiarity is consistent with certain visions of federalism, and other constitutional provisions—most obviously rights of association and religious liberty, but potentially privacy and substantive due process rights as well—are essential to the cultivation of autonomy for community-centered visions of the good that diverge from individualist norms.

This does not require Catholics to embrace the outcome of every lawsuit that purports to further individual autonomy, but we should weigh carefully what is gained and what is lost before we write off entire rights-driven theories of constitutional interpretation. As evidenced by the Catholic Charities debacle, the ability of Catholics to appeal to the common good in the political forum as a means by which to defend their institutional autonomy is rapidly being overtaken by the expanding individualist norms of the liberal project, and the electorate does not seem particularly sympathetic. If service providers are to continue functioning as moral agents, as both solidarity and subsidiarity compel them to do, a framework of meaningful legal rights may be the last line of defense.

Finally, Catholic social teaching will always most dramatically display its transformative capacity in the heart of the human person, regardless of whether the surrounding political or legal cultures recognize—or even allow for—that capacity. To account fully for the real-world power of solidarity and subsidiarity, we must understand them as invitations to relationship, to

57. See, e.g., Richard W. Garnett, "Taking Pierce Seriously: The Family, Religious Education, and Harm to Children," *Notre Dame Law Review* 76 (2000): 109.

be implemented person by person, community by community. The teaching, at its core, is a blueprint more for everyday human interaction than for grand culture war strategizing. Solidarity invites us to recognize God in our neighbor, coworker, estranged family member, or nameless face we pass on the street, and to act accordingly; subsidiarity calls us not only to support social structures that facilitate personal responses to human need, but to provide those personal responses ourselves. As witnesses to the truth of the Incarnation, we are compelled to live out the power and wisdom of the Church's teachings, regardless of how difficult that may be under the prevailing norms of American law.

[6]

THE CONSTITUTION AND
THE COMMON GOOD

A Perspective on the Catholic Contribution

ROBERT JOHN ARAUJO, S.J.

*We the People of the United States, in Order to form a more perfect Union, establish
Justice, insure domestic Tranquility, provide for the common defence, promote the
general Welfare, and secure the Blessings of Liberty to ourselves and our Posterity,
do ordain and establish this Constitution for the United States of America.*

Preamble to the Constitution of the United States

With these words, the Constitution of the United States outlines the purposes for which the Constitution was created. The goals to which the American people commit and bind themselves in a political union are identified in
this pledge. But what do these words mean from a Catholic perspective? That
is the subject of this short chapter. This chapter will first consider how the
words of the Preamble contribute to establishing a framework in which the
Constitution and the laws promulgated in accordance with it were intended
and are designed to promote the common good,[1] an idea that has long been a
part of the Catholic perspective on legal systems and structures.

1. In his inaugural address of January 20, 2001, President George W. Bush twice mentioned the importance and relevance of the common good to the American people. First, he

To develop this point, I shall briefly explain the concept of the common good as it has been construed in the Western world. Next, I shall provide a concise analysis of the Preamble to demonstrate how its content can promote the common good. I shall then apply these principles by contrasting two U.S. Supreme Court decisions, *Jacobson v. Massachusetts*, which held that the government can subject an individual to vaccination against communicable disease against his will,[2] and *Stenberg v. Carhart*,[3] which struck down a Nebraska law that prohibited the gruesome procedure commonly known as partial-birth abortion. I shall argue that *Jacobson* is largely consistent with the underlying principles of the common good while *Stenberg* is not. I conclude this chapter by viewing these cases from a Catholic perspective of the common good. I suggest that appropriation of the Catholic understanding of the common good would remedy the impoverished views of *Stenberg* and lead to a broader protection of all individuals, which in turn would enhance the community at large.

THE COMMON GOOD: A BRIEF INTRODUCTION

The concern about the common good as a social, political, and legal issue extends back to biblical times and the chronicles of God's people seeking right relation with God and one another. In a religious context, the early texts of Deuteronomy and Leviticus express concern about the common good through the development of the Mosaic Law. Classical Athens and Rome, which have also had an impact on the Catholic perspective, made their respective contributions as well.

As one turns to the classical era of ancient Greece and Rome, one will find that the ancient philosophers also addressed the common good and the

---

stated that "[o]ur national courage has been clear in times of depression and war, when defending dangers defined our common good. Now we must choose if the example of our fathers and mothers will inspire us or condemn us. We must show courage in a time of blessing by confronting problems instead of passing them on to future generations." Second, he called all Americans to an important challenge when he said, "What you do is as important as anything government does. I ask you to seek a common good beyond your comfort; to defend needed reforms against easy attacks; to serve your nation, beginning with your neighbor. I ask you to be citizens: citizens, not spectators; citizens, not subjects; responsible citizens, building communities of service and a nation of character." George W. Bush, "Inaugural Address of 20 January 2001." http://www.whitehouse.gov/news/inaugural-address.html.

2. *Jacobson v. Massachusetts*, 197 US 11 (1905).

3. *Stenberg v. Carhart*, 530 US 914 (2000).

polis's response to it. Among the earliest to tackle this issue was Aristotle, who noted that "[e]very state is a community of some kind, and every community is established with a view to some good."[4] In looking at the state or the political institution established to govern the community, he suggested that just governments are those "which have a regard for the common interest."[5] In assessing what Aristotle considered "just," one can turn to his discourse on ethics, in which he supplied the foundation of a theme that justice is reciprocity and mutuality amongst human beings through their relationship with one another.[6] In placing the notion of reciprocity into the human community, Aristotle contended that the truest or best form of justice is the reciprocal display of friendship between persons.[7] Aristotle emphasized that the best form of this friendship would look to the interests of the other before considering the interests of one's self.

While critical of the conditions of political community practiced in the Rome of his time, Marcus Tullius Cicero shared some of Aristotle's attitudes when he suggested that a commonwealth or social order emerges from the social spirit of people who make the commonwealth their "property," which is established on the principles of "respect for justice" and "partnership for the common good."[8] Cicero was not, according to Frederick Copleston, a writer of new or original ideas but rather a Roman reflection or adaptation of his Greek teachers. His presentation clarified Greek political and philosophical thought for a Roman audience.[9] It would follow that his explanation of the common good was influenced by his Greek predecessors, from whom he learned. As Sabine points out, the state constitutes the affairs of the people and should be guided by the moral law of God, that is, a natural law "which transcends human choice and human institution."[10]

4. Aristotle, *Introduction to Aristotle,* 2nd ed., ed. Richard McKeon (Chicago: University of Chicago Press, 1974), 589.

5. Ibid., 629–30.   6. Ibid., 433–34.

7. Ibid., 502–3.

8. Cicero, *De Re Publica De Legibus,* trans. Clinton Walker Keyes (Cambridge: Harvard University Press, 1928).

9. Frederick Copleston, *A History of Philosophy,* vol. 1 (New York: Doubleday, 1993), 418–19.

10. George H. Sabine, *A History of Political Theory,* 4th ed. (n.p.: Oryden Press, 1993), 166.

AN ANALYSIS OF THE PREAMBLE
OF THE CONSTITUTION

The drafters of the Constitution were men of learning, and many were familiar with the ancient Greek and Roman canon of political philosophy.[11] While they did not elaborate on the doctrine in great detail, both James Madison and, perhaps, Alexander Hamilton raised concerns about the common good in their advocacy for the adoption of the 1787 Constitution. For example, in addressing the problem of factions, Madison argued that they:

> divided mankind into parties, inflamed them with mutual animosity, and rendered them much more disposed to vex and oppress each other than to co-operate for their common good. So strong is this propensity of mankind to fall into mutual animosities, that where no substantial occasion presents itself, the most frivolous and fanciful distinctions have been sufficient to kindle their unfriendly passions and excite their most violent conflicts.[12]

Either Madison or Hamilton later submitted another important point in the context of the virtues of a bicameral representative legislature when he stated:

> Of all the objections which have been framed against the federal Constitution, this [the criticism leveled at the House of Representatives] is perhaps the most extraordinary. Whilst the objection itself is leveled against a pretended oligarchy, the principle of it strikes at the very root of republican government. The aim of every political constitution is, or ought to be, first to obtain for rulers men who possess most wisdom to discern, and most virtue to pursue, the common good of the society; and in the next place, to take the most effectual precautions for keeping them virtuous whilst they continue to hold their public trust.[13]

For those who drafted the Constitution and advocated its adoption, the pursuit of the common good was vital to the establishment, sustenance, and success of the federal union. While these brief references to the common good found in the Federalist Papers do not explain what was meant by the "common good," they do indicate its significance in the minds of the Founders.

The Preamble of the Constitution identifies the purposes for which the

---

11. For example, Professor Max Farand notes references to both Aristotle and Cicero presented by Hamilton during the Constitutional Convention of 1787, see Max Farand, *The Records of the Federal Convention of 1787*, vol. 1 (New Haven: Yale University Press, 1966), 308.

12. James Madison, "Federalist #10," in *The Federalist Papers*, ed. Clinton Rossiter (New York: New American Library, 1961), p. 78.

13. Madison, "Federalist #57," in ibid.

federal government of a legislative, an executive, and a judicial branch was established. While the Preamble does not necessarily serve as a source of power,[14] it does provide the basic objectives for which the framers drafted and implemented the Constitution. A parsing of the text within the framework of the common good would help illustrate this point.

The Preamble identifies "We the People of the United States" as the persons most directly involved with or concerned about the Constitution. The language suggests that "We the People . . ." are individual persons united in a community. The text uses the first person plural pronoun "we" to reinforce this suggestion. It further defines the pronoun "We" by adding the inclusive modifier that states that these individuals are "the People of the United States." This language of identification then proceeds to explain that the integrated community, as opposed to a collection of autonomous individuals, is a national community bound together for a set of reasons. An explication of the reasons follows.

The community, which identifies itself as "the People of the United States," exists for a set of purposes that is preceded by the phrase "in Order to . . ." This language, which begins to explain the raison d'être of the union, then specifies six categories of activities that are connected with the coordinating conjunction "and." The significance of this conjunction implies that the reasons for which the Constitution exists are to achieve all, not just some, of the listed goals. These goals identify the purposes for which the community of "the People of the United States" has come together.

The first goal that the Preamble identifies is to "form a more perfect Union." Rather than electing to advance the separate interests of autonomous individuals or autonomous states, the initial objective toward which action is to be taken is to develop a union, a community—but not just any union, a more perfect one.[15] A second goal follows, and it is geared to the establishment of justice. Again, it should be noted that the justice to be pursued is the

14. See *Jacobson v. Massachusetts*, 197 US 11, 22 (1905), where the Court stated that the Preamble "indicates the general purposes for which the people ordained and established the Constitution, it has never been regarded as the source of any substantive power."

15. Prof. Mary Ann Glendon has made an important observation of this phenomenon. As she stated, "Our overblown rights rhetoric and our vision of the rights-bearer as an autonomous individual channel our thoughts away from what we have in common and focus them on what separates us. They draw us away from participation in public life and point us toward the maximization of private satisfactions." See Mary Ann Glendon, *Rights Talk: The Impoverishment of Political Discourse* (New York: Free Press, 1991), 143.

justice for the community of "the People of the United States," who strive to perfect their union.

The third purpose for which the community exists is to "insure domestic tranquillity." Again, the tranquility to be pursued is not for the advantage of some. Rather, it is for the benefit of the entire community of individuals who identify themselves as "the People of the United States." This third justification for the union is related to and paves the way for the fourth objective, that is, those actions pursued to "provide for the common defence." In short, the other goals for which the Constitution was established, including domestic tranquility, cannot be attained unless measures are taken to secure by a "common defence" "the People of the United States." Once more, this protection cannot be limited to the benefit of some but must be extended to safeguard all. To ensure this, the framers provided the fifth goal of the Constitution, which are those steps taken to "promote the general Welfare." The use of the modifier "general" intensifies the significance that the actions taken for the achieving the purposes of the union are for every one of the people who comprise the United States. This welfare cannot be realized if the beneficiaries do not include all of the individuals who compose the federation.

The sixth and final goal is connected to the previous five with the coordinating conjunction "and." The purposes for which the Framers ordained and established the union under the Constitution are incomplete or imperfect if the blessings of liberty are not secured. Again, there is little dispute that these blessings are for all, not just some, of "the People of the United States." This last goal reminds us that the attaining this liberty is not just for the people of a particular—the present—generation; it is a goal for all succeeding generations of Americans, which is made clear by the use of the phrase "our posterity." Indeed, as the text makes clear, these aspirations were for the benefit of all succeeding generations who would continue the existence of "the People of the United States." Now, a question must be posed: how do these goals, which provide guidelines for pursuing the common good in our culture, relate to issues surrounding abortion? The protection of the human person and human dignity at all stages of human life requires insertion and participation in, not insulation and separation from, the community. The community prospers when its members give of themselves contributing to the whole, making it prosper. The community withers when they turn within and tend only to their private cares. Benjamin Barber has argued that there can be no fraternal feeling, no general will, no selfless act, no mutuality, no species identity, no gift relationship, no disinterested obligation, no social empathy, no love or belief or commitment if a person goes through life emphasizing the significance of privacy and its zealous protection.[16]

This point of view bears directly on the issue of abortion. There is a deep irony in the fact that the right to abortion is founded on the so-called right of privacy. This right, fabricated in 1965 in *Griswold v. Connecticut*, "guaranteed" married couples the "right" to prevent pregnancy.[17] In 1972, this "right" was expanded in *Eisenstadt v. Baird* to include all individuals, married or not.[18] In 1973 in *Roe*, the Supreme Court gave this "right to privacy" a new twist by creating a near absolute legal right to abort a pregnancy. In subsequent decisions, the Supreme Court made clear the truly radical nature of this right. Indeed, in *Stenberg*, the Court held that the right of "privacy" includes the right to kill a child in the process of being born. How can this result be squared with the obvious concern for the common good set forth in the Preamble and the Federalist Papers?

THE CONSIDERATION OF THE COMMON GOOD
IN SUPREME COURT JURISPRUDENCE

Aristotle commented that the state achieves greatness when its leaders promulgate law that promotes or enhances the common good.[19] One practical way of implementing this noble goal is for a state to take those steps necessary to protect each of its members regardless of status, hierarchy, class, or other category of identification.[20] A fundamental reason justifying this approach is that as each person is protected, the protection of all will necessarily follow. And when all are protected, each in turn is safeguarded by the State even though some may have to forgo the exercise of particular liberties within specific contexts.

16. Benjamin Barber, *Strong Democracy: Participatory Politics for a New Age* (Berkeley: University of California Press, 1984), 71–72. Barber further argues, "From this precarious foundation [of individualism and privacy], no firm theory of citizenship, participation, public goods, or civic virtue can be expected to arise." Ibid., 4.

17. *Griswold v. Connecticut*, 381 US 479 (1965).

18. *Eisenstadt v. Baird*, 405 US 438 (1972).

19. See Aristotle, *Politics*, Book I, trans. Benjamin Jowett (Oxford: Clarendon Press, 1926).

20. H. A. Rommen, *The State in Catholic Thought: A Treatise in Political Philosophy* (St. Louis: B. Herder, 1945), 349.

This principle was illustrated by the Supreme Court's decision in *Jacobson v. Massachusetts*. This early-twentieth-century case involved a Massachusetts statute that authorized cities and towns to require mandatory vaccinations free of charge if these municipalities determined that inoculations were necessary to protect public health and safety.[21] Jacobson refused to comply with the order of his city to subject himself to the required immunization, and he was found guilty of violating the regulation promulgated to enforce the state statute.[22] In his defense, Jacobson argued that he was immune from prosecution on two constitutional grounds: (1) under the rights secured to him under the Preamble of the Constitution of the United States,[23] and (2) under the rights of liberty, due process, and equal protection guaranteed under the Fourteenth Amendment.[24]

Over the dissents of Justices Brewer and Peckham, Justice Harlan, writing for the majority, affirmed the conviction.[25] The majority quickly set aside Jacobson's first defense, which was based on the Preamble of the Constitution. The Court noted that the Preamble was not the source of any substantive power, but that it expressed "the general purposes for which the people ordained and established the Constitution."[26] This conclusion is significant because, as the text of the Preamble makes clear, one of the purposes for which the Constitution was "ordained and established" is the promotion of the common good.

The Court spent considerably more time discussing Jacobson's second defense, which was based on the protection of liberty under the Due Process Clause of the Fourteenth Amendment. In rejecting Jacobson's personal liberty argument, however, the Court relied on the state's interest in protecting the common good and, thus, on the purposes of the Constitution set forth in the Preamble.

At the outset of its examination of Jacobson's liberty claim, the majority explored Jacobson's argument that the state invaded his constitutionally protected liberty when it prosecuted him for failing to undergo the mandated vaccination. In essence, he claimed that the state authorities trammeled the exercise of his autonomy to protect his own health in the way he determined was best.[27] While the majority acknowledged that there could be cases where

21. *Jacobson v. Massachusetts*, 197 US 11, 12 (1905).
22. Ibid., 13–14.   23. Ibid., 13–14.
24. Ibid., 14.   25. Ibid., 39.
26. Ibid., 22.   27. Ibid., 26.

a liberty argument could prevail,[28] this defense was not available in Jacobson's circumstances. The majority stated that the rights of liberty enjoyed by each person do not confer an absolute right to be free from all restrictions because "[t]here are manifold restraints to which every person is necessarily subject for the common good."[29] In other words, the liberty of the individual must cohere with the liberty of everyone else. But since liberty is not the only issue addressed in the Preamble, the liberty of each person must also be considered in the context of legitimate concerns about other vital issues. Thus the majority made clear that the rights to liberty exercised and enjoyed by each person are subject to "such reasonable conditions . . . essential to the safety, health, peace, good order, and morals of the community. Even liberty itself . . . is not unrestricted license to act according to one's own will. It is only freedom from restraint under conditions essential to the equal enjoyment of the same rights by others."[30] In essence then, the rights properly belonging to the individual must be understood in the context of rights properly belonging to all persons. A well-ordered society requires that the civil authorities take account of the welfare of all "and not permit the interests of the many to be subordinated to the wishes or convenience of the few."[31] This is precisely what the Preamble of the Constitution establishes as the purpose for which the framers established the Constitution of the United States.

Although the Court's decision in *Jacobson* remains good law and its rationale remains intact, the state's ability to promote and enhance the common good was put aside in *Stenberg v. Carhart*. As noted above, in *Stenberg* the Court held that the state may not ban a particularly gruesome form of abortion know as partial-birth abortion. *Stenberg* is the latest in a long line of abortion cases in which the place of the common good in constitutional adjudication has been eroded. In *Planned Parenthood of Southeastern Pennsylvania v. Casey*[32] the Court gave a sweeping definition to the meaning of "liberty," one that is at odds with the constitutional understanding of "liberty" presented here. In *Casey*, the Court stated that there is "a promise of the Constitution that there is a realm of personal liberty which the government may not enter."[33] This personal liberty is premised on a fundamental belief: "At the heart of liberty is the right to define one's own concept of existence, of

28. Ibid., 38–39.   29. Ibid., 26.
30. Ibid., 26–27.   31. Ibid., 29.
32. *Planned Parenthood of Southeastern Pennsylvania v. Casey*, 505 US 833 (1992).
33. Ibid., 847.

meaning of the universe, and the mystery of human life. Beliefs about these matters could not define the attributes of personhood were they formed under compulsion of the State."[34] Here the Court embraces the very notion of liberty it rejected in *Jacobson*. Indeed, *Casey*'s formulation of liberty accentuates the interests of the isolated, autonomous individual. This formulation of constitutional liberty fails to provide any means of resolving the conflict between competing liberty claims of different individuals, and it ignores the claims of the community as a whole.

In *Stenberg v. Carhart*, a majority of the Supreme Court again sacrificed the common good for the interests of the isolated, autonomous individual. The majority opinion concluded that state legislation banning a particularly repugnant method of abortion (intact dilation and extraction—know as the D&X method) was unconstitutional on several grounds.[35] Justice Breyer acknowledged "the controversial nature of the problem" and the "virtually irreconcilable points of view" presented in the case.[36] Nonetheless, the majority based its decision on the "Constitution's guarantees of fundamental individual liberty" that protect "the woman's right to choose" as founded in previous decisions of the Court.[37]

A detailed critique of the *Stenberg* Court's decision and its application of *Casey*'s principles to the statute in question is beyond the scope of this chapter. Instead, I wish to demonstrate how the *Stenberg* majority's conception of individual liberty trumped the common good, disregarded the precedent of *Jacobson*, and is at odds with the fundamental objectives of the Constitution identified in the Preamble.

At issue in *Stenberg* was the legality of the statute enacted by the State of Nebraska to outlaw the D&X method of abortion—a method in which the skull of a partially delivered child is split open and its brains suctioned out with a vacuum. In his majority opinion, Justice Breyer acknowledged that this procedure "may seem horrifying" to some.[38] Of course, this could be said of virtually every method of abortion, for they all destroy innocent human life at its most vulnerable stage. Indeed, the intentional mutilation of any human being is a serious matter. In the Court's view, however, it is not serious

34. Ibid., 851, quoted in *Lawrence v. Texas*, 539 US 558, 574 (2003).

35. *Stenberg v. Carhart*, 530 US 914, 922 (2000).

36. Ibid., 920–21.

37. Ibid. The previous decisions were identified as *Roe v. Wade*, 410 US 113 (1973) and *Planned Parenthood of Southeastern Pennsylvania v. Casey*, 505 US 833 (1992).

38. US 914, 922 (2000).

enough to overcome the constitutional infirmity of curtailing liberty. At several points Breyer acknowledges that the D&X procedure is performed "on a living fetus"[39] or "of a still living fetus."[40] Still the majority found that the state's efforts to regulate the D&X method were unconstitutional for two independent reasons: (1) the statute failed to provide for an exception "for the preservation of the . . . health of the mother";[41] and (2) it imposed an "undue burden" on the mother's liberty to pursue other types of abortion not specifically regulated by this statute.[42]

In a concurring opinion Justice Stevens attempted to reinforce the majority's opinion by arguing that the State irrationally attempted to regulate only one of "two equally gruesome procedures."[43] For Stevens, the outcome of this case was mandated by *Roe v. Wade* because "the word 'liberty' in the Fourteenth Amendment includes a woman's right to make this difficult and extremely personal decision—makes it impossible . . . to understand how a State has any legitimate interest in requiring a doctor to follow any procedure other than the one that he or she reasonably believes will best protect the woman in her exercise of this constitutional liberty."[44] As a result of this kind of justification, the liberty of a woman to choose an abortion, regardless of its repugnance, was of paramount interest to the majority of the Justices. Although liberty is an important constitutional concept, it is not an *absolute* objective that must prevail above all other considerations, including the common good.[45] What the majority failed to grasp was that they exalted one particular form of liberty—the liberty to kill a child in the process of being born, insulating it from other vital considerations. In doing so, the majority also failed to acknowledge that the purpose of constitutional protection of liberty is not just for the benefit of particular individuals, but for the benefit

---

39. Ibid., 928.   40. Ibid., 939.

41. Ibid., 930.   42. Ibid.

43. Ibid., 946.

44. Ibid. Justice Ginsburg later stated in her own concurring opinion joined by Justice Stevens, "Chief Judge Posner [in *Hope Clinic v. Ryan*, 195 F3d 857, 881 (1999), dissenting opinion by Posner, C.J.] correspondingly observed . . . that the law prohibits the D & X procedure 'not because the procedure kills the fetus, not because it risks worse complications for the woman . . . , not because it is a crueler or more painful or more disgusting method of terminating a pregnancy . . .' Rather, Chief Judge Posner commented, the law prohibits the procedure because the State legislators seek to chip away at the private choice shielded by *Roe v. Wade*, even as modified by *Casey*." Ibid., 952.

45. *Catechism of the Catholic Church*, ¶ 1738.

of all. To hold otherwise is to render unintelligible the text of the Preamble "for ourselves and our Posterity."[46]

In short, the majority in *Stenberg* was singularly attracted to the same kind of absolute individual liberty that caused Mr. Jacobson to disobey the vaccination laws. Indeed, as Justice Scalia noted in his dissent, in giving constitutional protection to the D&X "method of killing a human child," the majority gave "live-birth abortion free rein,"[47] Furthermore, Scalia's dissent makes clear that this sort of exaggerated liberty is at odds with the Preamble: "The notion that the Constitution of the United States, designed among other things, 'to establish Justice, insure domestic Tranquility, . . . and secure the Blessings of Liberty to ourselves and our Posterity,' prohibits the States from simply banning this visibly brutal means of eliminating our half-born posterity is quite simply absurd."[48]

Chief Justice Rehnquist and Justices Thomas and Kennedy also dissented. While Rehnquist, Scalia, and Thomas had previously noted their opposition to a constitutionally protected "right to abortion," Justice Kennedy had not.[49] For this reason, Kennedy's *Stenberg* dissent merits special attention. He begins with the recognition that the Preamble to the Constitution establishes the purposes for which the rest of its text and the laws made under it are to achieve. These include the promotion of the common good—the good for everyone rather than the good for the isolated, autonomous individual.

46. Again, Prof. Glendon's work is most informative on this point. As she has insightfully argued, "The strident rights rhetoric that currently dominates American political discourse poorly serves the strong tradition of protection for individual freedom for which the United States is justly renowned. Our stark, simple rights dialect puts a damper on the processes of public justification, communication, and deliberation upon which the continuing vitality of a democratic regime depends. It contributes to the erosion of the habits, practices, and attitudes of respect for others that are the ultimate and surest guarantees of human rights. . . . Rights talk in its current form has been the thin end of a wedge that is turning American political discourse into a parody of itself and challenging the very notion that politics can be conducted through reasoned discussion and compromise. For the new rhetoric of rights is less about human dignity and freedom than about insistent, unending desires. Its legitimization of individual and group egoism is in flat opposition to the great purposes set forth in the Preamble to the Constitution: 'to form a more perfect Union, establish Justice, promote the general Welfare, and secure the Blessings of Liberty to ourselves and our Posterity.'" See Glendon, *Rights Talk*, 171–72.

47. *Stenberg v. Carhart*, 530 US 914, 953 (2000) (Scalia, J., dissenting).

48. Ibid.

49. See, e.g., *Planned Parenthood of Southeastern Pennsylvania v. Casey*, 505 US 833 (1992).

Kennedy notes that much of the language used in discussing abortion employs "clinically neutral terms" such as "reduction procedure."[50] However, this neutral, sanitized language is akin to other neutral terms—including "the final solution" and "ethnic cleansing"—that have been employed to mask genocide. Plainly, the wholesale destruction of millions of human beings constitutes a definite threat to the common good. If "the final solution" and "ethnic cleansing" were forms of genocide, the D&X procedure is, as Kennedy stated, a type of "infanticide"—and the statute involved here was a legitimate barrier to "one of the most serious crimes against human life."[51]

Justice Kennedy recalled that the three-Justice plurality of *Casey* had acknowledged that the State has substantial interests that directly relate to the common good. These interests include continuing pregnancy and caring for the mother and child before and after birth.[52] He also noted that the State retains a proper interest to ensure that the medical profession and society do not become insensitive to the taking of human life, including that of the fetus.[53] His concern goes beyond one person or even a few—it seems to encompass the entire community and future communities. As Justice Kennedy observed, states can take those steps needed to ensure that the medical profession focuses on the necessity to preserve rather than take life and to take those compassionate and ethical steps to make society's members "cognizant of the dignity and value of human life."[54]

Perhaps not surprisingly, Kennedy heavily relies on *Jacobson v. Massachusetts*. In doing so, he acknowledged that it is the province of the legislature, not a doctor exercising a medical opinion in an individual case, to determine the content of the law and policy for protecting "public health and safety."[55] With proper deference to doctors, he further argued that "this . . . is the vice of a health exception resting in the physician's discretion."[56] Such discretion places in the hands of the few a momentous decision that affects, sometimes quite adversely, the many—and perhaps even all. It poses unnecessary threats to the common good not only for those in the present but for those of the future as well.

---

50. US 914, 960 (2000) (Kennedy, J., dissenting).
51. Ibid., 979.   52. Ibid., 961.
53. Ibid.   54. Ibid.
55. Ibid., 971–72, quoting from *Jacobson v. Massachusetts*.
56. Ibid., 972.

THE CATHOLIC PERSPECTIVE

In *Stenberg,* The Supreme Court banished the notion of the common good to the margins of American law. In its place, the Court has enshrined the sweeping notion of liberty articulated in *Casey.* When one attempts to understand the objectives of the Constitution by relying on such an approach one is left with an impoverished legal environment that considers only the disconnected individual's exaggerated liberty, a liberty of isolation, a liberty that zealously protects the constitutional claims of the self while simultaneously denying the same claims of other human beings—especially the unborn and the partially born.

By contrast, the Catholic perspective on the common good and its place in constitutional adjudication offers a far richer understanding of how individual and community interests are simultaneously protected. The Catholic perspective of the common good does not endorse the exaggerated individualism and autonomy that are emphasized in *Casey* and *Stenberg.* Rather, it supports the vital position that the interests of the individual are inextricably related to the interests of all the other members of the community or society to which he or she belongs. Moreover, the terms of these relationships are not based solely on positivist principles, but are founded on a transcendent and objective moral order.

The idea of the common good has a rich tradition within Catholic philosophy and social thought as developed by philosophers and theologians. Evidence of a distinctively Catholic perspective begins to emerge in the work of Augustine of Hippo. St. Augustine's view reflected some of the preceding thinking of Aristotle and Cicero when he suggested that the human race is not simply united "in a society by natural likeness," but it is or should be "bound together by a kind of tie of kinship to form a harmonious unity, linked together by the 'bond of peace.'"[57] Unlike Aristotle and Cicero, however, Augustine's thought developed within the context of a Christian milieu. Whereas the political philosophy of the ancients was typically viewed as an end in itself (and in the context of Plato's Republic, a perfect end), Augustine viewed the human state and institution as imperfect. As the Church was superior to the State, so the City of God was superior to the City of Man. The

---

57. St. Augustine, *The City of God,* trans. Henry Bettenson (New York: Penguin Books, 2003), 547.

Church or Christian society had the duty of informing the imperfect State so that it might at least be able to improve itself and become more perfect.[58]

During the late Middle Ages, Thomas Aquinas, who was influenced not only by Aristotle, but by sacred Scripture, the liturgy, and Augustine himself, continued the investigation into the common good. For Aquinas, the object of justice is to keep people together in a society in which they share relationships with one another: "Justice is concerned only about our dealings with others."[59] The notion of justice as being the mutuality or reciprocity shared among the members of society was further refined by Aquinas when he argued that "the virtue of a good citizen is general justice, whereby each person is directed to the common good."[60] Aquinas understood the connection between virtue and the common good as directed by justice "so that all acts of virtue can pertain to justice in so far as it directs [each person] to the common good."[61]

Jacques Maritain brought Aquinas's understanding of the common good forward into modern political discourse. He recognized the need to separate the dignity of the individual human being from the errors of exalting the primacy of the isolated individual and the promotion of his or her private good. The common good, for Maritain, is "the human common good," which includes "the service of the human person."[62] In large part, Maritain was responding to the threats posed to the dignity of the human person by three forms of the state that existed in the first half of the twentieth century: (1) the bourgeois liberal state, (2) the communist state, and (3) the totalitarian state. Thankfully communism and totalitarianism are now largely things of the past. The bourgeois liberal state, however, is still with us. Maritain concluded that "bourgeois liberalism with its ambition to ground everything in the unchecked initiative of the individual, conceived as a little God,"[63] was also a threat to the dignity of the human person and the common good. Maritain stated that the emphasis on individualism at the expense of community results in "the tragic isolation of each one in his or her own selfishness or helplessness."[64] The morbid effect of this "tragic isolation" in our own law can be

---

58. Copleston, A History of Philosophy, 89–90.

59. St. Thomas Aquinas, Summa Theologica, Q. 58, A.2.

60. Ibid., A.6.   61. Ibid., A.5.

62. Jacques Maritain, The Person and the Common Good (Notre Dame, IN: University of Notre Dame Press, 1966), 29.

63. Ibid., 91–92.   64. Ibid., 92–93.

seen in the Supreme Court's decisions going back to *Roe* and culminating in *Stenberg*.

Maritain understood the social conditions of his time, which impacted his thinking and writing. Consequently, he acknowledged that evil arises when "we give preponderance to the individual aspect of our being."[65] Moreover, he recognized that exaggerated individualism can be a major problem for society because the reality of human nature recognizes that each human being is simultaneously both an individual and a member of a community. For Maritain, a constitutive element of being human is the "inner urge to the communications of knowledge and love which require relationship with other persons."[66] In plain terms, Maritain advanced the basic position that the human person and the community are not in conflict with one another because their vital interests are complementary rather than contradictory. Of course, this reflects the nature of the human person recognized by political philosophers going back to Aristotle that the human person is a social being. The interests of the individual and the community do not conflict but coincide. One principal reason for this is each needs the other to survive: the individual cannot provide all that the self needs; and the community cannot exist without the presence of a group of individuals. The interests of the individual, then, are inextricably related to the interests of the community. This point is fundamental to the Catholic perspective of the common good. Maritain's words are compelling in this regard:

There is a correlation between this notion of the person as social unit and the notion of the common good as the end of the social whole. They imply one another. The common good is common because it is received in persons, each one of whom is a mirror of the whole. . . . The end of society is the good of the community, of the social body. But if the good of the social body is not understood to be a common good of human persons, just as the social body itself is a whole of human persons, this conception also would lead to other errors of a totalitarian type. The common good of the city is neither the mere collection of private goods, nor the proper good of a whole which, like the species with respect to its individuals or the hive with respect to its bees, relates the parts to itself alone and sacrifices them to itself. It is the good human life of the multitude, of a multitude of persons; it is their communion in good living.[67]

Maritain submitted that the rights of the individual human person and the interests of the community are compatible and harmonious. What is

65. Ibid., 43.   66. Ibid., 47.
67. Ibid., 49–50 (footnote omitted).

good for one is simultaneously desirable for the other. While, writing from the perspective of the eve of World War II, Maritain suggested that

[i]t is up to the supreme effort of human freedom, in the mortal struggle in which it is today engaged, to see to it that the age which we are entering is not the age of the masses, and of the shapeless multitudes nourished and brought into subjection and led to the slaughter by infamous demigods, but rather the age of the people and the man of common humanity-citizen and co-inheritor of the civilized community—cognizant of the dignity of the human person in himself, builder of a more human world directed toward an historic ideal of human brotherhood.[68]

In short, each person's rights coincide with the needs of the community. In isolation, a person is cut off from the others. The solitary person must provide for the self alone without expecting assistance from others in times of need. In community, however, the individual person can rely on the generous support of others. This generosity is not simply material. The communion of persons in relationship enables the individual to be more, not less, of a human being.

In the context of the abortion issue, the mother and child, the individuals whose interests are most directly at stake, would be better served if society would do more to help both of them simultaneously with the respective challenges each faces. Programs providing concrete assistance to the mother would constitute attractive alternatives to abortion that respect the interests of both the woman and the child whom she bears. Similarly, programs that benefit the child encourage the child's coming into the world. One illustration of such a program is that provided by the Archdiocese of Oklahoma City in which access to prenatal and postnatal care for the mother and child, adoption strategies, and assistance to unwed mothers come together in a comprehensive and coordinated activity sponsored by the Church.[69]

In a specifically legal context, the Catholic view of the common good was carefully examined by Heinrich Rommen, a lawyer and legal philosopher who fled Nazi Germany for the United States in the late 1930s. In 1945 he published his comprehensive *The State in Catholic Thought*.[70] He describes the common good as:

68. Jacques Maritain, *Christianity and Democracy* (San Francisco: Ignatius Press, 1944), 97–98.

69. See Catholic Charities of Oklahoma, *Family Support Services,* http://www.catholic-charitiesok.org/family_support.html.

70. Rommen, *The State in Catholic Thought.*

the creative principle, the conserving power of the body politic; it is the final cause of the state, its intimate end; it and nothing else gives the political, sovereign power its moral authority and legitimacy. Therefore the common good is the directive rule and the last unappealable norm of the acts of the sovereign power, as the object of this power is nothing but to produce, in collaboration with the citizens, the actual realization of the common good. The common good is the first and the last law.[71]

The common good for Rommen is not simply the sum of the goods for each private individual.[72] It is, in essence, a relational concept in which the good of the one must be understood in the context of the good for all other members of the society.[73] In several instances, Rommen, like Maritain, acknowledges the essential interrelation of the private or individual good and the common good.[74] He recognizes this connection in the concept of the *suum cuique* where everyone receives his or her due.[75] To this perspective I would add that what is due one person cannot be determined until that which is due all other individuals concerned with the same issue is taken into account. This point will be developed shortly.

In the late twentieth and early twenty-first centuries, Catholic scholars have continued to examine the common good in a wide variety of contexts, including economic issues, the use of armed force, bioethics, and other topics. Some build on the tradition of their predecessors in faith; others, while identifying themselves as Christian writers, rely principally on the work of contemporary authors who have little or no relation to a Christian or Catholic context.[76]

71. Ibid., 310–11.

72. Ibid., 314, 316.

73. See Robert John Araujo, "Justice as Right Relationship: A Philosophical and Theological Reflection on Affirmative Action," *Pepperdine Law Review* 27 (2000): 377, 448–50 and 474–6.

74. Rommen, *The State in Catholic Thought*, 332.

75. Ibid., 334.

76. See, e.g., David Hollenbach, *The Common Good and Christian Ethics* (Cambridge: Cambridge University Press, 2002) (examining "pressing" contemporary social problems); Michael Novak, *Free Persons and the Common Good* (Lanham, MD: Madison Books, 1989) (investigating the common good as a social order in which the proper exercise of human liberty, guided by reflection, takes into account the public interest and the social order that is essential to human liberty); John A. Coleman, "Pluralism and the Retrieval of a Catholic Sense of the Common Good," speech at Loyola Marymount University, Los Angeles, Commonwealth Symposium, May 12–14, 2000, treating three principal points: the first is that the notion of the common good moves deeply against the American individualist grain; second, that appeals to the common good have become increasingly rare in law and politics

Within the social teachings of the Catholic Church, the common good is a frequent theme. The Church's overall view of the common good must be understood simultaneously from two perspectives: the individual and the relational. This is because the Church recognizes that the nature of the human person is both social and individual at the same time.[77] The Church acknowledges and teaches that no one lives an entirely isolated life. Therefore, the good of the individual requires the realization of the common good, which can be brought about only in conjunction with others.[78]

The nature of the common good has also been a topic frequently addressed in papal and other magisterial texts in recent years. Beginning with Leo XIII and continuing through the pontificate of John Paul II, modern popes have stressed the inextricable relation between the good of the individual and the good of society as a whole—one cannot exist without the other, and each balances the other. In his most well known encyclical, *Rerum novarum,* Leo XIII addressed workers' demands for just wages, safe working conditions, and the right to organize. Leo's response to these concerns reflects the prominent role that the common good plays in Catholic social teaching.[79] Leo recognized that it is the duty of the political authority to protect the public good and to intervene when the common good is threatened. Moreover, Leo noted that if the state failed to act in support of the common good, the justification for its sovereignty would disappear.[80]

Many of Leo's successors have made similar points. Commemorating the fortieth anniversary of *Rerum novarum,* Pope Pius XI noted in his encyclical *Quadragesimo anno* that there is an essential connection between the pursuit of the common good and the realization of social justice.[81] In his first encyclical, *Summi pontificatus,* promulgated in 1939 on the eve of the Second World War, Pius XII pointed out that

---

largely due to the fact that the dominant voices in jurisprudence dismiss as meaningless or authoritarian any appeal to the common good; and, third, massive institutional and sociological changes in American society do not cultivate any uncomplicated assumptions about any received cultural sense of the common good; Kevin Quinn, "Viewing Health Care as a Common Good: Looking Beyond Political Liberalism," *Southern California Law Review* 73 (2000): 277 (focusing on new political developments to health care issues and relating them to Catholic teachings).

77. *Catechism of the Catholic Church,* ¶ 1905.

78. Ibid.

79. Pope Leo XIII, *Rerum novarum,* ¶ 51 (1891).

80. Ibid., ¶¶ 35, 36 (1891).

81. Pope Pius XI, *Quadragesimo anno,* ¶ 58 (1931). See also ¶¶ 25, 45, and 49.

it is the noble prerogative and function of the State to control, aid and direct the private and individual activities of national life that they converge harmoniously towards the common good. That good can neither be defined according to arbitrary ideas nor can it accept for its standard primarily the material prosperity of society, but rather it should be defined according to the harmonious development and the natural perfection of man.[82]

Pope Pius XII elaborated on this point three years later in his 1942 Christmas broadcast to the whole world when he noted that reason, enlightened by faith, recognizes that the State must harness its political and social activities to realize permanently the common good.[83] Similar points have been made by Pope John XXIII,[84] Pope Paul VI,[85] and Pope John Paul II.[86]

During the Second Vatican Council, the Church fathers defined the common good as "the sum of those conditions of social life by which individuals, families, and groups can achieve their own fulfillment in a relatively thorough and ready way."[87] The council concluded that the common good is that synthesis of social conditions that enables people both as individuals *and* as members of groups to reach their fulfillment.[88] The fulfillment of the individual and the group is the same—it is that "human dignity lies in man's call to communion with God."[89] As a consequence, the Church is concerned about the temporal dimensions of the common good insofar as they ordered toward this ultimate end of each human being.[90] The State has a principal role in protecting the temporal dimensions of human dignity and advancing the common good as defined by the Church; however, it is also clear that

82. Pope Pius XII, *Summi pontificatus,* ¶ 59 (1939).

83. Pope Pius XII, "1942 Christmas Address of Pope Pius XII," in *Principles for Peace-Selection from Papal Documents: Leo XIII to Pius XII,* ed. Harry Koenig (Washington, DC: National Catholic Welfare Conference, 1943).

84. Pope John XXIII, *Pacem in terris,* ¶¶ 56, 57, 132 (1963).

85. Pope Paul VI, *Populorum progressio,* ¶ 24 (1967); *Octogesima adveniens,* ¶ 20, 46 (1971).

86. Like Pope Leo XIII, Pope John Paul II was a prolific writer. His encyclicals often refer to the common good. For example, see *Evangelium vitae,* ¶¶ 56, 70, 71, 72, 90, 101 (1995); *Veritatis splendor,* ¶ 52 (1993); and *Centesimus annus,* ¶ 6, 11, 13, 14, 34, 40, 43, 47, 48, 51, 52, 58 (1991).

87. Pope Paul VI, *Gaudium et spes,* ¶ 74 (1965). See also ¶ 26, where the common good is similarly described as "the sum of those conditions of social life which allow social groups and their individual members relatively thorough and ready access to their own fulfillment."

88. Ibid., ¶ 26.

89. Ibid., ¶ 19.

90. *Catechism of the Catholic Church,* ¶ 2420.

everyone also has the "dignity" to pursue the common good by establishing and sustaining institutions that improve the conditions of human life.[91] This understanding of the common good is inevitably related to the protection and preservation of human life. Indeed, the Council emphatically taught that "whatever is opposed to life itself, such as any type of murder, genocide, abortion, euthanasia or willful self-destruction . . . are infamies . . . [which] poison human society . . . [and] are a supreme dishonor to the Creator."[92] These actions, which mock and cheapen the dignity of every human existence, are the grist for the mill of the State.

Time after time, Pope John Paul II presented this Catholic perspective on the common good with great clarity as it bears on the topic of abortion. He demonstrated the nexus between the common good and the civil law, especially that involving human nature and human life. Like the Second Vatican Council, he acknowledged that the taking of unborn human life is not only morally illicit but criminal.[93] With illegal abortion, it is the actors who are responsible for this evil. However, the pope noted that the sinister nature of abortion is enhanced when the legal mechanisms of the State authorize it.[94] In short, it is the State, through its sanction of abortion, that establishes "legal" mechanisms that nonetheless perpetrate an evil—the taking of human life. This point stands in stark contrast to the perspective offered in *Stenberg* and the earlier cases upon which it relies. He rhetorically asked that while few would question whether the actions perpetrated by twentieth-century tyrants against fellow human beings were crimes against humanity, would they reach the same conclusion if genocide were "legitimated" by popular consensus?[95] Acknowledging the presence of the ethical relativism frequently evident in the societies of the present day, John Paul II formulated an answer to this question by stating that the value of democratic institutions stands or falls upon the values that these societies embody and promote.[96]

91. Ibid., ¶¶ 1926, 1927.

92. Pope Paul VI, *Gaudium et spes,* ¶ 27 (1965).

93. Pope John Paul II, *Evangelium vitae,* ¶ 70 (1995).

94. Ibid., ¶ 4. He further states that while abortion may become as a result of the law "socially acceptable," it is nevertheless evidence of "grave moral decline." Ibid., ¶ 2. Thus, "the very nature of the medical profession is distorted and contradicted, and the dignity of those who practice it is degraded." Ibid. In addition the Holy Father uncompromisingly declares that "a law which violates an innocent person's natural right to life is unjust and, as such, is not valid as a law." Ibid., ¶ 90.

95. Ibid., ¶ 70.

96. Ibid.

In the particular context of the United States, Pope John Paul II, upon receiving the credentials of Lindy Boggs as the new U.S. ambassador to the
Holy See on December 16, 1997, acknowledged that the American founders
based their claims to freedom and independence on "certain 'self-evident'
truths about the human person" and the system of "ordered liberty" that
would promote and sustain these truths.[97] In reflecting on this element of
the pope's message, one can consider the likelihood that an "unordered liberty" leads to chaos since it leads to the exercise of individual license without regulation. An ordered liberty also is consistent with the notion of the
suum cuique that justice for the individual is whatever that person is due.
As noted above, what is "due" a particular individual depends in part upon
what is "due" those other individuals with whom the first comes in contact.
An environment of "ordered liberty" is conducive to a just, or relatively more
just, society in that the liberty of each person must cohere with the liberty to
which every other person is equally entitled.

John Paul further indicated that Americans lived freely so as "to fulfill their
duties and responsibilities toward the family and toward the common good
of the community."[98] The pope continued by drawing attention to the link between true freedom and moral responsibility and accountability. He emphasized that whenever any category of people (and he specifically mentioned the
unborn in this context) are excluded from the protection of the law, "a deadly
anarchy subverts the original understanding of justice. The credibility of the
United States will depend more and more on its promotion of a genuine culture of life and on a renewed commitment to building a world in which the
weakest and most vulnerable are welcomed and protected."[99] In a more general discussion of democratic institutions, John Paul noted that "[a]uthentic democracy is possible only in a State ruled by law, and on the basis of a correct
conception of the human person . . . [and] if there is no ultimate truth to guide
and direct political activity, then ideas and convictions can easily be manipulated for reasons of power. As history demonstrates, a democracy without values easily turns into open or thinly disguised totalitarianism."[100]

97. "Address of John Paul II to H.E. Mrs. Corine (Lindy) Claiborne Boggs: New Ambassador of the United States of America to the Holy See—16 December 1997," http://www.vatican
.va/holy_father/john_paul_ii/speeches/1997/december/documents/hf_jp-ii_spe_19971216_
ambassador-usa_en.html.
98. Pope John Paul II, *Evangelium vitae,* ¶ 70 (1995).
99. Ibid.
100. Pope John Paul II, *Centesimus annus,* ¶ 46 (1991).

CONCLUSION

In *Stenberg v. Carhart,* the Supreme Court embraced an impoverished view of individual liberty and sacrificed the common good to the caprice of the individual. Indeed, Stenberg may rightly be regarded as a manifesto for a "thinly disguised totalitarianism." The liberty argument advanced by the majority in *Stenberg* essentially places the perceived interests of one person over the interests of every other human being, including those who are being born. Although the desires of individuals must be considered, they are not the only interests that are at stake when the rights to life, liberty, and property hang in the balance. *Stenberg* presents a bankrupt understanding of liberty by focusing only on the desire of the isolated individual, insulated from any relationship with another person and even with one's own authentic self. The Preamble to the Constitution makes clear that the law can be used to promote and protect the common good. All human life demands the attention and protection of society and its law. Specifically, the desire of some to exterminate the lives of others cannot trump this concern for the common good to which each individual's existence is tied. The Constitution does not give the powerful unfettered discretion to decide who lives and who dies. Instead, the Constitution declares that it was adopted to "establish Justice" and to secure "the blessings of Liberty" for all of us and "for our Posterity."

Since the founding of the republic, liberty has been a value of central concern in our institutions of government, in the American political tradition, and in the laws that govern our nation. Indeed, as the Preamble to the Constitution makes clear, securing "the blessings of liberty" was one of the reasons why "We the People" adopted the Constitution as our fundamental law. At the same time, the Preamble also makes clear that the liberties and freedoms protected by the Constitution are not restricted to some subset of the populace. They are guaranteed to all Americans. Exaggerated claims of liberty upon which the legal right to abortion is based bankrupt the noble principles set forth in the Constitution's Preamble.

Catholic thought concerning the common good provides us with a way of understanding the U.S. Constitution and the proper role of liberty in our constitutional order. The Preamble to the Constitution frames the rights and duties of American citizens so that present and future generations may experience the universal opportunities for human flourishing that the framers hoped to secure in adopting the Constitution. This is what the common good is all about—the ability of the single individual to enjoy the liberties protected by our founding legal text can be understood only in the context of all other individuals participating in and seeking the same protections to which all human beings are equally entitled by their very nature. This Catholic perspective on the common good of all humanity acknowledges that the uniqueness and sanctity of every human being is shared by every other human being of yesterday, today, and tomorrow. As Martin Niemöller indicated about a half century ago, an attack on one is ultimately an attack on all. He is said to have remarked:

In Germany, they first came for the Communists and I didn't speak up because I was not a Communist. Then they came for the Jews, and I didn't speak up because I was not a Jew. Then they came for the trade unionists, and I didn't speak up because I was not a trade unionist. Then they came for the Catholics, and I did not speak up because I was a Protestant. Then they came for me—and by that time no one was left to speak up.[101]

Niemöller's reflection on people's response to the Nazi horror reminds us of the consequences of silence. In facing the horrors of *Stenberg* and other direct assaults on innocent human life, are we willing to speak up today? The Catholic understanding of the common good gives us a way to speak so that we might be heard. The voice of the common echoes through our constitutional history. It is the voice of the founders and the voice of St. Augustine. We should join our voices with theirs today in speaking truth to power.

101. See www.bit.umkc.edu/vu/course/cs451/bits.html.

PART III

CATHOLICISM IN DIALOGUE WITH POLITICAL AND LEGAL THEORY

[7]

WHY WE SHOULD (AND SHOULD NOT) BE LIBERALS

CHRISTOPHER WOLFE

I want to ask in this essay whether "we" should be liberals. The "we" of the title has three dimensions. First, it refers to Americans generally. Should we as Americans want to have liberalism as the foundation of our public philosophy? Second, it refers more specifically to Americans who believe in classical or traditional (not Lockean) natural law. And third, it refers to Americans who take the Catholic intellectual tradition as their overarching perspective on political life. Should we think of ourselves as liberals, as advocates of a liberal public philosophy, or should we think of ourselves as opponents of liberalism and liberal public philosophy?[1]

To these questions, I want to respond "yes" and "no." First, I want to show why, by and large, it is appropriate for us to consider ourselves liberals. Second, I want to show why we should not be willing to think of ourselves simply as liberals, without reservations about liberalism. To accomplish these goals, after first indicating some difficulties understanding what liberalism is, I will try to show the considerable truth in core liberal principles (relying on

---

1. The categories of "advocates of natural law" and "Catholics" are by no means identical, of course, and for purposes of this essay I should say that I will be using natural law as the primary point of reference, emphasizing what Catholics have in common with many of their fellow citizens.

a description of liberalism from Peter Berkowitz). Then I will highlight some parts of the truth that liberalism overlooks.

UNDERSTANDING LIBERALISM

The term "liberal" today, as it always has, describes both a political philosophy (or perhaps several different ones) and a political program. For the typical American, it implies, for example, particular political stances, or at least strong inclinations, on abortion and homosexual rights, economic regulation, social welfare programs, gun control, censorship of pornography, and church-state separation. Why this particular constellation of policy views or orientations deserves the term "liberal" is not immediately clear, especially in light of the fact that, in the past, persons considered liberals had quite different views on some of these issues. In the nineteenth century, for instance, liberals would have had attitudes toward economic regulation virtually the opposite of those considered liberal today.

The best explanation for the use of the term at any given time comes from looking at liberalism as a tradition of political thought extending over centuries. This enables us to examine the historical process by which liberals passed on to their successor-liberals a generally consistent set of political views, but with each generation modifying the received liberal wisdom in certain ways, as they confronted new circumstances and issues, or worked through older, unresolved problems of liberal theory. In such a process, the movement of thought from one generation to another might be limited, but over the course of a number of generations, the changes could be, and have been, quite substantial.

In general, liberalism refers to a family of political philosophies whose origins date to about the seventeenth century. It has been a broad movement in politics and society, whose primary purpose has been to expand freedom through enlightenment. Liberals have sought to achieve their goals by displacing older hereditary and established hierarchies and authorities (political, social, and religious)—regarded as forms of despotism—with limited government based on equality before the law and broad personal freedoms, especially freedom of religion, thought, and discussion.

But liberalism also refers, in a somewhat different way, to the specific, dominant late-twentieth-century expression of liberal political philosophy, represented most importantly in the thought of John Rawls. This version of liberalism, which claims to be the proper working out of the liberal political tradition, maintains that government should be neutral with respect to the question of the human good, embracing a notion of justice that prescinds from the truth of "comprehensive" philosophical, theological, or moral views. This approach has been characterized by one of its critics, Michael Sandel, as creating "the procedural republic," that is, a nation that provides a broad framework or procedure for individuals to pursue their own goals, without attempting to influence the substance of those pursuits (except insofar as they interfere with the similar rights of others to pursue their own goals). It can also be referred to as "anti-perfectionist" liberalism, because it denies that political life should aim to perfect its citizens, according to some standard of human excellence. While this term is useful, it is important to note that many contemporary anti-perfectionist liberals do recognize that liberalism ultimately must be understood, and defended, as contributing to moral improvement in important ways.

What is the relationship between these two meanings of liberalism, between the broad tradition of liberal political theory and its dominant contemporary form? It seems to me that there are three main answers. One possible relationship is that contemporary liberal political theory is the logical fulfillment of the aspirations of the broad liberal tradition, one that has thought through and realized the implications of earlier liberal thought and achieved a more coherent political theory that is also properly adapted to the circumstances of our time. This has involved winnowing out some elements of earlier expressions of liberalism that were unconsidered remnants of pre-liberal thought now understood to be inconsistent with liberalism.[2]

A second position on the relation between liberalism old and new is that contemporary liberalism is merely one possible working out of broad liberal principles. It is not logically and necessarily implied by the most important principles of earlier forms of liberalism, but it is a defensible or plausible development of them.[3]

---

2. This position can be subdivided into those who reject contemporary liberalism—and therefore also the principles from which it ineluctably flowed—and those who embrace contemporary liberalism, and who therefore view earlier forms of liberalism somewhat critically, as incomplete liberalism, but also somewhat benignly, as the first steps toward a fuller form of it.

3. And, again, people with this view can divide as to whether the development is a good one.

A third position would be that contemporary liberalism is a departure from, or even a betrayal of, the broad liberal tradition. Its efforts to sort through elements of earlier liberal thought and to discard parts that are inconsistent with what it holds to be the central logical thrust of the tradition are actually destructive of a proper coherence or balance represented by that earlier liberalism. Those who hold this position can, of course, vary on the question of which earlier strand of liberalism (or combination of parts of them) is considered to be a more adequate expression of liberalism.

Most of contemporary political thought can be viewed as representing variants of one of these three different positions, which is to say that contemporary political thought and discussion can be understood as competition among various forms of liberalism, all within the broad context established by the liberal tradition broadly understood. The "liberalism-communitarianism" debate, therefore, is not really a debate between liberals and non-liberals, but a debate within liberalism, as is the "liberalism-republicanism" debate, and even the "liberalism-postmodernism" debate.[4] And, finally, I want to argue that the same framework may be adopted in examining the ongoing debate between liberalism and classical natural law theory.

THE TRUTH IN LIBERALISM

I think that people of sound judgment and good will, including American natural law theorists and Catholics, should be willing to be considered liberals. The main principles of liberalism are not just defensible, but good. It is also true that certain tendencies of liberalism are more problematic, but these can be sufficiently countered to make liberalism, on the whole, valuable rather than objectionable.

Let us begin by asking how a believer in natural law might evaluate the various tenets of liberalism. For this purpose, I want to employ the following description of liberalism from Peter Berkowitz:

Seen in the light of both its fundamental premise and its overriding aim, liberalism is a tradition that extends over centuries, cuts across national boundaries, and finds eloquent advocates in parties of the left and the right. It is wide enough to include not only such standard-bearers as Locke, Kant, and Mill, but also thinkers more eclectic

4. Peter Berkowitz makes a similar point in his chapter "Liberalism, Postmodernism, and Public Philosophy" in *Public Morality, Civic Virtue, and the Problem of Modern Liberalism,* ed. T. William Boxx and Gary M. Quinlivan (Grand Rapids, MI: Eerdmans, 2000), 158–60.

and difficult to categorize such as Montesquieu, Madison, and Tocqueville. It is a tradition that has articulated a set of characteristic themes including individual rights, consent, toleration, liberty of thought and discussion, self-interest rightly understood, the separation of the private from the public, and personal autonomy or the primacy of individual choice; has elaborated a characteristic set of political institutions including representative democracy, separation of governmental powers, and an independent judiciary; and, less noticed these days but vital to understanding liberalism's possibilities and prospects, has provided a fertile source of reflections on such non-political supports of the virtues that sustain liberty as commerce, voluntary association, family, and religion.[5]

If this is a fair description of liberalism (and I think it is), let us ask how someone who takes his orientation from natural law will view the various components that Berkowitz describes as its "characteristic themes" and its "characteristic set of political institutions."

NATURAL LAW AND LIBERALISM'S CHARACTERISTIC THEMES

Individual Rights: Should We Believe in Rights?

Some people argue that there are dangers in the adoption of rights-language, that it may be imprudent to employ language whose origin is in philosophical systems (such as Hobbesian and Lockean natural rights theory) that are antithetical in so many respects to classical natural law theory and that may encourage some of the defects of those systems (such as individualism).[6] For the moment, though, putting aside such prudential questions, let me simply ask whether a natural law theorist should consider it *true* that, for example, unborn children have "rights." I think the answer is "yes."

While the classic natural law tradition, especially in the work of Thomas

---

5. Ibid., 157. I use this formulation partly because it was as I sat listening to him deliver this paper at a conference that I realized how much of a "liberal" I am! For a more extensive discussion of the core principles of liberalism, justifying the general understanding of liberalism I share with Berkowitz, see chapter 7 of my *Natural Law Liberalism* (Cambridge: Cambridge University Press, 2006).

6. See, for example, Ernest Fortin, *Human Rights, Virtue, and the Common Good*, ed. J. Brian Benestad (Lanham, MD: Rowman and Littlefield, 1996); and Robert Kraynak, *Christian Faith and Modern Democracy* (Notre Dame, IN: University of Notre Dame Press, 2001). For an approach that has deep concerns about potential problems with overemphasizing rights, but that accepts them more readily in principle (an approach I share), see Mary Ann Glendon, *Rights Talk: The Impoverishment of Political Discourse* (New York: Free Press, 1991).

Aquinas, did not speak much about rights, there clearly are grounds in that tradition for embracing rights. If it is wrong for A to hit B, then B can be said to have a right not to be hit by A. If it is a principle of justice that A ought to give x to B, then B can be said to have a right to x from A. This explains why Catholic social thought, rooted in natural law, has been willing to embrace rights so strongly in the twentieth century.

Consent: Should We Accept the Notion of Consent?

There are serious reasons to hesitate about fully embracing a theory of consent. First, there is the highly artificial character of most theories of consent. Most nations have never undertaken to secure consent explicitly from their citizens, and, more importantly, few of those that have have been willing to regularly re-collect this consent, opting instead to rely on theories of tacit consent, with all the difficulties entailed by it.[7]

Moreover, if consent is understood to be the actual source of authority, we should have misgivings about it. A natural law theory of political authority considers political power to be just that—"natural"—rather than the artificial or conventional creation of human beings in some pre-social state of nature.

Nonetheless, as Yves Simon showed in his classic discussion,[8] the idea of consent makes good sense if it is understood as popular participation in the *designation* of who holds political authority. And in this respect Simon is only harkening back to a tradition at least as old as Aristotle, who notes that collecting the opinions of those who experience the effects of rule (asking the person who is wearing the shoe how it feels) is quite sensible. The idea of requiring consent also draws support from its tendency to contribute to political stability (a notion supported by de Tocqueville's discussion of the advantages of democracy).[9] And, finally, it has a very strong ground-

---

7. For a discussion of consent noting some of these difficulties (but more favorable to the theoretical utility of the concept than I am), see Jeremy Waldron, *Liberal Rights* (Cambridge: Cambridge University Press, 1993), ch. 2. See also the classic exchange between Jefferson and Madison on the prudence of requiring each generation to explicitly consent to the fundamental laws: letter of Jefferson to Madison, September 6, 1789, and letter of Madison to Jefferson, February 4, 1790.

8. Yves Simon, *The Philosophy of Democratic Government* (Chicago: University of Chicago Press, 1951), chapter 3.

9. Alexis de Tocqueville, *Democracy in America*, vol. 1 (New York: Alfred A. Knopf, 1945), chapter 14, on the advantages of democracy, where he shows that popular participation in

ing in the severe objections that can be lodged against any theory that makes political power hereditary or limits the choice of rulers to a particular social class, because no such class is particularly trustworthy to hold such power, unchecked by others.

Toleration: Should We Embrace Tolerance?

Classic natural law thought has typically been associated with Catholicism, and Catholic teaching was long regarded as either outright intolerant, or as tolerant only under certain conditions, but not in favor of a principled tolerance. Is this true?

I think the basic historical facts are the following. Christian doctrine has always required a free and uncoerced faith. That is why, for example, during the Middle Ages, it was not the systematic policy of "Christian" countries to require all citizens to adopt Christianity. However, many Catholics—both political authorities and ecclesiastical authorities who directed them—sometimes persecuted non-Christians and other Christians, acts for which Pope John Paul II asked forgiveness.[10] While some of this persecution was not

---

the making of laws contributes to the sense of the people that it is *their* law and therefore worthy of obedience (even when they have lost the legislative battle to determine the content of the law).

10. "While we praise God who, in his merciful love, has produced in the Church a wonderful harvest of holiness, missionary zeal, total dedication to Christ and neighbour, we cannot fail to recognize the infidelities to the Gospel committed by some of our brethren, especially during the second millennium. Let us ask pardon for the divisions which have occurred among Christians, for the violence some have used in the service of the truth and for the distrustful and hostile attitudes sometimes taken towards the followers of other religions." Pope John Paul II, "Homily for the Day of Pardon" (March 12, 2000), available at http://www.vat ican.va/holy_father/john_paul_ii/homilies/documents/hf_jp-ii_hom_20000312_pardon_ en.html.

See also the report of the International Theological Commission, *Memory and Reconciliation: The Church and the Faults of the Past* (December 1999), especially section 5.3. "The Use of Force in the Service of Truth":

To the counter-witness of the division between Christians should be added that of the various occasions in the past millennium when doubtful means were employed in the pursuit of good ends, such as the proclamation of the Gospel or the defense of the unity of the faith. "Another sad chapter of history to which the sons and daughters of the Church must return with a spirit of repentance is that of the acquiescence given, especially in certain centuries, to intolerance and even the use of force in the service of truth." This refers to forms of evangelization that employed improper means to announce the revealed truth or did not include an evangelical discernment suited to the cultural values of peoples or did not respect the con-on grounds of religious heterodoxy per se, but rested on political grounds (namely, the politically seditious activities of nonbelievers or heretics), intolerance of different religious belief did occur on many occasions.

Contemporary liberals such as Jeremy Waldron and Brian Barry have accurately identified the theoretical arguments that provided a ground for suppressing not false religious belief per se, but the public expressions of it.[11] The point of suppression, according to this rationale, was not to compel individuals to adopt true religious belief, but to protect those who held true religious beliefs from those who sought to spread false ones. This rationale for a certain measure of intolerance is not as easily dismissed as the argument for direct religious compulsion.

I think that this line of reasoning has been rejected by the Catholic Church in *Dignitatis humanae,* which declared that people have a right not only to religious belief, but also to religious speech. (To be more precise, there is a right *not to be compelled* in these matters.) The right to religious belief entails a broad right to religious actions (subject to the requirements of public order), and those religious actions include efforts of evangelization.

What is the ground for this right? Is it only a right in certain circumstances, as a matter of prudence? That is, does it rest on the fact that, in the circumstances of the modern world (i.e., religious pluralism), true religious belief is better off with a policy of religious tolerance—leaving open the possibility that, if conditions changed, the policy of toleration might be dropped? If so, then it might fairly be said that such tolerance would be merely "tactical" and not "principled."

My suggestion for resolving these questions is that we not distinguish so sharply between "prudential" and "principled" arguments. I would argue that a limited number of prudential arguments (i.e., arguments that do not depend on the intrinsic immorality of an act) hold so broadly that they are really principled arguments (i.e., arguments that hold universally). For example, some of the prudential arguments against religious intolerance are that (1) in a world that accepts the principle of intolerance, that intolerance will more

---

sciences of the persons to whom the faith was presented, as well as all forms of force used in the repression and correction of errors.

Ibid., available at http://www.vatican.va/roman_curia/congregations/cfaith/cti_documents/rc_con_cfaith_doc_20000307_memory-reconc-itc_en.html.

11. Waldron, *Liberal Rights,* ch. 4; and Brian Barry, "How Not to Defend Liberal Institutions," in *Liberalism and the Good,* ed. R. Bruce Douglass, Gerald R. Mara, and Henry S. Richardson (New York: Routledge, 1990), 48.

often be visited on true religious belief than on false religious belief (e.g., on Christians in Islamic countries); (2) there is little reason to suppose that political authorities will be likely to discern religious truth; (3) reliance on the secular authority to enforce religious orthodoxy will undermine reliance on the more important, "spiritual weapons" of religious truth (e.g., the tendency toward a sort of bourgeois and lazy established religion portrayed in Trollope's novels about English society); and (4) a policy of persecution will cause deep animosities that will be passed down from generation to generation, poisoning the atmosphere for future apostolic efforts to regain people for the true religion. Taken together, I believe that these arguments (especially the last two) provide for religious tolerance a strong, principled argument, rather than a selective or tactical one dependent on conditions (even against the argument for religious intolerance in its narrower form—limits on religious proselytism by those who hold false religious beliefs—that seems most defensible).

Liberty of Thought and Discussion: Should We Believe in a Very Broad Liberty of Thought and Discussion?

This question is tied somewhat closely to the previous one, since the teaching of the Catholic Church was for a long time considered opposed to such liberty, as it is currently understood. For example, in the nineteenth century, Pope Leo XIII in his encyclical *Libertas praestantissimum* defended free speech and press rights for both "what things so ever are true and honorable" and for "all matter of opinion which God leaves to man's free discussion," but denied such rights to false or "lying opinions," arguing that "right is a moral power which . . . it is absurd to suppose that nature has accorded indifferently to truth and falsehood."[12] But restricting free speech to true opinions, most would say, is a denial of free speech.

---

12. Pope Leo XIII, *Libertas praestantissimum,* ¶ 23 (1888):

We must now consider briefly liberty of speech, and liberty of the press. It is hardly necessary to say that there can be no such right as this, if it be not used in moderation, and if it pass beyond the bounds and end of all true liberty. For right is a moral power which—as We have before said and must again and again repeat—it is absurd to suppose that nature has accorded indifferently to truth and falsehood, to justice and injustice. Men have a right freely and prudently to propagate throughout the State what things so ever are true and honorable, so that as many as possible may possess them; but lying opinions, than which no mental plague is greater, and vices which corrupt the heart and moral life should be diligently repressed by public authority, lest they insidiously work the ruin of the State. The excesses of

Again, however, it seems to me that a strong argument for free speech can be constructed from Catholic or natural law thinking.[13] Once "the cat is out of the bag" and we have left behind a world in which education was restricted to a very small part of the population—and it is good, as a general principle, that education is no longer so restricted—then restrictions on speech beyond those required by public order are likely to be more harmful than helpful to the cause of truth. The same reasons that justify religious free speech would apply more broadly: the likelihood that speech limits would be imposed on the truth, the unlikelihood of political authorities having special insight into what is true, the encouragement of intellectual sloth among those who believe what is true, and the creation of deep passions among those who hold heterodox opinions, which would create deep and abiding obstacles to their openness to the truth.

One should not downplay the requirement of public order, which will be the source of legitimate, if controversial, limits on free speech and press rights. This would include not only cases of "clear and present danger," but also cases where public order is threatened more indirectly, such as pornography.[14] Still, sound political reasoning will justify a right to free speech (a right against being coerced in matters of speech) in many cases where the speech itself is not intrinsically good speech.

---

an unbridled intellect, which unfailingly end in the oppression of the untutored multitude, are no less rightly controlled by the authority of the law than are the injuries inflicted by violence upon the weak. And this all the more surely, because by far the greater part of the community is either absolutely unable, or able only with great difficulty, to escape from illusions and deceitful subtleties, especially such as flatter the passions. If unbridled license of speech and of writing be granted to all, nothing will remain sacred and inviolate; even the highest and truest mandates of natures, justly held to be the common and noblest heritage of the human race, will not be spared. Thus, truth being gradually obscured by darkness, pernicious and manifold error, as too often happens, will easily prevail. Thus, too, license will gain what liberty loses; for liberty will ever be more free and secure in proportion as license is kept in fuller restraint. In regard, however, to all matter of opinion which God leaves to man's free discussion, full liberty of thought and of speech is naturally within the right of everyone; for such liberty never leads men to suppress the truth, but often to discover it and make it known.

13. For another natural law argument for free speech, see Robert George, *Making Men Moral: Civil Liberties and Public Morality* (Oxford: Clarendon Press, 1993), 192–210.

14. "The sum of experience . . . affords an ample basis for legislatures to conclude that a sensitive, key relationship of human existence, central to family life, community welfare, and

*Self-Interest Rightly Understood: Should We
Favor Political Arrangements Resting Not on Disinterested
Dedication to the Common Good, but on Self-Interest, Even with
the Qualifying "Rightly Understood"?*

Certainly there are forms of self-interest that are wrong. Those who pursue their own interest without regard for the common good and the well-being of others are properly criticized. But "self-interest rightly understood," if not as noble a formula as "public-spiritedness," or "civic virtue," is not only an acceptable, but to some extent a necessary, element of political life. It reflects, in part, what traditionally had been called "the order of charity." Why, for example, should a person dedicate more efforts to helping his or her child than other children? Because we have responsibilities to ourselves and others in a certain order, depending on the closeness of the relation. We have a naturally deeper "interest" (in both senses of the word) in those closely related to us. So we ought to support ourselves and our families before (though not instead of) attending to the needs of others. We should take care of the property that supports our families before taking care of others' property.

Yves Simon goes so far as to make the controversial argument that a good wife, who happens to be the wife of a murderer

hates the prospect of her husband's being put to death; she is normally and virtuously concerned with the good of her family, and, from the standpoint which is and ought to be hers, the death of the murderer is an evil [as opposed to the viewpoint of the judge, who stands for society and the common good]. . . . The common good, of course, shall prevail, but, significantly, Aquinas considers altogether sound and honest the opposition made to the requirements of the common good by the person in charge of the particular good. The common good itself demands that wives should want their husbands to survive, even though the latter happen to be criminals. *That particular goods be properly defended by particular persons matters greatly for the common good itself.* The wife of the murderer, as she fights for the life of the man whom the common good wants put to death, does precisely what the common good wants her to do.

That is, Simon says, she desires the common good formally in this case, but not materially.[15]

---

the development of human personality can be debased and distorted by crass commercial exploitation of sex." *Paris Adult Theatre v. Slaton*, 413 US 49, 63 (1973).

15. Simon, *The Philosophy of Democratic Government*, 41–441 (emphasis in original text).

Self-interest also is an inevitable part of social life, given man's fallen nature. So, for example, Pope Leo XIII buttresses the argument for private property with an appeal to the importance of self-interest:

And in addition to injustice, it is only too evident what an upset and disturbance there would be in all classes, and to how intolerable and hateful a slavery citizens would be subjected. The door would be thrown open to envy, to mutual invective, and to discord; *the sources of wealth themselves would run dry, for no one would have any interest in exerting his talents or his industry;* and that ideal equality about which they entertain pleasant dreams would be in reality the levelling down of all to a like condition of misery and degradation.[16]

Self-interest, then, from a natural law perspective, can be considered a legitimate aspect of good government.

Separation of the Private from the Public: Should We Consider the Private Separate from the Public?

The distinction between the private and the public is one to which Christianity made a significant contribution. It is not central to classical political philosophy. In the ancient world, there was typically not a separation, but a union of religion and political life.[17] Christianity was persecuted by Roman political authorities precisely because it insisted on a fundamental private sphere into which the public could not intervene: the sphere of faith.

Moreover, natural law theory has articulated the principle of subsidiarity, according to which higher or more general associations should intervene in the life of lower or more particular associations only when the latter are incapable of performing a task adequately.[18] One implication of this is that public authorities ought not to insert their authority into the private world of families and voluntary associations, except when this is necessary for the common good.

Of course, the private and the public are not completely independent. They are distinct, but they have an impact on each other. The private world

---

16. Pope Leo XIII, *Rerum novarum,* ¶ 15 (1891) (emphasis added).

17. See, for example, Fustel des Coulanges, *The Ancient City* (Baltimore: Johns Hopkins University Press, 1980).

18. See my "Subsidiarity: The 'Other' Ground for Limited Government," in *Liberalism, and Communitarianism: Essays on the Catholic Intellectual Tradition and the Moral Foundations of Democracy,* ed. Kenneth L. Grasso, Gerard V. Bradley, and Robert P. Hunt (Lanham, MD: Rowman and Littlefield, 1995), 81–96.

of the family is obviously deeply influenced by the "social ecology" within which it exists, as any parent knows only too well. The public world is affected by the conduct of people in their private lives (especially when attention is paid to the aggregate pattern of private actions). That is why some acts that look simply "private" may not be so, as in the case of adult consensual acts, such as hiring someone for less than the minimum wage, or selling or using pornography.

Personal Autonomy or the Primacy of Personal Choice: How Important Is Personal Autonomy?

It seems to me that we should agree that personal autonomy is a very important *means*. Without genuine freedom and choice, it is not possible to lead a moral life. Liberals are right to think that what is important is not just *what* we do, but *how* we do it, that *we choose* to do it.

What we do does matter, and so personal autonomy cannot be absolutized. First, the autonomy of one person must be compatible with that of another, so in some cases it is good that autonomous action be suppressed, as when one person seeks to curtail the legitimate autonomy of another. This is no minor qualification, as some liberals tend to treat it. It demonstrates that autonomy is not an ultimate and unqualified good: it must yield to the moral imperative of respecting the rights of others. Autonomy itself cannot account for that moral imperative.

Second, virtually everyone realizes that certain autonomous actions can undercut genuine autonomy, simply as a factual matter. One can freely choose to get drunk, but in doing so one loses genuine autonomy—self-determination—while in that state. More importantly, one can freely choose to participate in the conception of a child, but in doing so one brings into existence obligations that limit one's autonomy. It is more controversial among liberals (unfortunately) whether one can contract into a relationship that permanently curtails one's autonomy, such as indissoluble marriage. Some liberals object that such an institution is incompatible with what they hold to be essential: the permanent revisability of one's commitments. Ironically, the same liberals tend to defend the right to suicide, though suicide, however autonomous, destroys the autonomous actor—it is the ultimate unrevisable act.

Note that, in the case of each of these characteristic themes of liberalism, an advocate of natural law (or Catholic social thought) would respond not by rejecting the principle, but by saying, "yes, that is right—if the principle is understood properly, if it is moderate and limited." That is, we would join what might be called the great ongoing internal dialogue of liberalism. We are part of the tradition of liberalism. We are liberals.

NATURAL LAW AND LIBERALISM'S CHARACTERISTIC POLITICAL INSTITUTIONS

I will only briefly note here that natural law theory has no trouble seeing value in what Berkowitz calls "liberalism's characteristic set of political institutions," namely, representative democracy, separation of governmental powers, and an independent judiciary.[19] While institutional questions always involve a measure of prudential judgment relative to the circumstances of a given political community, it is fair to say that natural law theory: (1) looks with favor on political arrangements, such as representative democracy, that promote the participation and therefore the capacities of as many citizens as reasonably possible, because this development of capacities is an important part of the common good;[20] and (2) in general looks with favor on arrange-

---

19. For an example of how natural law theory would evaluate these institutions, see my discussion of "Natural Law and Judicial Review" in *Natural Law and Contemporary Public Policy,* ed. David Forte (Washington, DC: Georgetown University Press, 1998).

20. In this respect, it follows Alexis de Tocqueville, who says of democracy:

I am less inclined to applaud it for what it does, than for what it causes to be done. . . . It is incontestable that the people frequently conduct public business very ill; but it is impossible that the lower orders should take a part in public business without extending the circle of their ideas, and quitting the ordinary routine of their thoughts. . . . When the opponents of democracy assert that a single man performs what he undertakes better than the government of all, it appears to me that they are right. . . . Democratic liberty is far from accomplishing all its projects with the skill of an adroit despotism. It frequently abandons them before they have borne their fruits, or risks them when the consequences may be dangerous; but in the end, it produces more than any absolute government; if it does fewer things well, it does a greater number of things. Under its sway, the grandeur is not in what the public administration does, but in what is done without it or outside of it. Democracy does not give the people the most skilful government, but it produces what the ablest governments are frequently unable to create; namely, an all-pervading and restless activity, a superabundant force, and an energy which is inseparable from it, and which may, however unfavorable circumstances may be, produce wonders. These are the true advantages of democracy.

Tocqueville, *Democracy in America,* 251–52. See also Simon, *The Philosophy of Democratic Government,* 130.

ments that provide checks on political power, such as separation of powers and a limited form of judicial review, because of its recognition of both good and evil in human beings.

NATURAL LAW, LIBERALISM, AND "VIRTUES SUSTAINING LIBERTY"

Berkowitz also points out that part of the liberal tradition is "liberalism's fertile source of reflections on such non-political supports of the virtues that sustain liberty as commerce, voluntary association, family, and religion." The first two of these, commerce and voluntary association, can be described as typically *modern* supports for the virtues that sustain liberty. Neither of them was salient in an earlier era, where status rather than contract determined relations in society.

The other two, however, family and religion, are not distinctly modern (though they may take typical forms in the modern world). Reflection on family and religion can, I think, be described as part of liberalism's continual internal debate about its relation to the pre-liberal world. This suggests, at the same time, that there is a permanent tension of sorts there. That in turn raises the question of the limits of liberalism.

WHAT LIBERALISM FAILS TO SEE

I said earlier that, given my description of the core of liberalism, "people of sound judgment and good will, including American natural law theorists and Catholics, should be willing to be considered liberals," and I really mean that. But I also want to say that they should be uncomfortable about being simply liberals. If liberalism has grasped much of the truth about political life, it has also found it difficult to embrace some of that truth, or perhaps has even simply missed some of it.

The first problem with liberalism is that it fails to recognize sufficiently the influence of "the regime," a notion that is so central to classical political philosophy.[21] The vision of political life in the liberal tradition is that it exists to establish a framework for the protection of individual rights. Government should remove the barriers to individual "pursuit of happiness." Even

21. The notion of the "regime"—which combines politics and sociology and economics and culture—is particularly central to and well set out in the work of Leo Strauss.

when it acts positively (e.g., in modern liberal economic redistribution), this is viewed simply as providing means to self-development, not actually determining that development—it is providing means rather than dictating ends.

Jeremy Waldron defends liberalism against a more modern form of this criticism:

Sometimes liberals are accused of taking the beliefs and preferences of individuals as given and hence of ignoring the fact that forms of society may determine forms of consciousness and the structure and content of preferences. But liberals need not be blind to the possibility of preferences changing, either autonomously or along with changes in social structure and social expectations. Provided this possibility of change is in principle something that people as they are can recognize in themselves and take into account in their reflective deliberations, then it can be accommodated perfectly well in a liberal account of freedom.[22]

The confident "can be accommodated perfectly well" may distract us from the tenuousness of the assumption on which it rests. Liberals can recognize, Waldron says, that people's ends may be chosen due to "changes in social structure or social expectations," that is, due to the shape and tone and influences of the community of which they are a part. This should not bother liberals, however, as long as "in principle" people "as they are" can recognize this fact and take it into account in their reflective deliberations. Waldron appears to assume that this condition is not problematic. It seems to me deeply so.

The force of the "in principle" is not clear. Is this to be opposed to "in practice"? If it is merely the theoretical possibility that people may recognize the influences in their society, that is unobjectionable, but it is not clear how that constitutes a defense of liberalism. How likely, in fact, are people to recognize such influences? Waldron appears to go beyond just theoretical possibility when he specifies that it must be people "as they are." So that is the question: *do* (not just "can") people, as they are, recognize the extent to which their preferences—their ends, their goals, their assumptions about what is good in life—are shaped by their social ecology?

This is the kind of empirical question that is very difficult to answer on the basis of anything other than our own experience with human beings. On the basis of my experience, I am simply puzzled that Waldron seems so confident that this condition is met. The people I have dealt with in the course of my life, the students I have taught—even, I confess, some of the scholars with

22. Waldron, in an omitted footnote, cites Rawls's use of this argument against utilitarianism. Waldron, *Liberal Rights*, 41.

whom I have interacted—have not *consistently* demonstrated this awareness and control over such influences in their "reflective deliberations." It is common to see reflection and critical awareness with respect to a certain range of issues—especially the ones that are more subject to controversy in our society at a given time—but this is compatible with little or no reflection on other broad attitudes toward life (especially where there is a broad social consensus). In fact, I am impressed over and over again with how many people seem simply to absorb many of their most important attitudes toward life from their surroundings, the culture or subcultures of which they are a part, with relatively little or no critical distance from those influences. The idea that people "as they are" engage in a high level of self-critical analysis, then, strikes me as an extraordinarily optimistic assessment. It seems to be a very good example of a kind of romanticism at the heart of much liberalism.

But someone might say, "So what if liberalism shapes people, as long as its shapes them well?" Should we be bothered about the way liberalism shapes people?

I should point out immediately that some of that influence is quite beneficent. For example, liberalism, on the whole, encourages people to be tolerant and peaceful, to be active in pursuit of opportunities, and to have an awareness of their own dignity and rights.

For the moment, though, I want to ask about some of the less attractive aspects of liberalism. I will just mention three tendencies in particular. The first is the tendency to emphasize freedom at the expense of an emphasis on truth about ultimate realities. The claim to know the truth about human purposes has so often been associated with abridgment of freedom that liberals are somewhat understandably suspicious of truth claims about human ends. The post-Reformation religious wars (international and domestic) are the most commonly invoked example, from Hobbes and Locke to Rawls, and today their place is admirably filled by Osama bin Laden and the dreaded "Religious Right" in America. (This suspicion of dogma in general, however, is compatible with the ready acceptance of certain truth claims, above all, the claims of modern science and liberalism's "procedural" principles.)[23]

Over time, the citizens of liberal democracies seem to move from toler-

23. For a good example of dogmatic commitment to the procedural principles by someone who is generally a skeptic, see Oliver Wendell Holmes Jr.'s ode to freedom of speech—replacing the "fighting faiths" of the past with a faith that the marketplace is the best test of truth—in *Abrams v. U.S.*, 250 US 616, 630 (1919).

ance of other people to relativism about ideas of the good. The virtue of non-judgmentalism eclipses the virtue of wisdom. Some people consider this one of liberalism's attractive features, but those of us who believe that human beings are very much worse off when they do not understand the most fundamental truths about human life cannot.

The second tendency, somewhat related to the first, is the tendency of liberal democracy to undermine religion. Alexis de Tocqueville is well known for his statements about the importance of religion in America. Indeed, he calls it the first of our political institutions, even though Americans embrace the separation of church and state. But there is another side to de Tocqueville that is less noted. In particular, it is interesting to note that at the end of *Democracy in America,* in his recommendations for how to prevent democratic despotism, he says nothing about religion. I think the explanation for this is that de Tocqueville was aware of the tenuous status of revealed religion in modern liberal democracy.

De Tocqueville suggested that liberal democracies would be suspicious of tradition and that the philosophical method of Americans would be to rely on themselves. But this strikes at the heart of revealed religion, which rests precisely on "the handing down" (*traditio*) of the good news that has been revealed to mankind by a God who has intervened in a particular moment of human history. De Tocqueville recognized that the natural tendency of modern liberal democracy was the more diffuse and indefinite religion of pantheism (prevalent in much "New Age" religion).

De Tocqueville likewise recognized that liberal democracies would incite and cater to the human desire for physical well-being. He specifically pointed out that one of the advantages of religion is its tendency to curb or moderate this desire, thereby facilitating pursuit of the greater and more glorious possessions of mankind. But a moment of reflection shows that this can be turned around. If religion can benefit democracy by acting *against* one of its strongest tendencies, democracy can undermine religion by propagating that tendency.

For these and other reasons, de Tocqueville had some doubts about how efficacious a restraint on liberal democracy religion might be in the long run. I think that American history bears out those concerns. Those who take a more benign view of that history point out the surprising strength of religion in America, especially when compared to Europe. While this strength should not be ignored, a closer attention to the character of that religious belief raises some questions. In many respects, traditional Christian beliefs, for example, seem to have been modified to accommodate liberal democratic tendencies. Nowhere is this seen more clearly than in the progressive decline of marriage as an institution in American society, a process in which many churches as well as religious believers have accommodated changing sexual mores.

This leads us to the third problematic tendency of liberalism, which is the undermining of the stability of the family. Many scholars argue that the family is just as strong as it has been in the past, but has simply assumed new forms. While it is true that we should resist the tendency to view the history of the family with an unjustified nostalgia—there were plenty of problems with families in the past—I think that they are wrong to think that there have not been dramatic changes that greatly weaken the family in performing its essential functions, most importantly, the raising of children.[24] And, while it is also true that many of the forces undermining the family are part of modernity in general, there seem to be reasonable grounds for finding in liberal democracy itself tendencies contrary to stable family life, such as individualism, affluent materialism, and doubt about absolute substantive moral principles.

It does not follow from my analysis that, because the influence of the regime is so great, we ought to abandon liberalism. The alternatives, after all, might be worse. I for one certainly have no desire to return to the Greek polis or the Roman republic. Medieval Christendom might seem to some people (especially Catholics) to be more attractive, but I would warn people not to romanticize the actual once-existent forms of that ideal either. As de Tocqueville suggested about the aristocracy of the *ancien regime,* one can be distracted by the high points so much that one fails to see the great amount of human misery and injustice.

What I would say, instead, is that we should help people as much as we can to be more self-critical about aspects of liberalism that are less attractive. And we should also try to "high-tone" liberalism to the limited extent that we can[25]—for there is a wide range of forms of liberalism, and some of them shape people in much better ways than others.

24. Elizabeth Fox-Genovese, "Thoughts on the History of the Family," in *The Family, Civil Society, and the State,* ed. Christopher Wolfe (Lanham, MD: Rowman and Littlefield, 1998).

25. See, for example, the sobering passage with which de Tocqueville concludes his discussion of the "advantages" of democracy in America, in which he notes the deep tendency

WHY DOES IT MATTER?

Someone may raise the question: why does it matter whether there is some phenomenon called "liberalism" and whether it is a good thing or a bad thing? Such an objector might argue that this discussion is primarily a semantic game—people fighting over whether they or others fall in a category that can be defined in very different ways—and that what matters is not semantics and names, but substance. So, he would argue, let's talk about substantive principles and not worry about whether this or that person or principle is "liberal," or "conservative," or whatever.

There is some truth to this, of course. "Liberalism" is a term that has been used to cover such a broad range of thinkers and programs that it might be wondered whether it is that useful a term at all. And, in the final analysis, what matters is not whether a particular principle or political practice is "liberal," but whether it is good.

But the discussion about liberalism is, I think, useful. Again, Peter Berkowitz has some useful observations:

Several reasons justify the effort to give liberalism its due. First, liberalism clarifies the contemporary intellectual scene by providing a framework which reveals that what appear to be rival and incompatible schools of thought in fact share a formal structure and governing moral intention. Second, giving liberalism its due means a substantial gain in self-knowledge, both for those who think of themselves as liberals and for those who do not recognize the liberalism of their ways. Third, the liberal tradition has untapped resources for understanding more precisely how to defend, and sustain a political life that rests upon, the premise of natural freedom and equality, a premise whose power not many would wish to deny and whose authority few can honestly resist.[26]

By his first point, Berkowitz means to point out that an understanding of liberalism demonstrates the similarities that get glossed over or lost in discussions of the differences between liberal and communitarian writers, and liberal and postmodernist writers. I would add that discussions of the differences between liberalism and natural law theory sometimes obscure what they have in common. Likewise, by his second point, Berkowitz suggests that it is important for communitarians and postmodernists to recognize their own liberalism,

---

of liberal democracy to gravitate toward what might be called the "middling state of things," the down side of which is "mediocrity." Tocqueville, *Democracy in America,* vol. 1, chapter 14, 252–53.

26. Berkowitz, "Liberalism, Postmodernism, and Public Philosophy," 161.

and I add that the same is true for advocates of natural law. By his third point, Berkowitz argues that the liberal tradition has resources that are often over-looked today, and I would argue that those resources are sometimes principles that classical liberals inherited from pre-liberal thought and practice, based on forms of natural law, and that they did not consider incompatible with liber-alism, but rather supportive of it. That is, not only is it true that natural law thinkers are often more liberal than they know, but also liberal thinkers (espe-cially the more moderate ones) are often more rooted in natural law than they know.

In the end, it matters whether we should consider ourselves liberals be-cause, if we don't, we may not think and speak as clearly about ourselves and others as we should. This is bad for at least three reasons. First, we won't un-derstand the truth about ourselves. Second, we will be less able to defend our own principles persuasively to others who value liberalism greatly. Third, we will not be able to defend and promote liberalism, with all its valuable as-pects, to those people who, for various historical and other reasons, are sus-picious of it, especially in its contemporary form (e.g., moderate Muslims). At the same time, we can be self-critical liberals who are aware of the limits of liberalism and help others to be the same.

One final point I should mention: this chapter is part of a larger over-all analysis of American public philosophy. A logical companion would be: "Why We Should (and Should Not) Be Conservatives."

[8]

REASON, FREEDOM, AND THE RULE OF LAW

Reflections on Their Significance in Catholic Thought

ROBERT P. GEORGE

The idea of law and the ideal of the rule of law are central to the Catholic (and, more generally, the Western) tradition of thought about public (or "political") order.[1] St. Thomas Aquinas went so far as to declare that "it belongs to the very notion of a people [*ad rationem populi*] that the people's dealings with each other be regulated by just precepts of law."[2] In our own time, Pope John Paul II has forcefully reaffirmed the status of the rule of law as a requirement of fundamental political justice.[3] For all the romantic appeal of "palm tree justice" or "Solomonic judging," and despite the sometimes decidedly unromantic qualities of living by preordained legal rules, the Catholic (and Western) tradition affirms that justice itself requires that people be governed in accordance with the principles of legality.

Among the core concerns of Catholic and other legal philosophers in recent decades has been the meaning, content, and moral significance of the

---

1. By no means am I suggesting that the idea of law or the ideal of the rule of law were Catholic inventions. On the contrary, this idea and ideal were articulated and developed in pre-Christian classical and Jewish traditions of thought. The treatment of the subject in the writings of St. Thomas Aquinas is, unsurprisingly, deeply indebted to Plato and, especially, Aristotle, as well as to the Hebrew Bible.

2. St. Thomas Aquinas, *Summa theologiae,* I-II, q. 105, a. 2c.

3. See the encyclical letter of Pope John Paul II, *Sollicitudo rei socialis* (1987).

rule of law. The renewal of interest in this very ancient question (or set of questions) springs from above all, I think, the unprecedented rise and fall of totalitarian regimes. In the aftermath of the defeat of Nazism, legal philosophers of every religious persuasion tested their legal theories by asking, for example, whether the Nazi regime constituted a *legal* system in any meaningful sense. In the wake of communism's collapse in Europe, legal scholars and others are urgently trying to understand the role of legal procedures and institutions in creating and sustaining decent democratic regimes. It has been in this particular context that Pope John Paul II has had occasion to stress the moral importance of the rule of law.

One of the signal achievements in legal philosophy in the twentieth century was Lon L. Fuller's explication of the content of the rule of law.[4] Although Fuller was not himself a Catholic, he unhesitatingly availed himself of the resources of the Catholic intellectual tradition in developing what he referred to as a "procedural natural law theory." Reflecting on law as a "purposive" enterprise—the subjecting of human behavior to the governance of rules—Fuller identified eight constitutive elements of legality. These are (1) the prospectivity (i.e., nonretroactivity) of legal rules; (2) the absence of impediments to compliance with the rules by those subject to them; (3) the promulgation of the rules; (4) their clarity; (5) their coherence with one another; (6) their constancy over time; (7) their generality of application; and (8) the congruence between official action and declared rule. Irrespective of whether a legal system (or a body of law) is good or bad, that is to say, substantively just or unjust, *to the extent* that it truly is a legal system (or a body of law) it will, to some significant degree, exemplify these elements.

It was a mark of Fuller's sophistication, I think, that he noticed that the rule of law is a *matter of degree*. Its constitutive elements are exemplified *to a greater or lesser extent* by actual legal systems or bodies of law. Legal systems exemplify the rule of law *to the extent that* the rules constituting them are prospective, susceptible of being complied with, promulgated, clear, etc.

Even Fuller's critics recognized his achievement in explicating the content of the rule of law. What they objected to was Fuller's claims—or, in any event, what they took to be Fuller's claims—on its behalf. Provocatively, Fuller asserted that, taken together, the elements of the rule of law, though in themselves procedural, nevertheless constitute what he called an "internal moral-

4. See especially Lon L. Fuller, *The Morality of Law* (New Haven, CT: Yale University Press, 1964).

ity of law." (Hence, the title of Fuller's major work on the subject of the rule of law, *The Morality of Law.*) Moreover, he explicitly presented his account of the rule of law as a challenge to the dominant "legal positivism" of his time. According to Fuller, once we recognize that law, precisely as such, *has* an internal morality, it becomes clear that the "conceptual separation of law and morality," which forms the core of the "positivist" understanding of law, legal obligation, and the practical functioning of legal institutions, cannot be maintained.

These claims drew sharp criticism from, among others, Herbert Hart, the Oxford legal philosopher whose magisterial 1961 book *The Concept of Law* both substantially revised and dramatically revitalized the positivist tradition in analytical jurisprudence.[5] In a now famous review essay in the *Harvard Law Review,* Hart accused Fuller of, in effect, engaging in a semantic sleight of hand.[6] According to Hart, there isn't the slightest reason to suppose that the constitutive elements of legality, which Fuller correctly and very usefully identified, should be accounted as a "morality" of any sort. As Fuller himself seemed to concede, unjust (or otherwise morally bad) law can exemplify the procedural elements of legality just as fully as just law can. But if that is true, then it is worse than merely tendentious to claim that these elements constitute an "internal *morality* of law."

Indeed, Fuller's critics have observed that even the most wicked rulers sometimes have purely self-interested reasons to put into place, and operate strictly in accordance with, legal procedures. Yet even the strictest adherence to the forms of legality cannot ensure that the laws they enact and enforce will be substantively just or even minimally decent. Replying to Hart and other critics, Fuller argued that the historical record shows that thoroughly evil regimes, such as the Nazi regime, consistently fail to observe even the formal principles of legality. In practice, the Nazis, to stay with the example, freely departed from the rule of law whenever it suited their purposes to do so. So Fuller defied Hart to provide "significant examples of regimes that have combined a faithful adherence to the [rule of law] with a brutal indifference to justice and human welfare."[7]

5. H. L. A. Hart, *The Concept of Law* (Oxford: Clarendon Press, 1961).

6. H. L. A. Hart, "Review of *The Morality of Law,* by Lon L. Fuller," *Harvard Law Review* 78 (1965): 1281–96.

7. Lon L. Fuller, *The Morality of Law,* 2nd ed., with "Reply to Critics" (New Haven, CT: Yale University Press 1969), 154.

Now, it is important to see that Fuller's claim here is not that regimes can never perpetrate injustices—even grave injustices—while respecting the desiderata of the rule of law. It is the weaker, yet by no means trivial, claim that regimes that respect the rule of law do not, and cannot so long as they adhere to the rule of law, degenerate into truly monstrous tyrannies such as the Nazis.

Still, Fuller's critics were unpersuaded. My own esteemed teacher, Joseph Raz, one of Hart's greatest students and now his literary executor, pursued a more radical line of argument to deflate Fuller's claim that the elements of the rule of law constitute an internal morality. Raz suggested that the rule of law is a purely instrumental, rather than any sort of *moral*, good. He analogized the rule of law to a sharp knife—an *efficient* instrument, and in that nonmoral sense "good," but equally serviceable in morally good and *bad* causes.[8] Indeed, according to Raz, insofar as the institution and maintenance of legal procedures improves governmental efficiency, they increase the potential for evildoing by wicked rulers.

Fuller's arguments have, however, won some converts. Most notably, perhaps, Neil MacCormick, who had once shared Raz's view that the requirements of the rule of law "can in principle be as well observed by those whose laws wreak great substantive injustice as by those whose laws are in substance as just as they can possibly be," eventually revised his opinion to give some credit to Fuller's claim that the elements of the rule of law constitute a kind of internal morality.

There is always something to be said for treating people with formal fairness, that is, in a rational and predictable way, setting public standards for citizens' conduct and officials' responses thereto, standards with which one can judge compliance or noncompliance, rather than leaving everything to discretionary and potentially arbitrary decision. That indeed is what we mean by the "Rule of Law." Where it is observed, people are confronted by a state which treats them as *rational agents due some respect as such*. It applies fairly whatever standards of conduct and of judgment it applies. This has real value, and independent value, even where the substance of what is done falls short of any relevant ideal of substantive justice.[9]

---

8. See Joseph Raz, "The Rule of Law and Its Virtue," *Law Quarterly Review* 93 (1977): 208.

9. Neil MacCormick, "Natural Law and the Separation of Law and Morals," in *Natural Law Theory: Contemporary Essays,* ed. Robert P. George (Oxford: Clarendon Press, 1992), 105–13, at 123 (emphasis supplied).

MacCormick's revised understanding strikes me as sounder than the contrary understanding of Hart and Raz, who refuse to accord to the requirements of the rule of law any of the sort of more than merely instrumental value that MacCormick labels "independent," and that I would bite the bullet and call "moral." Plainly it is the case that well-intentioned rulers who genuinely care for justice and the common good of the communities they govern will strive for procedural fairness—and will do so, in part, because they understand that people, as rational agents, are due the respect that is paid them when officials eschew arbitrary decision making and operate according to law. And we can understand this without the need for sociological inquiry into the way things are done by officials in more or less just regimes. Rather, it is the fruit of reflection on what such officials *ought* to do because they *owe* it to those under their governance. But if I am right about this, then respect for the requirements of the rule of law *is not a morally neutral matter*—despite the fact that the elements of the rule of law are themselves procedural. Rather, rulers or officials have *moral reasons,* and, inasmuch as these reasons are generally conclusive, a *moral obligation,* to respect the requirements of the rule of law.

Of course, respect for the rule of law does not exhaust rulers' or officials' moral obligations toward those subject to their governance. Nor, as Fuller's critics such as Hart and Raz correctly observe, does respect for the rule of law guarantee that the substance of the laws will be just. If Raz went too far in one direction by treating the rule of law as a morally neutral "efficient instrument," boosters of the rule of law can easily go too far in the other direction by supposing that the achievement and maintenance of the rule of law immunizes a regime against grave injustice and even tyranny.

Here historical and sociological inquiry is the antidote to overblown claims. Apartheid and even slavery have coexisted with the rule of law. And those legal positivists who claimed that even the Nazi regime worked much of its evil through formally lawful means were not without evidence to support their view. I would therefore venture on behalf of the rule of law only the following modest claim when it comes to the question of its alleged incompatibility with grave substantive injustice: an unjust regime's adherence to preannounced and stable general rules, so long as it lasts, has the virtue of limiting the rulers' freedom of maneuver in ways that will generally reduce, to some extent, at least, their capacity for evildoing. Potential victims of injustice at the hands of wicked rulers will generally benefit, if only to a limited extent, from their rulers' willingness, whatever its motivation, to respect the requirements of the rule of law.

Philosophers of law from Plato to John Finnis have warned that wherever the rule of law enjoys ideological prestige ill-intentioned rulers will find it necessary to—and will—adhere to constitutional procedures and other legal forms as a means of maintaining or enhancing their political power.[10] Plato himself had no illusions that adherence to such procedures and forms would *guarantee* substantively just rule. Nevertheless, he noticed that even apart from the self-interested motives of evil rulers sometimes to act in accordance with principles of legality, decent rulers always and everywhere have reason to respect these principles; for procedural fairness is itself a requirement of substantive justice—one that is always desirable in human relations and, in particular, in the relationships between those exercising political power and those over whom such power is exercised.

Where the rule of law is respected, there obtains between the rulers and the ruled a certain reciprocity. Now, this reciprocity will certainly be useful in securing certain desirable ends to which it is a means. I have in mind, for example, various elements of social order, including efficiency in the regulation and/or delivery of public services, and political stability, particularly in times of stress. But Plato's point, and I see no reason to doubt it, is the moral philosophical one that, given the dignity of human beings, this sort of reciprocity is more than *merely* a means to other ends. As such, it ought to be protected and advanced wherever possible, and it may not lightly be sacrificed even for the sake of other important goods.

Now, there is a lot packed into my little phrase—more Kantian in flavor, I suppose, than Platonic—"given the dignity of human beings." Although most people have moral objections to cruelty toward animals, we do not consider that pets or farm animals are to be governed in accordance with the requirements of the rule of law? Within the bounds of decency, we hope, the farmer resorts rather to Pavlovian methods, or, indeed, to whatever it takes to get the chickens to lay and the cows into pasture. Indeed, it would be pointless to attempt to rule nonhuman animals by law because laws cannot function for chickens and cows as *reasons* for their actions. The farmer, rather, causes (or, at least, attempts to cause) the animal behavior he desires. Humans, by con-

---

10. See Plato, *Statesman*, 291a–303d; John Finnis, *Natural Law and Natural Rights* (Oxford: Clarendon Press, 1980), 274.

trast, can be governed by law because legal rules can function in their practical deliberation as what Herbert Hart described—in an important break
with his positivist predecessors, Bentham and Austin, who conceived of legal rules as *causes* of human behavior, rather than as *reasons*—as "content-
independent, peremptory reasons for action."[11]

Virtually all philosophical accounts of human dignity stress the moral significance of human rationality. People are, in the phrase of Neil MacCormick's that I've already quoted, "due some respect, as rational agents." But if
this is true, as I believe it is, then perhaps it is worth pausing to consider why
and how governance in accordance with the requirements of the rule of law
treats people with some of the respect that they are due as *rational* agents.
What is it about human rationality that entails a dignity that is violated when
rulers treat those subject to their rule the way farmers treat livestock?

Today, when one speaks of human rationality (in virtually any context),
one will be understood to be referring to what Aristotle labeled "theoretical" rationality.[12] *Merely* theoretically rational beings, however, could not be
ruled by law and would, in any event, no more deserve to be ruled by law
than computers deserve such rule. It is hard to see how even theoretically
rational agents who, *unlike computers,* were capable of (1) experiencing feelings of desire and (2) bringing intellectual operations to bear in efficiently
satisfying their desires could be due the respect implied by the rule of law or
other requirements of morality.[13] Such agents would not be capable of exercising *practical* reason and making *moral* choices. Their behavior could only
be caused—ultimately either by external coercion or internal compulsion.[14]

11. See H. L. A. Hart, *Essays on Bentham* (Oxford: Clarendon Press, 1983), ch. 10. For a
particularly illuminating account of the differences between reasons and causes; see Daniel
N. Robinson, *Philosophy of Psychology* (New York: Columbia University Press, 1985), 50–57.

12. Theoretical, as opposed to what Aristotle labeled "practical," rationality inquires into
what is, was, or could be the case about the natural, social, or supernatural world; practical rationality identifies possibilities for choice and action and inquires into *what ought to be done.*

13. This is why instrumentalist theories of practical reason such as Hobbes's or Hume's—
not to mention the various contemporary reductionist accounts of human behavior that
understand human beings as computers with emotions—have difficulty providing an even
remotely plausible account of human dignity, and only rarely offer to do so. See Thomas
Hobbes, *Leviathan* (1651), ed. Michael Oakeshott (Oxford: Blackwell, 1957), pt. 1, ch. 8; and
see David Hume, *A Treatise of Human Nature* (1740), ed. David Fate Norton and Mary J.
Norton (Oxford: Oxford University Press, 2000), bk. 2, pt. 3, sec 3.

14. See Germain Grisez, Joseph M. Boyle Jr., and Olaf Tollefsen, *Free Choice: A Self-
Referential Argument* (South Bend, IN: University of Notre Dame Press, 1976).

Lacking the capacity ultimately to understand and act on the basis of more than merely instrumental *reasons,* they would literally be beyond freedom and dignity.

My proposition is that the rationality that entitles people to the sort of respect exemplified in the principles of the rule of law is not primarily the rationality that enables people to solve mathematical problems, or to understand the human neural system, or to develop cures for diseases, or to inquire into the origins of the universe or even the existence and attributes of God. It is, rather, the rationality that enables us to judge that mathematical problems are to be solved, that the neural system is to be understood, that diseases are to be cured, and that God is to be known and loved. It is, moreover, the capacity to distinguish fully reasonable possibilities for choice and action from possibilities that, while rationally grounded, fall short of all that reason demands.[15]

In short, the dignity that calls forth the respect due to rational agents in the form of, among other things, governance in accordance with the rule of law flows from our nature as *practically* intelligent beings, that is, beings whose nature is to understand and act on more than merely instrumental reasons. The capacity to understand and act on such reasons stands in a relationship of mutual entailment with the human capacity for free choice, that is, our capacity to *deliberate and choose* between or among open possibilities (i.e., options) that are provided by "basic human goods," that is, more than merely instrumental reasons.

Free choice *exists* just in case people have, are aware of, and can act upon such reasons; people have, are aware of, and can act upon such reasons just insofar as they have free choice. But if it is true that people possess reason and freedom, then they enjoy what can only be described as *spiritual* powers,[16] and, it might even be said, a certain sharing in divine power—namely, the power to bring into being that which one reasonably judges to be worth bringing into being (something "of value"), but which one is in no sense compelled or "caused" to bring into being.

What is Godlike, albeit, of course, in a very limited way, is the human

15. For an explanation of this point, see Robert P. George, "Natural Law Ethics," in *A Companion to Philosophy of Religion,* ed. Philip L. Quinn and Charles Taliaferro (Oxford: Blackwell Publishers, 1997), ch. 58. See also Robert P. George, *Making Men Moral: Civil Liberties and Public Morality* (Oxford: Clarendon Press, 1993), 8–18.

16. On the status of free choices as "spiritual" entities, see Germain Grisez, *The Way of the Lord Jesus,* vol. 1: *Christian Moral Principles* (Chicago: Franciscan Herald Press, 1983), 50–52.

power to be an "uncaused causing." This, I believe, is the central meaning and significance of the (otherwise extraordinarily puzzling) biblical teaching that man (unlike other creatures) is made in the very "image and likeness of God."[17] This teaching expresses in theological terms (and proposes as a matter of revealed truth) the philosophical proposition I have been advancing about the dignity flowing from the nature of human beings as *practically* intelligent creatures. Its upshot is not that human beings may not legitimately be ruled, but that they must be ruled in ways that accord them the respect they are due "as rational agents." Among other things, it requires that the rule to which human beings are subjected is the *rule of law.*

Reflection on the relationship of human reason and freedom—and the theological significance of this relationship in a religious tradition crucially shaped by the biblical account of man as a possessor of spiritual powers and, indeed, as an *imago dei*—helps, I believe, to make sense of the centrality of law, and the rule of law, in Catholic thought about political morality. In particular, it helps to explain the stress laid upon the ideal of the rule of law as a fundamental principle of political justice in the tradition stretching from early and medieval Catholic thinkers to John Paul II.

17. "[M]an is said to be made in God's image, insofar as the image implies *an intelligent being endowed with free-will and self-movement:* now that we have treated of the exemplar, i.e., God, and those things which come forth from the power of God in accordance with his will; it remains for us to treat of His image, i.e., man, inasmuch as he too is the principle of his actions, as having free-will and control of his actions." St. Thomas Aquinas, *Summa theologiae,* I-II, Prologue (emphasis in the original).

PART IV

CATHOLIC PERSPECTIVES ON
SUBSTANTIVE AREAS OF LAW

[9]

LABOR LAW

"Making Life More Human"—
Work and the Social Question

❦

THOMAS C. KOHLER

An expanding economy with an increasingly disproportionate distribution of income and markedly uneven rates of development, even within national boundaries. High rates of unemployment and increasing instability in employment relationships. Innovative forms of economic organization accompanied by unparalleled concentrations of economic power. An intensification of population shifts to urban areas, coupled with an unprecedented migration of people from East to West. An astounding disintegration of families and the progressive erosion of other forms of community life. These are the conditions captured by the term the "social question." They also represent the conditions in which unions and labor laws first developed during the nineteenth century, and to which Catholic Social Thought first responded. In an intensified guise, they characterize the contingencies that these institutions presently face.

This chapter will provide a cursory review of this development and assess the present situation in historical and comparative perspective. As John Paul II observed in his 1981 encyclical, *Laborem exercens,* "the question of human work" constitutes "a constant factor, both of social life and of the Church's teaching." Consequently, human work represents "the essential key" to the social question.[1] From the outset, work, its ordering, and its significance to authentic human development have been a central theme of Catholic Social Thought.

HISTORICAL DEVELOPMENT OF WORKERS' ASSOCIATIONS AND LABOR LAW

[W]orkmen may of themselves effect much . . . by means of such associations and organizations as afford opportune aid to those in distress. . . . The most important of all are workingmen's associations; for these virtually include all the rest.

Rerum novarum, ¶ 48–49

Introduction

No matter where one looks, the development of unions and of labor law has followed a remarkably similar pattern. Unions, of course, represent a reaction by workers themselves to industrialization and the thoroughgoing social dislocations that accompanied the development of liberal, market-oriented economies in the mid-nineteenth century. As Leo XIII observes, however, unions were hardly the only reaction, and their evolution, along with that of the institution of collective bargaining, was neither instantaneous nor linear. For the purposes of this brief overview, we can identify workers, employers, the state, and the Church as the four actors who played the most prominent roles in this development.

Writing in the last quarter of the eighteenth century, the great English legal commentator, Sir William Blackstone, observed that "three great rela-

---

1. The modern Catholic Social Thought tradition developed as a response to the wrenching social dislocations that followed in the wake of the French Revolution. The collapse of what Edmund Burke famously called society's "little platoons" gave rise to the issue of what would relate and unite individuals in the face of the disappearance of the venerable intermediary structures that once had anchored one's place in the world. These dislocations gave rise to the "social question," a matter that has been the focus of the Catholic Social Tradition from its beginning. As Pope John Paul II states in the encyclical *Laborem exercens* ¶ 3:

human work is *a key*, probably *the essential key*, to the whole social question, if we try to see that question really from the point of view of man's good. And if the solution—or rather the gradual solution—of the social question, which keeps coming up and becomes ever more complex, must be sought in the direction of "making life more human," then the key, namely human work, acquires fundamental and decisive importance. [footnote omitted]

For further discussion, see Thomas C. Kohler, "The Notion of Solidarity and the Secret History of American Labor Law," *Buffalo Law Review* 53 (2005): 883.

tions" characterize private life: husband and wife, parent and child, master and servant.[2] In this, he echoes a statement made by Aristotle in the *Politics* about the basic elements that constitute the household, and thereby, political society.[3] Family and employment continue to represent two of the most important (if imperiled) relationships of modern life. The ages-old model of relatively stable, largely intramoenial "employment," however, was being eradicated (particularly in England) even as Blackstone wrote. For many, the replacement would be work in large-scale, increasingly bureaucratically organized institutions.[4]

Self-Help Associations

Workers made a variety of responses to these changes in their conditions. One of the first in England were the so-called friendly societies—mutual help groups that provided rudimentary insurance and other forms of aid to needy members. These hardy and popular associations began to appear in Britain in the mid-1700s. By the latter part of the nineteenth century,[5] they had become significant social institutions in all the industrialized nations of Europe but Germany. By the late 1880s, for example, French mutual aid associations had 1.4 million members, while their English counterparts were estimated to have nearly 4 million participants (membership in English trade unions during this period stood at 1 million).

2. William Blackstone, *Commentaries on the Laws of England,* vol. 1 (New York: Garland Publishing, 1978) (1765), 422.

3. *Politics,* Bk. I, ch. 2–4.

4. Large-scale industry was at the center of economic development, and employment within such industries would come to typify the idea of work. For example, one scholar has indicated that by the end of the 1890s, over half of the labor force of Germany, Belgium, and Britain worked for employers with more than 20 employees. See Bob Hepple, ed., *The Making of Labour Law in Europe: A Comparative Study of Nine Countries up to 1945* (London: Mansell, 1986), 22. Nevertheless, it is important to recall that much paid employment continued (and continues) to be in the service of small employers. Protecting the conditions of these employees, for whom collective representation often is not realistic, has confronted the law with continuing difficulties.

5. These mutual-aid societies were expressly excluded from the sorts of bans that restricted other forms of workers' associations. On these points, see generally Antoine Jacobs, "Collective Self-Regulation," in *The Making of Labour Law in Europe: A Comparative Study of Nine Countries, supra* note 4.

Programmatic Reform Organizations

Programmatic associations of various sorts that typically had as their aim the complete reconstruction of society and the replacement of capitalism represent a second sort of response to the dynamic changes in conditions that industrialization induced. By far the most significant of these organizations in the United States was the Knights of Labor. The Knights was a quasi-religious and fraternal association that had begun as an organization of tailors, but subsequently opened its membership to everyone but bankers, lawyers, and alcohol dealers. As the noted labor scholar Msgr. George Higgins put it, as an organization, the Knights were "fundamentally revolutionary in purpose, but non-revolutionary in method."[6]

The Knights sponsored an ambitious program of moral, social, and economic reform. For example, equal pay for equal work for men and women was one of the stated goals of the Knights' 1878 constitution. Similarly, the Knights by 1886 had sixty thousand African-American members, and when black delegates were refused accommodations during a convention, white delegates walked out of the offending hotel. As part of its efforts to develop alternatives to capitalist forms of economic organization, the Knights also sponsored a substantial number of producer-cooperatives, particularly in the smelting industry. The geographical scope of the Knights' activities was no more circumscribed than the range of their interests. By 1880, the Knights had established affiliations in both Great Britain and Belgium, the latter of which remained vibrant for several years.

The Rise of the Modern Trade Union in the United States and England

The diffuseness of its goals and disagreements over its political directions assisted in the collapse of the Knights. Preceding the collapse was the establishment in 1881 of the first enduring national organization of workers' associations in the United States, the American Federation of Labor (AFL). The constituent member unions that composed the AFL represented skilled workers who were organized strictly along trade lines. From the start, the AFL abjured all political ties—particularly socialist ones. Instead, it adopted a policy of so-called business, or "bread and butter," unionism that has char-

---

6. George G. Higgins, *Voluntarism in Organized Labor in the United States, 1930–1940* (N.p.: Arno, 1960), 20.

acterized American unionism to the present. Although organization of unskilled and semiskilled workers subsequently would occur, the AFL unions established the patterns for labor law and collective bargaining in the United States.

The affiliated unions that constituted the AFL represented what Sidney and Beatrice Webb referred to as the "new model" trade unions. These were large-scale organizations with full-time leadership, increasingly specialized staffs, and highly pragmatic orientations. They emphasized the negotiation of agreements with employers, used strikes sparingly, and accepted the principles of voluntarism.[7]

Continental Socialist Workers' Movements

In contrast to those in England or the United States, workers associations with socialist orientations have played an important role in the development of unions, labor law, and the practice of collective bargaining on the Continent. In Germany, for example, the first national workers' organization, the General German Workers' Association *(Allegemeinen Deutschen Arbeiterverein)* was founded in 1863. Led by Lassalle, it had the chief goal of obtaining universal suffrage. A few years thereafter, Bebel and Liebknecht founded the strongly Marxian influenced Social Democratic Workers' Party *(Sozialdemokratische Arbeiterpartei)*. The merger of these two associations in 1875 marks the founding of the present Social Democratic Party. These parties also supplied the foundation for the development and spread of the so-called free or socialist unions, which typically had as part of their aims the overthrow of capitalism. It was not until the shift to a reformist social strategy in the 1890s that the free unions would engage in collective bargaining or other representational and participative activities in the workplace.

In addition to the free unions, Germany had two other programmatic workers' associations. These were the liberal Hirsch-Duncker unions (found in 1869) and the Christian unions (which were formed after the issuance of *Rerum novarum* in 1891). Both groups were meliorist: they accepted capitalism and sought to improve the standards of workers through collective bargaining and other forms of self-help activities. In terms of numbers at least, these later two associations were far weaker than their socialist counterparts.

---

7. See Jacobs, "Collective Self-Regulation," 216–17; Sidney Webb and Beatrice Webb, *The History of Trade Unionism* (Revised Edition, Extended to 1920) (New York: Longmans Green, 1935), 180–233.

At the turn of the century, the socialist unions counted over 680,000 members. In contrast, the liberal and Christian unions had fewer than 100,000 members each.

Socialist-oriented workers' associations also had important roles in the development of union movements and labor law in France and Italy. In both nations, however, Catholic social thought and Catholic unions exerted a stark influence as well. Perhaps not surprisingly, the Italian Catholic labor movement enjoyed massive growth during the later years of Leo XIII's papacy, which ended in 1903.

Non-Western Workers' Movements

Of course, unions exist outside of Europe and North America, and their rise has typically accompanied the development of mass industry or large-scale agricultural operations. Nevertheless, special problems often have obtained. For example, despite Japan's relatively early and quick industrial development during the first decades of this century, all attempts at establishing any sort of workers' movements there were strongly repressed. It was not until the postwar period that the formation of independent unions and the practice of collective bargaining appeared under the sponsorship of the American occupation government.

In the industrialized West, however, union affiliation surged nearly everywhere in the period between 1890 and 1920. For example, membership in the "free" unions in Germany grew from 50,000 in 1890 to more than 2.5 million by 1913, and more than 7 million in 1922. Similarly, in 1897, at the end of a short but severe depression, American trade unions had 450,000 members. By 1904, their constituency exceeded 2 million, and by 1920, spurred in part by the end of the war, over 5 million persons (about 19 percent of nonfarm workers) held membership.

Employer Responses to Employee Self-Organization

The waxing power of unions drew responses from management that followed similar patterns everywhere. One was simple resistance, which took various forms including blacklists, discharges, "yellow" or "yellow dog" contracts,[8] violence, and various forms of organized antiunion propagandizing efforts. More creatively, management also earnestly sought alternatives to

8. These terms denote a contractual agreement by which an employee agrees not to join a union during the term of his employment.

employee self-organization and collective bargaining. In England, Germany, France, and the United States alike, various forms of employee representation and participation schemes were developed, many of them quite elaborate. These participation schemes were directed at establishing an attitude of trust and willing cooperation with management on the part of employees and a sense of identity with their employer. They thereby would obviate the need for unions, while providing a channel of communication between employees and management, thereby increasing morale and, consequently, productivity and product quality. The present German works-council system is a direct outgrowth of these efforts. Joint employer-employee consultation and productivity committees, semiautonomous work teams, and other "employee involvement" devices (the forerunners of today's participatory schemes) likewise stem from these endeavors. The use of these devices was especially popular in the United States until the passage of the National Labor Relations Act in 1935 made the legality of their use by nonunionized employers highly dubious.[9]

The Role of the State and the Influence of Liberal Anthropology

The role of the state in the evolution of labor law and labor relations systems is a changing one and reflects the shifts in decision-making power that accompanied industrialization. Particularly in Germany, that development went hand-in-hand with the efforts to ground a representative democracy and the social institutions necessary to its support. Indeed, across industrialized nations, the entire struggle over the "social question" can be understood as an endeavor to develop an ordering system for the employment relationship appropriate to conditions in which the large institutions of market and state increasingly had come to predominate. Put slightly differently, workers' associations represent an effort to elaborate an entirely new kind of mediating institution[10] through which individuals could be enabled to participate in the promulgation and administration of the law that most directly affects the day-to-day conditions of their lives. The rise of unions has far less to do

9. On the development of these participative devices and the role of the law in regulating their use, see Thomas C. Kohler, "Models of Worker Participation: The Uncertain Significance of Section 8(a)(2)," *Boston College Law Review* 27 (1986): 499.

10. The term "mediating institution" refers to families, religious congregations, service and fraternal associations, unions, grass-roots political clubs, and the like that mediate the relation between individuals and the large institutions of market and state that characterize so much of contemporary public life.

with some sort of class consciousness than it does with the innate sociality and political nature of the human being—an application of phronesis to an unprecedented set of social contingencies. In short, unions are far more than economic institutions, and their significance as social bodies extends far beyond the bounds of market analysis.

Writing on the eve of the eruption of the industrial revolution in England, Adam Smith well described the initial position of the state and the law toward workers' associations. "We rarely hear," he wrote, "of the combinations of masters, though frequently those of workmen. But whoever imagines, upon this account, that masters rarely combine, is as ignorant of the world as of the subject." When employees do organize themselves, Smith continued, "The masters upon these occasions . . . never cease to call aloud for assistance of the civil magistrate, and the vigorous execution of those laws which have been enacted with so much severity against the combinations of servants, laborers, and journeymen."[11] In fact, these bans had two distinct sources. The first might be called traditional, and its typical expression can be found in judicially crafted bans against workers' combinations in the English common law, and in prohibitions such as those contained in the Prussian General Code[12] that forbade journeymen to form guilds or other organizations to represent their interests.

The second, and more important, source lies at the heart of modern liberalism, and the anthropology that informs it. In this framework, mediating groups of nearly every description are regarded as posing an imminent threat to individuals and the state alike. Indeed, this is one of the few things on which Thomas Hobbes and his greatest critic, Jean-Jacques Rousseau, agreed. Hobbes likened mediating associations to "wormes in the entrayles of a natural man,"[13] and counseled that they were every bit as pernicious. Similarly, Rousseau warned that "for the general will to be well-expressed" it is "important that there be no partial society in the State."[14] These views

11. Adam Smith, *An Inquiry into the Nature and Causes of the Wealth of Nations,* vol. 1, ed. R. H. Campell and A. S. Skinner (Indianapolis: Liberty Classics, 1981) (originally published 1776), 84.

12. «*Die Gesellen machen unter sich keine Kommune oder priviligierte Gesellshaft aus*» preußishes Allgemeines Landrecht II. Teil 8. Abschnitt ¶ 396 (1794).

13. Thomas Hobbes, *Leviathan,* ed. C. B. MacPherson (New York: Penguin Books, 1981), 375.

14. Jean-Jacques Rousseau, *On the Social Contract or Principles of Political Right,* ed. Roger D. Masters, trans. Judith R. Masters (New York: St. Martins Press, 1978), 61.

found their expression in the law that followed in modernity's wake, perhaps most famously in the Loi Le Chapelier of 1791,[15] which banned all forms of workers' associations.[16] Similar restrictions on workers' associations can be found in the English Combination Acts (1800), and like statutes throughout Europe, as well as judicially developed restraints on worker association in American common law.

As the American legal scholar Archibald Cox long ago observed, labor historically has demanded two things from the state: the right to organize and the right to strike. Achieving the de jure (as opposed to the de facto) recognition of these rights, and working out the systems within which they would be protected and circumscribed, would be the work of several decades. During this period, a rather large amount of legal (or extralegal) experimentation with various regimes for ordering the employment relationship would occur.

The Changing Character of Labor and Employment Law

Until the latter part of the nineteenth century, the employment law of England, France, Germany, Sweden, and several of the leading state jurisdictions in the United States was strikingly similar; employment was presumed to be for a period certain (generally fixed by custom) and was terminable only for good cause and after reasonable and customary notice. The emergence of mass markets and large-scale economic organizations dissolved the feudal notions of a personal and ongoing relationship between employer and employed that was the basis for the old employment law model. Its replacement was the so-

15. As formulated and introduced in the French National Assembly, the intentions of Le Chapelier's law were far reaching, and its wording could have come from the mouth of Rousseau himself: "The guild no longer exists in the state; there exists only the particular interests of each individual and the general interest. No one is permitted to encourage an intermediate interest that separates citizens from the community interest through a corporative spirit." (*Il n'y a plus de corporation dans l'état; il n'y a plus que l'intérêt particulier de chaque individu, et l'intérêt général. Il n'est permis á personne d'inspirer aux citoyens un intérêt intermédire, de les séparer de la chose publique par un esprit de corporations*).

16. Article 1 of the Decree stated: The destruction of all forms of guilds constituted by citizens of the same trade or profession being one of the fundamental goals of the French Constitution, it is forbidden to reestablish them under any pretext and under any form whatsoever. (*«L'anéantissement de toutes espèces de corporations de citoyens de même état et profession, étant l'une des bases fondamentales de la Constitution francaise, il est défendu de les rétablir de fait, sous quelque prétext et sous quelque forme que ce soit»*). A decree of 13–19 November 1790 had given workers the right to assemble and combine that the *Loi Le Chapelier* revoked.

called employment-at-will doctrine,[17] which made a roughly contemporane-
ous appearance in Continental, English, and American law alike. The at-will
doctrine began to shift employment law away from the law of domestic relations within which it had first developed to the then quickly developing area
of the law of contracts, in which it in large part has remained.

Like marriage, employment long had been conceived as a relationship
that represented some mixture of status and consent. Depending on the persons and the circumstances, the characteristics of both relationships could
be fixed somewhere on a continuum between these two poles. As the newly emerging law portrayed it, the employment relationship existed almost
wholly at the consent end of this continuum. In the common and civil law
alike, the notion of mutuality provided the justification: the employer or the
employed was free to terminate the relationship at any time. Like the modern
contract theories of political society that preceded them, the development of
the contract theories for legal ordering required a fair amount of inventiveness, which in this instance would come from continental legal scholars and
common-law judges alike. In their full-blown forms (which appeared in the
late nineteenth century), these contract theories exemplify a species of law
that Max Weber characterized as a system of logical rational formalism, that
is, a system that expresses its rules through abstract concepts that are the
creation of the legal theory itself. These rules are regarded as constituting a
complete, "gapless" system that encompasses all contingencies.

Employers undoubtedly appreciated the flexibility the new employment
law extended to them. Nevertheless, as an ordering system, it was unaccept-
able to employers and employees alike. Oddly enough, despite their differences, the new contractually based employment-at-will model of the employment
relationship shared a crucial characteristic with its family law–based prede-
cessor: the notion of a direct, "one-on-one" relationship between employer
and employed. This notion supported a legal fiction central to the new contract model, which portrayed the employment relationship and its conditions
as the result of ongoing bargaining between the employer and the employee.

Of course, this fiction did not reflect the reality of mass employment in
increasingly bureaucratically organized enterprises. What was sought after by employers, employees, and lawmakers alike was some sort of ordering system that would be appropriate for group dealings between employees

17. The doctrine presumes that unless specifically agreed, employment is freely and unre-
strictedly terminable at the will of either party.

and the organizations that employed them. In all parts of the industrialized world, the search after that system would remain a major societal preoccupation until the first two or three decades of the twentieth century. Unions, employer-sponsored worker participation plans, producer cooperatives, various schemes of "welfare capitalism,"[18] and calls for the complete reorganization of society along socialist lines all represent aspects of this search. The collective bargaining models that eventually would emerge represent one important outcome of these experiments in ordering, and their attributes are the product of employers and workers alike. Before turning to a brief consideration of the characteristics of these models, and to a comparative sketch of employment ordering systems, it is appropriate briefly to discuss the role of the Church in the evolution of labor law.

The Role of the Church: The American Example

An adequate description of the influence of the social teachings on the development of employment ordering systems far exceeds the limited bounds of this chapter. Succinctly stated, their impact has been both substantial and pervasive. Naturally, the character of this impact and the means of its expression has varied with time and place. Perhaps nowhere is the influence of the social teachings more palpable, however, than in the United States.

To take but a few scenes from a rich and complex story: Unlike most of Europe, the United States has never had a divided labor movement with separate Catholic or Christian trade unions. In fact, nearly from the start, the relations between the Church and workers' movements in the United States essentially have been friendly and (particularly through the first six decades the twentieth century) markedly cooperative. Once again, brief reference to the Knights of Labor is illuminating.

To protect its members from employer retaliation, the Knights began as a secret organization. Like many fraternal groups, it also maintained various covert rituals. Concerns raised by the activities of clandestine organizations such as the Masons, as well as the Marxist orientations of many workers' associations in Europe, led the Canadian bishops to condemn the Knights. Well-informed about the Knights' actions and programs in the United States,

---

18. This term describes a broad variety of activities from company-built model towns, such as Pullman, Illinois (which was erected in the late 1880s and inspired by employer-sponsored housing developments in Europe), to company-sponsored education and recreation programs.

and fearful that Rome might prohibit American Catholics from involvement in the organization, the American bishops, led by Cardinal Gibbons, successfully came to the defense of the Knights. In 1886, Gibbons drafted a statement on behalf of the bishops, which he took to Rome. The statement explained the role of the Knights and of trade unions in the American context, and admonished that a condemnation of such workers' association might drive a wedge between the Church and its poorest members. The distinguished historian John Tracy Ellis judged this document as one of the most significant the American bishops have produced, since it assisted in preventing any sort of fragmentations within the Church, within the developing labor movement, and between the Church and labor.

The way opened to them, Catholics have remained an integral part of the American labor movement. Indeed, Catholics—and Jews—in the United States have been distinctly more hospitable to becoming members of unions than any other group, and they also have dominated union leadership positions in numbers far disproportionate to their representation in the general population. There are undoubtedly a great many reasons for this, the most obvious being that as members of immigrant groups, many Catholic and Jews had strong financial reasons to become active in and to support unions.

Nevertheless, there appears to be more involved in all this than simple economic interest. For example, workers in the southern United States (where the numbers of Catholics and Jews historically were small) have had similar financial reasons to join unions, yet they traditionally have resisted organization. To condense a lot into a sparse description: habits of thought related to and inculcated by these two religious traditions appear to have had rather a lot do with the general willingness of Catholics and Jews to become involved in or to support unions. Both traditions, for example, place an enormous emphasis on community.[19] Similarly, neither would tend to understand community—at least in its most profound forms—simply in terms of a vol-

---

19. Briefly stated, rather than the sovereign, self-defining self of the Enlightenment, the Catholic or Jewish self is situated by obligation and exists through a web of associational ties with others. In contrast to a self that can know itself in Cartesian isolation, the Catholic self is a "mediated" self, which comes to know God, or anything else, only through participation in a community. Indeed, in this perspective, God discloses himself through others, and it is in serious conversation with others, within and across time, that one literally is inserted into the conversation among the Trinity. In other words, the Catholic and Jewish anthropology of the self, as well as the image of community, stands in stark relief to the images that one finds in secular modernity.

untary association of like-minded individuals. Accordingly, neither tradition emphasizes the supremacy of individual conscience over the norms author-itatively transmitted through the community.[20] As Tocqueville noted, "Ca-tholicism may dispose the faithful to obedience, but it does not prepare them for inequality." In contrast, "Protestantism in general orients men much less toward equality than toward independence."[21]

The "Catholic" attitude toward associational activities and communal ties generally (which might be termed the "subsidiarity attitude"),[22] as well as the American Church's early sympathy for and support of workers' associations (which is an expression of this attitude), set the groundwork for the special character of the relation between the Church and labor in the United States. Added to these factors is one that Tocqueville was the first to point out: the early separation of church and state in the United States has given religion and the religious voice a distinct and special function in American public life. That voice has played an important role in both the labor and the civil rights movements in the United States. These are large topics, however, that are better pursued in another place. It is appropriate here instead to turn to a sketch of labor and employment law systems.

CHARACTERISTICS OF LABOR LAW AND LABOR RELATIONS SYSTEMS

This teaching also recognizes the legitimacy of workers' efforts to obtain full respect for their dignity and to gain broader areas of participation in the life of industrial enterprises so that, while cooperating with others and under the direction of others, they can in a certain sense "work for themselves" through the exercise of their intel-ligence and freedom.

Centesimus annus, ¶ 43

Introduction

As a separate area of law, the law of employment is relatively new. For ex-ample, the first legal treatise dealing strictly with the employment relation-

20. In short, whether they themselves were in any sense "religious," unions and the sorts of habit they require to sustain themselves may have been particularly intelligible to persons of Jewish or Catholic backgrounds. As both groups have become more assimilated into Ameri-can culture, the special intelligibility of unions (and other mediating bodies) has faded.

21. Alexis de Tocqueville, *Democracy in America*, ed. J. P. Meyer, trans. George Lawrence (Garden City: Anchor Books, Doubleday, 1969) (originally published 1835), 276.

22. On the concept of subsidiarity, see chapter 5 in this volume.

ship did not appear in the United States until 1877. Similarly, the first work to treat the individual contract of employment in Italy was published only in 1901. One legal scholar has noted that in many European countries, labor law became recognized as a discrete field only after World War II.

This observation raises a definitional problem. Nearly everywhere, the term "labor law" refers to the law of collective bargaining and collective agreements. In some places, however, and particularly in Germany, the term more widely indicates the entire body of legal regulation that affects the private employment relationship. Broadly speaking, this includes both individual and collective labor law, as well as the law of social security. These operate together as part of an articulated whole, and it is misleading to assess the law regulating the individual employment relationship in isolation from collective labor law.

In contrast, in the United States context, labor law typically designates solely collective bargaining, while employment law specifies protections for the individual employee. These latter include statutory prohibitions of employment decisions based on factors such as race, sex, age, or disabilities, as well as judicially developed protections against unfair dismissal for individual employees. While labor and employment law are not wholly distinct fields, they rest on different bases, and in the final analysis, are intended to achieve rather different goals. Unlike the German system, American employment law has had a piecemeal development, and its various aspects often stand quite independent from one another, and from the law of collective bargaining.

In part, these terminological differences reflect the lack of systemization that is characteristic of common-law methodology, which unlike the approach of the continental civil law systems, is heavily analogic. More importantly, they exemplify two distinctly different responses to the issues raised by the "social question," and to the problems in employment ordering that have risen during the past quarter-century. In many ways, the U.S. and German models represent opposing "ideal types," between which the employment ordering regimes of other industrialized nations fall. For this reason, and because of the influence of Germany and the United States on the legal, social, and economic orders of other nations, they provide useful models for describing and comparing the characteristics of labor and employment law.

The late appearance of labor and employment law is hardly surprising. As has been seen, the search for an ordering regime appropriate to mass employment took several decades to develop. In typical fashion, the law did not lead these developments, but chiefly followed them. The key characteristics of collective bargaining systems had crystallized in most industrialized nations before the outbreak of the First World War. The time for formally instituting what the parties themselves had developed would occur in the decade or so that followed.

The German Model as Continental Prototype

The principal lines of present-day German labor relations law were laid down during the Weimar period (1919–1933). The Central Commission of Co-operation *(Zentralarbeitsgemeinschaft)* reflects the role of the parties in the law's promulgation. The employers' associations and the trade union federation established the committee at the war's end. In so doing, the employers pledged the unhindered recognition of unions, and both parties asserted that collective bargaining should serve as the chief means for ordering the employment relationship. The pathbreaking work of legal scholars such as Phillip Lotmar and, particularly, Hugo Sinzheimer also assisted in establishing the theoretical basis for German labor law and elaborating its contents. The Works Councils Act of 1920, the creation of the labor courts system (1926), and the establishment of a comprehensive unemployment insurance and job placement system (1927) are considered to be some of the most significant legacies of the Weimar era.

Individual Labor Law

German labor law developed as protective law, that is, as law to protect the weaker party to the employment contract. The idea that the state should play a positive role in supporting the individual's development of his or her personality[23] (in part, through assisting to stabilize the employment relationship) runs throughout. Consequently, German labor law presents an imposing edifice of extensive protections for the individual employee. These include broad protections against dismissal, the right to an annual vacation (twenty-four days), regulations concerning maximum daily working hours, the guarantee of continued remuneration in case of sickness, as well as a impressive variety of other statutorily guaranteed rights. Freedom of contract remains the basis of German employment law. However, by creating a statu-

---

23. This right to "the free unfolding of one's personality" *(die freie Entfaltung seiner Persönlichkeit)* is also guaranteed by Article 2 of the German constitution.

tory "scaffolding" that conditions, qualifies, or fixes the permissible terms, the state plays a large role in shaping the nature of the employment relationship.

Collective Labor Law

This relatively high level of state intervention affects but hardly displaces the significance of collective bargaining in the German employment ordering scheme. In the German conception, collective bargaining represents an autonomous lawmaking scheme that both embodies and operates according to the principle of subsidiarity.[24] As the German Constitutional Court characterizes it, the collective bargaining process entrusts to the parties the crucial task of the "meaningful ordering of working life" *("sinnvolle Ordnung des Arbeitslebens").*[25]

In keeping with the idea of contractual freedom, the collective bargaining agreement sets only the minimum employment conditions,[26] which become part of the terms of the contract between the individual employee and the employer. These minimum terms may be improved, but not reduced, through individual agreement. Similarly, by operation of the law, the collective agreement binds only an employer who has assented thereto and the employees who are actual members of the union that negotiated it. In actual practice, however, employers generally extend the collectively bargained conditions to all employees in the workplace. According to the so-called principle of contractual unity *(Prinzip der Tarifeinheit),* only one collective bargaining contract will govern the conditions of a given workplace.

Although they are possible, collective agreements between a single employer and a union are unusual. Typically, collective agreements are concluded between individual unions and an association of employers at a branch or regional level. This pattern of settlement precludes collective agreements from taking into consideration the particular problems and conditions of a

---

24. Thus, as one scholar and member of the German Constitutional Court notes, "the collective bargaining system proves to be a sensible restriction of governmental lawmaking. . . . With the negotiation of pay and other conditions of employment, the parites to the collective agreement truly take on tasks whose fulfillment by the state in a free democracy hardly would be possible." A. Söllner, *Grundriß des Arbeitsrechts* 121 (11. Auflage 1994).

25. BVerfGE 4, 107; 18, 27.

26. Accordingly, Germany has no minimum wage legislation. Minimums are set through the patterns established in collective bargaining.

specific business or workplace, and complicates, if not forecloses, direct employee involvement in the employment ordering process. It is at the latter, grass-roots level that the distinctive German labor relations institution, the works council *(Betriebstrat)*, exists and exerts its influence. The works council represents the chief means by which workers participate in management decision making. As such, it constitutes a central feature of the German employment relations system.

The Works Council and Workers' Participation

As previously noted, the works council traces its development to management efforts to develop alternatives to autonomous, self-organized employee associations. After World War I, the Weimar Constitution (Art. 165) called for the creation of establishment workers' councils *(Betriebsarbeiterräte)*, which would become part of a hierarchical system of workers and economic councils. These were to culminate in an Imperial Economic Council *(Reichswirtschaftsrat)*, comprising employers' and workers' representatives, which would review and give opinions on any draft legislation concerning social or economic matters. The Economic Council was to have the power to propose legislation as well. With the enactment of the 1920 Works Councils Act, only the first level of this scheme was realized. To secure its passage, however, the act had to be tailored in a way to make it acceptable to the conservative majority in Parliament. This resulted in the works councils standing separately from the unions, and being confined to representing the employees of only one employer. Thus, the works councils established by the 1920 act closely resembled the alternatives to collective bargaining that employers had developed in the nineteenth century. Not surprisingly, the unions had many misgivings about and objections to this structure, which strongly were reiterated with the reintroduction of the works councils system in the Works Constitution Act of 1952. These concerns and dissatisfactions were at least to some extent addressed in the 1972 amendments to the statute.

The institutional separation between the unions and the works councils continues to exist in form, but substantially less in fact. Presently, an overwhelming majority of the members of works councils are also union members. This gives the unions influence over and direct communication with the works councils. It also permits the works councils to serve as direct grass-roots links between the unions and individual workplaces. In short, the works councils system largely is grounded by its relationship with autonomous employee associations. While the employer is responsible for their economic support, the works councils consist solely of employee representatives who are selected by their colleagues.[27] Unlike the unions, which represent only their actual members, the works council represents the entire employee complement in the workplace. Although the law requires them in every workplace with five or more employees, many small and medium-size employers have no works council.

The works councils have extensive participatory rights that include personnel and economic as well as social matters. These rights are backed up by the employer's duty to supply the works council with any information necessary to the effectuation of its tasks. The law also establishes several areas where the works council has a codetermination right. The employer may effect no decision on matters that fall within the scope of this right without having received the express consent of the works council. In other words, on these topics, the works council has a managerial right that is coextensive with the employers'. The works council and the employer may also promulgate a "works agreement" *(Betriebsvereinbarung)*. The agreement constitutes a contract between the employer and the works council and may settle matters over which a codetermination right exists. In some ways, however, the works agreement resembles the collective bargaining agreement because it may also establish minimum conditions that have a normative effect on the individual employees' contract with the employer. To prevent the undermining of the collective bargaining system, however, works agreements are prohibited over topics that are treated in a collective agreement. This is a very broad prohibition. So long as an employer operates in a geographical region or a branch of industry where a collective agreement exists, works agreements over subjects treated in the collective agreement are banned. This is true even if the employer is not itself a party to the collective agreement. This rule reflects the importance of the collective bargaining system in the German scheme of labor relations.

The Anti-type: The American Model of Collective Labor Law

Several aspects of the American system of "free" collective bargaining stand in rather sharp relief to the German model. In the American scheme, the state establishes and sanctions a voluntary ordering system, but leaves

---

27. The law has been interpreted broadly; generally speaking, only persons who exercise significant managerial discretion are foreclosed from works council participation.

the outcomes achieved through the process to be determined wholly by the parties, free of governmental influence. This regime represents an example of what Gunther Teubner terms a "reflexive" legal scheme. The goal of reflexive law, Tuebner states, is "regulated autonomy" or controlled self-regulation. Reflexive legal schemes entail minimal state intervention in the ordering of relationships because they rely on market mechanisms to shape their results.[28]

In the United States, the term "collective bargaining" virtually is synonymous with the Wagner Act. The core goal of the statute is to protect and enhance individual status through the defense and maintenance of freely formed and autonomous employee groups. This feature defines the statute and characterizes the unique position that it holds in American law. The Act represents the only place in an otherwise highly individualistically oriented jurisprudence where the law has encouraged the formation of mediating bodies through which to promote individual empowerment and to foster self-determination. In the final analysis, the Wagner Act rests on a distinctly different idea of the character of human personhood than that which typically informs American law.

Congress enacted the Wagner Act in 1935. In so doing, and in contrast to the rest of the industrialized world, Congress deliberately opted for a system that would involve minimal state intervention in the employment relationship. As in the German conception, collective bargaining in the United States can be understood as a private lawmaking system. In contrast to the German conception, however, the chief function of the collective agreement in the United States context is not to establish a set of minimum employment conditions that strictly apply only to the union's members. Instead, the American collective bargaining agreement elaborates in a binding fashion all aspects of the employment relationship for all the employees in the affected workplace. Thus, the United States Supreme Court has described the collective bargaining agreement as not just a contract, but "a generalized code" through which the employment relationship can be "governed by an agreed-upon rule of law."[29]

The promulgation and administration of this law is largely the responsibility of the affected parties alone. Consequently, American collective bar-

28. Gunther Teubner, "Substantive and Reflexive Elements in Modern Law," *Law and Society Review* 17 (1983): 229, 254-55.

29. *Steelworkers v. Warrior and Gulf Navigation Co.*, 363 US 574, 580 (1964).

gaining agreements typically erect a private dispute resolution system—the grievance arbitration process—that the employer and union jointly administer. These systems generally have jurisdiction over nearly every sort of dispute that might arise concerning the employment relationship. The presence of an arbitration system normally precludes the courts or other arms of the state from adjudicating matters that come within the parties' dispute resolution scheme.

The so-called exclusivity principle bottoms the American model of collective bargaining. It also marks one of the starkest differences between the American and German industrial-relations systems. The exclusivity principle rests on the idea of majority rule. The principle establishes the association formed by a majority of employees in the affected workplace unit as the exclusive representative of them all. The principle prohibits an employer from attempting to bypass the majority-designated representative by unilaterally changing the terms or conditions of employment, or by dealing with individuals or groups of employees independently of the union. The preferred status the majority representative enjoys in this scheme carries with it the obligation to represent all employees fairly, regardless of their support for or membership in the union.

The exclusivity doctrine prevents the fragmentation and dissolution of the strength employees achieve through collective action. It thereby acts to protect the principles of majoritarianism that underpin the act's scheme. The exclusivity principle also reflects the fact that American workers generally organize and bargain on a workplace or employer basis, and not on a regional or industry-wide basis. To a substantial degree, the principle is a function of the emphasis in American-style collective bargaining on local, "bottoms-up" lawmaking. The centrality of exclusivity to the act's scheme reveals the statute's preoccupation with the removal of impediments to the free formation of autonomous, self-organized employee associations.

In adopting the act, Congress intended to institute a comprehensive, uniform, and flexible system through which the employment relationship could be ordered. Hence, rather than attempting to adjust specific problems legislatively, the Wagner Act left it to the parties themselves to promulgate arrangements appropriate to their circumstances. The chief significance of the American collective bargaining scheme lies in the opportunity it provides to involve people in making and administering the law that most directly determines the details of their daily lives. The process both permits and requires people to decide for themselves the kind of people they will be, and to explain and justify those choices to one another. Succinctly stated, American-style collective bargaining provides employees with a powerful means to participate in a broad spectrum of managerial decisions, which it accomplishes through establishing the lawmaking process at a grass-roots basis. Accordingly, the American labor law scheme also represents a concrete embodiment of the subsidiarity principle.

American Employment Law

During the past twenty years, the practice of collective bargaining in the United States steadily has declined. In contrast to "traditional" labor relations law, two sources of employment law have become of increasing significance in the American context. The first of these are statutorily guaranteed protections against discrimination in employment decisions based on factors such as race, color, creed, sex, or the national origin of an employee. These are far-reaching protections that are primarily contained in the famous Title VII of the Civil Rights Act of 1964. The Age Discrimination in Employment Act of 1967 (which prohibits age-based employment decisions and covers all employees over the age of 40) and the recent Americans with Disabilities Act (1992) are modeled after Title VII and extend that statute's protections against discrimination in employment. Unlike the Wagner Act, however, the rights created in these employment discrimination statutes are not intended to involve workers in the ordering process. Rather their goal is to open and extend employment opportunities, particularly for socially disadvantaged groups, by prohibiting management from the use of the statutorily outlawed criteria as the foundation for employment-related decisions. The rights these enactments create are individual rights that exist as a matter of positive law. With very limited exceptions, these rights are held by all persons, regardless of their status in the workplace hierarchy. The American employment discrimination statutes, and the remedies that have been developed for their enforcement, and especially affirmative action programs, have had substantial influence on foreign legal systems. Germany, England, the European Union, Canada, and India are a few examples of jurisdictions where the American model has been used as a pattern for lawmaking.

Judicially developed restrictions on unfair discharge represent a second source of contemporary American employment law. These restrictions began to be developed by the courts during the late 1970s and early 1980s. These developments were conscious reactions to two phenomena: the decline of unions and the practice of collective bargaining in the United States, and the growing instability in employment relationships, particularly among long-term, relatively well compensated managerial employees. Like the employment discrimination statutes, the remedies these judicially developed doctrines provide are chiefly litigation driven. Once more, their goal is not to provide employees with an opportunity to engage in the employment ordering process, but to prevent employment termination for arbitrary reasons. The protections they afford individuals against discharge are nowhere near as generous as those available under German law. In short, the United States remains, formally at least, a "hire and fire" society, with opportunities to dispute the discharge if one has the access to legal help and the ability to endure the arduous litigation process. Capital mobility, and not employment stability, represents an attitude that stamps the character of American employment law generally.

THE SIGNIFICANCE OF LABOR
AND EMPLOYMENT LAW

For the "health" of a political community—as expressed in the free and responsible participation of all citizens in public affairs, in the rule of the law and in respect for the promotion of human rights—is the necessary condition and sure guarantee of the development of the "whole individual and of all people."

Sollicitudo rei socialis, ¶ 44

The significance of the employment order for the authentic development and unfolding of our personhood lies at the heart of the entire social tradition. From the first, the social encyclicals have reiterated, illuminated, and explicated this crucial theme in a variety of ways, in light of "the signs of the times." Developing and responding to the implications of this insight constituted the life's work of such luminaries as Bishop Wilhelm Emmanuel von Ketteler, Albert-Maria Weiss, Albert de Mun, Oswald von Nell-Breuning, Cardinal Henry Manning, and Dorothy Day, to name but a very few. Consequently, an extended discussion of this theme is neither necessary nor appropriate. Instead, it may be useful to select from this rich and nuanced body of teachings a few points that bear particular emphasis in the present economic and social context.

A distinct set of insights into the anthropology of the human person orients and conditions the social teachings. One of the key understandings is the fact that humans are self-constituting beings. As such, we make ourselves to be what we are through the activities in which we habitually engage. Consequently, as Aristotle, Aquinas, and Augustine (among others) were at pains to remind us, it is the seemingly insignificant routines and actions of daily life that make all the difference. For it is through them that we literally are forming ourselves as individuals and as a society.

It is precisely its impact on the everyday, the concrete, and the particular that marks the real significance of the order governing the employment relationship. This law touches individuals more directly and frequently than virtually any other aspect of a public or private ordering regime. This has been true at least since the time of the industrial revolution. But presently, it is true for far more people, and a far greater proportion of the world's populace. For better or for worse, men and women are tied to the market and to paid employment in a way never before seen. The worldwide increase in labor force participation, particularly among women, is one of the most striking social developments of the past fifty years.

A few statistics help to illustrate this point. In the United States, for example, about 93 percent of adult males participate in the labor force, a figure that has remained roughly constant for several decades. Since 1950, however, women's workforce participation has risen by more than 200 percent. Nearly three-quarters of all women aged 25 to 54 are employed, the overwhelming proportion of them full-time (i.e., working thirty-five or more hours per week). Not surprisingly, the great majority of mothers presently are also active (and mostly full-time) workforce participants. Working hours for women have been increasing steadily during the past twenty years. Additionally, one major study shows that after years of gradual decline, the normal American workweek has increased to the point where the average employee works the equivalent of an additional month more than was worked in 1970.

In short, working for pay now occupies more of the time of more people in industrialized nations than ever. The job has become a central part of most adults' lives, and being employed or seeking employment is the way people spend the lion's share of their waking hours. Simply put, the employment order involves far more than simply wage rates, power relationships, "competitiveness," productivity, or workplace voice. It quite literally involves the constitution of human beings.

The preoccupation of the Church and the social teachings with such apparently mundane and unfashionable institutions as unions and employment law may seem surprising, even nostalgic. Whether and how people participate in decisions about the criteria for promotions, job training, health benefits, the dismissal of a fellow employee, or the best way to handle a novel or sensitive employment-relations question can appear trivial. But it is a tremendous error to regard such matters as being unworthy of serious attention. Individuals and societies alike become and remain self-governing only by repeatedly and regularly engaging in acts of self-government. It is the habit that sustains the condition. This point represents part of the significance of collective bargaining as an institution. By affording individuals the means to participate in administering the order of the employment relationship, collective bargaining can instill and strengthen the habits of direct responsibility and authentic self-rule.

The real worth of unions lies in the contributions they can make in assisting the full development of human personality, the proper unfolding of which can be determined only through a set of values that truly are intelligible. To consider how we are to live together, in concrete, daily situations, forces us to ask what it truly means to be a person. The institutions that support this sort of workplace self-determination, and that provide employment protections generally, are coming under increasing stress. A brief outline of these problems is appropriate here.

THE CURRENT STATUS OF LABOR LAW AND
LABOR RELATIONS SYSTEMS

[T]he highly developed social life, which once flourished in a variety of prosperous and interdependent institutions, has been damaged and all but ruined, leaving virtually only individuals.

Quadragesimo anno, ¶ 78

Since the onset of modernity, the farseeing among us have warned about the spread of a particular sort of individualism that would erode the mediating bodies that constitute civil society. Nevertheless, Tocqueville believed that the family would be one institution that could survive modernity's atomizing forces, while Durkheim thought that the employment relationship would provide people with the stable bonds to others that the disappearing institutions of social life once had supplied. Neither has proved to be the case. A quick glance over the social and work-life landscape reveals the following:

(1) Membership in autonomous employee organizations is declining nearly everywhere. For example, union membership in the private sector in France presently stands at 5–6 percent, a figure that one noted French labor scholar

describes as a "critical threshold." Similarly, union density in the United States has declined from a level of about 35 percent in the late 1950s to a bit under 8 percent in the private sector today. In 2004, Japanese union density rates declined to under 20 percent. Although Germany is the home of the world's largest trade union, and despite the centrality of collative bargaining to its labor relations system, German unions also have experienced substantial membership losses.

(2) In the United States at least, union decline is part of the generalized decline of all the mediating groups in society. In fact, union decline has been something of a leading indicator for the decline of mediating bodies in the United States as a whole. The fact that union decline has occurred at roughly the same time that families, churches, fraternal and service groups, grassroots political clubs, and similar mediating institutions began to deteriorate should come as no surprise. No single mediating structure is likely to flourish in the absence of others. All require and can engrain the same sorts of habits: decision, commitment, self-rule, and direct responsibility. No single institution alone can inculcate or restore these habits. The existence and decline of all these bodies is mutually conditioning. The collapse or deformation of any one of them threatens the rest.

(3) The employment relationship is changing and in many cases is much less a "relationship" than formerly:

(a) In the U.S., so-called contingent employment arrangements (part-time, temporary and limited-term contractual arrangements) are on the rise. One well-known observer of labor market trends characterized these arrangements as "just-in-time" employment. As American businesses seek to become more competitive, she predicted, "all employment relationships are going to become more fluid." Many commentators forecast that businesses increasingly will have only a "core group" of long-term employees, supplemented as needed by contingent workers.

(b) Likewise, employment leasing arrangements also are becoming increasingly popular. Under these arrangements, an employer contracts with a third-party to supply its employee complement. These arrangements pose challenges to collective bargaining and related employee representation and participation systems.

(c) "Self-employment" is also a rising phenomenon, at least in the U.S. Lawrence Mishel and Jared Bernstein[30] state that "Much self-employment is disguised underemployment, as can be seen from the fact that self-employed workers earn far less than those on regular payrolls." According to the authors, the self-employed have more education than their wage-earning counterparts. Nevertheless, self-employed women earn only 63 percent as much as salaried women. The income differences between self-

---

30. *The State of Working America*, 1994–95 (Armonk, NY: M. E. Sharpe, 1994).

employed and salaried men are negligible. However, the educational gap between the two groups of men is greater than between self-employed and salaried women. The self-employed also typically have fewer benefits.

(4) The workplace itself is increasingly less one "place." So-called telecommuter arrangements are on the rise, both in the United States and in Germany. For example, as early as 1989, 10 percent of the Chicago area employees of AT&T were working at locations other than company facilities, many of them at home. The term "virtual workplace" describes what many believe will typify the work world, which will be accompanied by an increasing isolation from one's coworkers.

(5) The newly emerging patterns of work organization mean that it will be increasingly difficult to distinguish between "employees" and nonemployee "independent contractors," who are owed no benefits and with whom no expectations of continuing work relationships are created.

(6) It is also becoming increasingly common for the employees of several businesses to work together at one workplace; thus, some employees simply do not work at a site owned or controlled by their own employer. In Germany, for example, such arrangements have put the works council system under great stress.

(7) Job stability is a major preoccupation everywhere. For those with jobs, however, pay instability may also be a matter of increasing concern. So-called variable pay plans, which tie pay to continuous profit or productivity improvements, are becoming increasingly popular with management.

(8) In light of the changes in employment, one German scholar has described German labor law as "a tanker in the fog." If so, the various aspects of American labor and employment law appear more like a disorganized squadron of boats, several of which have struck shoals. As the practice of collective bargaining has declined in the United States, there has been a corresponding increase in the piecemeal and ad hoc regulation of employment through the states and Congress. A blue-ribbon presidential commission on the future of U.S. labor relations has urged that non-litigation-based models be used to handle employment disputes. Similarly, a U.S. federal court system report has recommended that all non–civil rights employment matters be removed from federal court jurisdiction.

Of course, not all aspects of the above-described developments are undesirable. Telecommuting and flexible working hours may permit employees more freedom to determine their own working conditions. They also may afford women with young children more opportunities for participation in the workforce. Flexible employment arrangements and pay plans also give skilled and so-called knowledge workers greater ability to select the sorts of projects and tasks they wish to work on, and to earn considerably more. New patterns of work organization have done away with multiple levels of supervision, thereby giving some employees more ability to determine for themselves how to perform their work, and a greater range of tasks to perform. For the skilled and well-educated, such changes may be liberating. One pressing question is how equitably these chances for greater self-determination will be distributed.

CONCLUDING OBSERVATIONS

Toward the end of last century the Church found herself facing an historical process which had already been taking place for some time, but which was by then reaching a critical point. . . . A traditional society was passing away and another was beginning to be formed—one which brought the hope of new freedoms but also the threat of a new forms of injustice and servitude.

Centesimus annus, ¶ 4

Two decades ago, Czeslaw Milosz observed that "contrary to the prediction of Marx, this is the central problem of the twentieth century. Instead of the withering away of the state, the state, like a cancer, has eaten up the substance of society."[31] No doubt exists about the corrosive impact of the state on the institutions of civil society. Nevertheless, markets appear increasingly to be consuming the ordering capacity of the state, and to have outstripped its power of initiative. This does not mean, *pace* Marx, that we are being carried helplessly along by the tides of some ineluctable historical or natural force that lies beyond our control. It does mean that old patterns of ordering are breaking down, and that new patterns are seeking to emerge.

What emerges is not simply a matter of blind chance. Humans are free, reasonable, and responsible beings. As such, we play a constitutive role in history. The legal, social, and economic orders that condition our lives are the products of human choice and reflect series of judgments that certain ways of being are preferable to others. Each of our choices, as individuals and

---

31. Nathan Gardels, "An Interview with Czeslaw Milosz," *N.Y. Review of Books* (20 Feb. 1986): 34.

as societies alike, shifts probabilities. By making choices and acting on them, we bring situations into being that did not have to exist. At the same time, those choices establish conditions that make certain consequences more or less likely. In short, as St. Paul teaches, the fact that we are free means that we bear the awesome responsibility of working out our salvation "in fear and trembling."[32] We cooperate as active agents in the completion of history.

All of this may sound rather removed from labor and employment law. It is not. As Cardinal Newman pointed out over a century ago, economics embodies a set of claims about the character of our personhood. As such, it represents a moral system, a point that was very clear to Adam Smith, who grounded his economic writings on his extensive work in moral theory. Hence, as Smith observed, there is a reflexive relationship between market arrangements and liberal social institutions. The purpose of free markets is to promote individual self-determination and material well-being, thereby supporting the conditions for self-rule.

Authentic freedom and self-rule require a background. Modern capitalism, however, has a strong tendency to overwhelm and eventually to dissolve the discrete, local, and particular institutions—which Edmund Burke called the "little platoons" of social life—that provide this background. These grassroots institutions are the places where the habits of self-rule are practiced and learned. Regrettably or otherwise, there is no invisible hand that guarantees their existence, nor that automatically checks the centripetal forces that modern markets exert.

The future contours of labor and employment law are unclear. Increasingly, however, the trend has been the cabining and dissolution of opportunities for working men and women actively to participate in the promulgation and administration of the order that most directly affects their day-to-day conditions. Briefly stated, working people at nearly all levels of the economy are becoming the objects of administration rather than active and self-determining agents. Such conditions are in the most serious sense inhuman.

One thing is certain. Institutional orders inconsistent with our human character will not survive. Consequently, the most pressing question of our time is whether, and to what degree, the prevailing notions of our personhood are accurate. Everything turns on our answers to this query. The emergence of new patterns of ordering provides the perfect opportunity to revisit this question, in light of the Church's tradition.

---

32. *Philippians* 2:12.

[10]

CONTRACT LAW

A Catholic Approach?

JAMES GORDLEY

I am going to describe the approach to contract law of an influential group of jurists in the sixteenth and early seventeenth centuries. Historians call them the "late scholastics," or the "Spanish natural law school." As I have shown elsewhere, they were the first to give the law of contract a theory and a systematic doctrinal structure.[1] Before they wrote, the Roman law in force in much of Europe had neither. For all their subtlety, the Romans were not theorists. Neither were the medieval professors of Roman law, who were concerned chiefly with reconciling every Roman legal text with every other. In contrast, the late scholastics tried to explain Roman law by philosophical principles drawn from their intellectual heroes, Thomas Aquinas and Aristotle. Some have called their intellectual movement a Thomistic revival. Some of the leading figures were Catholic theologians as well as jurists, and priests as well as professors: for example, the Dominican Domingo de Soto (1494–1560) and the Jesuits Luis de Molina (1535–1600) and Leonard Lessius (1554–1623). Nevertheless, their work deeply influenced the Protestant founders of the northern natural law school, Hugo Grotius (1583–1645)

This essay was presented March 4, 2001, at a symposium on Catholic perspectives on American law at The Catholic University of America's Columbus School of Law.

1. James Gordley, *The Philosophical Origins of Modern Contract Doctrine* (Oxford: Clarendon Press, 1991), 69–111.

and Samuel Pufendorf (1632–94) who adopted many of their conclusions and disseminated them through northern Europe, paradoxically, at the very time when the spread of modern critical philosophy was discrediting the Aristotelian and Thomistic philosophical principles on which these conclusions had been based. Indeed, in its broad outlines, the approach of the late scholastics can still be seen in the work of eighteenth-century natural lawyers[2] and the drafters of the French Civil Code,[3] although by then, its philosophical origins had been forgotten. A sharp break with the past was not made until the rise of so-called will theories of contract in the nineteenth century.

Elsewhere, I have argued that we need to understand contract law much as the late scholastics did if we are to make sense of it at all.[4] Here, I will merely outline their approach and describe how it enables one to solve some problems concerning contracts of exchange that puzzle modern theorists. In particular, I will show how it enables one to explain why such contracts are enforced at all, why they are not enforced when they are unfair, and how the intention of the contracting parties can extend to matters that the parties never consciously considered. I will then ask whether one can describe the approach of the late scholastics as a "Catholic" one.

These three questions have been notoriously difficult since the rise of the nineteenth-century will theories. As A. W. B. Simpson has said, these theories treated the will of the parties as a sort of *Grundnorm* from which as many rules of contract law as possible were to be inferred.[5] Yet the will theorists did not explain why the will of the parties should be respected. Contracts, by definition, were binding obligations that, by definition, were formed by expressing the will to be bound. As Valérie Ranouil said of the French will theorists, "[t]he contract is obligatory simply because it is the contract."[6] If the contract was merely the will of the parties, its fairness was not a matter about which the courts should be concerned. As Joseph Story said: "Every person who is

---

2. Ibid.

3. Ibid.

4. James Gordley, "Contract Law in the Aristotelian Tradition," in *The Theory of Contract Law: New Essays*, ed. P. Benson (Cambridge: Cambridge University Press, 2001), 265.

5. A. W. B. Simpson, "Innovation in Nineteenth Century Contract Law," *Law Quarterly Review* 91 (1975), 266.

6. Valérie Ranouil, *L'Autonomie de la volonté: naissance et évolution d'un concept* (Paris: Presses Universitaires de France, 1980), 72, quoting Eduard Gounot, "Le principle de l'autonomie de la volonté en droit privé: contribution a l'étude critique de l'individualisme juridique" (thesis, Paris, 1912), 129.

not from his peculiar condition under disability is entitled to dispose of his property in such manner and upon such terms as he chooses; and whether his bargains are wise and discreet or profitable or unprofitable or otherwise, are considerations not for courts of justice but for the party himself to deliberate upon."[7] As a result, the conception of will on which contract law was supposed to be founded was a narrow one. The parties willed whatever they had consciously decided, whatever their reason for deciding it might be. It therefore became puzzling that the law holds the parties to many obligations that they never consciously considered. The reason the law does so, from the standpoint of the will theories, could be neither that these obligations are fair nor that the parties intended to assume them.

Today, the will theories are in discredit, in large part because they were unable to solve problems such as these. When jurists address them today, they are more likely to step outside their own discipline and use the language of economics. For that reason, I will be concerned with economic explanations. I will outline why I think they do not work, and why, to find solutions, we need to turn to the older tradition in which the late scholastics were writing.

In this tradition, contracts of exchange were described as acts of commutative justice. While distributive justice secures, for each citizen, a fair share of "honor or money or other things that fall to be divided among those who have a share in the constitution," commutative justice preserves the share that belongs to each. In involuntary transactions, in which one person has taken or destroyed what belongs to another against the other's will, commutative justice requires the one who did so to pay compensation so that his victim's original share will not have been diminished. In voluntary transactions, in which each party agrees to give something to the other in order to receive something in return, commutative justice requires that the resources exchanged be of equal value so each party's share remains the same.[8] One of the core concepts with which the late scholastics built their theory was this idea that sale, lease, and other contracts of exchange were acts of commutative justice in voluntary transactions.

The resources a person received mattered because for Aristotle, Aquinas, and the late scholastics, man has an end that they help him to realize. This

7. Joseph Story, *Commentaries on Equity Jurisprudence as Administered in England and America*, 14th ed., vol. 1 (Boston: Little, Brown, 1918), 337.

8. Aristotle, *Nicomachean Ethics* V.iv 1130b–1131a; St. Thomas Aquinas, *Summa theologiae* II-II, Q. 61, aa. 1–3.

end is to live a distinctively human life, a life that realizes, so far as possible, one's potential as a human being. Because man is a social animal, part of living such a life is helping others to live it as well. Living such a life is the ultimate end to which all actions are a means, either instrumentally or as constituent parts of such a life. In identifying the actions that contribute to such a life, a person exercises an acquired ability—a virtue—that these writers called "prudence." In following the dictates of prudence, the person may need other virtues as well, such as the courage to face pain and danger or the temperance to forgo pleasure. External things are of value to the extent that they contribute to such a life. Distributive justice secures for each person the wealth he needs to obtain them. Commutative justice enables him to obtain them while at the same time being fair to others by not diminishing their share of wealth.

One of the merits of this account, in my view, is that it identifies the conditions under which enforcing contracts of exchange will contribute to human happiness or welfare. One condition is that people use their purchasing power to acquire the resources they should in order to live such a life. Another is that they have the purchasing power they should have to acquire these resources. In Aristotelian terminology, contract contributes to human welfare to the extent people exercise the virtues of prudence and distributive justice.

If most American lawyers were asked why the law enforces contracts of exchange, they would probably not mention prudence and distributive justice. They would probably speak the way economists do. For an economist, contracts of exchange increase welfare because they make both parties better off, at least in their own judgment, at the time they make the contract. Welfare is maximized when the parties have entered into every possible mutually beneficial exchange. At that point there is no way to make one party better off without making another worse off. Such a state is said to be "efficient," or more technically, "Pareto efficient."

To me, one advantage of the approach of the late scholastics is that it becomes possible to see why the economists would be right about welfare if they made one small addition to their account: if they explained that there are virtues of prudence, courage, temperance, and justice, and that their account is correct only to the extent people actually practice these virtues.

Let's begin with the virtues concerned with making and sticking with a choice: prudence, courage, and temperance. If there is an end to human life, and all the things we acquire are a means to it, and if we have an ability to choose the things that serve this end, then there is a reason why contracts of exchange will promote human welfare. They enable each party to obtain things that help him toward his end.

An economist would not explain the matter that way. Once, many economists were utilitarians. They spoke of quantities of satisfaction and thought that a person chose in order to obtain the largest amount he could. Satisfaction need not be physical: a person could choose to be a martyr or a scholar, and if he did so, the reason was that he obtained the most satisfaction that way. Otherwise, he would have done something else.

That approach runs counter to our moral intuitions. If a boy tears wings off flies, or a man commits a rape, we do not think the tragedy is mitigated to any degree by his own satisfaction. Moreover, there is no reason to imagine that such choices, or the choices of the martyr or the scholar, or that of a thirsty man to drink beer on a hot day, are all made to obtain one single thing called "satisfaction," which accompanies each of them and for the sake of which each choice is made.

In any case, few economists today are utilitarians. As Paul Samuelson noted fifty years ago, most no longer believe in quantities of satisfaction—"in the existence of any introspective magnitude or quantity of a cardinal, numerical kind." They have discovered that to draw their supply and demand curves and build their models, they merely need to assume that people do prefer some courses of action to others. Preference is defined in terms of what a person actually chooses: he always chooses what he prefers at the time. As noted earlier, welfare is then defined in terms of enabling more people to choose what they prefer.

But why, then, is welfare supposed to be good, and a reason for enforcing contracts? One possibility is that it is good for people to get what they prefer if what they prefer is good, and that they have some ability to tell whether or not it is. But then we are talking about prudence in the Aristotelian sense whether we use that word or not. Another answer would be that people choose what they find most satisfying for themselves, and that increasing their own satisfaction is good, at least for them. But then we are back to utilitarianism. A third answer is that getting what one chooses is good ipso facto. One is, by definition, better off. That seems to be the answer of economists who define welfare in terms of preference and preference in terms of choice, and then assume that welfare is a good thing.

But that seems to defy common sense. I have put a hypothetical case to six leading economists, one of whom won the Nobel Prize. A man whose yacht was sinking radioed his position to the Coast Guard. He was told that, for whatever reason, it could not reach him for six days. He stepped into a life-boat with a six-pack of beer, which is all he had on the yacht to drink. He knew (never mind how) that if he drank only one can a day, he would survive. Instead, he drank four the first day and two the second, and was found dead on the sixth. Is this "efficient" in the sense that it satisfies his preferences without making anyone else worse off? Five economists said yes. The sixth (as it happens, the Nobel Prize winner) said that it couldn't happen.

Economists who take this position are making claims more radical than Aristotle, Thomas Aquinas, and the late scholastics, who merely said that *we* sometimes choose rightly, and we have abilities that enable us to do so. The economists' position seems to be that ipso facto we always choose what we prefer, and therefore what is welfare-maximizing, without any presuppositions about our abilities.

We can say, then, that a person's choices promote his welfare, properly understood, insofar as they are made prudently, courageously, and justly. Before we conclude that contracts of exchange promote welfare insofar as they are the product of such choices, however, we must ask how wealth is distributed. Our wealth sets limits to the choices we can make, and consequently, it may limit our ability to acquire things that enable us to live the distinctively human life that is our ultimate end. In the extreme case, if we cannot buy food, we cannot live at all. Aquinas and the late scholastics said that if a person finds himself in such extreme necessity, he is entitled to take what he needs to survive.[9] It would not be stealing. His right to live trumps another's right to live better. Aquinas also said that if a person has more than he needs to live the life that he should, he is obligated to give the rest away.[10] In between these extremes, one can speak of better or worse distributions of wealth, or to put it another way, of distributive justice. According to Aristotle and Aquinas, which distribution is just will depend on the kind of society one lives in. In a democracy, the ideal is an equal distribution. In an aristocracy in their sense—meaning rule of the virtuous, not the rich or well born—the ideal is that each has wealth in proportion to virtue, which means, in proportion to his ability to lead a distinctively human life.[11] But that is the ideal. On a practical level, they understood that one purpose of private property is to give

9. St. Thomas Aquinas, *Summa theologiae* II-II, Q. 66, a. 7.

10. Ibid., a. 2.

11. Aristotle, *Nicomachean Ethics* V.iv 1131b–1132b; St. Thomas Aquinas, *Summa theologiae* II-II, Q. 61, a. 2.

people an incentive to work.[12] Those who do work that pays more will have more, whatever their needs. They implicitly recognized that many random events can affect how wealthy a person is, such as whether his property is destroyed by chance. Presumably, they thought that in an imperfect world, one could not always attain the ideal. Still, one could speak of a just distribution of wealth, however much practical considerations made it necessary to compromise the ideal. To the extent that the distribution is just, people are able to acquire what they need to live as they should. Because, to that extent, there is a reason why people should have the wealth they do, there is a reason why goods should go to those who pay most for them.

Economists, however, do not say that to the extent wealth is justly distributed, welfare is increased when people contract. Once, utilitarian economists did think the distribution of wealth mattered to welfare. If spending an additional dollar brought less satisfaction to a rich man than a poor one, wealth should be distributed more evenly. An even distribution may seem fair to people in a democratic society. The utilitarian's reason, however, is that money should go to whoever derives the most satisfaction from spending it. That is an ideal which would appeal to few. According to this ideal, a person who likes to buy art only to destroy it should have less money, not more. Moreover, as before, to think of maximizing people's satisfaction is to imagine that people choose to obtain one thing, satisfaction, which accompanies each choice.

As mentioned, most economists have given up utilitarianism. They do not claim one can compare the importance of one person's preferences to that of another. Consequently, most of them cannot see how one distribution of resources could be better than another. They merely claim that given any initial distribution of resources, a contract of exchange is "efficient" in the sense that it will increase welfare. It will make both parties better off without making anyone else worse off. That is an improvement, given the initial distribution of wealth.

Actually, it is quite possible that those who enter into these contracts will make others worse off by bidding up the price of goods that others could have afforded more easily.[13] But the more fundamental objection, it seems to

---

12. Aristotle, *Politics* II.v.; St. Thomas Aquinas, *Summa theologiae* II-II, Q. 66, a. 2.

13. As noted by Michael Trebilcock, *The Limits of Freedom of Contract* (Cambridge: Harvard University Press, 1993), 58; Richard Posner, "Utilitarianism, Economics and Legal Theory," *Journal of Legal Studies* 9 (1979): 103, 114.

me, is that those who take this approach are not merely taking the initial distribution of wealth for granted. They are also taking for granted the rule of law that says that people may sell what they own to the highest bidder. If that rule is enforced, then, indeed, whatever the distribution of wealth, a contract will make both parties better off (although I would add, only assuming those parties choose rightly). But why should we take it for granted that, whatever the distribution of wealth, this rule promotes welfare? And, indeed, to do so assumes the very thing to be proven. For we are seeking a reason why welfare is improved if goods go to whoever pays most for them.

To illustrate, imagine a world in which nearly all the wealth is held by a small group who live in decadence while the rest go hungry. Suppose that one of the wealthy people buys a side of beef. Many people might think it a definite improvement in welfare if someone like Robin Hood took the beef and gave it to someone who is poor. If the rich person then tried to buy it back, many might think it a further improvement if someone took the money he offered away and gave it to the poor person as well. Admittedly, if goods must go to whoever pays the most, the poor person with the beef will be better off (if he has chosen rightly) selling it to the rich person. But why should we assume that it increases welfare to have that rule in force? And if we assume it does, then we have assumed that welfare is increased when goods go to whoever pays the most, which was the proposition in dispute.

Moreover, this proposition is far from obvious. As noted earlier, Aquinas and the late scholastics believed that it would not be stealing for a person in desperate want to take what he needed. In times of war or famine, governments suspend the rule that goods go to whoever will pay the most. They ration. An economist could say these are aberrational cases. But what they indicate is that the normal rules do not apply when the distribution of wealth or its consequences are sufficiently aberrational.

We should not conclude that economics is a false science. We should merely conclude that economists' conclusions about welfare maximization are valid only on the assumption that people are practicing virtues that the economists never mention. The late scholastic approach to contract law does not overlook that point. That is one of its advantages.

A second advantage is that it explains how a contract can be unfair. Modern American law recognizes that it can be. In some cases, American courts have refused to enforce a contract because the price was unfair. In others, they have refused to enforce unfair auxiliary terms.

Following Aristotle and Thomas Aquinas, the late scholastics said that a contract of exchange is an act of voluntary commutative justice. The parties exchange at a just price, a price at which the value of what each gives equals the value of what he receives. As modern scholars have noted,[14] writers in this tradition thought that normally, unless public authority set a price, the fair price was the market price under competitive conditions. They knew that this price varies from day to day and from region to region. It has puzzled scholars that these writers expected exchange at such a price to preserve equality.

That problem did not trouble most people before the nineteenth century, and, in my opinion, it should not trouble us. For Aquinas, the late scholastics, and, for that matter, for the seventeenth- and eighteenth-century natural lawyers, the fair price of goods was the market price at the time and place of the sale. They understood perfectly well that this market price had to fluctuate to reflect factors that they called need, scarcity, and cost, which correspond to what we today call supply and demand.[15] Normally or eventually, they thought, the seller who charged the market price would recover his costs. Therefore, normally or eventually an exchange at the market price does not make either party richer at the other's expense. In that sense, it is a fair price. Often, they knew, prices will fluctuate and the seller will recover more or less than his costs. But that situation had to be tolerated. In their view, prices had to fluctuate because they had to reflect not only cost but need and scarcity. They seem to have regarded the market price as the fairest price practicable.[16] Moreover, they realized that exchange at the market price is fair in the same way a bet can be fair: the party who wins if prices change could

14. John Noonan, *The Scholastic Analysis of Usury* (Cambridge: Harvard University Press, 1957), 82–8; Raymond de Roover, "The Concept of the Just Price and Economic Policy," *Journal of Economic History* 18 (1958): 418; Giovanni Ambrosetti, "Diritto privato ed economia nella seconda scolastica," in *La seconda scolastica nella formazione del diritto privato moderno*, ed. P. Grossi (Milan: Giuffrè, 1973), 28.

15. See Thomas Aquinas, *In decem libros ethicorum expositio*, ed. A. Pirotta (Turin, 1934), lib. 5, lec. 9; *Summa theologiae* II-II q. 77 a. 3 ad 4; Leonardus Lessius, *De iustitia et iure, ceterique virtutibus cardinalis libri quatuor* (Paris, 1628), lib. 2 cap. 21 dub. 4; Ludovicus Molina, *De iustitia et iure tractatus* (Venice, 1613), disp. 348; Domenicus Soto, *De iustitia et iure libri decem* (Salamanca, 1556), lib. 6 q. 2 a. 3; Hugo Grotius, *De iure belli ac pacis libri tres*, ed. B. J. A. de Kanter–van Ketting Tromp (Leiden, 1939), II.xii.14; Samuel Pufendorf, *De iure naturae et gentium libri octo* (Amsterdam, 1688), V.i.6.

16. See Gordley, *Philosophical Origins*, 98–101.

just as easily have lost. As Soto observed, "as the business of buying and selling is subject to fortuitous events of many kinds, merchants ought to bear
risks at their own expense and, on the other hand, they may await good for-
tune."[17]

I have argued elsewhere that this theory makes sense of the relief that
our courts now give when a price is so high or low as to be "unconsciona-
ble."[18] Nearly always the person who gets relief paid more or took less than
the market price. In some cases, he agreed to such a price because, like a
shipwrecked sailor in need of rescue, he was physically cut off from normal markets. In some cases, he agreed out of ignorance. For example, a New
York court gave relief to a man who had bought a refrigerator from a door-
to-door salesman for three times the price he would have paid in a nearby
store.[19] In contrast, our courts would not give relief, and we ourselves would
have little sympathy, if a person complained that he had been cheated on the
price of his house because six months after he bought it, housing prices fell,
so that he lost money by buying when he did. He could just as easily have
won. Moreover, there is no way to eliminate the risk he ran without freezing
housing prices and facing the evils that economists describe: stocks of un-
sold housing or queues of buyers. It seems to me, then, that this older theory explains our own intuitions and those of our courts about when a price is
fair. Moreover, far from contradicting a modern economic understanding of
prices, the theory can actually be sharpened by the insights of modern economics. We can see more clearly today how, in a long run, the seller would
recover his costs, and what evils would ensue if we tried to eliminate price
fluctuations by freezing prices.

For Aquinas and the late scholastics, the principle of equality also explained how the auxiliary terms of a contract could be unfair. The performance terms of the contract specify what is to be exchanged. Auxiliary terms
govern other matters: for example, whether the seller warrants his goods
against defects. In Roman law, the seller was liable for defects unless the con-

17. *De iustitia et iure* lib. 6, q. 2, a. 3.

18. James Gordley, "Equality in Exchange," *California Law Review* 69 (1981): 1587.

19. *Jones v. Star Credit Corp.*, 298 NYS2d 264 (Sup Ct 1969). See also *Frostifresh v. Reynoso*,
274 NYS2d (Sup Ct 1966), rev'd as to damages, 281 NYS2d 964 (App 1967) (relief given when
refrigerator that had cost the seller $300 sold for $900 plus $250 credit charges); *American
Home Improvement Co. v. MacIver*, 201 A2d 886 (NH 1964) (relief given to party who agreed
to pay $1,750 plus $800 in credit charges for purchase and installation of fourteen windows, a
door, and coating for sidewalls to his house).

tract specified otherwise. Aquinas explained that unless the seller is liable, equality would be violated since a party would have paid the price for sound goods and received defective ones.[20] According to Molina, the parties could agree that the seller would not be liable. But they could do so only if the seller reduced his price and so preserved equality.[21]

Here again, it seems to me that the teachings of modern economics not only are compatible with those of the late scholastics but can clarify them. Suppose the parties to a contract were fully aware of the risks and burdens that its auxiliary terms place on them and of the cost of bearing them. According to an economist, the parties would place the risks and burdens on the party who could bear them most cheaply and adjust the price to compensate him. If a buyer would pay $100 to be rid of a risk, a seller who wishes him to assume it must offer at least a $100 reduction in the price. A seller would do so only if he could not bear the risk himself more cheaply. It might be he could eliminate the risk by some preventative measure that costs only $80. Or it might be that he would be willing to bear the risk for $80 for the same reason that an insurance company can better bear a risk than its customers. It can better bear the risk of fire than a homeowner because it runs the same risk over and over and can set off the extra money it makes when it wins against its losses when it loses. If, for either reason, the seller were willing to bear the risk for $80, he would never transfer the risk to someone who would only bear it for $100. Agreeing to reduce the other party's risk is like improving a product: anyone who can do it for $80 and sell it for up to $100 will do so. That is so independent of any assumptions about the bargaining power of buyers or the competitiveness of the market.

An economist would say that a contract that compensates each party for the risks and burdens that he assumes would be efficient. We can now see, however, that it would also preserve commutative justice as these earlier authors understood it. The price would have been adjusted for the risks and burdens placed on each party. Conversely, if, in a particular case, we are convinced that a contract places a risk or burden on the party least able to bear it, we can conclude that both parties did not fully understand the risks and burdens the contract entailed, and that the party bearing them was not fully compensated for doing so. The other party was able to take advantage of his ignorance. I have argued elsewhere that the cases in which courts have held

20. St. Thomas Aquinas, *Summa theologiae* II-II, Q. 77, aa. 2–3.
21. Molina, *De iustitia et iure* disp. 353.

terms to be unfair are precisely those in which it seems clear that a risk or burden was placed on the party least able to bear it.[22] That party could not have been fairly compensated. The late scholastic approach explains why he should be entitled to relief.

We can now see why the late scholastic approach has yet another advantage. It can also explain how the intention of the contracting parties can extend to matters that they never consciously considered. There are a host of auxiliary terms that the law reads into a contract when the parties have not otherwise specified. Such terms make up a large part of the law of sales, the law of leases, the law of partnership, and so forth. They are sometimes called the "implied terms" of a contract. Given what we have said, we can see how a court should determine which terms to read in. They should be the terms that are fair. Fair terms place the risks and burdens of a contract on the party who can most easily bear them. An economist would agree that such terms should be read into the contract, although he would say they are efficient rather than fair. According to Richard Posner, one of the founders of the law and economics movement: "The task for a court asked to interpret a contract to cover a contingency that the parties did not provide for is to imagine how the parties would have provided for the contingency if they had decided to do so."[23] As we have seen, an economist would expect the parties to place risks or burdens on whoever could bear them most easily. But let us now consider the relationship between these terms which the court reads in and the terms to which the parties consciously agreed.

In the technical language of the late scholastics and Aquinas, when a person acts for an end he consciously intends, he "virtually" intends the means to it. Suppose I buy a car. Do I intend to buy a cam shaft? I may never have heard of one. But the car won't work properly without the cam shaft, and I intend to buy a properly working car. I "virtually" intend to buy the cam shaft. And, of course, I would consciously intend to buy it if the matter were explained to me and I were asked.

It is the same with the terms of the contract if the parties intend an act of commutative justice. If so, they want not only to exchange but to do so on fair terms. For Aquinas or the late scholastics, this is the one intention they could have that the law would respect. The purpose of contracts of exchange is to enable the parties to exchange without either party enriching himself at

---

22. Gordley, "Contract Law in Aristotelian Tradition," 318–23.
23. Richard Posner, *Economic Analysis of Law*, 6th ed. (New York: Aspen, 2003), 105.

the other's expense. Of course, one of the parties might not intend to treat the other fairly. In that case, however, the law must treat him as though he did. It is as though one of the parties contracted with no intention of carrying out his side of the bargain. He is using a legal institution—contract—for a purpose of his own that the law does not respect rather than for the purpose for which it is intended. The law must treat him as though he had an intention that the law will respect.

We have seen, then, that this older approach to contract law had solutions to problems that became perennially troublesome after it was abandoned. My final question is to what extent it can described as Catholic. The architects were Catholic jurists participating in a revival of Thomistic philosophy. As we have seen, at the pinnacle of the theory was the idea that human life has an ultimate end. As Catholics, these jurists believed that this end is to know, to love, and to serve God. Contact enables us to obtain the external things we need for that end while treating others fairly, which belongs to that end as well. Love of God and neighbor, however, are not specifically Catholic ideals, nor specifically Christian ones. Thomas Aquinas and the late scholastics themselves thought that their conclusions about contracts were matters of natural law, not divine law, and therefore valid wherever people make contracts. That is why they thought they could learn from non-Christians such as Roman jurists and Greek philosophers. It is why non-Catholics such as Hugo Grotius could learn from them. Grotius turned to their work to find principles that both Protestants and Catholics could respect.

Indeed, Grotius and the late scholastics thought that these principles could be respected by nontheists. In a famous passage, Grotius said, "all we are about to say [of law] would still hold if one were to accept, which one cannot without the utmost wickedness, that there is no God or that He has no interest in the affairs of men."[24] Scholars have observed that here again, he echoed the words of the late scholastics.[25] As Catholics, we wish a nontheist had a clearer idea of his ultimate end. Yet a nontheist who is not a moral agnostic could believe that there are better and worse ways of living of our lives; that we have a capacity, albeit an imperfect one, to know which ones are better; that external things can contribute to a better life; that we there-

---

24. *De iure belli ac pacis* prol. § 11.

25. Anton-Hermann Chroust, "Hugo Grotius and the Scholastic Natural Law Tradition," *New Scholasticism* 17 (1943): 101, 114–16; Michel Villey, *La formation de la pensee juridique moderne,* 4th ed. (Paris: Montchrestien, 1975), 346–47, 611–13.

fore should choose wisely what we acquire; that respect for others is part of living a better life; that others should have a fair share of the resources they need to live a good life, and that we should respect the share they have. These are the principles on which the older approach to law was founded. It was not rejected because it was Catholic. It was rejected because these principles were called into question with the rise of modern critical philosophy. If this older approach is useful, and I believe it is, we can be proud as Catholics that is was built by Catholic authors, but also proud that it can speak to others.

PROPERTY LAW: CATHOLIC SOCIAL THOUGHT AND THE NEW URBANISM

A Shared Vision to Confront the Problem of Urban Sprawl?

❦

VINCENT D. ROUGEAU

A STORY OF A SPRAWLING AMERICAN PLACE

South Bend, Indiana, is a city of close to 100,000 people that lies some ninety miles east of Chicago, just south of the Michigan state line. Its smaller sister city of Mishawaka, which is home to about 50,000, is immediately adjacent to the east. Together, the two form the urban center of St. Joseph County, which has a total population of around 250,000. Strategically located between Chicago and Detroit, South Bend and Mishawaka were once thriving centers of automobile-related manufacturing, but that era ended over forty years ago when the Studebaker Corporation, long a South Bend institution, closed its doors for the last time. After a difficult period of economic decline, the region has found new life in recent years as a center for retail, transportation, and medical care. It is also home to the University of Notre Dame, which is now the largest employer in the county.

Apart from a few affluent enclaves, South Bend and Mishawaka contain most of the region's lower-income, blue-collar, and nonwhite households. With a few exceptions, the white-collar middle and upper-middle class has fled both cities. This has fueled a housing explosion in the surrounding unincorporated parts of the county, creating a hodgepodge of subdivisions—from standard to deluxe in their housing styles—loosely tied or completely unconnected to any municipal government, public services, or community institutions. Although suburban flight came late to this region—it began in earnest in the 1970s and 1980s—it nonetheless followed a highly predictable pattern. What started as a trickle for bigger houses, more land, and the ever-so-elusive piece of the "American dream" became a flood when the South Bend schools were placed under a desegregation order in the early 1980s. Once school busing began, housing construction outside of South Bend exploded, and the fastest growing areas of the county were those in school districts not covered by the desegregation plan. A separate school system and a virtually all-white population allowed Mishawaka to benefit from some of this flight, primarily through aggressive annexation of suburban shopping areas, and Mishawaka has now become the retail shopping hub for north central Indiana and southwest lower Michigan.

Although county services and government, designed for a farming community, were woefully inadequate to the task of serving tens of thousands of suburban newcomers, legislators from the newly affluent county pushed bills through the state house designed to make it extremely difficult for South Bend and Mishawaka to annex additional territory.[1]

Despite the lack of sewers, adequate roads, and public water systems, the subdivision dwellers were unwilling to be annexed into existing jurisdictions where needed services were already in place. They did not want to pay additional taxes, nor do they want to participate in the difficult interracial and interclass interactions of city governance. They wanted to be left alone. Thus began the "sprawling" of St. Joseph County, Indiana, a story so ordinary in modern American history that it hardly bears reporting in detail.[2] Like so many other American cities, South Bend is now the unattractive hole in a

1. In 1993, the Indiana annexation statute was amended to make it easier for landowners in certain jurisdictions to defeat an annexation attempt. The only jurisdiction that met the population requirements necessary to be covered by the legislation is St. Joseph County. See Ind. Code 36-4-3-13(e) (1993) (amended 1999, current version at Ind. Code 36-4-3-13(g) (2003)). A 1999 amendment to the same legislation allowed a simple majority of affected landowners to defeat an annexation in St. Joseph County, whereas 65% of affected landowners are required to defeat annexation in the rest of Indiana. Ind. Code § 36-4-3-13(g) (2003). In 2003, this latter provision was found to violate the Indiana Constitution's provisions against special legislation. See generally *Municipal City of South Bend v. Kimsey*, 781 NE2nd 683 (Ind 2003).

2. "Sprawl" has become a widely accepted term for describing the low-density American

doughnut of suburban affluence, home to poorly functioning public schools and the site of the vast majority of the region's poverty-related social problems. Cheap gasoline, cheap rural land, limited land use regulation, changing lifestyles, and America's unresolved racial demons dispersed the bulk of the region's population into larger homes on former farm fields and woodlands outside the city limits. Rural roads designed for tractors have become clogged with commuter and shopping traffic, and a once distinctive agricultural and wooded countryside has been transformed into a fairly typical American suburban tableau.

Although most people do not associate Indiana with the history of Catholic immigration to the United States, South Bend and Mishawaka have always been ethnic, Catholic towns, and the names in the telephone book have more in common with those in Chicago than with those in Indianapolis. Early settlers included French fur trappers, who were followed in the nineteenth century by Poles, Italians, Hungarians, and Belgians, who came to staff the growing factories. For ethnic Catholics, American suburban sprawl has raised particularly troubling issues, since many of these people found themselves on the front lines of urban social change in the 1950s, '60s, and '70s. Although some were happy to leave their city neighborhoods (whatever the reasons), many others have lived to regret the loss of the coherent urban parishes that fostered the rich community life so essential to living out an authentic Catholic faith. Indeed, the physical structure of a community, like the structure of government, has an important role to play in the creation and maintenance of a communal social life:

> A human is not an individual who lives for himself or herself alone. The modern idea of the autonomous person misses the reality of that which is social. Certainly, the Christian conception about humans has always held fast that they possess an independence and a personal responsibility for what they do. At the same time it has emphasized that a human is a social being. . . .
>
> Social life does not develop of its own doing. The solidarity and unity in values and goals need a judicial-organizational structure.[3]

---

metropolis. Indeed, academics have begun to measure the "sprawl phenomenon." In "Measuring Sprawl and Its Impact," researchers from Cornell and Rutgers Universities defined sprawl as "low-density development with residential, shopping and office areas that are rigidly segregated; a lack of thriving activity centers; and limited choices in travel routes." Reid Ewing et al., Smart Growth America, *Measuring Sprawl and Its Impact* (2002), 7, http://www.smartgrowthamerica.org/sprawlindex/MeasuringSprawl.PDF.

3. A. Rausher, "Institutions of Social Organization: Family, Private Property, State," in

One of the worst features of American suburban sprawl is that it is a strikingly concrete representation of a broader retreat of individuals from the nation's communal life. As the pursuit of private comforts and the realization of personal preferences has become a priority for most people, many of the structures of our nation's common life have been allowed to atrophy.[4] In the face of this privatization of American life, more people have begun to question the nation's ability to actualize fundamental common values and goals that support our democracy.[5] Indeed, when one examines the response of American law to the phenomenon of sprawl, it is quite apparent that certain legal regimes have enhanced the retreat into private suburban enclaves and semiprivate municipalities, fostering the deterioration of a sense of common purpose in America's metropolitan areas.

In the pages that follow, I will discuss the New Urbanism, a response to suburban sprawl that has come from the architectural profession. After a brief description of the new urbanist movement, which, although still in its infancy, has become quite influential in real estate development around the world, I will consider the challenges New Urbanism has encountered in the areas of American local government and zoning law. I will conclude with an analysis of New Urbanism and metropolitan sprawl from the perspective of Catholic social thought and argue that Catholic visions of the human person and community have been undermined in the sprawling American metropolis. Although New Urbanism has been legitimately criticized for certain elitist tendencies, I will argue that its broad principles are fairly consistent with Catholic visions of the common good, subsidiarity, and solidarity. Indeed, Catholic thought provides a theoretical underpinning to New Urbanism that gives intellectual substance to the aesthetic vision New Urbanism hopes to create, and challenges certain traditional understandings of American local government that have encouraged selfish individualism, wasteful materialism, and abandonment of communal responsibilities to the poor.

Principles of Catholic Social Teaching, ed. David A. Boileau (Milwaukee: Marquette University Press, 1998), 71–72.

4. See, e.g., Robert D. Putnam, *Bowling Alone: The Collapse and Revival of American Community* (New York: Simon and Schuster, 2000).

5. See, e.g., Mary Ann Glendon, *Rights Talk: The Impoverishment of Political Discourse* (New York: Free Press, 1991); Christopher Lasch, *The Revolt of the Elites* (New York: W. W. Norton, 1995); Michael Sandel, *Democracy's Discontent* (Cambridge: Harvard University Press, 1996).

THE NEW URBANISM

The movement now known as New Urbanism traces its beginnings to a meeting in 1993 in Alexandria, Virginia. At that time, a group of 170 architects and urban designers met to discuss their concerns about "the placelessness of modern suburbs, the decline of central cities, the growing separation in communities by race and income, the challenges of raising children in an economy that requires two incomes for every family, and the environmental damage brought on by development that requires us to depend on the automobile for daily activities."[6] By 1996, the group had formed the Congress for the New Urbanism (CNU) and had developed a charter for the organization ("Charter") that outlined a vision for "an American movement to restore urban centers, reconfigure sprawling suburbs, conserve environmental assets, and preserve our built environment."[7]

The Charter is directed primarily to the fundamentals of a New Urbanist vision for development and design. Its twenty-seven principles are divided into three sections entitled "The Region: Metropolis, City, and Town"; "Neighborhood, District, and Corridor"; and "Block, Street, and Building." Each section has nine principles that serve to explain the foundational concepts of New Urbanism. The Charter begins with a preamble, which functions like the general clause of a civil code. It is in this preamble that one finds the animating ideas of New Urbanism. Thus, in order to understand what the New Urbanism is all about, it is useful to consider the preamble in full:

The Congress for the New Urbanism views disinvestment in central cities, the spread of placeless sprawl, increasing separation by race and income, environmental deterioration, loss of agricultural lands and wilderness, and the erosion of society's built heritage as one interrelated community-building challenge.

We stand for the restoration of existing urban centers and towns within coherent metropolitan regions, the reconfiguration of sprawling suburbs into communities of real neighborhoods and diverse districts, the conservation of natural environments, and the preservation of our built legacy.

We recognize that physical solutions by themselves will not solve social and economic problems, but neither can economic vitality, community stability, and environmental health be sustained without a coherent and supportive physical framework.

6. Shelley B. Poticha, "Foreword to the Charter of the New Urbanism," in *The Charter of the New Urbanism,* ed. Michael Leccese and Kathleen McCormick (New York: McGraw-Hill Professional, 2000), 1.

7. Ibid., 2.

We advocate the restructuring of public policy and development practices to support the following principles: neighborhoods should be designed for the pedestrian and transit as well as the car; cities and towns should be shaped by physically defined and universally accessible public spaces and community institutions; urban places should be framed by architecture and landscape design that celebrate local history, climate, ecology, and building practice.

We represent a broad-based citizenry, composed of public and private sector leaders, community activists, and multidisciplinary professionals. We are committed to re-establishing the relationship between the art of building and the making of community, through citizen-based participatory planning and design.

We dedicate ourselves to reclaiming our homes, blocks, streets, parks, neighborhoods, districts, towns, cities, regions, and environments.[8]

Anyone who has spent time in a city designed prior to mass automobile ownership will recognize that the New Urbanism is not really "new" at all, but an attempt to reclaim a traditional, human-scale urban design that reflects and respects local culture and enhances the social integration of the community. In other words, the planning assumptions in New Urbanism use human beings as the point of reference for development decisions, and its models are the great cities of Europe, as well as early American cities such as Boston, Charleston, Annapolis, or New Orleans. In the United States, however, the point of reference for most development since World War II has been the automobile. Planners and architects have assumed that most people will drive rather than walk to the places they want to go, and that most people prefer to live in enclaves that are segregated by income and lifestyle.

Furthermore, since the 1950s, most suburban local governments have implemented a type of zoning that mandates rigid separations between residential, commercial, and industrial land uses.[9] When automobile use is assumed as the primary mode of transportation, commerce can be segregated at some distance from residential development, and industrial development can be

---

8. *The Charter for the New Urbanism*, v–vi.

9. "The institution of zoning may be said to be inherently discriminatory because it is exclusionary by nature. The heart of the zoning process is to separate land uses by districts, which necessarily means that all uses will be excluded from a particular district except those which are specifically or conditionally provided." Robert R. Wright and Morton Gitelman, *Land Use: Cases and Materials*, 4th ed. (Eagan, MN: West, 1991) 2, "Zoning, from the point of view of the average citizen, created a hierarchy of districts, culminating in the single-family residential district. This 'highest' district was to be protected, not only from commercial and industrial incursions, but also from structures which might house more than one family, such as duplexes, townhouses, and apartments." Ibid., 940.

placed even farther away in "industrial parks." This segregation of uses helped to enhance socioeconomic and racial segregation as the suburbs expanded by creating a model that encouraged monolithic, geographically isolated developments of homes in specific price ranges. Whereas traditional urban living required a certain amount of social mixing, particularly on public transportation and in major shopping and employment districts, long distances, the need for an automobile, and exclusionary zoning fostered the creation of suburban developments that were designed to appeal to fairly narrow socioeconomic groups, such as upper-middle-class families with children. Initially, de jure and de facto segregation kept these areas racially monolithic as well, but since the 1980s, there has been a notable increase in the racial and ethnic diversity of many suburban areas, particularly around the nation's larger cities.[10]

NEW URBANISM CONFRONTS AMERICAN LOCAL GOVERNMENT

The legal structures imposed by American local government, particularly in the area of zoning, were, and continue to be, a formidable obstacle to the New Urbanist movement. As is clear from the preamble, three important goals of New Urbanism are (1) the creation of mixed-use developments that combine living, working, and commerce in a coherent urban community of walkable neighborhoods; (2) the mixing of incomes, classes, and ethnic groups within individual neighborhoods, villages, towns, and cities; and (3) the orientation of planning and government policy to the metropolitan region. Yet, because exclusionary zoning has now become the legal standard in most American jurisdictions, many of the architectural and design techniques that the New Urbanism employs to encourage these goals are difficult to implement or illegal.

---

10. The results of Census 2000 suggested that "racial and ethnic diversity is rising in America's suburbs." William H. Frey, *Melting Pot Suburbs: A Census 2000 Study of Suburban Diversity* (Washington, DC: Brookings Institution, 2001), 2. Overall, suburban minority populations within the country's 102 largest metropolitan areas rose from 19.3% in 1990 to 23.7% in 2000. Ibid. Some of these gains, however, were concentrated in a relatively small number of cities known as "melting pot metros." Ibid. Yet, even outside of these areas dramatic increases in suburban minority populations occurred. For example, in the area around Portland, Oregon, the percentage of African Americans living in the suburbs doubled during the 1990s. Gordon Oliver, "Suburbs Suit Portland, Ore., Residents of Color; Minorities Snap up Homes," *Oregonian* (29 October 2001).

In his book *City Making,* Gerald Frug has argued that in the area of land use and zoning, most American suburban communities view themselves as autonomous entities, as opposed to "situated subjects" that exist in an intimate relationship with a central city and broader metropolitan region.[11] Exclusionary zoning has developed out of this framework of false autonomy:

> The United States Supreme Court and most state courts have allowed localities to decide their zoning policies in the interests of their own residents with little regard to their effect on outsiders. . . . The impact of this aspect of local government law on America has been profound. It has fostered not only the suburbs' ability to exclude potential residents but also their ability to recruit them: in a country where people frequently move, racial, ethnic, and class segregation can survive only if there are clear boundary lines that indicate where the "right" kind of people live. Suburban boundaries have also helped to engender a suburban consciousness that combines the felt legitimacy of suburban separation with an acceptance of the benefits of race and class privilege. Fears of racial and class integration, desires to protect "home and family, property, and community," and allegiance to suburban separateness have defined and reinforced each other.[12]

Confirmation of Frug's observations is easily found in any American metropolitan area, and the experience of South Bend/Mishawaka as described earlier fits squarely within this model. Hostility toward the cities from St. Joseph County residents provided the necessary political support for the anti-annexation legislation, and the two cities have done little to improve the situation. Despite their being contiguous, there is very little meaningful cooperation between predominately white Mishawaka and more racially diverse South Bend.

In the suburbs, mixed-use and mixed-income development designed to appeal to a broad cross-section of a metropolitan population strikes at the heart of a key aspect of local autonomy that has long been accepted in American law—the ability to exclude. Furthermore, because much of the funding of public goods and services in the United States takes place at the local as opposed to the state or federal level, the democratic rhetoric of localism in the United States has provided an egalitarian cover to a structure that inhib-

---

11. Gerald E. Frug, *City Making: Building Communities without Building Walls* (Princeton: Princeton University Press, 1999), 76–77. Frug draws on the work of Charles Taylor, Michael Sandel, Michael Walzer, and others to develop the idea that the identity of a suburb is meaningful only in its relationship to a city, drawing parallels to the philosophical treatments that argue that the identity of the "self" can be understood meaningfully only when situated in relationship to other persons. Ibid., 73–74.

12. Ibid., 77.

its the downward distribution of wealth in American society.[13] Lacking a hereditary class hierarchy, Americans have tended to use "ability to pay" as an important means of exclusion in suburban localities, and as a way of maximizing the benefits they receive from local tax expenditures. Most suburban jurisdictions manipulate their zoning and planning legislation to prevent the introduction of poorer or socially disfavored groups into the community. Social segregation based on wealth is generally seen as a reasonable expression of private personal preferences based on income and, unlike racial segregation, is both legally and socially sanctioned.[14]

New Urbanist developments hope to encourage economic mixing by incorporating design principles that have long been rejected by most American suburbs. For example, traditional urban neighborhoods tended to offer a mix of housing styles in close proximity. Row houses on side streets might

13. The history of localism's impact on American politics is well documented. For example, in *Democracy In America* (ed. Harvey C. Mansfield and Delba Winthrop [Chicago: Chicago University Press, 2000]), Alexis de Tocqueville argued that the township played an integral role in preserving American democracy by providing both a mechanism for the expression of individual freedom and a political structure in which to breed a "spirit of freedom." Ibid., 57–58. Indeed, it was America's respect for the equality of individuals' freedom and autonomy created in the township that de Tocqueville saw as integral to the emphasis American society placed on the acquisition of wealth and, in particular, individual self-sufficiency. Ibid., 267–74.

14. Many commentators have pointed out the tendency for suburban municipalities to become enclaves of privilege under the legal cover of local autonomy. Huge disparities exist among jurisdictions in terms of the level of public services offered, and there is a tendency to concentrate the least desirable land uses in jurisdictions with high concentrations of poor or minority residents. For example, Richard Briffault argues that "[m]ore affluent localities can . . . use their regulatory authority to maintain their preferred fiscal position. To the extent that more affluent localities are able to deploy exclusionary zoning techniques as an informal wealth test that keeps out newcomers who bring less to the locality in tax base than they cost in local services, these localities can continue to offer better services and/or hold down their taxes." Richard Briffault, "The Local Government Boundary Problem in Metropolitan Areas," *Stanford Law Review* 48 (1996): 1115, 1136. Building on Briffault, Sheryll Cashin notes that this phenomenon creates a "tyranny of the favored quarter," whereby certain high-growth, high-income suburbs representing about 25% of the population of many American metropolitan regions capture the lion's share of the regions' infrastructure expenditure and job growth: "theoretical justifications for local governance should be tested against the empirical reality of the favored quarter. The collective action problem wrought by fragmented local governance creates a system in which the 'free riders' are the most privileged people in our society." Sheryll D. Cashin, "Localism, Self-Interest, and the Tyranny of the Favored Quarter: Addressing the Barriers to New Regionalism," *Georgetown Law Journal* 88 (2000): 1985, 1990.

be mixed in with large homes on main boulevards and apartment buildings at major intersections. Retail shops catering to the neighborhood would be placed at these same intersections, perhaps on the ground floors of the apartment buildings. Additionally, the large homes might have separate ancillary structures like garage apartments, on alleys, that could be leased to a tenant. New Urbanists have attempted to reintroduce many of these principles in their neighborhood design, but most American suburbs forbid all of these things. Zoning laws do not allow the mixing of retail and residential development, attached housing and detached housing are generally disfavored within the same neighborhood, and most local ordinances or subdivision covenants in suburban areas forbid the creation of more than one living space on one lot.[15] In fact, the tendency toward socioeconomic segregation in American suburbs is so strongly entrenched that many New Urbanist developments have been absorbed into the existing structure rather than offering an alternative to it.[16]

HOW SHOULD CATHOLICS RESPOND TO NEW URBANISM?

One of the most compelling ways to evaluate New Urbanism and the issue of suburban sprawl from a Catholic perspective is through the rich body

15. Developers have had to go to tremendous lengths to gain exceptions from traditional zoning codes or comprehensive plans in order to create communities under the principles of New Urbanism. In many cases communities have rejected the developments outright, but through the use of a process called a "charette," which is a visioning and planning meeting opened to the general public, New Urbanists have been able to convince many communities to change their zoning rules. When people are asked what they want in new communities during the charette process, they often describe communities that emphasize New Urbanist principles, which tends to weaken the resistance to the necessary changes in the zoning and planning regulations. Nevertheless, the tendency toward socioeconomic segregation in American suburbs cannot be underestimated. Gated communities, in particular, have flourished throughout all economic strata of American society by offering their residents a mix of personal security, the prestige of exclusivity, and a manufactured sense of community. Rebecca J. Schwartz, Comment, "Public Gated Communities: The Rosemont, Illinois, Approach and Its Constitutional Implications," *Urban Law* 29 (1997): 123, 123–26.

16. Some of the best-known New Urbanist developments are suburban "greenfield" (constructed on undeveloped land) projects that have become relatively expensive when compared to similar housing in the same area. For example both the Kentlands, in the Maryland suburbs near Washington, D.C., and Celebration, near Orlando, have developed reputations

of Catholic social teaching that has been developed since the late nineteenth century. At its most basic, Catholic social teaching announces the Church's intention to be present in the affairs of the world in a meaningful way. In particular, the articulation of the concepts of the common good, solidarity, and subsidiarity in Catholic social teaching allows us to evaluate social, political, and economic structures as they impact the lived tradition of the Catholic faith.[17]

Catholic social teaching grew out of the social and political unrest that accompanied Europe's transition from an agrarian to an industrial economy. The plight of working people was of particular concern to the Church, and for over one hundred years Catholic social teaching has assessed social and political developments in the modern world from the perspective of the poor and the dispossessed. One of the earliest "new" ideas that sprang from the social teaching was the concept of subsidiarity. Developed in part to respond to the growing influence of the statist ideologies of fascism and communism, subsidiarity stresses the need for individuals and small communities to retain power over issues and decisions best handled at lower levels in the social and political hierarchy.[18] An issue of particular importance to the Church was the intervention of the state in the life of the family and in the education of children, but subsidiarity also recognizes that certain functions must be performed at the level of larger bodies, sometimes even beyond the state.[19]

The creation of human-scale neighborhoods that encourage the develop-

---

as rather exclusive, upper-middle-class developments with little ethnic diversity. See, e.g., Jack Snyder, "Celebration, Florida Marks 5 Years," *Orlando Sentinel* (17 June 2001), noting that the average home price in Celebration is well above the Orlando median and that 87% of the residents are white, as compared to 51% of the population of Orlando.

17. For a comprehensive collection of the documents of Catholic social teaching, see David O'Brien and Thomas Shannon, eds., *Catholic Social Thought: The Documentary Heritage* (Maryknoll, NY: Orbis Books, 1995).

18. "It is an injustice . . . to transfer to the larger and higher collectivity functions which can be performed and provided for by lesser and subordinate bodies." Pope Pius XI, *Quadragesimo anno*, ¶ 79 (1931), reprinted in O'Brien and Shannon, *Catholic Social Thought*, 60.

19. For example, in his encyclical *Pacem in terris*, Pope John XXIII saw the modern nation state as incapable, on its own, of securing the universal common good:

This means that the worldwide public authority and the public authorities [of individual nation-states] must tackle and solve problems of an economic, social, political, or cultural character which are posed by the universal common good. For, because of the vastness, complexity and urgency of these problems, the public authorities of the individual States are not in a position to tackle them with any hope of positive solution.

ment of an ethos of community and locality is a key goal of New Urbanism that resonates strongly with the subsidiarity principle. On the higher level, New Urbanism sees the neighborhood as an integrated part of the larger village, town, city, or metropolitan area, not an independent entity geared primarily to a narrow market niche. This allows for an upward aspect of the principle of subsidiarity to operate in which the New Urbanist neighborhood is connected to, and can rely upon, key amenities of the metropolitan community, such as public transportation. Within the New Urbanist community itself, the design principles allow various types of households, from single individuals to large families with children, to gain a certain measure of independence. For example, elderly people and pre-teenage children can get themselves to basic places like school or the grocery store. At least in theory, a multigenerational family could actually live in a New Urbanist community, allowing the members to support one another, and lessening the need for social services provided by government agencies.

Johann Verstraeten, a theologian at the Catholic University of Leuven who is an expert in the social teaching, has noted that over recent decades, the late Pope John Paul II theologized Catholic social teaching by stating that the social doctrine is part of a "radical conversion to a 'lived faith,' to an 'experienced faith,' and for an integral humanistic engagement."[20] Catholics cannot live out their Christian vocation in retreat from the world, particularly when that retreat allows them to abandon solidarity with the poor and discourages them from cooperating for the common good of society. Thus, the concept of solidarity also has important implications for a Catholic evaluation of New Urbanism.

In *Sollicitudo rei socialis,* John Paul II wrote that "solidarity is undoubtedly a Christian virtue. . . . In the light of faith, solidarity seeks to go beyond itself, to take on the *specifically Christian* dimension of total gratuity, forgiveness, and reconciliation. One's neighbor is then not only a human being with his or her own rights and a fundamental equality with everyone else, but becomes the *living image* of God the Father, redeemed by the blood of Jesus Christ

---

Pope John XXIII, *Pacem in terris,* ¶ 140 (1963), reprinted in O'Brien and Shannon, *Catholic Social Thought,* 153. This situation of nation-states in an increasingly complex and interdependent world would appear to be analogous to the situation of small localities within the modern American metropolis.

20. Johann Verstraeten, "Solidarity and Subsidiarity," in *Principles of Catholic Social Teaching,* supra note 3, 142.

and placed under the permanent action of the Holy Spirit."[21] Solidarity and working for the common good cannot be understood without a particular reference to the needs of the poor. In the same document John Paul II notes that the "option or love of preference for the poor" is "an option, or a *special form* of primacy in the exercise of Christian charity to which the whole tradition of the Church bears witness. It affects the life of each Christian inasmuch as he or she seeks to imitate the life of Christ, but it applies equally to our *social responsibilities* and hence to our manner of living, and to the logical decisions to be made concerning the ownership and use of goods."[22]

In many ways, modern American suburban development represents a retreat from society and the human engagement it requires. Separate, highly autonomous local governments have encouraged the development of a suburban ethos that rejects the notion of a broad metropolitan community that encompasses the poor. An eerily escapist pattern of movement seems to be at work in American metropolitan areas. As the earliest suburban communities have aged, many are now suffering fates similar to the cities their earliest residents once abandoned. In an effort to find communities that are "cleaner," are "safer," and have "better schools," Americans have pushed the boundaries of the metropolis ever outward, creating newer suburbs farther away that meet these needs.[23] How much longer can this trend continue, and is it something Catholics ought to accept as inevitable or benign?

Inasmuch as suburban sprawl is a product of fear, exclusion, racism, distrust, and withdrawal from communal obligations, Catholics should be deeply suspicious and concerned about it. In his recent book on Christian ethics, David Hollenbach considered the American urban/suburban divide in the context of Catholic conceptions of solidarity and the common good:

One of the most important meanings of the concept of the common good, therefore, is the good that comes into existence in a community of solidarity among active, equal

21. Pope John Paul II, *Sollicitudo rei socialis,* ¶ 40 (1987), reprinted in O'Brien and Shannon, *Catholic Social Thought,* 423.

22. Ibid. at ¶ 42.

23. It is important to point out that another important reason for sprawl has been population growth, particularly in the Sunbelt and in the coastal cities. Nevertheless, most cities contain vast underutilized areas that could have absorbed much of the population increase if they had been thoughtfully redeveloped. Indeed certain metropolitan areas that have had relatively modest population growth over the last twenty years, such as Rochester and Albany, N.Y., Hartford, Conn., and Detroit, rank relatively high in terms of sprawl. Ewing, *Measuring Sprawl and Its Impact,* 15.

agents. . . . When a society not only falls short of the level of solidarity it could reasonably aspire to but is shaped by institutions that exclude some members from agency altogether, the resulting interdependence becomes a genuine evil. . . . The kind of interdependence that exists between US suburbs and core cities today provides a regrettable example of such shared harm. In the cities it leads to unemployment, inadequate housing, inferior education, drugs, crime, and despair for many of the poor: In the suburbs it leads to fear, the building of fences and gates, urban sprawl with its accompanying environmental degradation, and to what has been called a "frantic privacy" which makes the very notion of citizenship problematic.[24]

Certainly there is nothing wrong with a desire to live in safety and comfort. Indeed, some commentators have defended urban sprawl by arguing that it actually serves the public good because it is economically efficient, as well as a reasonable response to people's desires and freely-made choices. These commentators also reject the contention that sprawl imposes excessively high infrastructure, environmental and social costs, and argue that as the suburbs have expanded geographically, living situations and community choices for the poor, new immigrants, and for typical members of the middle-class have been enhanced.[25] Yet, it is also quite clear that American suburban sprawl grows out of a deeply materialistic and selfish strain in American culture. Much of modern suburban development is wasteful and excessive, and it plays to a consumerist ethos that believes bigger is better and that newer is better still. Surely Catholics cannot stand by mute when the law, the economy, and the political system are manipulated in ways that create opulence and comfort in the suburbs ahead of decent public services for the poor in the cities.

At least in its principle, New Urbanism suggests that it is possible to develop a desirable built environment for all, while enhancing our opportunities to live in community and solidarity with those who are different, particularly the poor. Although to date New Urbanism has had trouble making good on this promise, possibilities for community exist through New Urbanism that could never be achieved under the current dominant patterns of suburban

24. David Hollenbach, *The Common Good and Christian Ethics* (Cambridge: Cambridge University Press, 2002), 189–90.

25. See, e.g., Peter Gordon and Harry Richardson, "Critiquing Sprawl's Critics," *Cato Institute* (20 June 2003); Clint Bolick, "Subverting the American Dream: Government Dictated 'Smart Growth' Is Unwise and Unconstitutional," *University of Pennsylvania Law Review* 148 (2000): 859; Gregg Easterbrook, "The Case for Sprawl," *New Republic* (15 March 1999); Peter Gordon and Harry Richardson, "Defending Urban Sprawl," *Public Interest* 139 (Spring 2000), 65.

development and local government. New Urbanism alone will not dislodge members of the middle-class's longstanding apprehensions about living near the poor, nor can it redress economic inequities between American cities and suburbs. Yet, by attempting to create communities that seek in their scale, their function, and their aesthetic to engage and respect the human person, New Urbanism makes a direct and compelling connection to the humanistic values of Catholic thought. Furthermore, by directing its vision to metropolitan as opposed to local planning, New Urbanism envisions the American metropolis as an integrated whole and attempts to respect the poor as equal participants in the life of the American metropolis. This offers a hope for the future of American metropolitan life and, indeed, for American democracy, that localism and exclusionary zoning have failed to provide.

[12]

TORT LAW

Toward a Trinitarian Theory of Products Liability

๛

AMELIA J. UELMEN

It may come as a surprise to theologians and philosophers who are experts in Catholic Social Thought that its profound and multilayered social critique has not yet been fully integrated into American jurisprudence. Among legal specializations, several obvious candidates for integration leap to mind. The Church's extraordinarily deep and extended reflections on human labor could do much to enrich theories of labor law. The principle of subsidiarity, and reflections on the dignity of the human person and on the role of religion in public life, readily go hand in hand with the theoretical underpinnings of many aspects of constitutional law. The preferential option for the poor could easily inform many areas of governmental regulation, from immigration to health care policy and tax law, just to name a few.

In the list of obvious candidates, however, many might not include products liability. How would such seemingly technical and scientific standards for the production of material goods intersect with Catholic Social Thought? Similarly, no one would be surprised that legal theorists have not yet identified the deeply mysterious theological doctrine of the Trinity as a lens for products liability analysis. Yet spurred on by the conviction that Catholic

A slightly expanded version of this essay is published in *Journal of Catholic Social Thought* 1 (2004): 603–45.

Social Thought can offer profound solutions to the knottiest dilemmas in products theory, and encouraged by recent challenges to move beyond the "ordinary" and "conventional" in order to probe the depths of the unique resources that Christian theology may offer to legal theory,[1] this chapter sets out a few initial ideas as a first step toward a "Trinitarian" theory of products liability.

It begins with a brief outline of some of the overarching themes in products liability and a story that illustrates what could be considered one of the principal tensions: the profound disconnect between how economic analysts and the ordinary citizens who make up civil juries define the standard for a "reasonably designed" product. The second section pursues the somewhat modest goal of showing that the philosophical and analytical framework of Catholic Social Thought can do much to help flesh out the critique of predominating products liability theories, which are largely influenced by economic analysis. The more ambitious final sections move beyond critique, zeroing in on a relatively new current of thought in Catholic theology that sets out the Trinity as a model for social life. Then, considering two hotly debated areas in products theory, they test whether Catholic Social Thought viewed through a Trinitarian lens might promise creative solutions.

AN OVERVIEW OF THE LAW OF PRODUCTS LIABILITY

General Background

Products liability is the area of tort law that deals with the liability of the supplier of a product to the person who is injured by the product. Although key elements of its doctrine date back to the early twentieth century,[2] products liability theory is a relatively contemporary development. Following World War II, as mass markets for products were rapidly expanding, courts increasingly resonated with strong policy arguments that consumers should be assured of greater protection against dangerous products than was afford-

---

1. See, e.g., William J. Stuntz, "Christian Legal Theory," *Harvard Law Review* 116 (2003): 1707, 1721 (reviewing *Christian Perspectives on Legal Thought*, ed. M. McConnell and A. Carmella, [New Haven, CT: Yale University Press, 2001]); George M. Marsden, *The Outrageous Idea of Christian Scholarship* (Oxford: Oxford University Press, 1998).

2. See, e.g., *MacPherson v. Buick Motor Co.*, 217 NY 382, 389 (1916); *Thomas v. Winchester*, 6 NY 397 (1852).

ed by the contract law of warranty. Thus they began to flesh out a more flexible framework for the analysis of liability for injuries from defective products.

For example, in a seminal 1963 case, *Greenman v. Yuba Power Products*,[3]
the plaintiff was injured while using a power tool that had been given to him
by his wife. The plaintiff himself could not show that he had read and relied
on the warranty. The California Supreme Court found the law of warranty
entirely too cramped. In a world of mass production, why should it make any
difference, the court reasoned, whether the plaintiff had actually purchased
the product or whether he had actually read the warranty? Thus the court
held that under a theory of "strict" products liability, the plaintiff need only
show: (1) that he was injured by the power tool while using it a way it was intended to be used; and (2) that his injury was caused by a defect in the product.[4] As the doctrine developed, courts emphasized that as a matter of policy a plaintiff should not have to jump through the hoops of showing exactly
what went wrong in the manufacturing process. It was enough to show that
the product was marketed in a "defective condition unreasonably dangerous
to the user or consumer," and that such defect caused the plaintiff's injury.[5]

Two principal theories began to take shape: manufacturing defect and design defect. When the product injury is due to an alleged manufacturing defect, the analysis is relatively simple because the standard of safety is that of
the manufacturer's own design. A product is defective when a flaw in the
manufacturing process caused it to emerge defective as compared to the intended design.[6]

When the injury is due to an alleged defect in the product design itself,
the analysis is much more complex. In evaluating a manufacturer's conscious
judgments about product design, how safe is "reasonably" safe? Compared to
what? According to whose perspective? Some aspects of the balance are intuitively obvious. For example, the risk of paper cuts does not prevent the mar-
keting of paper. While automobiles could be designed as crash-proof tanks,
that would also make them prohibitively expensive, slow, awkward, and in-
efficient in fuel consumption, with consequent damage to the environment.

---

3. Cal 2d 57 (1963) (Traynor, J.).

4. Ibid., 62, 64.

5. See *Restatement (Second) of Torts* (1965) [hereinafter *Second Restatement*] § 402A, 347–
48.

6. See generally *Restatement (Third) of Torts: Products Liability* (1997) [hereinafter *Third Restatement*] § 2(a), 14.

Injury from accidents might even be augmented if these tank-type models were to crash into less sturdy models designed earlier. Some products are so dangerous that no "balance" ever seems appropriate.

But beyond the obvious, where and how to draw the line defining a product design as "unreasonably dangerous" is one of the most difficult conundrums in American tort law. Whose perspective and whose values should determine the correct balance for a "reasonably safe" design? Manufacturers and consumers may differently value the risks and benefits at stake. Manufacturers and victims of product accidents may have even more divergent views.

The Ford Pinto Case

The 1978 case of the exploding Ford Pinto illustrates the tension. In *Grimshaw v. Ford Motor Company*,[7] a stalled Ford Pinto was struck from behind by a car that had braked to a relatively slow speed of about thirty miles per hour. The impact resulted in a rear-end fire in the Pinto that killed the driver and left thirteen-year-old plaintiff Richard Grimshaw with serious injuries.

In the course of discovery, the Ford Motor Company produced a document that indicated that it was aware of certain risks, but because of a "cost-benefit" calculus, the company had determined it would be cheaper to compensate for resulting injuries and death rather than alert the public and recall the Pinto for repair. The jury awarded Grimshaw over $2.5 million in compensatory damages and $125 million in punitive damages as well. The punitive damages award was later reduced by the court to $3.5 million, but the case took on somewhat mythical dimensions, and remains an important symbol.[8]

Was it "unreasonable" for Ford to make such a calculation? According to some theories, of course not. As Professor Gregory Keating describes, a "powerful and influential tradition of thought asserts that reasonable care in the law of negligence is, and ought to be, economically efficient care."[9] Extrapolating from Judge Learned Hand's famous "formula" for determining the amount of care due, Professor (now Judge) Richard Posner described the

7. Cal App 3d 757 (1981) (affirming 1978 jury decision).

8. See Gary T. Schwartz, "The Myth of the Ford Pinto Case," *Rutgers Law Review* 43 (1991): 1013.

9. Gregory C. Keating, "Pressing Precaution beyond the Point of Cost-Justification," *Vanderbilt Law Review* 56 (2003): 653, 655.

"economic meaning of negligence" as asking the judge or jury "to measure three things: the magnitude of the loss if an accident occurs; the probability of the accident's occurring; and the burden of taking precautions that would avert it."[10] According to Posner, "[i]f the cost of safety measures or of curtailment—whichever is lower—exceeds the benefit in accident avoidance to be gained by incurring that cost, society would be better off, in economic terms, to forgo accident prevention."[11] In such cases, a "rational profit-maximizing enterprise will pay tort judgments to the accident victims rather than incur the larger cost of avoiding liability."[12]

But as the Ford Pinto case illustrates, more often than not this line of analysis just does not sit well with a civil jury. As Professor Michael Green graphically explains, the market for "a broken arm, shattered brain, or a life" is "quite thin"—not only because it is problematic to compare items that do not align on a common scale or measure, but also because on an even more basic level, "the stark balancing of lives and limbs with money strikes many as jarring, inappropriate, even absurd."[13]

Might this tension and confusion be simply a blip on the screen of the development of a relatively new legal theory? Probably not. The Ford Pinto narrative continues to repeat itself, with exponential increases in punitive damages. For example, in a 1999 trial against General Motors for an accident involving the Chevy Malibu, where the evidence included an internal cost-benefit analysis noting it would be cheaper to pay $2.40 per car to settle lawsuits than $8.59 per car to make the fuel system safer, the jury awarded $5 billion in punitive damages.[14] In an interview following the verdict, one juror proclaimed: "We wanted to let them know that no matter how large the company may be, we as jurors, we as people all over the world, will not stand for companies having disregard for human life."[15]

---

10. Richard A. Posner, "A Theory of Negligence," *Journal of Legal Studies* 1 (1972): 29, 32.

11. Ibid., 32.

12. Ibid., 33.

13. Michael D. Green, "The Schizophrenia of Risk-Benefit Analysis in Design Defect Litigation," *Vanderbilt Law Review* 48 (1995): 609, 617.

14. Jeffrey Ball and Milo Geyelin, "GM Ordered by Jury to Pay $4.9 Billion: Auto Maker Plans to Appeal Huge California Verdict in Fuel-Tank-Fire Case," *Wall Street Journal* (12 July 1999): A3.

15. Juror Billy Lowe, Jr., interview by Janan Hanna, "Paying the Price for Profits: Jurors in Liability Cases Are Sending Corporate America the Message that Covering up Product Risks Will Cost Big Money," *Chicago Tribune* (17 July 1999): Business Section, 1.

What is going on here? Professor Schwartz saw how the patterns of the debate over the standard of reasonable safety in product design reflect a clash between two radically different cultures: on the one hand, policy analysts, who see cost-benefit analysis as obviously acceptable, and on the other, the general public, which finds such analysis deeply disturbing.[16]

How can two such radically different views of "reasonable" be reconciled? According to the number-crunchers, the ordinary folks who serve on civil juries are simply incapable of understanding the technical complexities of product design decisions. Because jurors wreak havoc on any hope for an objective analysis, the whole tort system should be reformed, either to excommunicate them, or at the very least to greatly curtail their discretion.[17] According to the ordinary folks on civil juries, companies who crudely and cruelly exchange dollars for safety should be severely punished with multi-billion-dollar punitive damages awards, even though this response may effectively lead to bankruptcy.[18]

While most manufacturers and consumers would agree that lines must be drawn somewhere—it cannot possibly be the case that "reasonable design" means that manufacturers have to spend an infinite amount on safety to avoid liability and punitive damages—the debate on where and how to draw the line reveals a profound and seemingly irreconcilable cultural rift.

CATHOLIC SOCIAL THOUGHT AND PRODUCTS LIABILITY THEORY

With this background in mind, the goal of this section is to show how Catholic Social Thought might help to describe the tensions and flesh out a critique of an economic analysis of products liability theory. The analysis that follows is by no means the only way to explain the tension or dig into the layers of the debate. Complex critiques of legal theorists and scholars in other disciplines, such as sociology, psychology, and analytic philosophy, have already enriched the dialogue in important ways.[19]

16. Schwartz, "The Myth of the Ford Pinto Case," 1041.

17. See, e.g., Franklin Strier, "The Educated Jury: A Proposal for Complex Litigation," *De-Paul Law Review* 47 (1997): 49 (advocating requiring a minimum number of college-educated individuals on juries trying complex cases).

18. See, e.g., Schwartz, "The Myth of the Ford Pinto Case," 1029.

19. For an excellent application to products liability of cultural studies theorists' analyses

However, in contrast to critiques based on other disciplines, most legal scholars may not have considered Catholic Social Thought as a resource for reflection on products liability theories. Even from an initial reading of the most recent social encyclicals, it is astounding to see the number of passages that not only reflect the Church as an "expert in humanity"[20] looking broadly at human work and economic systems, but also contain specific and in-depth discussion of criteria for the production of material goods.

The analysis that follows is neither a complete and exhaustive compilation of all the relevant documents of Catholic Social Thought—it focuses on two of the more recent encyclicals, *Sollicitudo rei socialis* and *Centesimus annus*—nor an in-depth survey of all the nuances of design defect theory. It does, however, hope to offer a few initial ideas about the intersection between Catholic Social Thought and products theory so as to spark further research, discussion, and analysis.

A Broader Cultural Framework for Product Design Decisions

What the jury was reaching for in the Ford Pinto case, and what Catholic Social Thought could offer to the field of products liability theory, could be described in a nutshell as a broader cultural framework for evaluating decisions about the production of material goods. In classic "both/and" style—or perhaps here best described as "yes, but"—Catholic Social Thought recognizes the positive aspects of economic development and production, but insists that such must be placed within a broader ethical and cultural context. Embedded within this insistence on a broader cultural context is a profoundly substantive critique of the current framework.

"Yes": Appreciation for the Commercial Endeavor

To start with the "yes," Catholic Social Thought includes a deep appreciation for the advantages and benefits of the modern business economy and for technological and scientific development. Economic initiative is "important not only for the individual but also for the common good."[21] The production

---

of consumers as "socially situated," see Douglas A. Kysar, "The Expectations of Consumers," *Columbia Law Review* 103 (2003): 1700, 1757–61.

20. Pope John Paul II, *Sollicitudo rei socialis,* ¶ 41 (1987) (quoting Pope Paul VI, *Populorum progressio,* ¶ 13 [1967]).

21. Ibid., ¶ 15; see also Pope John Paul II, *Centesimus annus,* ¶ 32 (1991).

of material goods not only is practical and necessary,[22] but also reveals something affirmative and favorable regarding the truth about the human person. "Indeed, besides the earth, man's principal resource is *man himself.*"[23] *Centesimus* highlights how the commercial endeavor can lead to human growth and fulfillment: "disciplined work in close collaboration with others" gives rise to the development of "[i]mportant virtues . . . such as diligence, industriousness, prudence in undertaking reasonable risks, reliability and fidelity in interpersonal relationships, as well as courage in carrying out decisions which are difficult and painful but necessary, both for the overall working of a business and in meeting possible set-backs."[24]

Although the analysis is complex, in the most recent documents one finds nothing of a yearning for a simpler, less industrialized past. As *Sollicitudo* highlights, "the ever greater availability of material goods not only meets needs but also opens new horizons."[25] Even though this same encyclical includes a cutting social critique, it also notes that "[t]he danger of the misuse of material goods and the appearance of artificial needs should in no way hinder the regard we have for the new goods and resources placed at our disposal and the use we make of them. On the contrary, we must see them as a gift from God and as a response to the human vocation, which is fully realized in Christ."[26]

"But": Elements of a Broader Cultural Context

While Catholic Social Thought appreciates the positive potential of the commercial endeavor, it also highlights the fact that production and economic development must be analyzed within the context of a broader cultural framework. Analogously, the Church has long affirmed the validity of private property[27] while highlighting the limits of this right. As the Second Vatican Council framed it in *Gaudium et spes,* "Private property or some ownership of external goods affords each person the scope needed for personal and family autonomy, and should be regarded as an extension of human freedom. . . . Of its nature private property also has a social function

---

22. *Sollicitudo rei socialis,* ¶ 29; *Centesimus annus,* ¶ 32.
23. *Centesimus annus,* ¶ 32.
24. Ibid.
25. *Sollicitudo rei socialis,* ¶ 29.
26. Ibid.
27. *Centesimus annus,* ¶ 30.

which is based on the law of the *common purpose of goods*."[28] Profit serves a legitimate role as an indication that a business is functioning well.[29] But it is not the only indicator of a firm's condition: "*other human and moral factors must also be considered which, in the long term, are at least equally important for the life of a business*."[30]

On a macro level, to strive for economic development and an expansion of product markets is legitimate, and can in some sense contribute to a life that is "qualitatively more satisfying."[31] But the process of "singling out new needs" must be "guided by a comprehensive picture of man which respects all the dimensions of his being and which subordinates his material and instinctive dimensions to his interior and spiritual ones."[32] For example, "an excessive promotion of purely utilitarian values, with an appeal to the appetites and inclinations towards immediate gratification, [makes] it difficult to recognize and respect the hierarchy of the true values of human existence."[33]

Catholic Social Thought's global embrace also brings to the fore the claim that criteria for economic development and expansion of markets must include their impact on "all and each person."[34] As *Sollicitudo* warns, "True development cannot consist in the simple accumulation of wealth and in the greater availability of goods and services, if this is gained at the expense of the development of the masses, and without due consideration for the social, cultural and spiritual dimensions of the human being."[35]

For the theoretical analysis of the process of production, the tools of economics are useful. But the documents consistently emphasize that economics is only one element of culture. As *Centesimus* observes, "Of itself, an economic system does not possess criteria for correctly distinguishing new and higher forms of satisfying human needs from artificial new needs which hinder the formation of a mature personality."[36] A broader cultural context is "urgently needed" to educate consumers in the responsible use of their power of choice, and to form "a strong sense of responsibility" among all those involved in the commercial endeavor.[37]

Yes, the Church has a profound appreciation for the commercial endeav-

---

28. Ibid., quoting Second Vatican Council, *Pastoral Constitution on the Church in the Modern World (Gaudium et spes)*, ¶ 71 (1965).

29. *Centesimus annus*, ¶ 35.   30. Ibid.

31. Ibid., ¶ 36.   32. Ibid.

33. Ibid., ¶ 29b.   34. *Sollicitudo rei socialis*, ¶ 33.

35. Ibid., ¶ 9.   36. *Centesimus annus*, ¶ 36.

37. Ibid.

or. *But,* to the extent that analyses of economic development and production lose their grounding in a broader moral, cultural, and spiritual framework, Catholic Social Thought offers a vigorous critique. *Centesimus* warns of the consequences when economic freedom loses its anchor in the truth about the human person: "[E]conomic freedom is only one element of human freedom. When it becomes autonomous, when man is seen more as a producer or consumer of goods than as a subject who produces and consumes in order to live, then economic freedom loses its necessary relationship to the human person and ends up by alienating and oppressing him."[38]

Perhaps the need for a broader cultural framework is best summed up in *Sollicitudo*'s citation of this passage from the Gospel of Matthew: "For what will it profit a man, if he gains the whole world and forfeits his life?"[39]

A Critique of Current Products Liability Theory through the Lens of Catholic Social Thought

The next section explores some implications for products liability of Catholic Social Thought's insistence on a broader cultural framework for economic development.

Products Liability Analysis Is a Moral Endeavor

When the principles of Catholic Social Thought are brought to bear on current products liability theory, what immediately emerges is the moral character of any business endeavor and of the choices that underlie the process of product design. Since its inception, products analysis has tended to obfuscate this characteristic. As the theory was developing, it seemed to be in some sense a leap ahead in consumer protection to move beyond the evidentiary obstacle course required to prove negligence, toward a more technical policy analysis. Since product accidents are simply the cost of doing business, manufacturers should simply pay; the plaintiff should not be required to jump through the additional hoops of determining fault.

Recent scholarship, however, has probed the theoretical line between negligence and strict products liability. Especially in design defect analysis, what emerges is that whether it is termed "strict" liability or negligence, the manufacturer has, at some point, made a conscious decision about how much money to spend (or not to spend) on safety. Whatever the determined dollar

---

38. Ibid., ¶ 39.
39. *Sollicitudo rei socialis,* ¶ 33 (citing Matt. 16:26).

amount may be, this decision is at bottom not a technical or scientific calculation but a moral decision: at the end of the day, the jury, charged with determining whether that decision was "reasonable," is asked to make a moral judgment. In the words of torts scholar David Owen, product accidents are always moral events.[40]

Catholic Social Thought provides a broad framework for emphasizing the moral dimension of production decisions. It highlights that true development can never be measured merely in terms of the greater availability of material goods. As *Sollicitudo* explains, "True development cannot consist in the simple accumulation of wealth and in the greater availability of goods and services, if this is gained at the expense of the development of the masses, and without due consideration for the social, cultural and spiritual dimensions of the human being."[41] Similarly, "the mere accumulation of goods and services, even for the benefit of the majority, is not enough for the realization of human happiness."[42] It further warns that "unless all the considerable body of resources and potential at man's disposal is guided by a moral understanding and by an orientation towards the true good of the human race, it easily turns against man to oppress him."[43]

Instead, as *Centesimus* defines it, "the purpose of a business firm is not simply to make a profit, but is to be found in its very existence as a *community of persons* who in various ways are endeavoring to satisfy their basic needs, and who form a particular group at the service of the whole of society."[44]

Against the backdrop of Catholic Social Thought's broader cultural framework, what comes into relief is that however the test is articulated, balancing the costs and benefits of safety expenditures is essentially a moral endeavor that implicates moral values. Of course technical and scientific knowledge about risks to safety contribute to the analysis in important ways. But that should in no way mask the moral nature of the underlying decisions about production.

---

40. David G. Owen, "The Moral Foundations of Products Liability Law: Toward First Principles," *Notre Dame Law Review* 68 (1993): 427, 430. See also *Sollicitudo rei socialis*, ¶ 41 ("[W]hatever affects the dignity of individuals and peoples, such as authentic development, cannot be reduced to a 'technical' problem.").

41. *Sollicitudo rei socialis*, ¶ 9.

42. Ibid., ¶ 28.

43. Ibid.

44. *Centesimus annus*, ¶ 35.

A More Complex Analysis of Whether "Society Would Be Better Off"

According to Richard Posner's economics analysis, "[i]f the cost of safety measures or of curtailment—whichever cost is lower—exceeds the benefit in accident avoidance to be gained by incurring that cost, society would be better off, in economic terms, to forgo accident prevention."[45] The rational profit-maximizing manufacturer would take "precautions whose benefits, measured by the losses averted discounted by the probability those accidents would occur in the absence of a precaution, outweigh their costs."[46] To be fair, Posner's formula could embrace more complex and relational human dimensions, such as emotional costs and enhancement to relationships of trust, and many economic theories of legal analysis do so.[47] Neither does Posner's description "in economic terms" necessarily preclude the contributions of other disciplines. As applied, however, the analysis often stops with "economic terms" in part because other elements are not easily quantifiable.

In contrast, Catholic Social Thought offers a profound critique of the extent to which "economic terms" can ever fully measure the health of a society. For example, in a sharp critique of both communism and the free market society, *Centesimus* notes that although the free-market society may achieve a greater satisfaction of material human needs than communism, "insofar as it denies an autonomous existence and value to morality, law, culture and religion, it agrees with Marxism, in the sense that it totally reduces man to the sphere of economics and the satisfaction of material needs."[48]

In fact, it places "side-by-side" with the miseries of underdevelopment an equally inadmissible "super-development" that, like the former, "is contrary to what is good and to true happiness."[49] As a cutting critique in *Sollicitudo* summarizes: "[a]n excessive availability of every kind of material goods for the benefit of certain social groups easily makes people slaves of 'possession' and of immediate gratification, with no other horizon than the multiplication or continual replacement of the things already owned with others still better."[50] Thus one could question the extent to which society is "better off"

45. Posner, "A Theory of Negligence," 32, and discussion supra, note 10.

46. Posner, "A Theory of Negligence," 32–33.

47. See, e.g., Guido Calabresi and Philip Bobbitt, *Tragic Choices* (New York: W. W. Norton, 1978), 32; Guido Calabresi, *Ideals, Beliefs, Attitudes and the Law* (Syracuse, NY: Syracuse University Press, 1985), 69–86.

48. *Centesimus annus*, ¶ 19.   49. *Sollicitudo rei socialis*, ¶ 28.

50. Ibid.

where a "blind submission to pure consumerism" leads to "crass materialism" and "radical dissatisfaction"—"the more one possesses the more one wants, while deeper aspirations remain unsatisfied and perhaps even stifled."[51]

Insight into What "Cost/Benefit" Analysis Fails to Capture

Perhaps one of the strongest attractions of economics-based legal analysis is its promise to articulate a quantifiably measurable, and thus seemingly more objective, standard. Here, too, Catholic Social Thought does not negate the utility of economic analysis and does not hesitate to affirm the "secure" advantages of the mechanisms of the market: "they help to utilize resources better; they promote the exchange of products; above all they give central place to the person's desires and preferences, which, in a contract, meet the desires and preferences of another person."[52]

However, as *Centesimus* also highlights, the numbers cannot hope to capture the full picture. A more complete cultural analysis must recognize the limits of the market: "there are collective and qualitative needs which cannot be satisfied by market mechanisms. There are important human needs which escape its logic. There are goods which by their very nature cannot and must not be bought or sold."[53] Further, it warns against an "idolatry" of the market "which ignores the existence of goods which by their nature are not and cannot be mere commodities."[54]

Catholic Social Thought's insistence on a broader cultural framework to analyze the process for producing material goods reveals the Achilles heel of many forms of law-and-economics analysis as applied to products liability design defect cases: since there are goods that, by their very nature, cannot be bought or sold, and perhaps, to some extent, not even measured, economic analysis alone can never produce an "objective balance."[55] Every step of the process—from assigning dollar amounts, to lining up various values, to weighing and balancing those values—takes place within the context of a very specific philosophical framework and anthropology; every step applies specific moral criteria to make value judgments.

---

51. Ibid.
52. *Centesimus annus*, ¶ 40.
53. Ibid.
54. Ibid.
55. See Kysar, "The Expectations of Consumers," 1766.

BEYOND CRITIQUE: CATHOLIC SOCIAL THOUGHT
THROUGH A TRINITARIAN LENS

To articulate a critique is much easier than to propose a positive contribution. This next section presents a few initial ideas on how Catholic Social Thought might offer positive and constructive solutions to some of the most difficult theoretical problems in design defect analysis. As its focal lens it zeroes in on the Trinity, the very life of God, and the fundamental pattern from which Catholic Social Teaching emerged. As the United States Bishop's Conference's Introduction to *Sharing Catholic Social Teaching* describes:

Catholic Social Teaching emerges from the truth of what God has revealed to us about himself. We believe in the triune God whose very nature is communal and social. God the Father sends his only Son Jesus Christ and shares the Holy Spirit as a gift of his love. God reveals himself to us as one who is not alone, but rather as one who is relational, who is Trinity. Therefore, we who are made in God's image share this communal, social nature. We are called to reach out to build relationships of love and justice.[56]

What might this mean, concretely? And in particular, what might this mean for products liability?

The Trinity as a Social Model

It is hardly understatement to describe as "undeveloped" the scholarship on the Trinity as a social model. As theologian Enrique Cambón describes, generally in the culture of Christian churches, when one must speak about the Trinity, there has been a tendency toward either abstract and incomprehensible discourse or refuge in eloquent silence.[57] Over the centuries, much of the Catholic theological reflection on the Trinity has emphasized its pattern found in the individual soul rather than in interpersonal relationships.[58]

More recently, however, scholars of various disciplines have begun to

56. United States Catholic Conference, *Sharing Catholic Social Teaching: Challenges and Directions*, 1 (Washington, DC: United States Catholic Conference, 1998) (hereafter *Sharing Catholic Social Teaching*). See generally Pontifical Council for Justice and Peace, *Compendium of the Social Doctrine of the Church*, ¶¶ 30–37 (Vatican: Libreria Editrice Vaticana, 2004).

57. Enrique Cambón, *Trinità Modello Sociale* (The Trinity as a Social Model) (Rome: Città Nuova, 1999), 16 (paraphrasing Hans Kung; translations from the Italian here, and throughout, are my own). See also Karl Rahner, *The Trinity* (New York: Herder and Herder, 1970), 10–11 ("We must be willing to admit that, should the doctrine of the Trinity have to be dropped as false, the major part of religious literature could well remain virtually unchanged").

58. This is certainly not to downplay the momentous insights and contributions of great

probe how the dynamic of the relationship between the Father, Son, and Holy Spirit might serve as a fascinating and profound model not only for theology and philosophy, but for every discipline.[59] Some of the cutting-edge work in this field is gestated by the Interdisciplinary Study Center of the Focolare Movement headquartered in Rome, Italy.[60] Because the analyses have emerged from decades of practical experience in living what Pope John Paul II termed the *spirituality of communion*,[61] the resulting descriptions of the Trinity as a social model are accessible even to those without theological or philosophical training. One can intuit how they might be applied to the most varied disciplines.

As Focolare founder Chiara Lubich describes, "the heart of Christian anthropology" can be found in a life based on Jesus' new commandment, "with which it is possible to live the Trinitarian life on earth: 'As I have loved you, so you also should love one another.'"[62] Further, "[w]hen we live the new commandment, seeking to receive the gift of unity in Jesus that comes to us from the Father, the life of the Trinity is no longer lived only in the interior life of the individual person, but it flows freely among the members of the Mystical Body of Christ."[63]

---

theologians such as Augustine. It is only to highlight that the "social" dimension of the theological model has emerged after—and building on—centuries of reflection.

59. See, e.g., Jacques Maritain, *The Person and the Common Good,* trans. John Fitzgerald (Notre Dame, IN: Notre Dame Press, 1966), 37–39; David Hollenbach, S.J., *The Common Good and Christian Ethics* (Cambridge: Cambridge University Press, 2002), 129–32.

60. The Focolare Movement is one of the relatively new ecclesial movements in the Roman Catholic Church. Founded in Italy in 1943, it is now known especially for its work in interreligious dialogue, and more generally as an effective instrument to build unity between people of different cultures, races, and social backgrounds. See generally http://www.focolare.org. The Interdisciplinary Study Center's bimonthly journal, *Nuova Umanità*, often includes essays and analyses on the application of the Trinity as a social model. See, e.g., "Symposium: La Trinità-Esperienza di Dio (The Trinity: Experience of God)," *Nuova Umanità* 24 (2002): 127–390.

61. See Pope John Paul II, *Novo millennio ineunte,* ¶ 43 (2001) ("A spirituality of communion indicates above all the heart's contemplation of the mystery of the Trinity dwelling in us, and whose light we must also be able to see shining on the face of the brothers and sisters around us. A spirituality of communion also means an ability to think of our brothers and sister in faith within the profound unity of the Mystical Body, and therefore as 'those who are a part of me.'").

62. Chiara Lubich, "Toward a Theology and Philosophy of Unity," in *An Introduction to the Abba School: Conversations from the Focolare's Interdisciplinary Study Center* [hereinafter *Abba School*] (Hyde Park, NY: New City Press, 2002), 19, 25 (citing John 12:32, 15:12).

63. Ibid., 25.

Specifically, an anthropology based on the model of a triune God whose very nature is communal and social offers a rich description of how to get from one person to another—in theological terms, *pericoresis,* or "mutual indwelling"—a union of persons without loss of individual identity.[64] How is this possible? Specifically, the commandment of love is "lived out and measured against Jesus' love for us, to the point of abandonment."[65] He who was God "emptied himself"—*kenosis.*[66] Mutual indwelling is possible through an essential attitude of openness to the other, of "making room" for the other, even to the point of "emptying" oneself for the other.[67]

In the life of the Trinity, this openness or emptiness is not a negative encroachment on one's personhood, but actually the positive key to self-fulfillment: "whoever loses his life for my sake will find it."[68] Reflecting on the mysterious cry that Jesus addressed to the Father before dying, "My God, my God, why have you forsaken me?"[69] Lubich probes the paradox: "There may be those who think that to affirm self is to struggle against all that is not self, because what is not self is perceived as limit and, what is more, as a threat to the integrity of the self. But Jesus forsaken, in that terrible moment of his passion, tells us that while the awareness of his subjectivity appears to be diminishing because it seems he is being annulled, in that very moment it *is* in all its fullness."[70]

Based on this example, she draws out striking implications for the philosophy of being: "[Jesus forsaken] shows us, by his being reduced to nothing, accepted out of love for the Father to whom he re-abandons himself ('Into your hands I commend my spirit,' *Luke* 23:46), that I am myself not when I close myself off from the other, but when I give myself, when out of love I am lost in the other."[71]

This, according to Lubich, is the interpersonal dynamic at the heart of the Trinity: "In the relationship of the three divine Persons, each one, being

64. Cambón, *Trinità Modello Sociale,* 30.

65. Lubich, *Toward a Theology and Philosophy of Unity,* 25.

66. See Philippians 2:6–7.

67. See *Novo millennio ineunte,* ¶ 43 ("A spirituality of communion means . . . knowing how to 'make room' for our brothers and sisters, bearing 'each other's burdens'") (citing Gal. 6:2).

68. Matthew 10:39, 16:25.

69. Matthew 27:46.

70. Lubich, *Toward a Theology and Philosophy of Unity,* 33.

71. Ibid.

Love, *is* completely by *not being*, each one mutually indwelling in an eternal self-giving."[72] And as the "heart of Christian anthropology," this is the dynamic that can inform all human relationships and social structures. Like a "divine immigrant" who retained the language and customs of his homeland, Jesus brought to humanity the pattern of life at the heart of the Trinity so that human relationships and human community could be "on earth as it is in heaven."[73]

Trinitarian Patterns in Catholic Social Thought

Against the backdrop of this description of "the heart of Christian anthropology," the Trinitarian dimensions of Catholic Social Thought come into relief. The Second Vatican Counsel highlights the powerful analogy between the life of the Trinity and life in human community, and as a consequence human fulfillment in relationships of self-giving:

[T]he Lord Jesus, when He prayed to the Father "that all may be one . . . even as we are one" (*John* 17:21–22), opened up vistas closed to human reason, for He implied a certain likeness between the union of the divine Persons and the union of God's sons in truth and charity. This likeness reveals that man, who is the only creature on earth which God willed for itself, cannot fully find himself except through a sincere gift of himself.[74]

If "I am myself when I give myself," to make room for the other is neither a sad concession to the realities of the social contract nor a simple nod of respect for the principle of equality. Rather, it is one's door to authentic freedom and human fulfillment. As *Centesimus* highlights: "When man does not recognize in himself and in others the value and grandeur of the human person, he effectively deprives himself of the possibility of benefitting from his humanity and of entering into that relationship of solidarity and communion with others for which God created him. Indeed, it is through the free gift of self that man truly finds himself."[75]

Similarly, at the core of its definition of an "alienated" society is the inca-

72. Ibid., 34. See also David Schindler, Introduction to *Abba School*, 8 (summarizing Lubich's analysis: "The fullness of each person [in the Trinity] coincides with the 'self-emptying' entailed in being *wholly for* the other.").

73. See Chiara Lubich, "Spiritualità dell'unità e vita trinitaria" (The Spirituality of Unity and Trinitarian Life), *Nuova Umanità* 26 (2003): 12–13; Chiara Lubich, *Essential Writings* (Hyde Park, N.Y.: New City Press, 2007), 98.

74. *Gaudium et spes*, ¶ 24.

75. *Centesimus annus*, ¶ 41.

pacity to offer the "gift of self": "its forms of social organization, production and consumption make it more difficult to offer this gift of self and to establish this solidarity between people."[76]

A close analysis of a text from *Sollicitudo* reveals the profoundly Trinitarian dimension of the definition of solidarity. Pope John Paul II describes solidarity as an invitation beyond equality, beyond equal respect for the rights of others, to a more profound recognition of the fundamental unity of the human race: "In the light of faith, solidarity seeks to go beyond itself, to take on the specifically Christian dimension of total gratuity, forgiveness and reconciliation. One's neighbor is then not only a human being with his or her own rights and a fundamental equality with everyone else, but becomes the living image of God the Father, redeemed by the blood of Jesus Christ and placed under the permanent action of the Holy Spirit."[77] The consequence of this vision is clear: "One's neighbor must therefore be loved, even if an enemy, with the same love with which the Lord loves him or her; and for that person's sake one must be ready for sacrifice, even the ultimate one: to lay down one's life for the brethren (cf. 1 John. 3:16)."[78]

What is the result of this love? A new awareness or "new criterion" for interpreting reality. *Sollicitudo* goes on to explain: "At that point, awareness of the common fatherhood of God, of the brotherhood of all in Christ—'children in the Son'—and of the presence and life-giving action of the Holy Spirit will bring to our vision of the world a new criterion for interpreting it."[79] This Trinitarian vision, then, is the ultimate source of inspiration for solidarity: "Beyond human and natural bonds, already so close and strong, there is discerned in the light of faith a new model of the unity of the human race, which must ultimately inspire our solidarity. This supreme model of unity, which is a reflection of the intimate life of God, one God in three Persons, is what we Christians mean by the word 'communion.'"[80]

As distinguished from philanthropy, solidarity "is not a feeling of vague compassion or shallow distress at the misfortunes of so many people, both near and far. On the contrary, it is a firm and persevering determination to commit oneself to the common good; that is to say to the good of all and of each individual, because we are all really responsible for all."[81]

76. Ibid.   77. *Sollicitudo rei socialis*, ¶ 40.
78. Ibid.   79. Ibid.
80. Ibid.   81. *Sollicitudo rei socialis*, ¶ 38.

☙

Through a Trinitarian lens, Catholic Social Thought presents so much more than a tool to manage fairly what would otherwise be clashes between varying interests in the market, and much more than a grudging acknowledgment of another's rights. Because a life of communion is the essence of the structure of reality, making room for the other, acting in a way that acknowledges the other as the living image of God, is a true positive good, and more characteristic of an authentically human life.

TRINITARIAN PRODUCTS THEORY

What might the Trinity as a social model offer to products liability theory? The next sections explore its potential contribution by considering two hotly debated issues in the field. First, it returns to the Ford Pinto case to discuss the tension between policymakers and ordinary citizens concerning the role of cost-benefit analysis. Second, it explores the debate as played out in the Third Restatement's recent formulation of the definition of a defective product.

The analysis posits not that the Trinity would take sides in the debate, but that the Trinitarian lens can function as a "new criterion for interpretation," or as Thomas Kuhn described, a paradigm shift to help products theorists see "new and different things when looking with familiar instruments in places they have looked before."[82]

As anthropologist Clifford Geertz poetically described, the heart of religious perspective, "of this way of looking at the world," is not so much to posit the theory of an invisible world beyond the visible, nor the doctrine of a divine presence, nor the existence of "things in heaven and earth undreamt of in our philosophies."[83] Rather, according to Geertz, the heart of religious perspective is "the conviction that the values one holds are grounded in the inherent structure of reality, that between the way one ought to live and the way things really are there is an unbreakable inner connection. What sacred symbols do for those to whom they are sacred is to formulate an image of the world's construction and a program for human conduct that are mere reflexes of one another."[84]

82. See Thomas S. Kuhn, *The Structure of Scientific Revolutions,* 2d ed. (Chicago: University of Chicago Press, 1970), 111.
83. Clifford Geertz, "The Struggle for the Real," in *Islam Observed: Religious Developments in Morocco and Indonesia* (Chicago: University of Chicago Press, 2004), 97.
84. Ibid.

To pose the Trinity as a social model applicable to products liability theory is not a recipe for tweaking economic analysis toward more generous and safety-concerned results. The distinction between law-and-economics and the cultural framework of Catholic Social Thought is best described not as a direct clash between the greedy industrialists obsessed with profit-maximization and the magnanimous producers who triple-check every safety concern. The novelty, rather, is a completely different framework and process for decision making—or better, a completely different description of reality, which then informs one's conduct.

With the "intimate life of God" as a model for human communion, there is, to paraphrase Geertz, an "unbreakable inner connection" between the life of communion at the heart of the Trinity and the "the way one ought to live." Or as *Sollicitudo* might frame it, "in the light of faith," judgments about product design and safety are to be based on "a new model of the unity of the human race, which must ultimately inspire our solidarity."[85] What emerges is not so much a list of criteria, or an extra weight on one side of the balance, but a conviction about the "inherent structure of reality," which then informs the decision-making process.

As Professor William Stuntz describes, the "core" of Christianity's distinctive contribution to legal theory is about "attitudes and relationships, not rules and standards."[86] He gives a wonderfully concrete example by discussing of two ways to think about Jesus' occupation for most of his adult life: making tables. "Were the tables he made distinctive? Did he use different wood or a different manufacturing process than other carpenters used? The likely answer is no—at least, the gospel accounts offer no reason to think otherwise."[87] He then invites the reader to "change the question—focus less on the noun and more on the verb": "Instead of asking whether Jesus' tables were different, ask whether he made the tables differently—whether his motivations and attitudes toward his work, the ways he treated his customers and his coworker, differed from the practices of other carpenters. The answer to that question is surely yes."[88]

In a sense, the following sections focus "more on the verb," highlighting how Catholic Social Thought through a Trinitarian lens brings to the fore

85. See *Sollicitudo rei socialis*, ¶ 40.
86. See Stuntz, "Christian Legal Theory," 1721.
87. Ibid., 1721–22.
88. Ibid, 1722.

how a broader cultural framework for the commercial endeavor might influence the decision-making process for the production of material goods. Through this lens, the production of material goods is "naturally interrelated with the work of others," *with others, for others:* "it is a matter of doing something for someone else."[89]

The Ford Pinto Case through a Trinitarian Lens

Turning back to the opening discussion of the exploding Ford Pinto, here we might ask, would Catholic Social Thought through a Trinitarian analysis have made any difference? Or better, through this lens might we see "new and different things" that might provide additional guidance to define the design defect standard?

In the defense bar, at this point it is clear that cost-benefit arguments generally do not go over well with juries. As Professor Schwartz described the tension, "What seems obvious enough is that there exists a basic belief held by many (indeed most) of the public that it is wrong for a corporation to make decisions that sacrifice the lives of its customers in order to reduce the corporation's costs, to increase its profits."[90] More generally, as Professor Michael Wells summarized, "[t]here is a growing body of evidence that laymen (who, after all, make up juries) do not evaluate risks in the way that economists and other policymakers do."[91]

But even if one is not enamored of number crunching as the key to social policy, one must admit that the development of useful products that can vastly improve human life will always entail some risk of injury. Practically, expenditures on safety cannot be placed at infinity; manufacturers must, at some point, draw a line. It would be irresponsible for them not to measure scientifically the probability and gravity of likely risks and bring these measurements to bear on the development of their products. But in their efforts to articulate predictable standards and measure risks objectively, they run head on into one of the most intractable problems in tort theory: because it is impossible to measure certain values, they cannot be compared in nu-

---

89. See *Centesimus annus,* ¶ 31.

90. Schwartz, "The Myth of the Ford Pinto Case," 1041; see also Calabresi and Bobbit, *Tragic Choices,* 32.

91. See Michael Wells, "Scientific Policymaking and the Torts Revolution: The Revenge of the Ordinary Observer," *Georgia Law Review* 26 (1992): 725, 736.

meric terms.[92] To appreciate further the conundrum of hard-to-measure values, it is enough to flip around the problem: in evaluating the consequences of products accidents, at some point juries do have to come up with a dollar amount for damages.

In addition to the rather general critique that economics is not all there is, might Catholic Social Teaching through a Trinitarian lens have a specific contribution to offer to this complex problem?

Defining the "Reasonable Person"

Catholic Social Thought through a Trinitarian lens offers not only insight into what cost-benefit analysis fails to capture, but also an alternative framework for defining what it means to be "reasonable." As Professor Posner sets out the "economic meaning of negligence," the "rational profit-maximizing enterprise" "should attempt to measure three things: the magnitude of the loss if an accident occurs; the probability of the accident's occurring; and the burden of taking precautions that would avert it."[93] If the cost of safety measures or of curtailment exceeds the benefit in accident avoidance to be gained by incurring that cost, it would be more "rational" to pay tort judgments to the accident victims rather than incur the larger cost of avoiding liability.[94]

As discussed above, within a cultural framework informed by Catholic Social Thought, one is under no illusion that the algebraic formula can fully capture all that should be taken into consideration. The dilemma of incommensurable values remains, but because Catholic Social Thought's cultural framework does not hinge on assigning numeric values to all the factors in the balance, it is less problematic. Catholic Social Thought would highlight the limitations of a Posnerian "rational profit-maximizer's" approach not so much because it applies the economic tools of cost-benefit analysis, but because the criteria are too impoverished to fully capture the decision-making process of a "reasonable" person.

Through a Trinitarian lens, something "new and different" comes into relief—an alternative definition of what it means to be "reasonable." Through this lens, the "inherent structure of reality" consists of the relationships of

92. See Cass R. Sunstein, "Incommensurability and Valuation in Law," *Michigan Law Review* 92 (1994): 779, 796; *Centesimus annus*, ¶ 40, and discussion supra, notes 52–55.

93. Posner, "A Theory of Negligence," 32.

94. Ibid., 33.

mutual love and gift that provide "a new model of the unity of the human race, which must ultimately inspire our solidarity."[95] To paraphrase Geertz, this is the model of "the way things really are" that informs "the way one ought to live"—the moral standard of due care.

Such an approach not only would explode models of consumers as primarily atomistic economic beings[96] but also would provide a thick description of alternative forms of rationality.[97] For one whose "inherent structure of reality" *is* the depth of one's connection to other human beings, it is evident that the Posnerian "rational profit-maximizers" might be missing out on the greatest richness of all. Through a Trinitarian lens, the heart of what it means to be a "reasonable person" is to open oneself to relationships of respect, service, and attentive care to all that solidarity calls for in the production process. Through this lens, it is "reasonable" that the production of material goods should express concern for others: "I am myself not when I close myself off from the other, but when I give myself, when out of love I am lost in the other."[98] Through a Trinitarian lens, it is *more* reasonable to let solidarity with those with whom one is called to live in relationships of communion permeate the decision-making process than to be guided by "rational profit-maximizing" formulas.

The Jury's Perspective as Normative Guide

The alternative definition of the "reasonable person" described above would probably not satisfy those in search of an objective anchor for product design decisions. The driving force behind much of the law-and-economics analysis is to provide a set of predictable standards that lend themselves to even and neutral application. What is often left out of the equation, however, is that those who evaluate the actual cases—civil juries—often reject these seemingly neutral and objective descriptions of the law. Or if this fact is recognized, it is often followed by the assumption that the reason ordinary citi-

---

95. See *Sollicitudo rei socialis*, ¶ 40.

96. See Luigino Bruni, "Toward an Economic Rationality 'Capable of Communion,'" in *The Economy of Communion: Toward a Multi-Dimensional Economic Culture* (hereafter *Economy of Communion*), ed. Luigino Bruni, trans. Lorna Gold (Hyde Park, N.Y.: New City Press, 2002), 41–67 *et seq.*; see also Kysar, "The Expectations of Consumers," 1757–58.

97. Kysar, "The Expectations of Consumers," 1774–82 (discussing whether lay [non-expert] judgments constitute a "rival rationality").

98. Lubich, *Toward a Theology and Philosophy of Unity*, 33. See also *Centesimus annus*, ¶¶ 41, 58.

zens reject such standards is because they are incapable of the technical and complex analysis required to appreciate and accurately apply them.

Through a Trinitarian lens, one can appreciate not only alternative definitions of what it means to be reasonable, but also reasons why the jury may already be intuitively operating according to this dynamic.[99] As Professor Stephen Gilles put it: "No one has suggested that jurors are deeply conflicted over whether the average person ought to take as much care for the average other person as for himself or herself."[100] Through this lens, Catholic Social Thought actually does a better job than economic analysis of capturing the operating definitions of "reasonableness" as applied by jurors within the context of the dynamic of a civil trial.

Studies indicate that when projected deaths are anonymous and statistical, the public seems more willing to balance risks and benefits; when victims are specific and identifiable, however, it is more likely to call for open-ended expenditures.[101] A tort suit, by nature, focuses on and dramatizes the individual victim with all his or her personal attributes: the victim's injury or death is the ultimate focus of the trial.[102] When jurors are brought face-to-face with accident victims and with managers who made decisions about safety, the context cannot help but put into relief the personal dimension of responsibility for decisions about safety and the personal consequences of product accidents. There are no "statistical people"—only flesh-and-blood human beings.

As Professor Charles Fried explains, in certain contexts a stranger may be seen as a "potential friend": "A person is a potential friend if we encounter him in some degree of particularity, as a person with concrete, individual attributes. Thus every stranger we encounter in a situation where personal interaction of some sort is possible—every person who appears to us as a particular person—is a potential friend."[103] Even if the jurors and parties are strangers at the start of the trial, the process of the trial brings them into a context in which the jurors are more likely to view these parties as "potential friends"— engaged in a personal interaction—rather than as "statistical lives."[104]

99. See Kysar, "The Expectations of Consumers," 1737–38.
100. Stephen G. Gilles, "The Invisible Hand Formula," *Virginia Law Review* 80 (1994): 1015, 1048.
101. See generally Charles Fried, "The Value of Life," *Harvard Law Review* 82 (1969): 1415.
102. See, e.g., Schwartz, "The Myth of the Ford Pinto Case," 1043.
103. Fried, "The Value of Life," 1429.
104. See ibid., 1430.

Through a Trinitarian lens, the preferred point of reference for a safety design decision would be the personal face-to-face dynamic of a civil trial, which highlights the impact that product accidents have on individual people. Because juries are the ultimate evaluators of product design decisions, the face-to-face encounter with the consequences of product accidents should actually carry more weight than a distanced statistical analysis. Observing the dynamic of a trial through a Trinitarian lens, one may intuit that jurors' enraged response to cost-benefit analysis is not so much a negative reaction to the process of assigning numeric values to probable risks as an indication that this kind of distanced and seemingly "objective" analysis does not fully capture the regard due to fellow human beings.

Considering the Ford Pinto dilemma, reading the design defect standard through a Trinitarian lens, the cost-benefit studies relevant to the design of the Pinto would have been placed within a much broader framework of attentive care to all that solidarity would require. With the Trinity as a model of the "unity of the human race," it is clear that solidarity requires more than a "feeling of vague compassion or shallow distress at the misfortunes of so many people, both near and far."[105] Rather, it inspires "a firm and persevering determination to commit oneself to the common good"—and a consequent concern for each person individually potentially affected by product accidents—"that is to say to the good of all and of each individual, because we are all really responsible for all."[106]

If the Ford Pinto manufacturers had looked at the design problem through a Trinitarian lens, they would have felt solidarity's pull toward responsibility for "the good of all and of each individual"—and would have been cautious not to let the seemingly anonymous and distant quality of the mass statistics distort the fact that their safety considerations could have drastic and fatal consequences in the lives of actual individual human beings. Through a Trinitarian lens, the universal bonds of human solidarity would inform design decisions to the point that the manufacturers might ask themselves, "Given realistic budget constraints on the amount one could spend on an automobile, would I want my child, my sister, or my father to drive this car?"

While manufacturers who do not open themselves to a broader cultural analysis run the risk of being blindsided by juries, the instrumental point should not be overemphasized. The power of Catholic Social Thought's anal-

105. See *Sollicitudo rei socialis,* ¶ 38.
106. See ibid.

ysis lies in its own philosophical structure and its deep appreciation for humanity's relational nature, not in its predictive capacity. However, the disconnect between current products theory standards and actual jury decisions does indicate that to highlight the need for a broader cultural analysis such as that offered by Catholic Social Thought is not a plea for manufacturers to magnanimously open the corporate coffers beyond the call of duty. Rather, it is a thick description of the legal standards to which they will be held, according to jurors' evaluations of "reasonableness." Thus even the law's theoretical "bad man," who is interested only in a description of the edges of legal duty so as to predict potential liability, may find something helpful in Catholic Social Teaching's description of the cultural criteria.[107]

The "Risk-Utility"—"Consumer Expectation" Debate through a Trinitarian Lens

A second hotly debated area of design defect theory revolves around the effort to define the test for a defectively designed product. As courts and scholars worked to articulate the test, two main contenders emerged: the consumer expectation test and the risk-utility balance.[108] As the California Supreme Court, long recognized as a leader in the development of products liability theory, explained in the relatively early case of *Barker*:

[A] product may be found to be defective in design, so as to subject a manufacturer to strict liability for resulting injuries, under either of two alternative tests. First a product may be found to be defective in design if the plaintiff establishes that the product failed to perform as safely as an ordinary consumer would expect when used in an intended or reasonably foreseeable manner. Second, a product may alternatively be found defec-

---

107. See Oliver Wendell Holmes, "The Path of the Law," *Harvard Law Review* 10 (1897): 457, 459, 461.

108. The consumer expectation test emerged from two comments to the Second Restatement, § 402A. In judging whether one had sold a product in an "unreasonably dangerous" defective condition, Comment *g* defined "defect" as occurring "where the product is, at the time it leaves the seller's hands, in a condition not contemplated by the ultimate consumer, which will be unreasonably dangerous to him." Comment *i* further described the consumer's perspective as according to the "ordinary knowledge common to the community as to [the product's] characteristics." The risk-utility balance emerged from early scholarship commenting on § 402A; a second test emerged in the effort to describe "reasonable" judgments about product design. See John W. Wade, "On the Nature of Strict Tort Liability for Products" (hereafter "On the Nature"), *Mississippi Law Journal* 44 (1973): 825, 837. For one of the best explanations of the risk-utility test, see *Cepada v. Cumberland Engineering Co.*, 386 A2d 816 (NJ 1978).

tive in design if the plaintiff demonstrates that the product's design proximately caused his injury and the defendant fails to establish, in light of the relevant factors, that, on balance, the benefits of the challenged design outweigh the risk of danger inherent in such design.[109]

Attempting to glean a "consensus" of the courts and leading torts theorists, the recently formulated Third Restatement indicates that the risk-utility balancing test seems to have won the day. Section 2(b) states the test for design defect: a product is defective in design "when the foreseeable risks of harm posed by the product could have been reduced or avoided by the adoption of a reasonable alternative design . . . and the omission of the alternative design renders the product not reasonably safe."[110] Comment d defines "reasonable" according to the risk-utility balance, and in comparison to an alternative design. Comment d states:

> Answering [the question of whether design specifications create unreasonable risks] requires reference to a standard outside the specifications. Subsection (b) adopts a reasonableness ("risk-utility" balancing) test as the standard for judging the defectiveness of product designs. More specifically, the test is whether a reasonable alternative design would, at reasonable cost, have reduced the foreseeable risks of harm posed by the product and, if so, whether the omission of the alternative design rendered the product not reasonably safe.[111]

Consumer expectations are tucked into a broad range of factors for evaluating not the product itself, but whether the alternative design was reasonable. Comment g explains: "Under Subsection (b) consumer expectations do not constitute an independent standard for judging the defectiveness of product design." While consumer expectations may be relevant to proof of a reasonable alternative design, "since reasonable consumers have a right to expect product designs that conform to the reasonableness standard," such expectations are not determinative.[112]

What would Catholic Social Thought through a Trinitarian lens bring to the debate? The following subsections note a few insights on various angles of the discussion.

---

109. *Barker v. Lull Engineering Co.*, 575 P2d 443, 455–56 (Colo App 1978).

110. Third Restatement, § 2(b), 14.

111. Ibid. § 2, comment d, 19.

112. See ibid., § 2 comment g, 27.

A Critique of the Alternative Design Requirement as an Expression of a Culture of Consumerism

One of the most controversial aspects of the Third Restatement's design defect standard was its articulation of reasonable alternative design as an element of the plaintiff's prima facie case.[113] As section 2(b) defines, the risk-utility balance is evaluated in comparison to the extent to which harm could have been reduced or avoided by the adoption of a reasonable alternative design. The Third Restatement's alternative design requirement has been criticized on several grounds, including its failure to accurately reflect the dominant trends in case law and the extent to which the requirement may dramatically increase the cost of proving a products liability case.[114]

Catholic Social Thought through a Trinitarian lens would push the inquiry back a number of steps to ask an even more fundamental cultural question: to what extent does the alternative design requirement presume the inherent goodness of an unending variety of material products, and perhaps even express a certain "blind submission" to "pure consumerism"?[115] As *Sollicitudo* warns: "an excessive availability of every kind of material goods for the benefit of certain social groups, easily makes people slaves of 'possession' and of immediate gratification, with no other horizon than the multiplication or continual replacement of the things already owned with others still better."[116]

The critique should not be overstated, especially in light of Catholic Social Thought's evaluation of economic initiative as "important not only for the individual, but also for the common good,"[117] and statement that an "ever greater availability of material goods not only meets needs but also opens new horizons."[118] But on balance it can shed light on the extent to which unarticulated cultural presumptions are often tucked into products liability theories such as the requirement of showing an alternative design.

Here too, Catholic Social Thought through a Trinitarian lens not only can point out the cultural drawbacks of "super-development"[119] and the "crass materialism" and "radical dissatisfaction" that result,[120] but also can highlight

---

113. See ibid., § 2(b) and § 2(b), comment d, 20.

114. See, e.g., Frank J. Vandall and Joshua F. Vandall, "A Call for an Accurate Restatement (Third) of Torts: Design Defect," *University of Memphis Law Review* 33 (2003): 909, 923; See also Kysar, "The Expectations of Consumers," 1720n84.

115. See *Sollicitudo rei socialis*, ¶ 28.   116. Ibid.

117. Ibid., ¶ 15.   118. Ibid., ¶ 29.

119. Ibid., ¶¶ 28, 31.   120. Ibid., ¶ 28.

the "new and different things"[121] that may form the basis of a positive alternative. In light of an "unbreakable inner connection" between the life of communion at the heart of the Trinity and the "the way one ought to live," one may begin to see the ways in which the production of material goods could be evaluated—and ordered—against the backdrop of a broader cultural framework.

Drawing an important distinction between "having" and "being," *Sollicitudo* explains: "To 'have' objects and goods does not in itself perfect the human subject, unless it contributes to the maturing and enrichment of that subject's 'being,' that is to say unless it contributes to the realization of the human vocation as such."[122] *Centesimus* draws out the moral consequences: "It is not wrong to want to live better; what is wrong is a style of life which is presumed to be better when it is directed towards 'having' rather than 'being,' and which wants to have more, not in order to be more but in order to spend life in enjoyment as an end in itself."[123] The challenge then becomes, *Centesimus* continues, "to create life-styles in which the quest for truth, beauty, goodness and communion with others for the sake of common growth are the factors which determine consumer choices, savings and investments."[124]

Decisions about the development of a variety of products should be evaluated against the backdrop of this imbalance: "there are some people—the few who possess much—who do not really succeed in 'being' because, through a reversal of the hierarchy of values, they are hindered by the cult of 'having'; and there are others—the many who have little or nothing—who do not succeed in realizing their basic human vocation because they are deprived of essential goods."[125]

Through a Trinitarian lens, one would see in the cultural shift an opportunity to further solidarity and human communion. The Trinitarian lens would highlight the ways in which broader questions about the production of material goods could constitute "a great opportunity for the moral, cultural, and even economic growth of all humanity."[126] In light of Trinitarian relationships of communion, this framework also offers to those hindered by the cult of "having" the possibility of "entering into that relationship of solidarity and communion with others for which God created [them]."[127]

---

121. Kuhn, *The Structure of Scientific Revolutions*, 111.
122. *Sollicitudo rei socialis*, ¶ 28.   123. *Centesimus annus*, ¶ 36.
124. Ibid.   125. *Sollicitudo rei socialis*, ¶ 28.
126. See *Centesimus annus*, ¶ 28.   127. See ibid., ¶ 41.

Through this lens, one might also see new advantages to the roads not taken in products theory. For example, in the influential article that set out the initial proposal for risk-utility factors, Dean John Wade included an inquiry into not only the manufacturer's ability to eliminate the unsafe character of the product, but also the availability of a substitute *product* "which would meet the same need and not be as unsafe."[128]

Beyond "Technical" Expectations to Highlight Relationships of Solidarity and Communion

A second area of debate that was especially heated in the formulation of the Third Restatement's design defect standard was the extent to which the "risk-utility" test is preferable to the "consumer expectation" test. One of the most pronounced criticisms of the consumer expectation test is that beyond the limited category of products that fail in their "manifestly intended" function, consumers may not be able to form any specific expectations, particularly regarding complex product design. As the manufacturer argued in another California case in which the plaintiff alleged injuries resulting from defective automobile design, *Soule v. General Motors,* the consumer expectation test is deficient and unfair because, among other reasons, it focuses "not on the objective condition of products, but on the subjective, unstable, and often unreasonable opinion of consumers" and because "it ignores the reality that ordinary consumers know little about how safe the complex products they use can or should be made."[129]

The Reporters for the Third Restatement agree that the consumer expectation test seems to pose a "totally unstructured standard of reasonableness."[130] Because the consumer expectation test relies heavily on intuition, they conclude, "it is so vague as to be lawless."[131] In contrast, it is argued, the more focused risk-utility test "relies less on intuition and more on a balanc-

---

128. Wade, "On the Nature," 837–38.

129. See *Soule v. General Motors,* 882 P2d 298, 309 (Cal 1994).

130. See Aaron D. Twerski, "From Risk-Utility to Consumer Expectation: Enhancing the Role of the Judicial Screening in Product Liability", *Hofstra Law Review* 11 (1983): 861, 864; James A. Henderson Jr., "Judicial Review of Manufacturers' Conscious Design Choices: The Limits of Adjudication" (hereafter "Limits of Adjudication"), *Columbia Law Review* 73 (1973): 1531.

131. See James A. Henderson and Aaron D. Twerski, "Achieving Consensus on Defective Product Design" (hereafter "Consensus"), *Cornell Law Review* 83 (1998): 867, 882; Henderson, "Limits of Adjudication," 1531.

ing of articulated considerations regarding the relative advantages and disadvantages of the product as designed and as it alternatively could have been designed."[132]

Further, the critique continues, even if the standard could be measured, it would be too fraught with individual preferences. "The concept of consumer expectations carries with it inescapable psychological connotations that frustrate attempts to objectify the appropriate standard. It is unrealistic to believe that one can surgically separate ordinary consumer expectations from the value preferences of flesh-and-blood human beings. . . . Even though risk utility confronts the same problem of objectifying a normative standard, it does a better job."[133]

In response to this analysis, Catholic Social Thought through a Trinitarian lens would offer both a critique and an alternative explanation. First, in response to its confidence that the complete set of risks and benefits can be "objectively" balanced, Catholic Social Thought would highlight the extent to which important human needs escape the logic of the market and the idea that "[t]here are goods which by their very nature cannot and must not be bought or sold."[134] It might even identify as "idolatrous" the extent to which a risk-utility balance tends to ignore "goods which by their nature are not and cannot be mere commodities."[135] To the extent that the risk-utility balance rests on the supposition that all the goods at stake could be objectively measured, Catholic Social Thought would unmask the illusion.

Catholic Social Thought would also highlight the ways in which this analysis tends to focus exclusively on the technical and mechanical aspects of consumer expectations. While this dimension is certainly relevant to product development, it nonetheless captures only one aspect of the inquiry and neglects an important set of "expectations" that embrace a universe beyond the technical concerns about a product's mechanical function.

While consumers may not be able to give a mechanically detailed explanation of how a product should have functioned, they can and do articulate their expectations about the care owed to relationships of respect and about the kind of judgments manufacturers should make when they know about certain risks to safety. As a juror in the Chevy Malibu case commented, "GM has no regard for the people in their cars, and they should be held respon-

---

132. Henderson and Twerski, "Consensus," 878–79.

133. Ibid., 881–82.   134. See *Centesimus annus*, ¶ 40.

135. See ibid.

sible for it. . . . We're telling [GM] that when they know that something . . . is going to injure people, then it's more important that they pay the money to make the car safe than to come to court and have a trial all the time."[136]

This is not to say that a general expectation about the "regard for people in their cars" will always be sufficient to fully analyze whether a product is defective in design. In *Soule*, for example, the plaintiff's own theory of design defect called for a technical and mechanical examination of "the precise behavior of several obscure components of her car under the complex circumstances of a particular accident."[137] In these cases, as the *Soule* court concluded, ordinary consumer expectations may not do much to advance the technical analysis of defect.[138]

But even in cases such as these the value judgments underlying technical design decisions should not be glossed over. Here Catholic Social Thought through a Trinitarian lens could highlight the ways consumer expectations about, for example, the regard due to "people in their cars" are neither unreasonable nor "so vague as to be lawless"—but actually in many ways capture the heart of the "law" as juries understand it.

Within a Trinitarian framework and process for decision making, appreciating the "unbreakable inner connection" between the life of communion at the heart of the Trinity and the "the way one ought to live," moral decisions about product design and safety can ultimately reflect "a new model of the unity of the human race, which must ultimately inspire our solidarity."[139] Even though ordinary consumer expectations may not be expressed in mathematical equations or formulas, they may nonetheless serve to form a robust and "reasonable" cultural framework that emphasizes the moral dimensions of decisions about product testing and development.

Finally, a Trinitarian lens would provide not only a cultural framework but a process for defining reasonable product design.[140] Of course, as the Reporters for the Third Restatement have observed, "one can never surgical-

136. Jury foreman Coleman Thornton and juror Sheila Nash, interview by Anne W. O'Neill, Henry Weinstein, Eric Malnic, "GM Ordered to Pay $4.9 Billion in Crash Verdict Liability," *Los Angeles Times* (10 July 1999): A1.

137. See *Soule v. General Motors*, 882 P2d 298, 309 (Cal 1994).

138. Ibid.

139. See *Sollicitudo rei socialis*, ¶ 40.

140. See Kysar, "The Expectations of Consumers," 1772. See also Stefano Zamagni, "On the Formation and Meaning of the 'Economy of Communion Experience,'" in *Economy of Communion*, 135.

ly separate ordinary consumer expectations from the value preferences of flesh-and-blood human beings." But neither is the seemingly "objective" risk-utility balance any less an expression of human value preferences.

Through a Trinitarian lens, the potential tug-of-war between values can become an occasion to further solidarity. By opening up the process to allow room *(kenosis)* for consumer expectations, in all their manifold dimensions—technical, mechanical, aesthetic, and moral—to permeate decisions about product design, the resulting "mutual indwelling" *(pericoresis)* could not only become a much more complete cultural foundation for economic development, and not only further and express the bonds of human solidarity and communion, but also serve as a substantive guide for the standards for product development.

CONCLUSION

A few years after the Third Restatement was published, the Reporters, Professors Henderson and Twerski, pondered the continued vitality of the consumer expectation test in some courts and among some commentators. They lamented that its influence could continue to wreak havoc in products litigation, allowing recovery "notwithstanding evidence that no feasible alternative design could have reduced or avoided the plaintiff's harm,"[141] and that it threatened to "abandon[] technology as the cornerstone of rational products litigation."[142] What is the great attraction? "Perhaps," they suggest, "the lure of such a doctrine is that it awakens in all of us a nostalgia for a world in which technology was not dominant."[143]

Catholic Social Thought through a Trinitarian lens would offer an alternative explanation. It would see in the recognition of the extent to which consumer expectations should inform design decisions, and more generally in a resistance to domination of economic analyses of the law, the expression of "an inherent structure of reality" in which technology *is not* dominant—because the human person is placed at the center of every aspect of productive activity. It would describe a world in which the cornerstone of products litigation is not technology, but the human person, morally responsible to other

141. James A. Henderson, Jr. and Aaron D. Twerski, "Intuition and Technology in Product Design Litigation: An Essay on Proximate Cause," *Georgia Law Journal* 88 (2000): 659, 689.
142. Ibid., 688–89.
143. Ibid., 689.

human beings for the consequences of product design decisions. If there is nostalgia for anything, it is for authentic relationships of solidarity and communion—because we are made in the image of God, who is not alone, who is relational, who is Trinity, "[w]e are called to reach out to build relationships of love and justice."[144] On earth as it is in heaven.

144. See *Sharing Catholic Social Teaching,* 1.

[13]

CRIMINAL LAW:
"EVERLASTING SPLENDOURS"

Death-Row Volunteers, Lawyers' Ethics, and Human Dignity

❧

RICHARD W. GARNETT

A few years ago, in an episode of the award-winning juris-drama *The Practice*, Rebecca Ward—one of the idealistic, if occasionally overzealous, young lawyers in Bobby Donnell's high-powered trial boutique—is asked to assist John Mockler, a legendary capital-defense lawyer, by serving as local counsel in a federal death-penalty case.[1] Rebecca's enthusiasm for the project wanes briefly upon learning that the condemned inmate, Walter Dawson, has elected not to fight his impending execution, but quickly waxes again as she sets out for the federal prison in Indiana, determined to convince him to cling to life.

She fails. Dawson insists that he is not afraid to die. He assures Rebecca

---

This essay is based on a longer one, which was included in the *Notre Dame Law Review*'s tribute to my colleague, teacher, and friend, Professor Thomas Shaffer. See "Sectarian Reflections on Lawyers' Ethics and Death Row Volunteers," *Notre Dame Law Review* 77 (2002): 795.

1. "Killing Time," an episode of *The Practice*, ABC, 30 September 2001. For another excellent television show's take on the death-row-volunteer problem, see "Bad Girl," an episode of *Law and Order*, NBC, 29 April 1998.

that, having accepted from Christ the gifts of redemption and forgiveness, and committed himself to God's service, he is ready to accept the punishment he believes his "atrocities" require. "But it's possible to serve God with your *life,* as well," she presses him. "Think how much good you could do! Think how many souls could you save!" Dawson hesitates. He appears to take these entreaties to heart. In the end, though, he is unmoved.

Later, outside the prison, Mockler scolds Rebecca: "Do you really think you did any good?" he asks. "The one thing he had, you just took away from him. . . . He *will* die, but perhaps more painfully now." Dawson, he reminds her, "is a human being, not a cause."

Rebecca's efforts, and Mockler's rebuke, raise the question: What should we lawyers think about, and how should we respond to, "death-row volunteers"? When a defendant accused of a capital crime attempts to plead guilty, or instructs his lawyer not to present a particular defense; when a convicted killer refuses to permit the introduction of potentially life-saving mitigating evidence—or even urges the jury to impose a death sentence—at the sentencing phase of a death-eligible case; when a condemned inmate refuses to file, or to appeal the denial of, habeas corpus and other postconviction petitions for relief; when he elects not to object to a particular capital-punishment method, to call into question his own competence to be executed, or to file an eleventh-hour, last-ditch appeal—what should lawyers do, and why? More specifically, what light might Catholic teachings and traditions cast on the death-row-volunteer problem?

Now, these are not questions of merely professional interest, narrowly conceived, for lawyers and judges. They are staples of headlines and news programs, both serious and sensational. They fascinate pop-culture purveyors and consumers alike, though little is novel about them. After all, Plato told us in the *Crito* that Socrates refused his friends' entreaties that he escape to Thessaly and thereby avoid execution for corrupting the youth, and Dickens contended that Sidney Carton did a "far, far better thing" than he had ever done in submitting to the death sentence imposed on another. More recently, Norman Mailer's sprawling "novel," *The Executioner's Song,*[2] relates the pathetic bravado with which convicted killer Gary Gilmore—a self-styled combination of Nietzschean *ubermench* and Marlboro man—demanded that the State of Utah strap him to an office chair, in front of a filthy mattress, fac-

---

2. Norman Mailer, *The Executioner's Song* (Boston: Little, Brown, 1979).

ing a black curtain with holes cut out for the executioners' rifles. And Professor Michael Mello has offered a gripping, if less lurid, account of the trial of the "Unabomber," Ted Kaczinski, and of his decision to risk a death sentence rather than to permit his lawyers to present his letter-bombing campaign and rambling neo-Luddite "manifesto" as the work of a madman.[3]

Still, notwithstanding his headliner status and prime-time appeal, the death-row volunteer is of particular interest *to* lawyers because he poses particularly chilling problems—"legal ethics" problems—*for* lawyers.[4] In fact, *The Executioner's Song* is a legal-ethics text as much as it is anything else. After all, at the end of Gilmore's life, lawyers were everywhere, doing and saying things that the reader is challenged to evaluate and to judge. Lawyers sought and won his death sentence and execution; they sold his story, marketed his death, and supervised his estate; they struggled creatively to keep him alive against his will, to protect other death-row inmates and to publicize opposition to the death penalty; and they tried to save taxpayers' money and to spare his mother the pain of losing her son to what looked like his shallow and deluded machismo.

Not surprisingly, then, more than a few lawyers and law teachers have attempted to map the "ethical" course for attorneys whose clients, in one way or another, elect or acquiesce in execution.[5] Still, it seems to me that something is missing from our thinking, and from our conversations, about the death-row-volunteer problem. It is not that we have misread the relevant canons and codes or misunderstood the relevant legal doctrine. The problem, instead, is that our arguments—which sound primarily in the register of choice, competence, and autonomy—tend to reflect and proceed from an unsound "moral anthropology." That is, they proceed from a flawed account of what it *is* about the human person that does the work in moral arguments about what we ought or ought not to do and about how we ought or ought not to be treated. They miss what it means, and what follows from the fact, that a condemned and resigned inmate "is a human being, not a cause." The

---

3. Michael Mello, *The United States v. Theodore John Kaczinski: Ethics, Power, and the Invention of the Unabomber* (New York: Context Books, 1999).

4. See Welsh S. White, "Defendants Who Elect Execution," *University of Pittsburgh Law Review* 48 (1987): 853, 855 (noting that the death-row volunteer presents a "special dilemma" for capital-defense specialists).

5. For a list of such efforts, see Garnett, "Sectarian Reflections," 798–99n15. See also John H. Blume, "Killing the Willing: 'Volunteers,' Suicide and Competency," *Michigan Law Review* 103 (2005): 939.

unfortunate result, it seems to me, is that the professed commitment to "human dignity" that drives and sustains so many capital-defense lawyers is often undermined by these same lawyers' responses to death-row volunteers.

My colleague and friend Professor Thomas Shaffer once offered the countercultural observation that "[e]thics properly defined is thinking about morals. It is an intellectual activity and an appropriate academic discipline, but it is valid only to the extent that it truthfully describes what is going on."[6] Morality, in other words, is about truth; it is about what *is*. Shaffer is right, I think. And this leads me to wonder if my own dissatisfaction with the death-row-volunteer literature is rooted in a nagging worry that it does *not* "truthfully describe what is going on," and that it has, in Pope John Paul II's words, missed the "moral truth about the human person"[7]—about what we are and why it matters.

It is appropriate, in a volume that gathers and presents "Catholic perspectives" on American legal problems, doctrines, premises, and traditions, to bring this "moral truth" to the conversation, and to propose—even if not to demonstrate—that the late Holy Father's Christian humanism and Catholic moral anthropology not only enable a more truthful description of "what is going on" in the context of the volunteer problem but also point toward a more promising solution to it. To be clear: This essay's aim is not to recount, defend, or attack the state and history of the Church's teaching on capital punishment generally. For present purposes, I assume that even a whole-hearted and clearheaded embrace and understanding of the Church's claims about the nature and destiny of the human person does not require one to reject categorically the death penalty.[8] Nor do I arrive at any definitive prescriptions for lawyers representing would-be volunteers or proposals for reforms of legal-ethics norms or death-penalty-related laws. My aim here is modest, but still valuable: to surface the possibilities that some capital-defense lawyers' arguments about volunteers—and, more generally, that some arguments for capital punishment's abolition—owe too much to a questionable understanding of what the person is and is for, and that the common

6. Thomas L. Shaffer, "The Legal Ethics of Radical Individualism," *Texas Law Review* 65 (1987): 963, 965.

7. Pope John Paul II, Ad Limina Address to the Bishops of Texas, Oklahoma, and Arkansas (6 June 1998).

8. Cf., e.g., E. Christian Brugger, *Capital Punishment and the Roman Catholic Moral Tradition* (Notre Dame, IN: University of Notre Dame Press, 2003).

practice of challenging one's client's competence merely because one disagrees with his decision to forgo challenges to his death sentence tends to undermine the very concept of human dignity that many death-row lawyers claim to serve.

DEATH-ROW VOLUNTEERS

The death-row-volunteer problem is not as exotic or anomalous as it might at first sound: five of the first eight men executed after the Supreme Court in 1976 reauthorized the death penalty were (in one way or another) volunteers, and according to one writer, "[o]f the 302 inmates executed between 1973 and 1995, thirty-seven, or twelve percent, gave up their appeals."[9] In fact, experienced capital-defense litigators report that *every* capital defendant, at one point or another, expresses a preference for execution over life in prison.[10] Most of them, though, change their minds.

The case of John Brewer, executed by the State of Arizona in 1993, is probably as typical of these cases as any one can be.[11] Brewer strangled his girlfriend, Rita Brier (and killed his unborn child), after she threatened to leave him in order to "prove [to him] he could live by himself." He confessed to the crime, was determined to be "competent," and pleaded guilty to capital murder. At his sentencing hearing, he refused to present evidence in mitigation (the court ordered his counsel to present such evidence anyway, over Brewer's objection). Instead, "throughout the[] proceedings, [Brewer] voiced his support for the state's death penalty statute and expressed his belief that he should be executed for the confessed crimes." He was, evidently, defiantly unrepentant. To ensure his own execution, he claimed—possibly falsely—to have engaged in sexual intercourse with Ms. Brier's corpse. He was sentenced to death; his guilty plea and death sentence were affirmed on mandatory appeal (over his objection); and he "then opposed every legal effort to save his life." In particular, he won the dismissal of a state-law petition for postconviction relief that was filed without his consent, and he never filed a federal habeas corpus petition. His mother tried, without success, in state and fed-

---

9. Christy Chandler, "Voluntary Executions," *Stanford Law Review* 50 (1998): 1897, 1902n42.

10. White, "Defendants Who Elect Execution," 855.

11. See *Brewer v. Lewis*, 989 F2d 1021 (9th Cir 1993); *Brewer v. Lewis*, 997 F2d 550 (9th Cir 1993) (Reinhardt, J., dissenting from denial of *en banc* review); *State v. Brewer*, 826 P2d 783, 788 (Ariz 1992), cert. *denied*, 506 US 872 (1992).

eral courts, to contest Brewer's competency and to proceed on her own behalf and as her son's "next friend." Although Brewer had apparently come to
believe that the co-deity and man-elf "Fro" had been reincarnated on Earth
as Brewer's murdered girlfriend and that he would rejoin "Fro" on the planet
Terracia after his execution, the federal court of appeals found no basis for
disturbing other courts' determinations that Brewer was competent to waive
further review. Through all this, Brewer continued to insist, "I'm here to pay
the penalty. . . . I just don't think I deserve to live."[12] He even informed the
Arizona Board of Pardons and Paroles that, if he had it to do over, he would
kill Ms. Brier again, in an even grislier fashion. On March 3, 1993, Brewer
was executed by lethal injection.

Why so many volunteers? There is no simple answer. We might start,
though, with this picture:

There are 2,859 people awaiting execution in the United States. . . . If death row were really a row, it would stretch for 2.6 miles, cell after six-foot-wide cell. In each cell, one
person, sitting, pacing, watching TV, sleeping, writing letters. Locked in their cells nearly twenty-four hours a day, the condemned communicate with each other by shouts,
notes, and hand-held mirrors, all with the casual dexterity handicapped people acquire
over time. Occasionally there is a break in the din of shouted conversations—a silent
cell, its inhabitant withdrawn into a cocoon of madness.[13]

Certainly, depression, mental illness, and psychological impairment—
"ranging from gentle neurosis to flamboyant talking-to-space-ships delu-
sional psychoses"[14]—are common on death rows and among those convicted
of capital crimes. There also is a grim awareness that the odds against securing a new trial or sentence through petitions and appeals are long and growing longer, as the courts iron out the remaining wrinkles in the substantive
law that governs the death penalty, as legislatures streamline and scale back
postconviction and habeas corpus remedies, and as competition increases for
the time of experienced—or even competent—capital-defense attorneys.[15] It
is understandable that condemned inmates facing the anxiety and tedium of

12. Abraham Kwok and Pamela Manson, "Brewer Is Executed, 1st Lethal Injection Given
in Arizona," *Arizona Republic* (3 March 1993): A2.

13. Michael Mello, "A Letter on a Lawyer's Life of Death," *South Texas Law Review* 38
(1997):121, 166.

14. Ibid., 167.

15. See generally Jim Dwyer, Barry Scheck, and Peter Neufeld, *Actual Innocence: Five
Days to Execution and Other Dispatches from the Wrongly Convicted* (New York: Doubleday,
2000).

waiting years—sometimes decades—under a death sentence might want to give up. Still, we should hesitate before chalking up a volunteer's choice to despair, fatigue, mental illness, or misplaced machismo. It could just as easily spring from stoic resignation, genuine remorse, the assurances of faith, or the peace that follows contrition. Gilmore himself insisted, "I know what I did. . . . I know the unlawful effect it had on the life of two families. I'm willing to pay ultimately. Let me!"[16]

Whatever the reasons that move volunteers, certainly there is little in the law that governs and structures the imposition of capital punishment and the review of death sentences that places much of an impediment in their way. Generally speaking, the law allows "competent" defendants to plead guilty to capital crimes, to represent themselves in capital cases, and to refuse to present mitigating evidence at sentencing.[17] And while it is true today that all death-penalty states require some form of appellate review in capital cases, nothing requires a convicted killer to file habeas corpus or other postconviction petitions for relief. What's more, courts are reluctant to allow family members, activists, clergy, taxpayers, attorneys, "uninvited meddlers,"[18] and other third parties to proceed with such petitions and appeals—either as "next friends" or to protect their own interests—when a competent inmate has opted against them. In Gilmore's case, for instance, the American Civil Liberties Union filed a taxpayers' suit to block the use of public funds for Gilmore's execution;[19] a lawyer tried to intervene to protect the interests of his own client who, he claimed, would be more likely to be executed under Utah's death-penalty statute if Gilmore gave up;[20] and the Supreme Court of the United States determined that even Gilmore's own mother lacked standing to second-guess him.[21] It is against this legal backdrop—decorated with the technical, bloodless language of standing, jurisdiction, "cases," and "controversies"—that condemned inmates volunteer and their lawyers struggle for a response.

Now, as a general matter, it strikes me as both reasonable and correct for

16. Gary Gilmore, "An Open Letter to the American Civil Liberties Union," in R. Cover, J. Resnik, and Owen M. Fiss, *Procedure* (New York: Foundation Press, 1988), 441, 442.

17. *Godinez v. Moran*, 509 U.S. 389, 392 (1993).

18. *Whitmore v. Arkansas*, 495 U.S. 149, 164 (1990).

19. Mailer, *The Executioner's Song*, 896–909. When Gilmore learned about this, he exploded, "A taxpayers' suit! I'll pay for it myself!"

20. Ibid., 846–64.

21. *Gilmore v. Utah*, 429 US 1012 (1976).

courts to let litigants control the course and the end of their cases, to treat such cases as discrete controversies between particular parties, and to resist the attempts of even well-meaning, deeply concerned outsiders to direct litigants in the direction and for the purposes the outsiders prefer. I am not convinced that lawsuits and litigation should serve as vehicles for the resolution of "big issues," and I worry about the patronizing elitism that can result when the client becomes a cause. Still, and especially in death-penalty cases, this backdrop and its individualistic—even atomistic—presuppositions are not uncontroversial. Professor Althouse, for example, in her essay on the *Gilmore* and *Whitmore* cases, criticized the Court for its "willful exclusion of emotion and real context from its decisions, its misguided characterizations of this exclusion as heroic, and its deliberate and activist narrowing of standing to serve the publicly stated goal of freeing the states to kill." In her view, while Mailer tells a story with a "maddening lack of boundary," he also "portrays the grand, interconnected mass of humanity that formed around even the least worthy person and illustrates how his fate included it all."[22]

Others might insist that we do not have to turn to Norman Mailer, but simply to the Eighth Amendment, for a critique of the law's apparent indifference to the volunteer. Our Constitution, the argument goes, is not simply a catalog of waivable privileges; it is also an exercise in self-paternalism, "our insulation from our baser selves."[23] It is, therefore, at least a hurdle, if not a barrier, in a would-be volunteer's path. As Justice Marshall put it, "[The volunteer] invites the State to violate two of the most basic norms of a civilized society—that the State's penal authority be invoked only where necessary to serve the ends of justice, not the ends of a particular individual, and that punishment be imposed only where the State has adequate assurance that the punishment is justified. The Constitution forbids the State to accept that invitation."[24] This was, actually, also the American Civil Liberties Union's response to Gilmore's demand, in an "open letter," that it "butt out of [his] life" and "butt out of [his] death"[25]: "We don't think the world is obliged to be governed by your preference. . . . We are not imposing our wants and attitudes on you; we are seeking to impose humanity and decency upon the State of

22. Ann Althouse, "Standing, in Fluffy Slippers," *Virginia Law Review* 77 (1991): 1177, 1178, 1180, 1183.

23. *Furman v. Georgia,* 408 US 238, 344–45 (1972) (Marshall, J., concurring).

24. *Whitmore,* 495 US at 173 (1990) (Marshall, J., dissenting).

25. Gary Gilmore, "An Open Letter to the ACLU," 441.

Utah."[26] And even one of Gilmore's many transient literary "agents" admitted that he "didn't see where any criminal had the right to tell society what to do with him . . . society, after all, set the rules."[27]

Now, Gilmore's death sentence was never reviewed and its constitutionality never evaluated. In most cases, though, the conviction of an inmate who decides not to resist his death sentence has, in fact, been reviewed—several times. In most cases, several courts have affirmed that he *is*, in fact, guilty of a crime for which the death penalty has been prescribed, and that whatever constitutional errors did taint his trial and sentencing are not likely to be corrected through further litigation. Even conceding that the Eighth Amendment is best regarded as a non-waivable constraint on the conduct of government, it is hard to see how even a self-paternalistic Constitution would require us to override his decision.

So, death-row inmates legally may, and for many reasons do, "volunteer" for execution. Still, that the law allows, and might even enable, defendants to elect execution does not answer lawyers' questions about what they should think and do in response. An attorney's awareness that few legal obstacles stand in a volunteer's way, and few legal avenues exist for second-guessing, does and should not end his ethical and *moral* inquiries.

LEGAL ETHICS ON DEATH ROW

What should lawyers think about, and how should we respond to, death-row volunteers? How *do* they, in fact, think and respond? We might begin by treating these as relatively straightforward "legal ethics" questions, and by turning for answers to the canons and codes of the profession. In this vein, one author (writing, appropriately enough, in the *Georgetown Journal of Legal Ethics*), after observing that "[a]ttorneys whose clients demand the death penalty are faced with a series of critical ethical decisions," and after examining thoroughly the possible "legal and ethical grounds for the attorney to

26. Barry Schwarzschild, Director, Capital Punishment Project, ACLU, "Open Reply to Mr. Gary Gilmore," in Cover, Resnik, and Fiss, *Procedure*, 442, 443. In a similar vein, Justice Holmes once stated that "[j]ust as the original punishment would be imposed without regard to the prisoner's consent and in the teeth of his will, whether he liked it or not, the public welfare, not his consent, determines what shall be done." *Biddle v. Perovich*, 274 US 480, 486 (1927).

27. Mailer, *The Executioner's Song*, 589.

act contrary to his or her client's wishes [to volunteer]," concludes that, although "[t]he guidelines for professional conduct direct the lawyer to represent the client's best interests and leave the direction of the litigation up to the client":

There is justification for an attorney to act contrary to the client's immediate wishes in a number of areas. Among the avenues open to the attorney are: persuading the client to appeal; negotiating plea options with the prosecution; raising the argument that mitigating evidence is constitutionally required; addressing the issue of incompetency; and proceeding through a next friend. Ultimately, the attorney may have to withdraw from representation, or she may be dismissed by the client.[28]

Let us start, then, with persuasion. Of *course* capital-defense lawyers try to persuade (or dissuade) the would-be death-row volunteers they represent. Such efforts are relatively uncontroversial, and certainly familiar. Supernovelist John Grisham, for instance, in his death-row novel *The Chamber,* describes the attempt of an earnest young attorney to convince his Klansman client (also his grandfather) not to give in to his impending execution.[29] And in the film *Murder in the First,* a crusading young public defender, hell-bent on bringing down Alcatraz, is forced to temporarily shelve his ambitions long enough to befriend and give hope to his miserable and lonely client, who is tired to the point of giving up.[30] It seems clear enough that one can concede that "the authority to make decisions is exclusively that of the client,"[31] yet still insist that *no* lawyer is "required to slavishly follow all the beliefs and goals of her client."[32] We may, and often should, put up a fight. The lawyer is, after all, not only a partisan, but also a counselor—even a friend.[33]

True to form, seasoned and creative death-penalty lawyers report having made every effort to convince, cajole, or even trick their clients into fighting their sentences, resisting resignation, and defeating despair. In fact, in an early examination of the problem, Welsh White found that, for most death-penalty specialists, an inmate's wish to accept execution is "an obstacle to ef-

28. Richard C. Dieter, "Ethical Choices for Attorneys Whose Clients Elect Execution," *Georgetown Journal of Legal Ethics* 3 (1990): 799, 819–20.

29. John Grisham, *The Chamber* (New York: Island Books, 1994).

30. *Murder in the First,* Warner Brothers, 1995.

31. Model Code of Professional Responsibility EC 7-7 (1980).

32. Dieter, "Ethical Choices," 811–12.

33. See Thomas L. Shaffer and Robert F. Cochran Jr., "Lawyers as Strangers and Friends: A Reply to Professor Sammons," *University of Arkansas Little Rock Law Review* 18 (1995): 69.

fective representation rather than an ethical dilemma."[34] That is, Professor White found that a client's decision to volunteer is generally regarded by the lawyer as something to negotiate, overcome, get around, or get past, and not—at least, not usually—as a time for soul-searching or as a crisis of conscience. As one attorney put it, "[w]hen a defendant says that he wants to die, I generally don't worry too much about it because I'm confident that I can persuade him to change his mind."[35]

Now, at first blush, such an attitude, and such efforts, seem to be in tension with the "sacred stories" of our profession, and with the "central and recurring theme in [our] narratives," namely, that of the "lawyer as champion" whose "duty [is] to client first."[36] Perhaps. Still, it appears that, for all the appeal the "lawyer as champion" story holds for the capital-defense bar, these lawyers look as much to Abraham Lincoln—who, as a young Springfield lawyer, reminded a prospective client that "some things legally right are not morally right"[37]—as to Lord Brougham.[38] It seems that they are inclined to ignore whatever constraints their role might otherwise impose on their exhortations. They are inspired and nourished by stories of resistance, and even regret, but not dutiful acquiescence, suspended judgment, and dogged selflessness.

34. White, "Defendants Who Elect Execution," 857.

35. Ibid. (quoting Oklahoma County Public Defender Bob Ravitz). I should add that, although I have also—thank God—been successful in helping to persuade my own client to "change his mind" on those occasions when he has taken steps to volunteer, I have to admit that I worried quite a bit about it—both about whether he *would* change his mind and about what I should do if he did not.

36. Susan P. Koniak, "The Law between the Bar and the State," *North Carolina Law Review* 70 (1992): 1389, 1447, 1448, 1456.

37. See David Luban, *Lawyers and Justice: An Ethical Study* (Princeton: Princeton University Press, 1988), 172 (citing to William H. Herndon and Jesse W. Weik, *Herndon's Life of Lincoln* [New York: Word Publishing, 1889], vol. 2, 345).

38. Brougham said, in support of his zealous defense of Queen Caroline against treason charges, that

[A]n advocate, in the discharge of his duty, knows but one person in all the world, and that person is his client. To save that client by all means and expedients, and at all hazards and costs to other persons, and, among them, to himself, is his first and only duty; and in performing this duty he must not regard the alarm, the torments, the destruction which he may bring upon others.

David Luban, "The Social Responsibilities of Lawyers: A Green Perspective," *George Washington Law Review* 63 (1995): 955, 973–74 (quoting *The Trial of Queen Caroline*, ed. J. Nightingale [London: J. Robins, 1821], 8).

Indeed, the death-row lawyer who is overly fastidious about his "station and its duties" tends to come off badly in the lore. Just by way of example, in *The Executioner's Song*, the often stoned and always uninspiring lawyer–media agent, Dennis Boaz, tells anyone who will listen about his respect for Gilmore's "intelligent decision." Later, though, he shares with Geraldo Rivera the ineffable revelation he had received that he could not, after all, help Gilmore die.[39] Another lawyer, Ron Stanger, is sick when he learns that the execution will proceed: "[He] wondered if he were going mad, because he would have bet a million Gary Gilmore would never be executed. It had made his job easy. He had never felt any moral dilemma in carrying out Gary's desires. In fact, he couldn't have represented him at all if he really believed the State would go through with it all. . . . He had seen himself as no more important than one more person on the stage."[40]

Volunteers' lawyers try to persuade volunteers to change their minds—but why? And what reasons for rethinking do they offer? They appeal to clients' self-interest, clearly, and might work to portray as less "long" the long-shot chances of success. They might warn would-be volunteers that they are irrational and depressed and that their judgments are not to be trusted. Clients might also be urged to turn outward, to think about their family, friends, communities[41]—even their lawyers. (When my own client expressed the desire to end legal proceedings and speed up his execution date, I responded by emphasizing the pain and demoralization that his execution would visit on *me*.) My impression, though, is that what really does the work in motivating lawyers' efforts to persuade volunteers is their own fierce opposition to and disgust with the death penalty itself. The litany of other reasons is, for the most part, makeweight. As one lawyer told Professor White, "[t]he state's goal of killing someone is immoral" and, therefore, "[my client's] desire to be

---

39. Mailer, *The Executioner's Song*, 522, 593.

40. Ibid., 946.

41. I am reminded here of the final scenes of the James Cagney film *Angels with Dirty Faces* (Warner Bros. 1938), where the Cagney character's childhood friend—now a parish priest in their old, still tough, neighborhood—pleads with Cagney to go against his character and act "yellow" at his impending execution, so that the neighborhood boys will not idealize and follow him. In the film, the priest says,

This is a different kind of courage, Rocky. The kind that's, well, that's born in heaven. Well, not the courage of heroics or bravado. The kind that you and I and God know about. . . . I want you to let them down. You see, you've been a hero to these kids . . . and now you're gonna be a glorified hero in death, and I want to prevent that, Rocky.

killed is not important to me."[42] In other words, the goal is not so much to assist a client who has misperceived his own interests, or miscalculated the best way to achieve them, but to prevent even a willing client from acceding to what is in fact an "immoral" punishment.

This goal and such arguments are, I think, quite reasonable—at least at the "persuasion stage." But what if persuasion fails (and, as we learned from *The Practice*, it sometimes does)? How can a lawyer continue to challenge an execution, in the teeth of a client's wishes to the contrary? Unpersuasive capital-defense lawyers respond in one of two ways: Either by acquiescing to the client's wishes, and perhaps even assisting him toward his objective; or by ignoring, and if necessary resisting, the volunteer's decision. My sense, though, is that these two very different responses proceed from common premises— "anthropological" premises—about human "dignity" and "autonomy."

Let's start with the first—and, maybe, the more difficult—option. Although, as I noted above, "[m]any lawyers who specialize in capital defense apparently take the position that their paramount obligation is to fight the executioner, regardless of their clients' wishes[,]" not all agree.[43] Richard Bonnie, for example, maintains that by honoring his client's decision to volunteer, he is "conforming to the traditional conception of the attorney's role."[44] As Professor Bonnie sees it, "the law's duty to respect individual dignity is heightened, not diminished, when choices are made in the shadow of death."[45] Michael Mello agrees: "Preventing executions is very important to me, but it's not the only thing that's important to me. There are choices and decisions that the person whose life is on the line ought to be allowed to make, as a basic part of human dignity and autonomy."[46] In the same vein, he has also written that, for him, "the issue of how to respond to execution volunteers comes down to a question of respecting the human dignity that remains in the person even after living for a time on death row."[47] As Professor

---

42. White, "Defendants Who Elect Execution," 859.

43. On the divisions in the capital-defense bar on this point, see, for example, C. Lee Harrington, "A Community Divided: Defense Attorneys and the Ethics of Death-Row Volunteering," *Law and Social Inquiry* 25 (2000): 849.

44. Richard J. Bonnie, "The Dignity of the Condemned," *Virginia Law Review* 74 (1988): 1363, 1367.

45. Ibid., 1391.

46. Michael Mello, "The Non-Trial of the Century: Representations of the Unabomber," *Vermont Law Review* 24 (2000): 417, 511.

47. Mello, "A Letter," 171.

Mello puts it, to achieve the "defining goal of [his] representation"—namely, client "empowerment"—he would even "help [his] client help our government kill him."[48]

It is not that Mello's opposition to the death penalty evaporates when matched against a volunteer's death wish. Like (evidently) all capital-defense counsel in that position, he *tried* to persuade Kaczynski. Still, "while it was important to me that Kaczynski have a choice . . . , I have been trying to persuade him not to exercise it. . . . [But] [b]ecause that decision is Kaczynski's, and his alone—not mine, not his lawyer's, not his family's—I will continue to support his right to make it, even though it could well result in an outcome I abhor."[49] For some lawyers, then, when persuasion fails, the same commitments to human "dignity" that animate their opposition to the death penalty, and that require them to at least try to rekindle resistance in their volunteering client, are thought, in the end, to require them to stand aside.

The other, apparently more common, option for volunteers' lawyers is to resist. But wait—did not all lawyers learn, while cramming for the multiple-choice legal-ethics exam, that "the authority to make decisions is exclusively that of the client and, if made within the framework of the law, such decisions are binding on his lawyer?"[50] Yes, but we also likely learned that a client's mental or physical condition may place additional responsibilities on a lawyer.[51] After all, even the "standard conception"[52] of the lawyer's role presumes competent clients and, in the minds of many capital-defense lawyers, a death-row volunteer's desire to die, or indifference toward death, raises a nearly irrebuttable presumption of incompetence.

It would be easy if this were true, if volunteers were always per se, or even presumptively, incompetent. After all, a lawyer need not worry about disregarding the stated wishes of an incompetent client any more than a parent need agonize over a child's objections to bedtime or Dostoyevsky. But it is *not* true. It is cheating to pretend otherwise. In fact, instead of claiming that death-row inmates are categorically incapable of making a decision that is sufficiently voluntary, knowing, and "autonomous" to warrant our respect, we ought to admit that it is precisely those conditions that are said to under-

48. Mello, "Non-Trial of the Century," 510, 511.

49. Ibid., 512.

50. Model Code of Professional Responsibility EC 7-7 (1981).

51. Id. at EC 7-12, EC 9-7, DR 4-101.

52. David Luban, *Lawyers and Justice: An Ethical Study* (Princeton University Press, 1988).

mine the competence of death-row volunteers that make life under a death sentence so intolerable, and the preference for execution understandable. "I have been close enough to smell the fear and despair of the place," Professor Mello writes, "and to imagine the utter lack of privacy or solitude that would be, for me, perhaps the worst part of living in that world."[53] We should concede that it is possible, even reasonable, for a condemned inmate, aware of the state of the law, aware of his own guilt, resigned to the inevitable, hoping for peace, and perhaps even eager for the Beatific Vision, the Communion of the Church Triumphant, or some other reward, to decide not to resist.[54]

Moreover, the failure or refusal to concede as much seems to undermine the values and commitments on which capital-defense attorneys' opposition to the death penalty rests. Rather than accept a client's submission to a punishment regarded by the lawyer as dehumanizing, the lawyer resists by calling into question his client's competence to exercise that autonomy, and by insisting that the substance of his client's choice is evidence of the unworthiness of that choice for respect. Echoing Augustine, perhaps, the volunteer's lawyer says "give me client control and autonomy, but not yet!" Of course, it is not so much that a capital-defense lawyer who ignores or resists a volunteer's decision *really* believes that his client is "incompetent." Instead, it is simply that the lawyer disapproves of the project, and wishes to thwart it, while continuing to profess loyalty to the profession's autonomy-based norms of client control.[55]

The problem has, as Professor White observed, "the elements of a tragic choice."[56] It seems that death-row volunteers who will not be swayed require their lawyers to participate in their dehumanization—either by acquiescing in, if not facilitating, their execution, or by deconstructing disingenuously their capacity to make choices worthy of respect.

---

53. Mello, "Non-Trial of the Century," 509.

54. Cf. 2 Maccabees 7:14, "It is better, being put to death by men, to look for hope from God, to be raised up again by him" (trans. Douay-Rheims, John Murphy Co., 1899).

55. For more on this point, see generally Joseph Goldstein, "For Harold Lasswell: Some Reflections on Human Dignity, Entrapment, Informed Consent, and the Plea Bargain," *Yale Law Journal* 84 (1975): 683.

56. White, "Defendants Who Elect Execution," 869.

WHO WE ARE AND WHY IT MATTERS

The observations and claims presented so far would seem to owe little to a distinctively "Catholic" perspective—death-row inmates sometimes decide to stop fighting their executions, the law (generally speaking) allows them to do this, and capital-defense lawyers wrestle with the dilemma that volunteers' decisions create. The point to be emphasized, here, is that the questions before us—that is, "what should we lawyers think about death-row volunteers, and how should we respond to them? What is the right thing to do?"— are not just technical points of professional responsibility, implicating only the "law about lawyers." They are *moral* questions, just as "legal ethics" is, properly understood, a *moral* enterprise. They are, accordingly, questions to which the Catholic tradition speaks and whose answers could well appear more clear from a Catholic stance.

What's more, they are *not* questions that are likely to be answered well *without* some "outside" help. We can agree, I think, that a tour through the applicable rules, canons, and maxims of professionalism would, for the most part, miss the point. This is not to say that it is not worth knowing the views of the relevant ethics committee. It is simply to note that these views—appealing, as they probably would, "not to conscience, but to sanction" and sounding, as they probably would, in "mandate rather than insight"—could not be the end of the matter.[57] Because they do not really purport or aspire to provide moral guidance to lawyers (though maybe they should), it is not necessarily a criticism to note that they do not. It is no insult to the profession to maintain that its regulatory minima have not preempted the ethical field. Nor need it be an insult to the academy to reject the academic convention that, when publicly speaking to difficult questions, one must translate religious themes, segregate religious commitments, and mute religious witness. A legal-ethics conversation from which religious beliefs, faith commitments, and "sectarian" language are excluded can be only empty and uninspiring.[58]

A requirement that religious believers who are also lawyers cordon off re-

---

57. Shaffer, "Radical Individualism," 963.

58. See H. J. Powell, *The Moral Tradition of American Constitutionalism: A Theological Interpretation* (Durham, NC: Duke University Press, 1993), 262n10 (1993) ("Christian theology . . . provides an intellectual and moral basis for a social criticism of American . . . law and politics that is both more radical and more truthful than that based upon secular leftist ideologies.").

ligious claims and obligations from deliberations about what they ought to do distorts ethical judgment no less than any other failure to "truthfully describe[] what is going on."[59] With respect to death-row volunteers, for example, I have come to believe that I cannot think about the problem except as a Christian. It seems clear to me that for a lawyer who is a believer, any purported resolution of an ethical question whose premise is that religious lawyers should hamstring their deliberations by disintegrating their lives is no resolution at all. After all, how can such a lawyer think about crime and punishment; about retribution, forgiveness, abuse of power, and the common good; about his client's despair, fear, contrition, and hope; or about corruption, redemption, damnation, and beatitude, if his faith is walled off from the conversation like a conflicted-out law partner?[60]

Once we are liberated from the constraints of deliberation-distorting demands that we either leave behind or translate religious—here, Catholic—commitments and premises, we can reengage the death-row-volunteer problem in a deeper, more promising way. More specifically, the Catholic tradition and a Catholic stance supply a different, richer moral anthropology—a better account of what it means to be human and of what it is about the human person that matters for moral inquiry.[61] After all, every legal problem, and every attempt at moral judgment, "reflects certain foundational assumptions about what it means to be human."[62] Similarly, as the late Pope John Paul II reminded us in his encyclical letter *Centesimus annus*, "[t]he guiding principle of . . . all the Church's social doctrine is a *correct view of the human person* and of his unique value, inasmuch as 'man . . . is the only creature on earth which God has willed for itself.'"[63]

I suggested earlier that while contemporary death-penalty lawyers whose

59. Shaffer, "Radical Individualism," 965. See also Powell, *The Moral Tradition of American Constitutionalism*, 264 ("The norm of Christian social ethics is the obligation to see and speak truthfully").

60. I was struck, for example, in the "Killing Time," episode of *The Practice*, by the fact that the lawyers seemed incapable of grasping (and, in fact, capable only of mocking) the inmate's desire to "accept punishment for [his] sins." This belief was, Bobby Donnell sputtered to a judge, evidence of "brainwashing." See note 1, above.

61. Cf., e.g., John Witte Jr., "Between Sanctity and Dignity: Human Dignity in Protestant Perspective," in *In Defense of Human Dignity: Essays For Our Times*, ed. Robert P. Kraynak and Glenn Tinder (Notre Dame, IN: Notre Dame Press,, 2003).

62. John J. Coughlin, "Law and Theology: Reflections on What It Means to Be Human from a Franciscan Perspective," *St. John's Law Review* 74 (2000): 609, 610.

63. See generally Francis Canavan, "The Image of Man in Catholic Social Thought," in

clients make moves toward volunteering respond differently when their efforts at persuasion fail, their anthropological assumptions—generally speaking—are the same: The person is and should be regarded as untethered and alone;[64] he is autonomous not simply in the obvious sense that his choices are not determined, but because it is taken as given that the only standards against which those choices can be evaluated are those that are generated, or endorsed, by the self. True, there is frequent and sincere talk of "human dignity," but this "dignity" consists precisely in his being a self-governing chooser. The dignity of the person not only includes, but is reducible to, the capacity to make, and the right to act on, what we are willing to recognize as "autonomous choices." On this view, the autonomy of atomized and rootless units is not only given, but is good in itself—its orientation unjudgeable; it is not regarded as a fragile gift that permits and facilitates the flourishing of the human person. Conduct is good because it is chosen, not chosen because it is good. We live, that is, in the world according to the Supreme Court, a world where we enjoy "the right to define [our] own concept of existence, of meaning, of the universe, and of the mystery of human life."[65]

Given these anthropological presuppositions, lawyers for would-be volunteers have three choices: first, acquiesce out of respect for autonomy in the client's submission to (in the lawyers' eyes) a dehumanizing penalty; second, oppose and obstruct, admitting candidly that autonomy is being sacrificed to the even more pressing obligation to prevent executions; or, third, resist by treating the client's decision as conclusive evidence of his incapacity to make it and of its unworthiness of respect. The choice is resisted not on the merits (at least, not explicitly), but by infantilizing the chooser. But given the autonomy-centered anthropological premises, and our elevation of choice and consent to "master concepts,"[66] each of these alternatives is bound to be unsatisfying. What is more, to the extent these lawyers hope to draw on notions

---

Catholicism, Liberalism, and Communitarianism: The Catholic Intellectual Tradition and the Moral Foundations of Democracy, ed. Gerard V. Bradley et al. (Lanham, MD: Rowman and Littlefield, 1995).

64. See Thomas L. Shaffer, "How I Changed My Mind," *Journal of Law and Religion* 10 (1993/1994): 291, 295 ("By 'liberal' I mean an adherent of the . . . philosophy that teaches . . . that every person is her own tyrant—that each of us is, most radically, all alone.").

65. *Planned Parenthood of Southeastern Pennsylvania v. Casey,* 505 US 833, 851 (1992) (joint opinion). For a provocative critique, grounded in faith, of the *Casey* anthropology, see generally Coughlin, "Law and Theology."

66. Peter H. Schuck, "Rethinking Informed Consent," *Yale Law Journal* 103 (1994): 899, 900 .

of "human dignity," there is the problem that their anthropological presuppositions are simply not up to the task of supporting such notions.[67] It is not so much that the dominant account is "wrong about the awesome dignity of the individual," but that "it cuts the self off from the source of that dignity."[68]

A Catholic approach, however, holds out the chance for something different and better, for a more edifying and inspiring account of the dignity of the human person. I tend to think that postmodern Americans have settled on "autonomy" as the moral gold standard primarily because we have lost the ability to articulate or believe in anything better.[69] We need something, after all, to assure us that all is well, and the consent of a self-governing chooser serves as our green light. We suspect, perhaps, that there is more to us than a sovereign self, but "autonomy" is the best we can do.

But lonely autonomy is *not* the best we can do. That freedom of choice is a gift, and even that its value is "inestimable,"[70] does not make it the only valuable thing. That we are distinguished by our capacity for choice does not mean that our dignity is reducible to that capacity. We are not merely agents who choose, we are also spouses, members, friends, and colleagues. We are people who belong, who exist in and are shaped by relationships. The "situations" lawyers confront—including the problem of death-row volunteers— are misshaped and misdescribed when framed to accord with the individualism reflected in our profession's rules.

Now, it is probably true, as Professor Elshtain has observed, that the *Casey*-based, autonomy-centered anthropology—however impoverished— is "so deeply entrenched that ... it is simply part of the cultural air we breathe."[71] Still, there is another account; one that turns our profession's (and,

67. See Wilfred M. McClay, "The Continuing Irony of American History," *First Things* 120 (Feb. 2002): 20, 25 ("Without a broadly biblical understanding of the sources of the dignity of the human person, it is hard to see how that dignity can continue to have a plausible basis in the years to come"); Alasdair MacIntyre, *After Virtue: A Study in Moral Theory,* 2d ed. (Notre Dame: University of Notre Dame Press, 1984), 1–5 (offering the "disquieting suggestion" that "the language and the appearances of morality persist even though the integral substantive of morality has ... been fragmented, and then in part destroyed").

68. Fr. Richard John Neuhaus, "The Liberalism of Pope John Paul II," *First Things* 73 (May 1997), 16.

69. Alasdair MacIntyre makes a similar point. See MacIntyre, *After Virtue,* 1–5.

70. See *Faretta v. California,* 422 US 806, 834 (1975) ("And whatever else may be said of those who wrote the Bill of Rights, surely there can be no doubt that they understood the inestimable worth of free choice.").

71. Jean Bethke Elshtain, "The Dignity of the Human Person and the Idea of Human Rights: Four Inquiries," *Journal of Law and Religion* 14 (1999/2000): 53, 58.

for the most part, our culture's) on its head. On this account, the dignity of the human person consists not so much in his capacity to choose, or his self-sovereignty, but in his status as a creature. On this account, we live less in a state of self-sufficiency than in one of "reciprocal indebtedness."[72] Our dignity derives, oddly enough, less from autonomy and sovereignty than from dependence and incompletion; the "greatness of human beings is founded precisely in their being creatures of a loving God,"[73] not self-styled authors of their own destiny. That which is our greatest source of pride is, at the same time, a constant call to humility.

Now, I am not sure what this would mean, or yield, in the death-row volunteer discussion. I am not sure what difference it would make to our perception of the obligations we have to our clients, and of the lives *and deaths* of our clients themselves, if our understanding of their worth, respect-worthiness, and destinies rested on these anthropological presuppositions. I *am* sure, though, that it should make a difference. As Professor Shaffer has observed, in another context:

> In our law offices, we lawyers begin as Solomon did with a view of human persons that precedes our being introduced to clients. The question during this prelude is, 'Who are those persons who will come to see me?' That question is certainly jurisprudential, but in this context it is also and primarily ethical.[74]

And I *do* know that we are not diminished by a faith-inspired shift in focus from autonomy and choice to creaturehood and dependence. As C. S. Lewis once wrote, in his essay, "The Weight of Glory":

> There are no ordinary people. You have never talked to a mere mortal. Nations, cultures, arts, civilisations—these are mortal, and their life is to ours as the life of a gnat. But it is immortals whom we joke with, work with, marry, snub, and exploit—immortal horrors or everlasting splendours.[75]

What, then, does a capital-defense lawyer owe the glory-burdened yet—to the world, anyway—"repulsive"[76] immortal who is resigned to his execution?

---

72. Gilbert Meilaender, "Still Waiting for Benedict," *First Things* 96 (October 1999): 48, 50 (reviewing Alasdair MacIntyre, *Dependent Rational Animals: Why Human Beings Need the Virtues* [Chicago: Open Court, 1999]).

73. Pope John Paul II, Ad Limina Address.

74. Thomas L. Shaffer, "Human Nature and Moral Responsibility in Lawyer-Client Relationships," *American Journal of Jurisprudence* 40 (1995): 1, 2.

75. C. S. Lewis, *The Weight of Glory*, 2nd rev. ed. (New York: MacMillan, 1980), 19.

76. Thomas L. Shaffer, "Should a Christian Lawyer Serve the Guilty?" *Georgia Law Re-*

What can he do to help secure "everlasting splendours" for them both? And, what difference would it make if he, his work, and his counsel were dedicated to the fundamental proposition that "the person is a good towards which the only proper and adequate attitude is love"?[77] The challenge, in the end, is to propose a truthful vision of the human person as "the noblest work of God—infinitely valuable, relentlessly unique, endlessly interesting,"[78] and to propose that the question of the death penalty stand or fall on that. Such a vision—"truthful Christian speech"—is required "if we are to be faithful to the God we worship."

A Catholic perspective on the death-row-volunteer problem—on its legal, ethical, and moral dimensions—is a challenging one. That it might not provide definitive prescriptions or clear rules for capital-defense lawyers, or for the rest of us, does not diminish its promise. What is proposed here, in other words, is not so much an answer to these lawyers' questions as a reorientation of the conversation around a Christian humanism, around a vision—a Catholic vision—of what we are and what we are for, and why it matters.

---

view 23 (1989): 1021, 1026 ("The interesting thing that the Gospel says about revulsion . . . is that the moral thing to do is to turn toward the repulsive person, to reach out to that person, to reach through his repulsiveness.").

77. Fr. Thomas Williams, L.C., "Capital Punishment and the Just Society," *Catholic Dossier* (Sept.–Oct. 1998): 30 (citing Karol Wojtyla, *Love and Responsibility,* trans. H. T. Willetts [Fort Collins, CO: Ignatius Press, 1981], 41–42).

78. Shaffer, "Human Nature," 2.

[14]

FAMILY LAW

Natural Law, Marriage, and the Thought of Karol Wojtyla

۞

JOHN J. COUGHLIN, O.F.M.

INTRODUCTION

At the midpoint of the last century, Dean Roscoe Pound wrote that the legal profession constituted "a learned art as a common calling in the spirit of public service."[1]

Yet, contrary to this wonderfully noble appreciation of our profession, lawyers may sometimes take an unreflective and mechanistic approach when counseling a client who is considering a divorce.[2] Over the course of the last five decades, the national divorce rate has risen to approximately 50 percent.[3]

This article is based upon on talk given at the Fordham Law School on March 8, 2001, as part of the Symposium on Natural Law and Counseling the Client.

1. Roscoe Pound, *The Lawyer from Antiquity to Modern Times* (St. Paul, MN: West, 1953), 5.

2. See Linda J. Waite and Maggie Gallagher, *The Case for Marriage: Why Married People Are Happier, Healthier, and Better Off Financially* (New York: Doubleday, 2000), 10; see also Robert H. Vasoli, *What God Has Joined Together: The Annulment Crisis in America* (New York: Oxford University Press, 1998), 23–26 (suggesting that canon lawyers in the United States have disregarded theological and canonical principles in order to make annulments widely available to American Catholics).

3. See Waite and Gallagher, *The Case for Marriage*, 187–88, citing *Bureau of the Census,*

Recent significant statistical evidence indicates that generally the culture of divorce has left neither divorced spouses nor their children in a more advantageous situation.[4] The natural-law tradition has long perceived a nexus between the general well being of society and the health of marriage and family life.[5] Consistent with the tradition, the societal foundation is destabilized to the extent that marriage is understood as a private and inner emotional experience rather than as an objective social reality.[6] This essay suggests that natural law affords a more complete and balanced understanding of marriage and family life than the present mainstream perspective, which has its roots in liberal theory.[7]

It is far beyond the modest aims of this discussion to provide a complete historical and philosophical analysis of the natural-law tradition on marriage or of the developments that have led to the demise of the traditional position in the United States.[8] Rather, in the limited space available, I shall briefly

---

Statistical Abstract of the United States, 117th ed. (Washington, DC: 1997), table 145 (noting the statistical indication that during the last years of the twentieth century the national divorce rate has leveled off and may be slightly declining).

4. See Judith S. Wallerstein, Julia M. Lewis, and Sandra Blakeslee, *The Unexpected Legacy of Divorce: A 25 Year Landmark Study* (New York: Hyperion, 2000), 294–316 (on the basis of a twenty-five-year longitudinal study of divorce, the authors have concluded that the "divorce culture" yields long-term negative consequences for individuals, families, and society); see also Waite and Gallagher, *The Case for Marriage,* 187–88 (indicating that married persons who have not been divorced, and their children, tend to be better off in terms of physical and emotional health as well as financial status than divorced spouses and their progeny.).

5. See John Finnis, *Natural Law, Natural Rights* (Oxford: Clarendon Press, 1980), 34, 64 (identifying marriage and family as a fundamental good for society) (1980); Karol Wojtyla, *Love and Responsibility,* trans. H. T. Willetts (Ft. Collins, CO: Ignatius Press, 1981) ("The point of departure must be the law of nature; legislation concerning the family must objectively express the order implicit in this nature."); Joseph Raz, *The Morality of Freedom* (Oxford: Oxford University Press, 1986), 162 ("Monogamy cannot be practiced by an individual. It requires a culture which recognizes it, and which supports it through the public's attitude and through its formal institutions.").

6. See Waite and Gallagher, *The Case for Marriage,* 10.

7. See Mary Ann Glendon, *Abortion and Divorce in Western Law, American Failures, European Challenges* (Cambridge: Harvard University Press, 1987), 115–16 (1987) (describing the influence of liberal theory on the rights language of family law); see also Mary Ann Glendon, *The Transformation of Family Law, State Law, and Family in the United States and Western Europe* (Chicago: University of Chicago Press, 1989), 188–90 (describing the philosophical change in divorce law during the last decades of the twentieth century).

8. On the natural law in general, see Pope John Paul II, *Veritatis splendor* (1993), *Acta Apostolicae Sedis (hereafter AAS)* 85 (1993): 1133–1228. To affirm the existence of the natural

discuss the loss of the natural law perspective from legal theory. Following this prolegomenon, I shall attempt to sketch in broad strokes two features of the tradition, especially as retrieved in the philosophical writings of Karol Wojtyla.[9] The first concerns marriage and family as the fundamental human community, and the second considers marriage as a virtuous relationship. The two features are juxtaposed to certain aspects of the understanding of marriage derived from liberal theory. The essay concludes with practical suggestions for the legal profession and legal education with regard to counseling clients about marriage.

At the outset, it must be mentioned that this essay is not intended to propose that divorce be eliminated from the law of the state.[10] To be sure, it would probably be impossible to return our present pluralistic society to a

---

law of marriage follows from reflection on human nature, as these universal and transcendent principles are said to be "written and engraved in the heart of each and every man." *Veritatis splendor,* ¶ 44. For a discussion of the role of natural law principles in jurisprudence, see, e.g., John Finnis, *Natural Law, Natural Rights;* Lloyd Weinrab, *Natural Law and Justice* (Cambridge: Harvard University Press, 1987), 224–65. Nonetheless, the role of natural law is far from settled in contemporary American jurisprudence. The chief objection to the theory seems to be that "[e]ither the allegedly universal ends are too few and abstract to give content to the idea of the good, or they are too numerous and concrete to be truly universal." Roberto Mangabeira Unger, *Knowledge and Politics* (New York: Free Press, 1975), 241; see also John Hart Ely, *Democracy and Distrust: A Theory of Judicial Review* (Cambridge: Harvard University Press, 1980), 48–54.

9. See Karol Wojtyla, *Person and Community: Selected Essays,* ed. Theresa Sandok, O.S.M. (New York: P. Lang, 1993); *Love and Responsibility; The Acting Person,* trans. Anna-Teresa Tymieniecka (N.p: Kluwer Academic Publishers Group, 1979).

10. Given its roots in medieval canon law, the original common law did not recognize divorce in the modern sense of that term, which indisputably dissolves marriage and carries with it the right of the parties to marry other persons. Rather, it permitted only separation, that is divorce *a mensa et thoro.* See John Witte Jr., *From Sacrament to Contract: Marriage, Religion and Law in the Western Tradition* (Louisville, KY: Westminster/John Knox Press, 1997), 159–61. During the nineteenth century in the United States, the development of divorce jurisdiction tended to imitate the English system of parliamentary or legislative divorce. See, e.g., *Maynard v. Hill,* 125 US 190 (1888) (upholding the competence of a territorial legislature to dissolve a marriage through a special act). Gradually, the device of legislative divorce ceded to judicial jurisdiction with rather limited grounds upon which a suit for divorce might be brought. In New York State, for example, the law permitted divorce to be granted only on the ground of adultery. See *Brady v. Brady,* 64 NY2d 339 (1985) ("Prior to 1966 amendments to the Domestic Relations Law, the sole ground for divorce in this State was adultery."). Since a legislative reform in 1966, New York's approach has permitted an action for divorce on any one of four fault grounds and two so-called no-fault grounds. See N.Y. Domestic Relations Law § 170.

time when divorce was not an option.[11] Yet, the culture of divorce and its consequences for individuals and society indicate that perhaps the legal profession ought to pause and reflect about the impact of the current state of affairs.[12] In contrast to an approach in which the lawyer unreflectively views facilitating a divorce as a mechanistic procedure, the natural-law alternative suggests that when lawyers counsel clients, both might benefit by appreciating the profound nature of the marital relationship. Such an appreciation would be beneficial in maintaining a balanced perspective on what is at stake for the individual, spouses, children, and the larger society.

THE DEMISE OF THE TRADITION

During the renaissance of law from the eleventh to the thirteenth centuries, the medieval canonists integrated various aspects of religious and secular thought to create a natural-law theory of marriage.[13] The theory held that marriage was a permanent association between a man and women intended to nourish the bond of conjugal love and to enable the procreation and education of children.[14] Among the principal effects of the new legal theory were

11. Cf. Wojtyla, *Love and Responsibility,* 217 ("[L]egislation concerning the family must objectively express the order implicit in its nature."). See also Alicia Brokars Kelly, "The Marital Partnership Pretense and Career Assets: The Ascendancy of Self Over the Marital Community," *Boston University Law Review* 81 (2001): 59, 64–75, 94–95 (observing that the triumph of "solitary individualism" over the marital community now characterizes the economics of marital dissolution). Divorce, in the sense of permanent separation, is unfortunately the only realistic alternative in some situations. Tragically, domestic violence remains a serious problem and threat to individuals, marriage, and the society. See Clare Dalton and Elizabeth M. Schneider, *Battered Women and the Law* (New York: Foundation Press, 2001), 5–7 (reporting on statistical studies that verify the serious problem of domestic violence, and noting that "[d]espite the proliferation of studies and statistics about domestic violence in the last decade, many of the findings remain highly contested and many are misleading unless carefully interpreted"); see also Waite and Gallagher, *The Case for Marriage,* 150–73 (reviewing the statistical evidence to indicate that single and divorced women are much more likely to be victims of domestic violence, perpetrated by boyfriends or former husbands, than women in traditional marriages).

12. See Robin Fretwell Wilson, "Children At Risk: The Sexual Exploitation of Female Children after Divorce," *Cornell Law Review* 86 (2001): 251, 262 (noting that the risk of sexual abuse of female children escalates following divorce).

13. See Harold Berman, *Law and Revolution: The Formation of the Western Legal Tradition* (Cambridge: Harvard University Press, 1983), 225–30; Witte, *From Sacrament to Contract,* 22–25.

14. See Witte, *From Sacrament to Contract,* 25.

greater equality for the wife; a focus on the mutual and free consent of the spouses as necessary to the validity of marriage; and the possibility of permanent separation from bed and board in cases of adultery, desertion, or protracted ill treatment.[15] Although the theory was consistent with the Christian view of marriage, it was thought to stand independent of revelation—viewing marriage as an association derived from nature for the good of individuals and especially for society.[16]

A sea change in the understanding of law itself during the eighteenth century belied the general concept of the natural law as well as its traditional position on marriage. A foundational principle of the common law recognized that there existed a superior body of law by the test of which all positive law was to be judged. While the sovereign might be above the positive law, he or she was bound by the natural law.[17] Blackstone wrote that the common law was "founded in principles that are permanent, uniform and universal . . . which every man has implanted in him."[18] This view of the common law, which considered the courts as the depositories of the custom and usage derived from, or at least consistent with, the natural law, was widely accepted in the colonies at the time of the American Revolution.[19] It was of particular importance in matters of equity, when the Chancellor's decision rested on

15. See Berman, *Law and Revolution,* 168; Witte, *From Sacrament to Contract,* 160–61.

16. See Berman, *Law and Revolution,* 228; and Witte, *From Sacrament to Contract,* 25.

17. See Weinrab, *Natural Law and Justice,* 15–126; see also John Locke, "Second Treatise on Government," in *An Essay Concerning the True, Original, and End of Civil Government,* ed. Peter Laslett (Cambridge: Cambridge University Press, 1988), § 135.

18. William Blackstone, *Commentaries on the Laws of England* (Oxford: Clarendon Press, 1775), vol. 4, 3. It has been suggested that Blackstone's deference to natural law was more as a "rhetorical figment" than a genuine application of its principles. After proclaiming that natural law is a higher law than the common law, Blackstone claimed that Parliament is omnipotent, and it would seem to follow that an act of the legislature could overturn the natural law. See Blackstone, vol. 1, 38 and 91. See George Whitecross Paton, *A Text-Book of Jurisprudence,* 4th ed., ed. G. W. Paton and David Derham (Oxford: Oxford University Press, 1972), 119.

19. See, e.g., *The Charges to the Grand Jury by the Chief Justice,* Quincy's Mass. Rep. 110, 113 (1765). The instructions given to the Grand Jury call for the indictment of participants in a protest against the Stamp Act, which protest degenerated into a riot. The Chief Justice instructed: "To relieve the Oppressed, to guard the Innocent, to preserve the Order of Society, and the Dignity of Government is a noble principle of the Mind. This is the Duty of every Individual of the Community." He continued that the riot "offended the Natural Law, that is the law which every man has implanted in him." Ibid. at 113. See also James Otis, "The Rights of the British Colonies," in *American Legal History: Cases and Materials,* ed. Kermit L. Hall, William M. Wiecek, and Paul Finkelman (Oxford: Oxford University Press, 1991) ("These are the bonds, which by God and nature are fixed.").

reason and conscience.[20] In *Wightman v. Wightman,* the famed Chancellor James Kent declared a marriage invalid on the ground of the lack of proper mental capacity of one of the parties:

That such a marriage is criminal and void by the Law of Nature, is a point universally conceded. And, by the Law of Nature, I understand those fit and just rules of conduct which the Creator has prescribed to Man, as a dependent and social being; and which are to be ascertained from the deductions of right reason, though they may be more precisely known, and more explicitly declared by Divine Revelation.[21]

Kent's reasoning reflected the classical notion of natural law as a set a reciprocal rights and responsibilities inherent in the nature of each human being and ordered by divine intention to advance the common good. The classical tradition, however, was gradually yielding to a new theory of individual rights.

An increasing secularization characterized the approach to legal and political questions during the "golden century of human reason."[22] The Protestant Reformation had led to a growing call for religious freedom as a matter of individual conscience.[23] Although Thomas Hobbes and John Locke acknowledged the validity of natural law, they considered the human being as a free individual who entered the social contract.[24] Additionally, the new economic theories of thinkers such as Adam Smith favored individual liberty to pursue private gain.[25] These various influences gave rise to a theory of law that focused on the rights and powers of the individual.

The eighteenth-century view of law was in harmony with the liberal the-

20. See G. Keeton and L. Sheridan, *Equity,* 3d ed. (N.p.: 1987), vol. 3, 33; see also F. Maitland, *Equity,* 2d ed. (N.p.: 1936), vol. 8, 2; Edward Yorio, "A Defense of Equitable Defenses," *Ohio State Law Journal* 51 (1990): 1201, 1205–6; see also Peter Schuck, "When Exception Becomes the Rule: Regulatory Equity and the Formulation of Regulatory Policy through an Exceptions Process," *Duke Law Journal* 1984 (1984): 163; John J. Coughlin, O.F.M., "Canonical Equity," *Studia Canonica* 30 (1996): 403–35 (describing the historical development of equity by the medieval canonists).

21. Johns. Ch. 343 (N.Y. Ch. 1820).

22. John Dickinson, *Administrative Justice and the Supremacy of Law* (Cambridge: Harvard University Press, 1959), 114.

23. See, e.g., Thomas Jefferson, "A Bill for Establishing Religious Freedom," in *The Portable Thomas Jefferson,* ed. Merrill D. Peterson (New York: Viking Press, 1975), 251–53.

24. See Locke, "Second Treatise on Government," §§ 143–44, 364–65; Thomas Hobbes, *Leviathan,* ed. Michael Oakeshott (Oxford: Blackwell, 1957), 82–84.

25. See generally Adam Smith, *An Inquiry into the Nature and Cause of the Wealth of Nations,* 2nd ed. (N.p.: 1778).

ory.[26] Government was by the consent of individuals, who entered a *"pactum subiectionis* rather than a *pactum unionis."*[27] The era witnessed a gradual shift away from the traditional conception of the common law as a fixed and determinate body of rules reflecting ancient custom and divinely designed principles. Supreme Court Justice James Wilson delivered a series of lectures in 1791 in which he "acknowledged the obligations derived from natural law," but "reduced them to private questions of conscience."[28] Wilson's view reflected the predominant conception of law, which held that it was the voluntary consent of individual men, instead of the authority of some higher law, that formed the obligatory basis of statutes, custom, and even the natural law itself.[29] The view was consistent with the theory of John Austin, who held that the state creates the law.[30] It marked the waning of the medieval and common-law solution that the sovereign had power over the positive law, but was bound by the higher principles of natural justice. Statutory law passed by the legislature was increasingly viewed as supreme, as it best reflected the consent of the people. No longer would judges understand their role as the guardians and interpreters of a higher, transcendent, and immutable corpus of law. Nor would they continue to understand the common law as primarily derived from these higher principles in order to furnish justice in individual cases.[31]

26. See David G. Ritchie, *Natural Rights: A Criticism of Some Political and Ethical Conceptions* (London: Allen and Unwin, 1895), 228.

27. Paton, *A Text-Book of Jurisprudence,* 108.

28. Morton J. Horwitz, *The Transformation of American Law 1790–1860* (Cambridge: Harvard University Press, 1977), 18–19.

29. See James Wilson, *The Works of James Wilson,* 2 vols., ed. Robert G. McCloskey (Cambridge: Belknap Press of Harvard University Press, 1967), quoted in Horwitz, *Transformation of American Law,* 19.

30. See John Austin, *Lectures on Jurisprudence, or The Philosophy of Positive Law,* Lecture 6, rev. 5th ed., ed. Robert Campbell (London: J. Murray, 1885). Commenting on Austin's concept of law, Hans Kelsen stated: "It can be said that the state creates the law, but this means only that the law regulates its own creation." Hans Kelsen, "The Pure Theory of Law and Analytical Jurisprudence," *Harvard Law Review* 55 (1941): 44, 65. Kelsen defined law as "the social technique which consists in bringing about the desired conduct of men through the threat of a measure of coercion which is to be applied in every case of contrary conduct." Hans Kelsen, *General Theory of Law and State,* trans. Anders Wedberg (New York: Russell and Russell, 1961), 19. Hence, for Kelsen, the state and the law are the same, since the state is only the legal order viewed from another direction.

31. See Horwitz, *Transformation of American Law,* 30. Rather, they began to function "as

The transformed view of law opened the prospect that traditional legal structures, such as the institution of marriage, would be eviscerated of the claim to an objective moral value.[32] Marriage could no longer avow a legitimacy based upon its status as a permanent institution derived from human nature, which transcended cultures and history.[33] To the contrary, the existential human situation at any given historical and cultural manifestation might give rise to law that regulated human sexuality and procreation in a variety of ways.[34] In addition to, or theoretically even to the exclusion of, lasting monogamous relationships between males and females, the law might recognize as privileged any number of possibilities such as cohabitation, polygamy, homosexual unions, or some other type of more advanced arrangement.[35] The demise of the natural-law tradition as affording the moral predicate for legal structures led to the relativity of value. It reduced marriage to merely a social convention, which two individuals elect based upon respective subjective preferences.

MARRIAGE AND FAMILY AS
FUNDAMENTAL COMMUNITY

In contrast to a focus on marriage as a mere social convention reflecting subjective preference, the natural-law tradition considers marriage and family to constitute the most fundamental form of human community.[36] This

---

equally responsible with legislation for governing society and promoting socially desirable conduct." The new view would ultimately lead to Holmes's realism that "the life of the law has not been its logic, it has been its experience." Oliver Wendel Holmes Jr., *The Common Law* 1 (Cambridge: Belknap Press of Harvard University Press, 1951), 1.

32. See Unger, *Knowledge and Politics*, 63 (criticizing liberal theory on account of the "inability to arrive at a coherent understanding of the relations between rules and values in social life").

33. See Witte, *From Sacrament to Contract*, 202–19.

34. See, e.g., *Planned Parenthood of Southeastern Pennsylvania v. Casey*, 505 US 833, 851 (1992) ("At the heart of liberty is the right to define one's own concept of existence, of meaning, of the universe, and of the mystery of human life.")

35. See Witte, *From Sacrament to Contract*, 215; see also Richard A. Posner, *Sex and Reason* (Cambridge: Harvard University Press, 1992), 435–42 (arguing on the basis of economic analysis for societal attitudes and laws that respect a "liberal" approach to sexuality); but see Robert P. George, *In Defense of Natural Law* (Oxford: Clarendon Press, 1999), 139–60 (arguing that the state should recognize only marriages between mature persons of the opposite sexes who have the capacity to "consummate marriage as a one-flesh communion").

36. See Aristotle, *Nicomachean Ethics*, bk. 8, ch. 12 (Princeton: Princeton University Press,

natural community flows from the unity of the person as body and spirit and the complementarity of the sexes. From a teleological perspective, the tradition identifies two inseparable ends of marriage.[37] First, conjugal love, or what Wojtyla describes as the sensual and spiritual intimacy of the spouses in marriage, demands a profound justification.[38] The depth of this community requires commitment on the part of the spouses to a lasting and exclusive fidelity to each other.[39] According to Wojtyla, this special form of love elicits from the participant the total gift of self.[40] It yields a kind of human friendship that prospers in the midst of the joys and sufferings of everyday life.

The second good commences with openness to the procreation of children.[41] As conjugal love flows from the complementarity of the sexes, procreation follows from the social nature of the human person. The bestowal of humanity upon those to whom the parents have given life fills the fundamental community with meaning and purpose. In describing this good, Wojtyla notes that from the moment of conception, the child presents him/

1984), 1162n. ("Between man and wife, friendship seems to exist by nature; for human persons are naturally inclined to form couples—even more than to form cities, inasmuch as the household is earlier and more necessary than the city.") See Wojtyla, "The Family as the Community of Persons," in *Person and Community: Selected Essays*, 315–27.

37. Thomas Aquinas, *Summa Theologica* III (N.p., 1926), q. 41, a. 1. (Thomistic thought describes two goods of marriage. "First, in relation to the principal end of matrimony, namely the good of the offspring. . . . Secondly, in relation to the secondary end of matrimony, which is the mutual services which married persons render one another in household matters. . . . For just as natural reason dictates that human beings should live together, since one is not self-sufficient in all things concerning life, for which reason the human person is described as being naturally inclined to political society. . . . Wherefore nature inculcated that society of man and woman which consists in marriage.").

38. See Wojtyla, *Love and Responsibility* (Thomistic thought emphasized the primacy of procreation over the *mutuum adiutorium*, which is referred to here as "conjugal love."). Neither the teaching of Vatican II, see Sacrosanctum Concilium Oecumenicum Vaticanum II, "Constitutio pastoralis de ecclesia in mundo huius temporis, *Gaudium et spes*," 51 (die 7 m. decembris a. 1965), AAS 58 (1966): 1025, nor of Paul VI, see Paulus PP VI, "Litterae Encyclicae *Humane vitae*," 12 (die 25 m. iullius a. 1968), AAS 60 (1968): 481–503, posited a hierarchy of the ends, but the later emphasized the inseparable connection between the ends. See also Wojtyla, "The Teaching of Humane Vitae on Love," in *Person and Community: Selected Essays*, 302. Cf. John T. Noonan Jr., *Contraception: A History of Its Treatment by the Catholic Theologians and Canonists* 582–97 (Cambridge: Harvard University Press, 1965) (prior to *Human Vitae*, suggesting that not every act of sexual intercourse need be open to procreation).

39. See Wojtyla, *Love and Responsibility*, 211–16.

40. Ibid., 125–26.

41. See Aristolte, *Nicomachean Ethics*, bk. 8, ch. 12, 1162a; Thomas Aquinas, *Summa Theologica* III, Supp., q. 41, a. 1.; Wojtyla, *Love and Responsibility*, 224–36.

herself for acceptance and participation in the community.[42] Deeply aware that the child belongs to them, the parents offer acceptance, care, and education to the child.[43] As the child discovers his/her humanity, the family unit develops and matures as a kind of organic and spiritual community.[44] Together with siblings, the child and parents form what Wojtyla identifies as a community of human persons.[45] The characteristic traits of this fundamental community might be said to include acceptance, participation, education, commitment, and fulfillment.

The reduction of the marriage to subjective experience stands in contrast to the natural-law tradition, in which marriage constitutes an objective value.[46] The primacy of individual experience over the objectivity of the fundamental human community has philosophical roots in classical liberal political theory.[47] As with the natural-law tradition, it is far beyond the modest scope of my remarks to trace the development and influences of liberal theory.[48] Suffice it to say that generally liberal theory emphasizes autonomy, individualism, subjectivity, and the relativity of moral value.[49] The seventeenth-

42. See Wojtyla, "Parenthood as a Community of Persons," in *Person and Community: Selected Essays*, 333.

43. See ibid., 332–35.   44. See ibid., 333.

45. See ibid., at 332–33.

46. See Thomas Aquinas, *Summa Theologica* II, Supp., III, q. 41, a. 1.

47. See, e.g., Drucilla Cornell, "Fatherhood and its Discontents: Men, Patriarchy and Freedom," in *Lost Fathers: The Politics of Fatherlessness in America,* ed. Cynthia R. Daniels (New York: St. Martin's Press, 1998), 199–200 (arguing that the law of the state ought not "to privilege or impose one form of family structure or sexuality over another").

48. See generally John Rawls, *A Theory of Justice* (Cambridge: Belknap Press of Harvard University Press, 1971), 3–53; Robert Nozick, *Philosophical Explanations* (Cambridge: Belknap Press of Harvard University Press, 1981), 27–114; see also Robert Song, *Christianity and Liberal Society* (Oxford: Clarendon Press, 1997), 9–48.

49. Liberal theory's emphasis on individualism seems evident in three well-known twentieth-century cases concerning marriage, procreation, and privacy. Starting with *Griswold v. Connecticut,* the United States Supreme Court has delineated a right of individual privacy based on the due process clauses of the fifth and fourteenth amendments. In *Griswold,* the Court struck down a state statute that criminalized the use of contraceptives "for the purpose of preventing conception." Appealing to the "sacredness" of marriage, the Court described the statute as "repulsive to the notions of privacy surrounding the marriage relationship." 381 US 479 (1965). The privacy right protecting the distribution and use of contraceptives was extended to nonmarried individuals in *Eisenstadt v. Baird,* 405 US 438 (1972). This legal reasoning then supplied the justification for the right of a women to have an abortion in *Roe v. Wade,* 410 US 113 (1973). Thus, the privacy right, which was claimed to be based on the "sacred character" of marriage, was extended to include constitutional protection for individuals to distribute and use contraception as well as to perform and have abortions.

century philosopher Thomas Hobbes expressed the understanding in its pristine form when he propagated the myth of Leviathan: the human being in the state of nature as an isolated, self-interested creature of fear and desire, engaged in a perpetual state of war with everyone else, and driven into political society only for the sake of self-preservation.[50] When applied to marriage and family, this image of the autonomous individual is precisely what gives rise to the primacy of subjective experience over the organic and spiritual reality of the community of persons that is the family.[51]

The family interacts with the larger society by affording the primary experience of participation in community.[52] For the large amount of good that it admittedly accomplishes in regulating business and rendering government benefits, the liberal state is incapable of supplying, and perhaps even militates against, a sense of solidarity and community.[53] Attempting to retrieve the natural-law tradition, Wojtyla recalls that marriage and the family compose the primary community.[54] In this regard, Wojtyla's position distinguish-

---

50. See Hobbes, *Leviathan*, 82–84. See also Locke, "Second Treatise on Government," §§ 143–44, 364–65 (the individual consents to a "social contract" pursuant to which the freedom of the state of nature is surrendered in order to procure societal protection of the "natural rights" of life, liberty, and property). Cf. Jean-Jacques Rousseau, *The Social Contract and Discourses*, bk. 1, trans. G. D. H. Cole (New York: E. P. Dutton, 1950), ch. 2, 4–18. (Concerning the social contract, the eighteenth-century philosopher Jean-Jacques Rousseau maintained that the family was the only "natural society.")

51. See Wojtyla, "The Problem of Experience in Ethics," in *Person and Community, Selected Essays*, 122–25.

52. See Wojtyla, *Love and Responsibility*, 217 ("The family is in itself a small society, and the existence of all large societies—nation, state, Church—depends on it.").

53. See Max Weber, *The Protestant Ethic and the Spirit of Capitalism*, trans. Talcott Parsons (London: Unwin, 1948). See also R. Jackson Wilson, *In Quest of Community: Social Philosophy in the United States 1860–1920* (New York: John Wiley and Sons, 1968) (criticizing liberal political theory on the ground that it fosters an impersonal and bureaucratic state, which encourages individual competition to the detriment of societal interests). See also Wojtyla, *The Acting Person*, 276–79, where the author suggests that participation in authentic communities, as opposed to the modern society, gives rise to words such as "brother," "sister," and "kinship." The reason, according to the author, is that authentic communities such as family, church and other subsidiary structures in society permit the individual person to experience "participation" rather than "alienation."

54. See Wojtyla, *Love and Responsibility*, 217 ("For although marriage in the natural course of things leads to the existence of a family, and although the possibility that it will do so must always be kept open, marriage itself is not as a result absorbed by and lost in the family. It retains its distinct existence as an institution whose inner structure is different from that of the family. The family has the structure of a society. . . . Marriage does not possess the struc-

es individualism from personalism.[55] Individualism denotes that the human person acts primarily to advance self-interest. In contrast, personalism refers to the constitution of the human person through acting in solidarity with others. Personalism posits the human person as created not for self-interest but for self-transcendence.[56] This leads to a second distinction, that between alienation and participation.[57] Membership in "society" ought not to be identified with that participation through which the human person experiences fulfillment. Such participation is possible only in those subsidiary structures that facilitate the formation of genuine "community."[58] The family is nature's primary structure to facilitate personalism and participation.

Wojtyla also draws attention to the semantic difference between the terms "society" and "community," as reflective of the difference between associational relationships and relationships that entail a deeper level of personal commitment and fulfillment.[59] In Catholic thought, subsidiary structures are considered a necessary condition for the creation of community.[60] Moreover,

---

ture of a society, but an inter-personal structure: it is a union and a communion of two persons.").

55. See Wojtyla, *The Acting Person*, 271–80.

56. See Wojtyla, "Catholic Sexual Ethics," in *Person and Community, Selected Essays*, 284–29; see also *Veritatis splendor*, 51 ("This universality does not ignore the individuality of human beings, nor is it opposed to the absolute uniqueness of each person. On the contrary, it embraces at its root each of the person's free acts, which are meant to bear witness to the universality of the true good.").

57. See Wojtyla, *The Acting Person*, 296–99; "Participation or Alienation," in *Person and Community, Selected Essays*, 204–6.

58. The Catholic concept of the common good thus holds that "[c]ollaboration in the development of the whole person and of every human being is in fact a duty of all towards all." Thus, the common good with its goal of authentic personal development mitigates against excessive individualism. "Progressioni <totius hominis> et <omnis hominis> cooperari est officium *omnium hominum erga omnes . . .*" Ioannes Paulus Pp. II, "Litterae Encylicae *Sollicitudo rei socialis*, 32 (die 30 m. decembris a. 1987)," *AAS* 80 (1988): 545 (emphasis in original).

59. See Wojtyla, *The Acting Person*, 277–79.

60. A constitutive element of the Catholic understanding of natural law has been the concept of the common good. The common good has been defined as "the sum of those conditions of social life which allow social groups and their individual members relatively thorough and ready access to their own fulfillment." The Pastoral Constitution on the Church in the World of Today defines the common good as "summam eorum vitae socialis condicionum quae tum coetibus, tum singulis membris permittunt ut propriam perfectionem plenius atque expeditius consequantur." *Gaudium et spes*, 26. It seems important to point out that the meaning of the common good in the Catholic tradition is not merely the good of the community. In contrast to an excessive focus on the community or the individual, the Catholic

it is recognized that the human person, as a social being, gravitates for authentic fulfillment to such subsidiary structures.[61] A significant subsidiary structure is that fundamental community of marriage in which the members recognize a source of meaning and value.[62] Here, personalism, participation, and solidarity flourish. The natural-law tradition holds that the special form of spousal love and the gift of new human life, which flows from it, constitute an objective reality upon which the larger society depends for its stability and well-being.

MARRIAGE AS VIRTUOUS

The predominance of subjective experience also mitigates the natural-law tradition that marriage is a virtuous relationship.[63] In Wojtyla's words, the contemporary view "proclaims the primacy of experience over virtue."[64] Pursuant to the tradition, the spouses' commitment to the two ends of marriage, conjugal love and procreation, is virtuous. In Wojytla's analysis, the human person finds fulfillment when the inner subjective elements of the person are brought into conformity with the objective and virtuous social reality through the person's free act of the will.[65] When the human person apprehends the natural goods of marriage in the intellect, the person understands that the basis for marriage is more than a subjective inner experience.[66] Rather, marriage exists as an outer objective social reality that represents virtue for the spouses, their children, and the larger society.[67] The moral life "calls for that creativity and originality typical of the person, the source and cause

---

position assumes a *"genuinely personalistic structure of human existence in community."* Wojtyla, *The Acting Person,* 282 (emphasis in original).

61. Pope Pius XI formulated what has become the classic statement of the principle of subsidiarity. Pius Pp. XI, "Litterae Encyclicae *Quadragesimo anno* (die 15 m. maii a. 1931)," *AAS* 23 (1931): 177–228.

62. See Finnis, *Natural Law, Natural Rights,* 398–410.

63. See Thomas Aquinas, *Summa Theologica* III, Supp., q. 41, a. 1; see also Wojtyla, *Love and Responsibility,* 197 ("Virtue can only come from spiritual strength").

64. Wojtyla, *Love and Responsibility,* 119.

65. See Thomas Aquinas, *Summa Theologica* III, Supp., q. 41, a. 1. ("That is said to be natural to which nature inclines, although it comes to pass through the intervention of free will; thus acts of virtue and the virtues themselves are called natural; and in this way matrimony is natural.").

66. See Wojtyla, *Love and Responsibility,* 119.

67. See ibid., 217.

of his own deliberate acts."[68] When the human person exercises free will to enter into and to sustain this fundamental community, the person acts in accord with natural virtue.

Liberal theory's emphasis on the autonomous individual results in a definition of freedom as the absence of government constraint.[69] Consequently, law is viewed as a constraint placed on individual freedom.[70] The fact that the state law requires a judicial judgment to dissolve a valid marriage places a burden on the freedom of the individual, who is not able to terminate the marriage at will by subjective choice. Pursuant to liberal theory, when such a restriction is justified by societal need, the burden must be the minimum necessary in order to produce the underlying purpose of the restriction. The natural law tradition, in contrast, understands law not so much as a burden but as an "enabling condition" of freedom. The tradition posits no necessary opposition between freedom and law. As already discussed, it understands marriage as a state of life entered into by free choice, which offers the spouses a deeper meaning. The meaning is located in the two ends of the conjugal love and new human life. To abide by this law based on human nature yields a deeper freedom than that which is available to the autonomous individual who acts principally to protect self-interest.

The primacy of subjective experience also results in the relativity of truth.[71] In liberal theory, freedom involves a subjective interpretation about truth. Each person is free to choose his/her own moral rules.[72] In contrast, the natural law tradition recognizes the truth of marriage not as a matter of speculative knowledge, but instead on the basis of "practical truth."[73] Practical truth is a truth to which the meaning of one's life is subject.[74] In other words, the day-to-day lived reality and the whole of one's life would be radi-

---

68. See *Veritatis splendor,* 40.

69. See Alasdair MacIntyre, "How We Can Learn What 'Veritatis Splendor' Has to Teach," in *Veritatis Splendor and the Renewal of Moral Theology,* ed. J. A. DiNoia, O.P., and Romanus Cesario, O.P. (Chicago: Midwest Theological Forum, 1999), 85.

70. See ibid.

71. See Wojtyla, *Love and Responsibility,* 119–121; see also *Veritatis splendor,* 101.

72. See *Veritatis splendor,* 101. See MacIntyre, *How We Can Learn What "Veritatis Splendor" Has to Teach,* 85.

73. See Thomas Aquinas, *Summa Theologica* I, q. 16, a. 4, ad II-II, q. 109, a. 2, ad 3; II-II, q. 109, a. 3, ad 3.

74. See Livio Melina, "Desire for Happiness and the Commandments in the First Chapter of 'Veritatis Splendor,'" in *Veritatis Splendor and the Renewal of Moral Theology,* ed. J. A. DiNoia, O.P., and Romanus Cesario, O.P. (Chicago: Midwest Theological Forum, 1999), 150.

cally impoverished in the absence of this truth. Marriage is such a practical truth as it shapes the destiny of the spouses. This is a truth that involves contemplation in the intellect, commitment in the will, and expression with the body.[75] To live in accord with the natural law requires a love for the true good. In living out their marital vows, the spouses love not only each other as autonomous individuals but the organic and spiritual reality that is created by their union.

Wojtyla's analysis retrieves this more profound understanding of marriage. The analysis starts with an appreciation of the value of the human person as "its own master" endowed with free will.[76] The experience of marital love, according to Wojtyla:

> forcibly detaches the person, so to speak, from its natural inviolability and inalienability. It makes the person want to do just that—surrender itself to another, to the one it loves. The person no longer wishes to be its own exclusive property, but instead to become the property of that other. This means the renunciation of its autonomy and its inalienability. Love proceeds by way of this renunciation, guided by the profound conviction that it does not diminish or impoverish, but quite the contrary, enlarges and enriches the existence of the person.[77]

This paradoxical aspect of marital love flows from the "work of the will," in which the mutual love of the spouses entices acts of self-sacrifice for each other and the family as a whole.[78] Wojtyla contrasts this profound "love that is gift of self" with "the superficial view of sex."[79] The superficial view involves "mutual sexual exploitation" in which the woman "surrender[s] her body to a man."[80] Instead, the profound love of the spouses in marriage demands the reciprocity of mutual surrender of both persons. When this love exists "the sensual and emotional experiences which are so vividly present in the consciousness" of marital union constitute the "outward gauge" of the self-giving of the persons.[81] The natural-law tradition recognizes that the spouses' self-gift to each other as well as the sacrifices the parents make for children constitute marriage and family life as virtuous.

---

75. See Wojtyla, *Love and Responsibility*, 195–208.
76. See ibid., 125.   77. See ibid., 125–26.
78. See ibid., 126.   79. See ibid.
80. See ibid.   81. See ibid.

CONCLUSION

Given the high rate of divorce that now characterizes American society, this chapter has attempted to retrieve certain aspects of the natural-law tradition about the meaning and purposes of marriage. The tradition understands the ends of marriage as the conjugal union of the spouses and the procreation and education of children. It sees marriage as a natural and virtuous relationship that elicits the gift of self from each of the spouses. It recognizes that natural goods of marriage lead to the family unity, which is the fundamental community of society. In light of the tradition, I offer two practical suggestions related to the issue of counseling clients who are thinking about divorce.

First, the attorney needs to understand his/her role as a "counselor-at-law." Certainly, the role of the attorney is not to serve as a therapist, minister, or social worker.[82] The attorney should realize, nonetheless, that a client who is faced with the possibility of divorce may be in a somewhat confused and vulnerable state of mind.[83] It may well be the case that referral to a religious and/or psychological counselor represents an important part of the process leading to an informed decision about the legal status of the client's marriage and family. The law of many states contemplates that prior to a final decree of dissolution, the parties experience a "cooling-off" period in which to view the situation in as balanced a way as possible under the circumstances of the case.[84] The legislative intent of the law is not to create a culture of divorce, but to facilitate reconciliation and keep families together when possible.[85] In accord with these considerations, the natural-law tradition affords the attor-

---

82. See Kenneth Kressal et al., "A Provisional Typology of Lawyer Attitudes towards Divorce Practice; Gladiators, Advocates, Counselors and Journeyman," in *Readings in Family Law,* ed. Frederica K. Lombard (New York: Foundational Press, 1990), 130 (distinguishing between family law attorneys as either counselors, who prefer a psychological and interpersonal approach, or advocates, who aim for the correct tactics to achieve victory for the client).

83. See William H. Simon, "Lawyer Advice and Client Autonomy: Mrs. Jones' Case," *Maryland Law Review* 50 (1991): 213n1 (noting a distinction between lawyers who focus on the client's autonomy in reaching decisions and those who adopt a more paternalistic view in guiding the client's decision-making process).

84. See, e.g., N. Y. Dom. Rel. Law § 170 (5) and (6).

85. See, e.g., *Sinha v. Sinha.* 515 Pa 14 (1987) (The goal of reconciliation that underlies the divorce law justifies the separation period of three years prior to a unilateral divorce.).

ney a historical background and perspective from which to counsel the client about legal options.

Second, law schools might consider including the natural-law perspective in courses that deal with domestic relations and family law.[86] It is not a matter of imposing a certain value system upon law students. The natural-law understanding of marriage is of significant importance to academic discussion of the family, if for no other reason than that the tradition has played such a central historical role in defining the institution of marriage in our society. It seems questionable that a student would complete a course about family law that culminates in the degree of doctor of law (juris doctor) and have never heard about the role of natural law in the historical development of the subject matter. The numerous law schools that have a Catholic tradition should be especially concerned to present the natural-law tradition, as it has been an important component of the Catholic intellectual heritage.

In this brief overview of the tradition, I have drawn heavily on the philosophical writings of Karol Wojtyla. Consistent with the natural-law tradition, Wojtyla's writings are primarily philosophical and most often do not appeal to the revelation of a specific religious tradition. In our pluralistic society, this kind of philosophical thinking affords hope in the face of skepticism about the possibilities for common agreement on the nature and ends of marriage. The fact that Wojtyla emerged as the successor to the Apostle Peter in the Catholic community should only enhance the importance of his pre-papal philosophical thought to the ongoing discussion about marriage in a society where broken marriages have become all too commonplace.

86. See John T. Noonan Jr., "A Catholic Law School," *Notre Dame Law Review* 67 (1992): 1037, 1040–41 (discussing the important role of natural law in Catholic law schools).

IMMIGRATION LAW

A Catholic Christian Perspective
on Immigration Justice

٭

MICHAEL A. SCAPERLANDA

Throughout recorded history individuals have left families, cultures, and nations to take up residence in foreign lands. Migration of individuals and families within and between nations occurs for multiple reasons. A variety of factors push people toward the decision to emigrate from their homes. These include lack of economic opportunity in the home region due to unemployment or underemployment; governmental instability or oppression; lack of educational opportunities; regional hostility toward one's religious, cultural, ethnic, or political identity; absence of family ties; famine; civil war; and, in a few cases, just plain adventure. At some point, these reasons for emigrating aggregate to the point of pushing an individual away from their place of origin.

Similarly, a variety of factors pull people toward certain immigration destinations. Family ties; political stability; economic and educational opportunity; cost and standard of living; absence of language barriers; religious, cul-

A version of this paper appeared as "Immigration Justice: Beyond Liberal Egalitarian and Communitarian Perspectives," *Review of Social Economy* 57 (1999): 523; and another version appeared as "Immigration Justice: A Catholic Christian Perspective," *Journal of Catholic Social Thought* 1 (2004): 535.

tural, and ethnic tolerance; and the cost of reaching the desired destination weigh against the resources available to effectuate the move. In contemplating the decision to leave one community and deciding among the possible destinations, the prospective émigré will factor in the formal legal barriers to exit and entry. In extreme cases, the benefits of migration outweigh even prohibitive legal barriers, and the migrant is willing to risk her life to migrate and will accept status as an undocumented shadow member of the receiving community.[1]

For as long as people have desired to migrate, others have created barriers to migration, prohibiting exit or refusing entry. Fear, protection of domestic labor, ethnic or religious purity, and multiple other factors contribute to migration barriers. Legalized segregation, zoning, deed restrictions, and gated communities create local barriers to entry in communities across the globe.

This chapter focuses on the formal legal barriers to transnational migration, exploring the ethical foundations for a socially just immigration policy. In it, I ask: By what criteria should we judge a country's barriers to exit and/ or entry? What factors go into deciding whether a state's e/immigration policies are morally just? The first part exposes the weaknesses in the currently fashionable attempt to anchor a socially just immigration policy in some version of liberal egalitarianism. This section also critiques a secular communitarian critique of liberal theory. The second part of this chapter provides a framework that looks beyond liberalism and communitarianism, outlining the contours of a socially just immigration policy founded upon the transcendent and common nature of humanity, giving due consideration to the understanding that the development of the human person requires community. Building on this foundation, in the third part, I make general observations about the justness of current United States immigration policy, remembering that the immigration issue cannot be viewed in a vacuum divorced from broader economic and political realities, especially the factors that push people into emigrating. I end with a critique of the draconian measures that lead to the virtually automatic deportation of so-called aggravated felons under United States immigration law.

---

1. See, e.g., Kevin Johnson, "Los Olvidados: Images of the Immigrant, Political Power of Noncitizens, and Immigration Law and Enforcement," *Brigham Young University Law Review* 1993 (1993): 1139; and Linda Bosniak, "Exclusion and Membership: The Dual Identity of the Undocumented Worker under United States Law," *Wisconsin Law Review* 1988 (1988): 955.

LIBERAL THEORY AND A COMMUNITIARIAN RESPONSE

Liberal Egalitarianism and Open Borders

Liberal egalitarianism, in its various permutations, dominates the immigration theory landscape. As Joseph Carens explains, "liberal egalitarians care about human freedoms. People should be free to pursue their own projects . . . as long as this does not interfere with the legitimate claims of other individuals to do likewise. In addition, liberal egalitarians are committed to equal opportunity, . . . keep[ing] economic, social, and political inequalities as small as possible."[2] Based on these ideas, liberal theorists struggle to justify immigration restrictions. Their own parameters—autonomy and equality—make it difficult for them to articulate why an accident of birth—being born in the United States or Haiti—ought to enhance or restrict a person's life chances. In the absence of a satisfactory explanation as to why would-be immigrants have an inferior claim to the economic, social, and political resources of the receiving state, "liberals ought to be committed to relatively unrestricted immigration policies."[3]

The liberal case for open borders derives from its conception of the state as procedural, devoid of substantive value judgments concerning what constitutes the good life. "The liberal state is not a private club; it is rather a public dialogue by which each person can gain social recognition of his standing as a free and rational being. I cannot justify my power to exclude you without destroying my own claim to membership in an ideal liberal state."[4] Building on Rawls, Carens posits that "[i]n the original position [behind the 'veil of ignorance'] one would insist that the right to migrate be included in the system of basic liberties [because] it might prove essential to one's plan of life. . . . So, the basic agreement among those in the original position would be to permit no restrictions on migration (whether emigration or immigration)."[5]

2. Joseph H. Carens, "Migration and Morality: A Liberal Egalitarian Perspective," in *Free Movement: Ethical Issues in the Transnational Movement of People and of Money,* ed. Brian Barry and Robert Goodin (University Park: Pennsylvania State University Press, 1992), 26.

3. Mark Tushnet, "Immigration Policy in Liberal Political Theory," in *Justice in Immigration,* ed. Warren Schwartz (Cambridge: Cambridge University Press, 1995), 155. See, e.g., Kevin Johnson, "Open Borders?" *UCLA Law Review* 51 (2003): 193, 195.

4. Bruce Ackerman, *Social Justice in the Liberal State* (New Haven: Yale University Press, 1980), 93.

5. Carens, "Migration and Morality," 26; Howard F. Chang, "Immigration Policy, Liberal Principles, and The Republican Tradition," *Georgetown Law Journal* 85 (1997): 2105, 2113.

Lacking a convincing "neutral" argument for exclusion, liberal egalitarian theory responds with an openness largely unconcerned with the consequences of migration on either the sending or receiving communities.

The Communitarian Response

A communitarian response to liberal theory's case for open borders is made most forcefully by Michael Walzer.[6] Rejecting the quest of Rawls, Ackerman, and others for abstract universal principles of justice, Walzer's theory of justice "is radically particularist" taking historically contingent "political community [as] the appropriate setting for" working out a theory of distributive justice.[7] To accept the universalist approach, "we would have to imagine what does not yet exist: a community that included all men and women everywhere. We would have to invent a set of common meanings for these people, avoiding if we could the stipulation of our own values."[8]

Walzer draws two important conclusions from his particularist choice: "distribution of membership is not pervasively subject to the constraints of justice"; and, therefore, "states are simply free to take in strangers (or not)."[9] Walzer states:

[T]he right to choose an admission policy is . . . basic. . . . At stake here is the shape of the community that acts in the world. . . . Admission and exclusion are at the core of communal independence. They suggest the deepest meaning of self-determination. Without them, there could not be *communities of character,* historically stable, ongoing associations of men and women with some special commitment to one another and some special sense of their common life.[10]

Most liberal theorists agree with Walzer—to an extent. Despite Carens's careless "so what" conclusion to the fact that "[o]pen immigration . . . might destroy old ways of life, highly valued by some, but it would make possible

6. Among the various communitarians, the focus here is on Walzer and his thought because "Walzer's analysis . . . has become the paradigm organizing concept for virtually all normative treatments of immigration law and policy, whether or not the substance of his views is actually embraced." Linda Bosniak, "Membership, Equality, and the Difference That Membership Makes," *New York University Law Review* 69 (1994): 1047, 1068. Carens criticizes Walzer's communitarianism for its lack of attention to the liberal traditions in the United States. Joseph H. Carens, "Aliens and Citizens: The Case for Open Borders," *Review of Politics* 49 (1987): 251, 264–70.

7. Michael Walzer, *Spheres of Justice: A Defense of Pluralism and Equity* (New York: Basic Books, 1983), 28.

8. Ibid., 29–30.   9. Ibid., 61.

10. Ibid., 61, 62.

new ways of life, highly valued by others,"[11] liberal theorists care so deeply about one value (maintaining the liberal state) that restrictive immigration laws can justify the use of force to keep out even innocent and needy aliens if their presence threatens to undermine that one value. In other words, liberals become markedly illiberal and intolerant of those who would threaten their highest value.[12] As Ackerman concludes, "[t]he *only* reason for restricting immigration is to protect the ongoing process of liberal conversation itself."[13] Liberal theorists such as Ackerman envision a particular community of character and will exercise whatever power they can muster to employ restrictive immigration measures along (1) ideological lines to keep out those who don't possess this liberal character, at least where admission threatens the liberal enterprise, and (2) numerical lines whenever the numbers of potential immigrants exceeds the absorption rate, thereby undermining the stability of the liberal dialogue.

Liberal theorists reject the breadth of Walzer's conclusions because his conclusions can be used to justify restrictive immigration policies that prefer certain groups on illiberal grounds. A discriminatory immigration policy based on these values fails the test of liberalism because it fails to treat "all human beings as free and equal moral persons,"[14] providing moral legitimacy to an impassioned population's xenophobic drive to exclude noncitizens on the basis of race, religion, ethnicity, or political opinion.[15]

11. Carens, "Aliens and Citizens," 251, 271.

12. James Dwyer, *Vouchers within Reason: A Child-Centered Approach to Education Reform* (Ithaca, N.Y.: Cornell University Press, 2001); James Dwyer, *Religious Schools v. Children's Rights* (Ithaca, N.Y.: Cornell University Press, 1998). See also Meira Levinson, *The Demands of Liberal Education* (Oxford: Oxford University Press, 1999). For my critique of *Vouchers within Reason*, see Michael Scaperlanda, "Producing Trousered Apes in Dwyer's Totalitarian State," *Texas Review of Law and Politics* 7 (2002): 175.

13. Ackerman, *Social Justice in the Liberal State,* 95.

14. Carens, "Migration and Morality," 25; and Chang, "Immigration Policy, Liberal Principles, and the Republican Tradition," 2105, 2113. Richard Rorty, *Contingency, Irony and Solidarity* (Cambridge: Cambridge University Press, 1989).

15. Given a history checkered with immigration laws that have excluded noncitizens on some of these grounds, the liberal theorists have legitimate fears. See, e.g., Johnson, "Open Borders?" 203–4 ("Historically, U.S. immigration laws have been overbroad in attacking the perceived evil of the day, whether it be racial minorities, the poor, political dissidents, or others"); ibid. at 206 ("Despite the nation's stated commitment to liberal ideals, U.S. immigration law has permitted ideological discrimination, suspect classifications in admission policies, and discrimination against noncitizens after admission, and continues to do so despite . . . liberal principles"); Victor Romero, "Proxies for Loyalty in Constitutional Immigration

Liberal and Communitarian Theories of Justice: Foundations Built on Sand

Where do these competing theories of justice and membership leave us? On the one hand, secular liberals, building subconsciously on Judeo-Christian values, emphasize the dignity and equal moral worth of each individual human being. Secular communitarians, on the other hand, realize that the full potential of the human being is developed and protected only within community, including political community. Can we mediate between these two positions in attempting to develop a socially and economically just immigration policy? Not on their own terms. The secular communitarian suggests that theories of justice are created out of the historical contingencies forming particular communities, while the liberal egalitarian abstracts humanity, creating universal principles of justice by envisioning a mythical state of nature or constructing a hypothetical "veil of ignorance" or *creating* solidarity out of human suffering. But neither liberal nor communitarian theory makes a claim to the truth about human nature and the relationship between the individual and the community, including the political community. Neither secular communitarians nor liberal egalitarians propose a criterion for measuring justice that transcends the rhetorical appeal of their own voices. As Walzer states, "[j]ustice is a human construction, and it is doubtful that it can be made in only one way."[16] He hopes that his appeal will lead the reader to prefer his vision of justice, but he makes no claim to truth, which seems irrelevant to his project.

Secular liberals and liberal communitarians celebrate our culture, which has gradually "substitute[d] Freedom for Truth as the goal of thinking and of social progress."[17] Divorced from truth, freedom and liberty are rootless and precarious concepts. As Rorty admits, the "insistence on contingency, and our consequent opposition to ideas like 'essence,' 'nature,' and 'foundation,' makes it impossible for us to retain the notion that some actions and attitudes are naturally 'inhuman.'"[18] In this world, where objective truth is de-

---

Law: Citizenship and Race after September 11," *DePaul Law Review* 53 (2003): 871 (exploring the "irrational" use of race and citizenship as proxies for disloyalty); and Gabriel Chin, "Segregation's Last Stronghold: Discrimination and the Constitutional Law of Immigration," *UCLA Law Review* 46 (1998): 1.

16. Walzer, *Spheres of Justice*, 5.

17. Rorty, *Contingency, Irony and Solidarity*, xiii.

18. Ibid., p. 189.

nied or ignored, we "cannot give a criterion for wrongness."[19] In other words, we give "up the idea that liberalism could be justified, and Nazi or Marxist enemies of liberalism refuted, by . . . argument."[20]

Rorty, Ackerman, and Walzer all prefer a liberal polity, but none of them provides a metaphysical foundation transcending historical contingency. In a world without objective truth, "self-knowledge" is "self-creation."[21] What they desire is a private life of self-creation coupled with a public life governed by the principles of toleration and equality. Liberal egalitarians and secular communitarians can continue their projects of building a liberal state where "all human beings" are treated "as free and equal moral persons" largely because they are free riders on a vision of the human person inherited in modified form from the Judeo-Christian ethic. What they desire is to keep the idea of human dignity but cast aside its foundations in a Creator. In their view, we should all agree to be nice to each other and treat each other as equal moral agents, but this is merely a matter of preference and agreement because nothing external to our contingent humanity obligates us to order justice in this fashion. This works, more or less well, because liberal egalitarians can coast on the remnants of Judeo-Christian culture and on the private piety of believers today. Without two thousand years of Christianity espousing, albeit imperfectly, the inherent worth of human beings it is doubtful that the liberal view of the individual would have gained legitimacy. The product of previous eras, Rorty says, including the Christian era, "is *us*—our conscience, our culture, our form of life."[22] Rorty acknowledges Christians as "toolmakers" whose "purpose was the alleviation of cruelty."[23] Now that Western society detests cruelty, "democracies are now in a position," he asserts, "to throw away some of the ladders [including Christianity] used in their own con-

19. Ibid., p. 75.

20. Ibid., p. 53.

21. "The process of coming to know oneself, confronting one's contingency . . . is identical with the process of inventing a new language—that is, of thinking up some new metaphors" (ibid., 27) because "human beings are simply incarnated vocabularies" (88). Without truth, "sexual perversion, extreme cruelty, ludicrous obsession, and manic delusion" becomes merely "the private poem of the pervert, the sadist, or the lunatic: each as richly textured . . . as our own life" (38). Since "[n]one of these strategies [for self-creation] is privileged over others" (38), "[t]he difference between genius and fantasy . . . is the difference between idiosyncrasies which just happen to catch on with other people" (37). "[P]olitical progress results from the accidental coincidence of a private obsession with a public need" (37).

22. Ibid.; 55.

23. Ibid.

struction."[24] As we have "de-theologized and de-philosophized" our vocabulary, "'human solidarity' has emerged as a powerful piece of rhetoric."[25] Upon this rhetoric, liberal egalitarians can build their vision of a just society.

Can liberalism maintain this "trick" in the long run, pretending that humanity is sacred in a de-divinized sense and that we ought to share a sense of solidarity in the face of avowed agnosticism and atheism? Rorty thinks so. Using his own version of liberal communitarianism, Rorty suggests that "[t]he social glue holding together the ideal liberal society . . . consists in little more than a consensus that the point of social organization is to let everybody have a chance at self-creation to the best of his or her abilities, and that the goal requires, besides peace and wealth, the standard 'bourgeois freedoms.'"[26]

Pope John Paul II echoes Rorty on the philosophical consequences of denying truth: "if there is no transcendent truth, in obedience to which man achieves his full identity, then there is no sure principle for guaranteeing just relations between people."[27] In contrast to Rorty, however, the Pope doubts that a de-divinized culture will promote respect for our fellow human beings: "self-interest as a class, group or nation would inevitably set them in opposition to one another. If one does not acknowledge transcendent truth, then the force of power takes over, and each person tends to make full use of the means at his disposal in order to impose his own interests or his own opinion with no regard for the rights of others."[28]

Ackerman foreshadows John Paul's ominous warning by suggesting that when "liberal institutions [are] in decay, it is only a matter of time before one or another zealot will seize the chance to impose his private nightmare on the rest of us."[29] In fact, Ackerman's own liberalism turns an ugly shade of illiberal as he would use all the power at his disposal to maintain his non-privileged

---

24. Ibid., 194.   25. Ibid., 192.

26. Ibid., 84. Of course, Rorty doesn't believe that everyone has an equal ability to self-create. In his ideal world, those who lack the ability to self-create will need to be anesthetized against the pain stemming from the lack of answers to life's ultimate questions. Ibid., 87: ("nonintellectuals would . . . be commonsensically nominalist and historicist. So they would see themselves as contingent through and through, without feeling any particular doubts about the contingencies they happened to be. . . . They would no more need to answer questions 'Why are you a liberal?' . . . than the average sixteenth-century Christian felt to answer the question 'Why are you a Christian?'").

27. John Paul II, "The Splendor of Truth" *(Veritatis splendor),* ¶ 99 (1993), in *The Encyclicals of John Paul II,* ed. J. Michael Miller (Huntington, IN: Our Sunday Visitor, 2001), 647.

28. Ibid.

29. Ackerman, *Social Justice in the Liberal State,* 313.

conception of the good life, which is living in a liberal state. In dire circumstances, he would even use force to ban non-liberals from the political offices to which they were elected.[30] And in his liberal society, the most unfortunate and innocent refugee fleeing a brutal regime could be cast from our shores to face almost certain death if her entry would threaten Ackerman's non-neutral conception of the good life.[31] In the absence of truth, power reigns supreme, and Ackerman would exercise it to exclude a number of human beings from citizenship in his liberal polity, denying them the rights of membership and, therefore, equal moral worth. In his liberal state, citizenship means everything: "the fate of noncitizens will be an appropriate subject for majoritarian politics."[32] For Ackerman, "[c]itizenship . . . is a concept in political—not biological—theory."[33] Any "individual who lacks dialogic competence fails to satisfy the necessary conditions for membership."[34] Persons who refuse to play his dialogic game excommunicate themselves from the community of citizens.[35] Persons whose language is unintelligible cannot be members of his club.[36] Those "unhappy creatures" who lack the mental capacity to engage in liberal dialogue live at the sufferance of the majority in this liberal state.[37] Fulfilling John Paul II's warning, Ackerman's non-neutral self-interest in maintaining a neutral dialogue allows the use of power to marginalize (a) those human beings who do not possess the capacity to engage in his dialogue and (b) those human beings who threaten the continuation of his dialogue.

Reconciling communitarian particularism with the universalist principles of liberal egalitarians is impossible on their own terms because each offers a different temporal conception of the good life with no external basis, no "grand sez who," objectively evaluating the competing claims for the moral ordering of society.[38] They stand side by side with their intellectual foundations built upon the sandy beachfront of political power. If the gale wind forces of totalitarianism buffet our shores with increasingly stronger waves of tyranny, communitarian justice and liberal egalitarian justice will be pulled from their sandy moorings to be ripped apart and carried out to sea in the undertow that follows the violent assault by those with less kind visions of justice.[39]

30. Ibid., 304.
31. Ibid., 95.
32. Ibid., 71.
33. Ibid., 74.
34. Ibid., 75.
35. Ibid., 78.
36. Ibid., 73.
37. Ibid., 79.
38. See Arthur Leff, "Unspeakable Ethics, Unnatural Law," *Duke Law Journal* 1979 (1979): 1229, 1230.
39. Heinrich Rommen's *Natural Law* is a practicing lawyer's attempt to make sense of law

What is the alternative? On what basis can we build a just society that includes a just immigration policy? By anchoring our vision of the good life and the common life in the transcendent nature of the human person, we can begin to escape our historical contingencies and lay a stronger foundation for a just immigration policy. In the next section, I view this foundation from the perspective of Roman Catholic teaching, and I address the objection that not everyone belongs to the Catholic Church or follows its teachings. Why, therefore, should its viewpoint be privileged above the rest in deriving a theory of justice? This objection is Ackerman's reason for advocating a neutral dialogue in which the Catholic would not be able to gain a privileged status in the argument by appeal to the divine. In response, I suggest that many of the ideas expressed in Catholic social doctrine are objectively available to all of us independent of our own faith (or non-faith) traditions.

SOCIAL JUSTICE, IMMIGRATION, AND THE NATURE OF HUMANITY

A Catholic Christian Perspective

Before developing and applying a theory of justice to immigration, we must begin to answer this central question: What is the source of human dignity? And what is required of individuals and institutions to guarantee that dignity? As Pope John Paul II said in his apostolic exhortation, *Ecclesia in America,*

[T]he foundation on which all human rights rest is the dignity of the person. God's masterpiece, man, is made in the divine image and likeness. Jesus took on our human nature, except for sin; he advanced and defended the dignity of every human person, without exception; he died that all might be free. The Gospel shows us how Christ insisted on the centrality of the human person in the natural order and in the social and religious orders

---

and legal systems in aftermath of the Nazi's rise to power. See Heinrich Rommen, *The Natural Law: A Study in Legal and Social History and Philosophy,* trans. Thomas R. Hanley and Russell Hittinger (Indianapolis: Liberty Fund, 1998), xi ("the reader will appreciate that the book was written by a lawyer in response to a political and legal crisis. As a practicing lawyer, Rommen watched with alarm as the Nazi party deftly used German legislative, administrative, and judicial institutions to impose totalitarian rule"). Some secular liberals, such as James Dwyer, tend toward totalitarianism in an effort to secure the liberal agenda. See note 14, supra. Jacques Maritain would not be surprised by Dwyer's type of liberalism; more than 50 years ago, he argued "that bourgeois liberalism with its ambition to ground everything in the unchecked initiative of the individual, conceived as a little God, . . . inevitably ends in statism." Jacques Maritain, *The Person and the Common Good* (Notre Dame, IN: Notre Dame Press, 1966), 91–92.

... defending men, women and even children who in his time and culture occupied an inferior place in society. The human being's dignity as a child of God is the source of human rights and of corresponding duties. . . . The dignity is common to all, without exception, since all have been created in the image of God. Jesus' answer to the question "Who is my neighbor?" demands of each individual an attitude of respect for the dignity of others and of real concern for them, even if they are strangers or enemies.[40]

From a Roman Catholic perspective, justice in immigration, like justice in other areas, requires a sense of solidarity built on our common status as "children of God." From this perspective, justice is *universal,* transcending national borders, but, unlike secular liberal theory, a Christian understanding of justice is based on the *reality* of the individual person, not mere *rhetoric* about an abstract theoretical human in the mythical state of nature or behind some "veil of ignorance." With liberal egalitarians, but for very different reasons, Catholic Christians conclude that all humans have equal moral worth.

The dignity, which each person possesses, takes form in community. The individual does not come into his or her full humanity in isolation. "Man's social nature makes it evident that the progress of the human person and the advance of society hinge on one another. . . . [T]he subject and goal of all social institutions is and must be the human person, which for its part and by its very nature stands completely in need of social life."[41] As Vatican II's "Pastoral Constitution on the Church in the Modern World" proclaims:

Man comes to a true and full humanity only through culture, that is through the cultivation of the goods and values of nature. . . . The word "culture" in its general sense indicates everything whereby a man develops and perfects his many bodily and spiritual qualities. . . . He renders social life more human both in the family and the civic community, through improvement of customs and institutions.[42]

Family life serves as the first school of community. "The first and fundamental structure for 'human ecology' is the family," where we receive our "first formative ideas about truth and goodness." Humans, however, "see the need for a wider community, within which each one makes his specific contribution every day towards . . . the common good. For this purpose they set

40. John Paul II, Post-Synodal Exhortation, Ecclesia in America, at ¶ 57 (22 January 1999), available at http://www.vatican.va/holy_father/john_paul_ii/apost_exhortations/documents/hf_jp-ii_exh_22011999_ecclesia-in-america_en.html.

41. Second Vatican Ecumenical Council, *Gaudium et spes,* ¶ 25 (1965) in *Vatican Council II: The Conciliar and Post Conciliar Documents,* ed. Austin Flannery (North Port, NY: Costello, 1975), 926.

42. Ibid., 958, ¶ 53.

up a political community which takes various forms. The political community exists, consequently, for the sake of the common good, in which it finds its full justification and significance, and the source of its inherent legitimacy."[43] Based in the reality of the human condition, "political community and the public authority are founded on human nature and hence belong to the order designed by God, even though the choice of a political regime and the appointment of rulers are left to the free will of citizens."[44] In this respect, the communitarians are correct: cultures flourish and "communities of character" are formed at a local level within the protective umbrella of the state.

There are "a plurality of cultures. Different styles of life and multiple scales of values arise from the diverse manner of using things, of labouring, or expressing oneself, of practicing religion, of forming customs, or establishing laws and juridical institutions, of cultivating sciences, the arts and beauty."[45] "*Peoples* or *nations* too have a right to their own full development, which while including . . . the economic and social aspects, should also include individual cultural identity and openness to the transcendent."[46] Therefore, each nation, each people, forms its own unique culture within which the individual members of the community can develop to their fullest potential.

Each citizen has the "right and the duty to contribute according to their ability to the genuine progress of their own community. Above all in areas of retarded economic progress, where all resources must be urgently exploited, the common good is seriously endangered by those who hoard their resources unproductively and by those who . . . deprive their community of much needed material and spiritual assistance."[47]

Because human development occurs within the family, the community, a culture's intermediary institutions, and the state, the emigration decision is fraught with consequences for the émigré and the community she leaves behind. As Pope John Paul II said:

43. Ibid., 980, 981, ¶ 74.

44. Ibid. See also John Paul II, Encyclical Letter, *Centesimus annus*, ¶ 39 (1991), in *The Encyclicals of John Paul II*, 544–45.

45. *Gaudium et spes*, ¶ 53, in *Vatican Council II: The Conciliar and Post Conciliar Documents*, 958.

46. John Paul II, Encyclical Letter, *Sollicitudo rei socialis*, ¶ 32.3 (1987), in *The Encyclicals of John Paul II*, 403.

47. *Gaudium et spes*, ¶ 65, in *Vatican Council II: The Conciliar and Post Conciliar Documents*, 971. A person has the right to emigrate even when such a departure endangers the public good by depriving the community of resources. See ibid.

Man has the right to leave his native land for various motives—and also to return—in order to seek better conditions of life in another country. This fact is certainly not without difficulties of various kinds. Above all it generally constitutes a loss for the country which is left behind. It is the departure of a person who is also a member of a great community united by history, tradition and culture; and that person must begin life in the midst of another society united by a different culture and very often by a different language. In this case, it is the loss of a subject of work, whose efforts of mind and body could contribute to the common good of his own country, but these efforts, this contribution, are instead offered to another society which in a sense has less right to them than the person's country of origin.[48]

To diminish the necessity of the laborer having to sever ties with his native schools of community, "[e]mployment opportunities . . . should be created in their own areas as far as possible."[49] Often, however, the local situation is so desperate that a person does not "become conscious of his dignity, and rise to his destiny by spending himself for God and for others. [H]uman freedom is often crippled when a man encounters extreme poverty."[50]

At a minimum, a Roman Catholic vision of justice requires that nation-states recognize and attempt to accommodate a person's decision to immigrate in those circumstances where economic, environmental, and political factors in the country of origin seriously undermine the full and authentic development of the individual as a human person.[51] The receiving community should make every effort "to ensure that [the migration] may bring benefit to the emigrants' personal, family, and social life."[52] Inequality between domestic and immigrant workers, for example, should be avoided.[53]

48. John Paul II, Encyclical Letter, *Laborem exercens,* ¶ 23.1 (1981), in *The Encyclicals of John Paul II,* 185.

49. *Gaudium et spes,* ¶ 66, in *Vatican Council II: The Conciliar and Post Conciliar Documents,* 972.

50. Ibid. ¶ 31, 931.

51. "[E]very human being has the right to freedom of movement and or residence within the confines of his own state. When there are just reasons in favour of it, he must be permitted to emigrate to other countries and take up residence there." Pope John XXIII, Encyclical Letter, *Pacem in terris,* ¶ 25 (1963).

52. John Paul II, Encyclical Letter, *Laborem exercens,* ¶ 23.1, in *The Encyclicals of John Paul II,* 185.

53. See Howard Chang, "The Immigration Paradox: Poverty, Distributive Justice, and Liberal Egalitarianism," *De Paul Law Review* 52 (2003): 759, 761 (article addresses the tension within liberal egalitarianism on this point).

Truth Accessible to All

Ackerman and Walzer, together with Rorty and Rawls, might be inclined to dismiss my Catholic-rooted understanding of human dignity as it relates to immigration because not everyone believes in Christ or even God. My response is threefold. First, their arguments are no more "neutral" than mine and rest on values and assumptions that many believing theists cannot accept because of the explicit denial or marginalization of God.[54] Liberal egalitarian and secular communitarian projects simply are not neutral.[55] Second, true pluralism allows a multiplicity of authentic voices to be heard in society. Requiring a large segment of the population (the religious segment) to mute the core of their being when they enter public dialogue renders pluralism hollow. Third, although the Catholic understanding of the person comes to fruition through revelation, this understanding is accessible and applicable, in some degree, to everyone whether or not they believe in God. In other words, the Catholic Christian approach to the nature of humanity and immigration justice is more inclusive than the approach of other political theorists.[56]

54. "Neutrality toward God ... implies ... a finite God: and a finite God is not really a God at all. Any such moment of simple neutrality ... implies the absence of God—implies, at least in that (logical—'onto-logical') moment, the death of God." David Schindler, "Modernity, Postmodernity, and the Problem of Atheism," *Communio* 24 (1997): 563, 567. In other words, neutrality toward God is impossible. "If God really does exist, then to lead a rational life a person has to take into account God and His purposes." Phillip Johnson, *Reason in the Balance* (Downers Grove, IL: InterVarsity Press, 1995), 7. See also Steven D. Smith, "The Restoration of Tolerance," *California Law Review* 78 (1990): 305, 317 ("privatization of religion ... is decidedly not neutral among competing religious beliefs; it flatly rejects the position of those who believe that religion serves an essential public role and therefore cannot be purely private in character").

55. See, e.g., Larry Alexander, "Good God, Garvey! The Inevitability and Impossibility of a Religious Justification of Free Exemptions," *Drake Law Review* 47 (1998): 35, 36 ("in the current philosophical literature on liberalism, there is a virtual cottage industry attempting to rebut the claims ... that liberalism can achieve neutrality among metaphysical views by rejecting a concern with Truth in favor of the 'political' notion of Reasonableness"); and Dwyer, *Religious Schools v. Children's Rights,* 82 (the "principle of state neutrality is not itself ideologically neutral [because] it reflects a partisan liberal position").

56. See Kevin Hasson, *God and Man at the Supreme Court: Rethinking Religion in Public Life* (1997), available at http://www.leaderu.com/socialsciences/hasson.html ("choosing the traditional anthropology allows the government to be genuinely neutral on cosmic questions. To say human beings thirst for the transcendent ... is merely to say something important about who human beings are. But that is not so for the existentialist position. ... It

This approach recognizes that humans through the centuries and across cultures have asked: "Does life have a meaning? Where is it going? . . . Each of us has both a desire and the duty to know the truth of our own destiny. . . . No one can avoid this questioning, neither the philosopher nor the ordinary person."[57] This thirst, which is common to all peoples and all cultures throughout history, must have an answer.

> It is unthinkable that a search so deeply rooted in human nature would be completely vain and useless. The capacity to search for truth and to pose questions itself implies the rudiments of a response. . . . Only a sense that they can arrive at an answer leads them to take the first step. This is what normally happens in scientific research. When scientists, following their intuition, set out in search of the logical and verifiable explanation of a phenomenon, they are confident from the first that they will find an answer, and they do not give up in the face of setbacks. . . . The same must be equally true of the search for truth when its comes to the ultimate questions. The thirst for truth is so rooted in the human heart that to be obliged to ignore it would cast our existence into jeopardy.[58]

When Pope John Paul II frames the question in this way, he is not speaking to and for only Roman Catholics. Indeed, he goes on to say: "These are the questions which we find in the sacred writings of Israel as also in the Veda and the Avesta; we find them in the writings of Confucius and Lao-Tze, and in the preaching of Tirthankara and Buddha; they appear in the poetry of Homer and in the tragedies of Euripides and Sophocles as they do in the philosophical writings of Plato and Aristotle."[59]

If we renew our sense of awe at the universe and recover a sense of play about ourselves and our surroundings, we may remember that all human beings share more in common than life, death, suffering, and the ability to communicate. In addition to the quest for meaning, human beings in all cultures across time have had some sense of right and wrong, good and evil. In application, we may disagree about what is good and what is evil, but we all have a sensor that tells us that there is right and wrong. "The source of our being places within us the vibration of good and the suggestion, the remorse of evil."[60] This universal and natural ability to decipher good from evil

---

necessarily assumes that there is no transcendent, but only alienated individuals who are anguished by false claims of one").

57. John Paul II, Encyclical Letter, *Fides et ratio,* ¶ 26–27.1 (1998), in *The Encyclicals of John Paul II,* 866.

58. Ibid., 867, ¶ 29.

59. Ibid., 850, ¶ 1.2.

60. Luigi Giussani, *The Religious Sense* (Montreal: McGill-Queens University, 1997), 107.

must lie at the heart of any authentic attempt to develop a theory of justice.

Humans possess in common an insatiable quest for meaning and a basic understanding of right and wrong. The written work of Rorty, Ackerman, Rawls, and Walzer each provide evidence that human beings have worth by the very nature of their being. These political philosophers might disagree with my Catholic Christian articulation of the sources of human dignity, but the fact that they go to such lengths to find commonality among human beings in what they see as only a contingent reality implies an insight into the human condition that they are not making explicit, perhaps even to themselves.

We also know that human beings require community for development. Although family and nationality are prior to the state, "[t]he social process of perfecting the idea of man reaches its fulfillment in the state, which since the time of Aristotle has been termed perfect society, i.e., a society which is genuinely self-sufficient, because in it the natural tendency to live in society finds its completion. The family . . . requires a higher social form for secure and permanent existence, for earthly happiness, for genuine self-sufficiency."[61] In short, the state is "a necessary society." Its essential function is "the establishment, maintenance, and promotion of the common good." It promotes, not creates.

Without benefit of divine revelation, we know by reason, observation, and collective experience that human beings have a commonality that transcends history and culture, binding us together as seekers of truth and of meaning. Our consciences, for instance, tell us that it is wrong to intentionally inflict unwarranted injury on another human being. We also know that humans require communities to fully develop. In the family—the first school of community—a young person learns the fundamentals of trust, mediation, property rights, negotiation, sharing, and much more. These skills are refined as the person applies them through interaction in broader social and political communities. We also know that consequences flow to the community from neglect of mentoring duties by parents and other leaders. From these observations of the reality of the human person, one can draw conclusions about the contours of a just immigration policy that parallel the conclusions drawn from within the Catholic faith tradition. Joseph Carens provides an excellent case study.

61. Rommen, *The Natural Law*, 211 (1998).

Earlier, I characterized Carens's statement that "[o]pen immigration . . . might destroy old ways of life, highly valued by some, but it would make possible new ways of life, highly valued by others" as "careless."[62] This "old ways, new ways, any way, its still immigration to me" attitude seems to have no regard for community, tradition, or the common good, or, indeed, any conception of public good.[63] Without completely abandoning liberalism's emphasis on individual autonomy, Carens has since developed a more nuanced approach, which acknowledges at some level the importance of community in human flourishing. "The central theme" of his book *Culture, Citizenship, and Community: A Contextual Exploration of Justice as Evenhandedness*, which was published in 2000, "is that a commitment to liberal democratic principles is often compatible with and may even require public recognition and support of different cultures and identities."[64]

In this project, Carens takes liberal theory out of the abstract and examines it at play in concrete situations to see "whether existing institutions and practices . . . embody forms of wisdom that are missed by . . . prevailing theories."[65] In contextualizing his theory, he makes some interesting observations.

First, Carens notes that it is impossible for the state to be completely neutral among competing conceptions of the good as expressed in different cultures. A nation's decisions as to language or internal political divisions, for example, are often culturally freighted.[66] In short, he says, the "ideal of cultural neutrality is an illusion."[67]

Second, and more importantly for our purposes, Carens appears to see that "the liberal freedom to choose one's own path in life, depends, in significant ways, upon" being within a particular culture "because it is only in the context of a [particular] culture that we can understand the options available to us and make intelligent judgments about which ones to pursue."[68] "A

---

62. See supra text at note 12.

63. See John Coughlin, "Law and Theology: Reflections on What It Means to be Human from a Franciscan Perspective," *St. John's Law Review* 74 (2000): 609, 613–615 ("the anthropological assumption of a radically autonomous individual may enshrine certain values as foundational to the law at the cost of excluding other significant values").

64. Joseph Carens, *Culture, Citizenship, and Community: A Contextual Exploration of Justice as Evenhandedness* (Oxford: Oxford University Press, 2000), 1.

65. Ibid., 3.   66. Ibid., 11.

67. Ibid., 53.

68. Ibid., 54–55. In contrasting liberal culture with Amish culture, Carens says that "one

sense of identity and of a shared history connected to their society of origin often constitutes a very important dimension of life for many immigrants and their descendants. Immigrants bring with them from their cultures of origin various values, conceptions, and commitments that shape the meaningfulness of the options open to them, sometimes in ways quite different from those of other members of society."[69] And, because "the transformation required to adapt to a new societal culture is normally very difficult and demanding, . . . it is reasonable for people to regard access to their native culture as a fundamental interest."[70]

These concrete observations cause Carens to modify his theory of the liberal state and its relationship with its inhabitants—both citizen and alien. Like other liberal theorists, he postulates certain universal requirements for a just state—at least a liberal democratic one. "Every liberal democratic political community must recognize certain principles such as freedom of speech, freedom of religion, majority rule, and so on."[71] But his contextual approach leads him to conclude that "there are many different ways of interpreting these principles and many different forms of practice among liberal democratic states. It seems plausible," he supposes, "that there is a range of disagreement about what the principles of democratic justice require, and that within that range different political communities are morally free to adopt different institutional arrangements and policies."[72]

This refined understanding leads Carens to two conclusions about justice in immigration policy. First, within undefined parameters it is morally legitimate for the members of the receiving country to form society in a non-neutral way that reflects the dominant culture. And, second, justice requires the state to be as evenhanded as possible in dealing with minority, including immigrant, cultures. For Carens justice and evenhandedness do "not mean that every cultural claim and identity will be given equal weight but rather that each will be given appropriate weight under the circumstances. . . . History [including religious history] matters, numbers matter, the relative im-

---

could . . . argue that the Amish way of life comes closer to realizing worthy human purposes in terms of a broad understanding of the human good and perhaps even in terms of fundamental liberal ideas itself than the conventional way of life in contemporary liberal societies. One might say, for example, that the Amish way of life has a purposiveness and rationality to it while liberal societies inculcate a blind dedication to acquisition and consumption, to meaningless and frivolous choice." Ibid., 96.

69. Ibid., 71.   70. Ibid., 55.
71. Ibid., 7.   72. Ibid.

portance of the claims to the claimants matters, and so do many other considerations."[73]

It is important to see how Carens has deviated from the liberal theorist's traditional dogma. Radical autonomy is softened by recognizing the importance of community to human flourishing. The individual's identity is relocated within the context of a particular community's culture, history, and tradition. And the liberal state can reflect the non-neutral values of the dominant culture, including, I assume, its religious heritage.

JUSTNESS IN AMERICAN IMMIGRATION POLICY

Individuals have inherent worth, which must be recognized by all. Because of the dignity inherent in every human person, there is a duty of solidarity with all peoples everywhere, and each person may be called upon to adjust his or her lifestyle in order to allow persons in another culture to have the basic tools necessary to develop more fully in their humanity. This sense of universal solidarity reinforces the reality that the human person develops fully only within a community—family, intermediate institutions, and the state. The state, like the family, is necessary for human development. Cultures flourish within but independent from the state.

General Observations

Emigration, because it entails an uprooting from one's community of origin, has serious consequences for the émigré and the community she leaves. Often a refugee experiences her new life as a spiritual, cultural, and economic amputee, cut off from that which shaped and nurtured her humanity. Therefore, a just immigration policy must begin by exploring and attempting to minimize the push factors, which cause people to leave their communities instead of staying to help form them more completely.

Peace, political stability, and economic development diminish the need to emigrate, and a just immigration policy should promote these goals. We should advocate "the policy of bringing the work to the workers, wherever possible, rather than bringing workers to the scene of the work. In this way many people will be afforded an opportunity of increasing their resources without being exposed to the painful necessity of uprooting themselves from

73. Ibid., 12.

their own homes, settling in a strange environment, and forming new social contacts."[74] Anthony Scaperlanda has written on the challenges and potential benefits of a properly ordered multinational enterprise expansion, which would raise the standard of living in the host country, encouraging workers to stay rather than emigrate in search of work, and promote solidarity across national borders through the development of reciprocal working relationships.[75] On a similar front, Pope John Paul II has expressed concern that foreign debt "is suffocating quite a few countries."[76] Under the weight of such debt, the cultures within those communities cannot thrive, forcing many people to live in desperate poverty while causing the strong and the adventurous to leave. Pope John Paul II has said:

Love for others, and in the first place love for the poor, in whom the church sees Christ himself, is made concrete in the *promotion of justice.* Justice will never be fully attained unless people see in the poor person, who is asking for help in order to survive, not an annoyance or a burden, but an opportunity for showing kindness. . . . It is not merely a matter of "giving from one's surplus," but of helping entire peoples which are presently excluded or marginalized to enter into the sphere of economic and human development.[77]

Our human ability can diminish but will never eliminate the push factors contributing to emigration. Transnational migration will occur, and a just immigration policy must concern itself with three issues: (1) who can enter, in what numbers, and on what conditions; (2) how to welcome and integrate these new members of the community into our society; and (3) what impact immigration will have on marginalized segments of the domestic population. Since a comprehensive study of the justness of United States immigration policy is beyond the scope of this chapter, what follows is one concrete instance of injustice in American immigration law and policy.

74. John XXIII, "Pacem in terris," ¶ 103 (1963).

75. Anthony E. Scaperlanda, "John Paul II's Vision of the Role of Multinational Enterprise Expansion in Building the Social Economy," *International Journal of Social Economics* (1998): 1764.

76. John Paul II, Post-Synodal Exhortation, Ecclesia in America at ¶ 59 (22 January 1999), available at http://www.vatican.va/holy_father/john_xxiii/encyclicals/documents/hf_ j-xxxiii_enc_11041963_pacem_en.html.

77. John Paul II, *Centesimus annus,* ¶ 58, in *The Encyclicals of John Paul II,* 558.

Injustice and the Criminal Alien

I'll end by taking the conversation from the general to the concrete, using Catholic Social Teaching to criticize one aspect of United States immigration law and policy.[78] Since 1988, Congress has pursued a course of action to rid the United States of its "criminal alien" population in an expedient manner. In the abstract this might seem like a worthy goal, especially if the noncitizen brought his criminal tendencies or habits with him from his country of origin. We might legitimately ask why we should put our society at risk by allowing an immigrant to abuse our freedoms when his criminal actions will likely hinder the flourishing and full human development of those who will be affected adversely (victimized directly or indirectly) by the criminal activity. On the other hand, if his criminal tendencies or habits developed in the United States or manifested themselves long after his taking up residence in the United States, is it moral to toss him into another society, even one where he holds formal citizenship? And if his crime is relatively minor, he has strong ties to the United States, and great hardship will be visited upon him or his family if he is removed, is it just to deport him?

For much of the twentieth century, our immigration law and policy attempted, albeit imperfectly, to balance these competing concerns. During this period, "the chief criminal deportation ground" required that the alien be: (a) convicted (b) of a crime involving moral turpitude; (c) within five years after the date of admission into the United States; and (d) be sentenced to confinement of one year or more.[79] Even if the criminal conviction made the alien deportable, he could seek multiple forms of relief from deportation, including INA § 212(c) relief, which allowed a deportable alien to remain in the United States if the alien merited a favorable exercise of discretion and had maintained a lawful unrelinquished domicile in the United States for seven consecutive years.[80] And an adverse decision by the

---

78. It should be kept in mind that some Catholic Christians will reject my particular observations and conclusions on prudential grounds. We may agree on the foundation for a just immigration policy but disagree in the way that it plays out in the practical life of the nation. I also suspect that many liberal egalitarians and secular communitarians will agree with my critique of our current immigration regime without any explicit agreement on the foundations.

79. See Thomas Alexander Aleinikoff et al., *Immigration and Citizenship: Process and Policy*, 4th ed. (Eagan, MN: Thompson West, 1998), 725.

80. See Elwin Griffith, "The Road between the Section 212(c) Waiver and Cancellation of

Board of Immigration Appeals was reviewable by the Court of Appeals.[81]

Beginning in 1988, Congress greatly expanded the list of removable offenses, made detention of many noncitizens mandatory after entry of removal orders, eliminated discretionary relief in many cases, and restricted judicial review.[82] The numbers alone demonstrate the increased significance of the immigration consequences of a criminal conviction. While "the INS removed 1,978 aliens for criminal violations" in 1986, that number had increased more than 36-fold to 71,597 by 2001.[83] Although the number of noncitizens removed from the United States in a given year, by itself, tells us little or nothing about the justness of our removal policy, it does provide an interesting backdrop upon which to view the substantive changes in the law. The Anti-Drug Abuse Act of 1988 added "aggravated felony" as a new but very limited ground for deportation, reserved for serious crimes, that is, murder and drug and weapons trafficking, regardless of the sentence imposed and the longevity of the alien's residence in the United States.[84] The Immigration Act of 1990 expanded the scope of crimes included within the definition of aggravated felony to include nonpolitical crimes of violence for which a prison sentence of at least five years was imposed and eliminated § 212(c) relief for certain aggravated felons.[85] In 1991, Congress further reduced the availability of § 212(c) relief.[86] And, in 1994, the definition of "aggravated felony" was further broadened to include such things as theft and burglary where a five-year sentence was imposed.[87] Finally, in 1996, Congress enacted the

---

Removal under 240A of the Immigration and Nationality Act—The Impact of the 1996 Reform Legislation," *Georgetown Immigration Law Journal* 12 (1997): 65.

81. See Michael Patrick, "Tell It to the Judge—Judicial Review of Immigration Decisions," *Immigration Briefings* 88-10 (1988): 1.

82. See generally Brent Newcombe, Comment, "Immigration Law and the Criminal Alien: A Comparison of Policies for Arbitrary Deportations of Legal Permanent Residents Convicted of Aggravated Felonies," *Oklahoma Law Review* 51 (1998): 697, 698–701 (brief history of congressional action since 1988). A full analysis of all the changes in criminal grounds for removal since 1988 is beyond the scope of this chapter. I will mention a few of the provisions to suggest that Congress's "throw 'em all out" mentality is unjust.

83. *Statistical Yearbook of the Immigration and Naturalization Service*, 236.

84. Pub. L. No. 100-690, 102 Stat. 4181 (1988).

85. Pub. L. No. 101-649, 104 Stat. 4978 (1990).

86. *The Miscellaneous and Technical Immigration and Naturalization Amendments of 1991*, Pub. L. No. 102-232, 105 Stat. 1733 (1991).

87. *The Immigration and Nationality Technical Corrections Act of 1994*, Pub. L. No. 103-416, 108 Stat. 4305 (1994).

Anti-Terrorism and Effective Death Penalty Act (AEDPA)[88] and the Illegal Immigration Reform and Immigrant Responsibility Act (IIRIRA),[89] which, among other things, eliminated § 212(c) relief altogether, greatly expanded the list of "aggravated felonies," and eliminated the possibility of discretionary relief from removal and deportation for aggravated felons.

Today, "[a]ny alien who is convicted of an aggravated felony at any time after admission is deportable."[90] The "aggravated felony" definition is so broad now that it includes "theft offense . . . for which the term of imprisonment is at least one year"[91] and "an offense that involves fraud or deceit in which the loss to the victim . . . exceeds $10,000."[92] Aggravated felons are ineligible for discretionary relief such as Cancellation of Removal.[93] They are also ineligible for asylum.[94] The term "aggravated felony" has been applied to a broad array of criminal convictions, including check kiting involving less than $25,000,[95] driving under the influence,[96] statutory rape,[97] and possession of a stolen vehicle.[98] Pursuant to our immigration laws, someone who came to the United States from Germany as a young child of say three or four, who does not speak German and has no ties to Germany, who has a citizen wife and three citizen children, one of whom has a serious medical condition, could be permanently banished from the United States upon conviction of any of the above crimes and a broad array of other crimes. The law provides no opportunity for discretionary relief even in those cases where (a) the immigration consequences of a conviction—permanent banishment from the United States—are clearly disproportionate to the crime and/or (b) there are serious equities weighing in favor of granting discretionary relief, such as strong community ties in the United States or extreme hardship to the noncitizen or his family if he is deported.[99]

88. Pub. L. No. 104-132, 110 Stat. 1214 (1996).

89. Pub. L. No. 104-208, Div. C., tit. III, 110 Stat. 3009 (1996).

90. U.S.C. § 1227(a)(2)(A)(iii).   91. Ibid. at § 1101(a)(43)(G).

92. Ibid. at (M)(i).   93. Ibid. at § 1229b.

94. Ibid. at § 1158(b)(2)(A)(ii).

95. *Khalayleh v. INS*, 287 F3d 978 (10th Cir 2002).

96. *Tapia Garcia v. INS*, 237 F3d 1216 (10th Cir 2001); and *In re Luis Manuel Ramos, I and N* 23 (Dec. 2002): 336 (where the offense was committed recklessly).

97. *Mugalli v. Ashcroft*, 258 F3d 52 (2d Cir 2001).

98. *Hernandez-Mancilla v. INS*, 246 F3d 1002 (7th Cir 2001).

99. The courts have exacerbated the problem in at least two ways. First, the majority of courts to address the issue have held that the Sixth Amendment's right to effective assistance of counsel is not violated when a criminal defense attorney fails to advise her client of the

It may be that the common good for the United States requires the permanent banishment of some criminal aliens. Justice, however, requires consideration of the well-being of the receiving community. And, it seems to me that the longer a noncitizen has lived in the United States (and especially if he was raised in the United States), the harder it is to justify dumping what are essentially our problems on another country merely because the noncitizen happens to carry that nation's passport. A system, such as our current system, which requires the deportation of even long-term permanent resident aliens, is unjust toward other countries when we exercise our legal right to remove without consideration of whether we *ought* to exercise that right at the expense of our neighbors. Justice also requires that the punishment be proportionate to the crime. Given the expansive definition of "aggravated felony," the punishment—permanent exile—is often grossly disproportionate to the crime. Finally, justice requires us to examine the effects of deportation on the noncitizen and the noncitizen's family and community. Often, as in the case of refugees, there are compelling reasons why a person should not be sent back to his country of origin. And often there are powerful circumstances that counsel in favor of allowing the person to stay in the United States. Family and other ties might counsel equitable relief from removal, allowing the alien to remain within his community. The post-1996 immigration regime unjustly makes no provision for discretionary relief even for a

---

immigration consequences of a guilty plea. See, e.g., *United States v. Fry*, 322 F3d 1198, 1200 (9th Cir 2003) (citing the cases from other circuits). Some of these courts reached their erroneous decisions by confusing the roles of the trial court and the defense counsel in informing the defendant of the consequences of his plea, and/or suggest that defense counsel owes a lesser duty to a client in the plea situation. See Gabriel Chin and Richard Holmes, "Effective Assistance of Counsel and the Consequences of Guilty Pleas," *Cornell Law Review* 87 (2002): 697, 724–35. A number of courts have held that although defense counsel may have no affirmative duty to advise a client of the collateral consequences of a guilty plea, affirmative misrepresentation does provide a basis for a claim of ineffective assistance. See, e.g., *U.S. v. Couto*, 311 F3d 179, 188 (2d Cir 2002). And a few courts have held that failure to advise constitutes ineffective assistance. See, e.g., *People v. Pozo*, 746 P2d 523 (Col 1987). Second, federal courts have consistently denied noncitizens the right to pursue a petition for habeas corpus to review an expired state conviction that serves as the predicate for deportation on the grounds that the person is no longer in state custody and that federal custody (Immigration Control and Enforcement) does not give courts the authority to review state convictions. See, e.g., *Drakes v. INS*, 330 F3d 600 (3d Cir 2003). See generally Gerald Neuman, "Habeas Corpus, Executive Detention, and the Removal of Aliens," *Columbia Law Review* 98 (1998): 961; and Lenni Benson, "Back to the Future: Congress Attacks the Right to Judicial Review of Immigration Proceedings, *Connecticut Law Review* 29 (1997): 1411.

long-time permanent resident who has strong ties to the United States and who was convicted of a relatively minor "aggravated felony."

CONCLUSION

Without denigrating United States immigration law, which, relatively speaking, serves internationally as a positive example of justice in immigration, we should consider whether we are doing all that we can, here and beyond, to foster the development of individuals and peoples who lack our material wealth. By reconnecting the quest for freedom to its only sure foundation, objective truth, we can continue constructing an immigration policy that is just and that can endure the shifting and often furious tides of domestic and international events. If pursued in this manner, our immigration policy can support a quest to guarantee every human being a chance to lead a dignified life.

[16]

INTERNATIONAL LAW:
FOUNDATIONS OF HUMAN RIGHTS

The Unfinished Business

𝇈

MARY ANN GLENDON

Over the two years it took them to draft the 1948 Universal Declaration of Human Rights, the eighteen members of the United Nations' first Human Rights Commission had surprisingly few discussions of why human beings have rights or why some rights are universal.[1] After the horrors of two world wars, the need for a minimal common standard of decency seemed evident. One of the first tasks assigned to the new commission chaired by Eleanor Roosevelt was the preparation of an "international bill of rights." The commissioners, in haste to complete their work before the deepening Cold War made its acceptance by the General Assembly impossible, left the problem of foundations for another day.

At the commission's first session in January 1947, China's Peng-chun Chang and Lebanon's Charles Malik did try to initiate a discussion of the premises on which such a document might be based.[2] Chang was a Confucian philosopher and educator who had done postgraduate work with John

1. For details of the framing of the Universal Declaration, see Mary Ann Glendon, *A World Made New: Eleanor Roosevelt and the Universal Declaration of Human Rights* (New York: Random House, 2001).
2. Human Rights Commission, First Session, Summary Records (E/CN.4/SR.7 p. 4).

Dewey, and Malik was a philosopher of science who had studied with Alfred North Whitehead and Martin Heidegger. Their suggestions precipitated the commission's first argument. The Yugoslav, French, and English delegates began to wrangle over the relation between man and society.

Several other commissioners became impatient with that sort of discussion. They just wanted to get on with the business at hand. After a time, India's Hansa Mehta broke in. She was one of two women on the commission, a pioneering human rights activist, a crusader against British colonialism, and an advocate for women's equality. She said, "We are here to affirm faith in fundamental human rights. Whether the human person comes first or the society, I do not think we should discuss that problem now. We do not need to enter into this maze of ideology."[3]

Charles Malik, who had been literally called out of his Beirut classroom and pressed into public service by the government of newly independent Lebanon, had not yet perfected the suave diplomatic style for which he would later become famous. He rebuked Mrs. Mehta as a professor of the old school would chide a student, saying: "Whatever you may say, Madam, must have ideological presuppositions, and no matter how much you may fight shy of them, they are there, and you either hide them or you are brave enough to bring them out in the open and see them and criticize them."[4]

The commission's chair, Eleanor Roosevelt, quickly realized that the group would have to concentrate on specifics if the project was to stay on course. She steered the discussion back to the problem of organizing the group's work schedule. Thereafter, the question of foundations surfaced only sporadically. One such occasion was the presentation of a discussion draft by the Secretariat of the U.N. Human Rights Division. Australia's Colonel Roy Hodgson demanded to know what was the philosophy behind the paper: "What principles did they adopt; what method did they follow?"[5] John Humphrey, the Canadian head of the Human Rights Division, replied that the draft "was based on no philosophy whatsoever." It was, he said, merely a collection from existing constitutions of "every conceivable right which the Drafting Committee might want to discuss."[6]

---

3. From "The More Important Speeches and Interventions of Charles Malik" (Papers of Charles Malik, Library of Congress, Manuscript Division), 38 (verbatim record).

4. Ibid., 44.

5. Human Rights Commission, Drafting Committee, First Session (E/CN.4/AC.1/SR.1 p. 5).

6. Ibid.

At the very end of the drafting process, and without much discussion, the commissioners did make a statement about the basis of human rights in the preamble to the 1948 Declaration. The preamble's opening line recites that "recognition of the inherent dignity and of the equal and inalienable rights of all members of the human family is the foundation of freedom, justice and peace in the world." The word "dignity" appears at so many key points in the Declaration that many scholars believe it represents the Declaration's ultimate value. Louis Henkin puts it this way: "Eschewing—in its quest for universality—explicit reliance on Divine inspiration or on Natural Rights, the Declaration provided the idea of human rights with a universally acceptable foundation, an *ur* principle, human dignity."[7]

But inquiring minds must ask what is this "dignity," and what is its basis? Its proximate source is easy to locate. The U.N. Charter professes "faith in freedom and democracy," which, according to the Charter, is grounded in another "faith"—"in the inherent dignity of men and women." That is a good deal of faith for a document that eschews divine inspiration. No wonder we find Nobel laureate Czeslaw Milosz musing ruefully about "those beautiful and deeply moving words which pertain to the old repertory of the rights of man and the dignity of the person."[8] Milosz continues, "I wonder at this phenomenon because maybe underneath there is an abyss. After all, these ideas had their foundation in religion, and I am not over-optimistic as to the survival of religion in a scientific-technological civilization. Notions that seemed buried forever have suddenly been resurrected. But how long will they stay afloat if the bottom is taken out?"

Milosz puts the question neatly as only a poet can. Is the universal-rights idea merely based on a kind of existential leap of faith? Or does it have some sturdier basis?

Such questions came to the surface when the Universal Declaration celebrated its fiftieth anniversary in 1998 amidst a barrage of attacks upon its aspiration to universality—mainly in the name of cultural relativism. Typically these assaults describe the Declaration as an attempt to universalize a particular "Western" set of ideas and to impose them upon people who were under colonial rule and thus not represented in its creation. The human rights

7. Louis Henkin, "Human Rights: Ideology and Aspiration, Reality and Prospect," in *Realizing Human Rights,* ed. S. Power and G. Allison (New York: St. Martin's Press, 2000).

8. Czeslaw Milosz, "The Religious Imagination at 2000," *New Perspectives Quarterly* (Fall 1997): 32.

project is dismissed as an instrument of "cultural imperialism" or "neo-colonialism."

An equally common retort is that cultural imperialism is the cry of the world's worst rights violators. That sort of response, however, is obviously inadequate: the allegations of cultural relativism and imperialism could be hypocritical or ideologically motivated, but nevertheless true. I propose therefore to take the accusations seriously.

My conclusions are as follows: (1) The Universal Declaration was an impressively, though imperfectly, multicultural document when it was adopted in 1948. It cannot be dismissed as "Western." (2) The framers of the Declaration did take account of the diversity of cultures by leaving room for a legitimate pluralism in interpreting and implementing its open-ended principles. (3) The danger of human rights imperialism is real, but its source is in the efforts of special interest groups to commandeer human rights for their own purposes, rather than in the Declaration itself. (4) The human rights project will rest on shaky foundations unless and until philosophers and statespersons collaborate on the business that the framers left unfinished.

IS THE UNIVERSAL DECLARATION "WESTERN"?

Those who label the Universal Declaration "Western" base the claim mainly on two facts: (1) many of the world's peoples, especially those still living under colonial rule, were not represented in the United Nations in 1948, and (2) most of the Declaration's rights first appeared in European and North and South American documents. Those statements are correct, but do they destroy the universality of the Declaration?

Contrary to what is often suggested, the participation by developing countries in the framing of the Declaration was by no means negligible.[9] At the United Nations' founding conference in San Francisco in 1945, it was chiefly the smaller or less-developed nations who were responsible for the prominent position of human rights in the U.N. Charter. Within the eighteen-member Human Rights Commission, China's Peng-chun Chang, Lebanon's Charles Malik, the Philippines' Carlos Romulo, and Chile's Hernan Santa Cruz were

9. See also Philip Alston, "The Universal Declaration at 35: Western and Passe or Alive and Universal?," *International Commission of Jurists Review* 30 (1983): 60, 61; and Johannes Morsink, *The Universal Declaration of Human Rights: Origins, Drafting, and Intent* (Philadelphia: University of Pennsylvania Press, 1999), especially the concise summary of the drafting process in pp. 1–12.

among the most influential and active members. It is sometimes said that the educational backgrounds or professional experiences of widely traveled men such as Chang and Malik "westernized" them, but their performance in the Human Rights Commission suggests something rather different. Not only did each contribute significant insights from his own culture, but each possessed an exceptional ability to understand other cultures and to "translate" concepts from one frame of reference to another. Those skills, which can hardly be acquired without substantial exposure to traditions other than one's own, are indispensable for effective cross-cultural collaboration and were key to the adoption of the Declaration without a single dissenting vote in 1948.

The Declaration itself was based on extensive comparative study. The first draft, prepared by the U.N. Secretariat, was accompanied by a 408-page document showing the relationship of each article to provisions of the world's existing and proposed constitutions and declarations. When the Human Rights Commission's second draft was submitted to U.N. members for comment, responses were received from a group of nations that included Brazil, Egypt, India, Mexico, Pakistan, South Africa, Sweden, and the United States.

Among the fifty-eight member states represented on the U.N. General Assembly's committee that reviewed the near-final draft in the fall of 1948, there was even greater cultural and ideological diversity. This Committee on Social, Cultural and Humanitarian Affairs (known as the Third Committee) was chaired by Charles Malik. It included six members from Asia, four from the African continent (Egypt, Ethiopia, Liberia, and South Africa), plus the large Latin American contingent. Six of the "European" members belonged to the communist bloc; Islamic culture was strong in eleven; and four had large Buddhist populations. Over the course of more than a hundred meetings, the members of this large committee went over every word of the draft. Each country's representatives were given, and most of them enthusiastically seized, the opportunity to participate.

At the end of this process, Charles Malik could justly say of the Universal Declaration that "[a]ll effective cultures in the world had a creative hand in the shaping of the document." As Malik put it, "The genesis of each article, and each part of each article, was a dynamic process in which many minds, interests, backgrounds, legal systems and ideological persuasions played their respective determining roles."[10]

10. Charles Malik, introduction to O. Frederick Nolde, *Free and Equal: Human Rights in Ecumenical Perspective* (Geneva: World Council of Churches, 1968), 12.

It was, of course, true that much of the world's population was not represented in the United Nations in 1948. Large parts of Africa and Asia in particular remained under colonial rule. The defeated Axis powers, Japan, Germany, and their allies, were excluded. On the other hand, subsequent actions by the nonrepresented countries suggest that cultural "diversity" has been greatly exaggerated where basic human goods are concerned. Most new nations adopted constitutions resembling the Universal Declaration as soon as they gained independence. Later, nearly all of these countries ratified the two 1966 covenants based on the Declaration. In 1993, virtually all countries in the world participated in the adoption of the Vienna Human Rights Declaration, which reaffirms the Universal Declaration. It is hard to dismiss this overwhelming endorsement of the principles of the Declaration as a mere vestige of the colonial mentality.

It is unlikely that any other political document in history has ever drawn from such diverse sources or received as much worldwide, sustained consideration and scrutiny as the Declaration underwent over its two years of preparation. Despite all the wrangling that occurred over specifics, moreover, there was remarkably little disagreement regarding its basic substance. At every stage, even the communist bloc, South Africa, and Saudi Arabia voted in favor of most of the articles when they were taken up one by one. The biggest battles were political, occasioned by Soviet concerns to protect their national sovereignty.

But what of the second objection mentioned above—the fact that several key ideas in the Declaration were initially described as rights in early modern Europe? On this point, the findings of a UNESCO philosophers' committee that included Jacques Maritain and University of Chicago philosopher Richard McKeon are instructive. After surveying leading philosophers and religious thinkers the world over, the UNESCO group discovered to its surprise that a few basic practical concepts of humane conduct were so widely shared that they "may be viewed as implicit in man's nature as a member of society."[11] Freedom, dignity, tolerance, and neighborliness, they found, were highly prized in many cultural and religious traditions.

Nevertheless, the elaboration of these concepts as "rights" was a relatively modern, and European, phenomenon. So, does that give human rights a

---

11. Richard P. McKeon, "The Philosophic Bases and Material Circumstances of the Rights of Man," in *Human Rights: Comments and Interpretations* (New York: Columbia University Press, 1949), 45.

genetic taint that prevents them from being "universal"? Surely, their origin ought not to be decisive. The question should be not who had the idea first, but whether the idea is a good one; not where the idea was born, but whether it is conducive to human flourishing. Moreover, if a legal-political idea originated in one country but was widely adopted and internalized elsewhere, for how long and in what sense does it still "belong" to its country of origin? Do not all vibrant, living cultures constantly borrow from one another?

Consider the civil-law tradition, which originated in ancient Rome. That tradition was in 1948, and remains, the most widely distributed legal tradition in the world.[12] The form and style of the Declaration gives it a familial resemblance not only to rights declarations in many continental European constitutions, but to the constitutions and charters that had appeared or were soon to appear in many Latin American, African, and Asian countries. Does that make all these instruments Roman? The French Civil Code of 1804 was widely copied by newly independent peoples in Latin America, who admired its clarity and were inspired by its consolidation of a Revolution that had abolished the old unequal statuses of feudalism. Does that make the law of all those countries French?

And what does the term "Western" mean anyway, if it is more than an epithet? The majority of the United Nations' membership in 1948, perhaps as many as thirty-seven countries, might have been described as "Western" in the sense of being influenced by Judeo-Christian traditions and Enlightenment thought. But how much sense does it make to lump together under a single label a group that comprises Latin Americans, North Americans, East and West Europeans, Australians, and New Zealanders? By the same token, such broad concepts as "Asian" or "Islamic" values are not very informative, given the great variety within traditions.[13] As the Chinese member of the first Human Rights Commission, P. C. Chang, observed long ago, "Culturally, there are many 'Easts' and many 'Wests'; and they are by no means all necessarily irreconcilable."[14]

12. See Mary Ann Glendon, Michael Gordon, and Christopher Osakwe, *Comparative Legal Traditions*, 2d ed. (St. Paul, MN: West, 1994), 58–62.

13. See Amartya Sen's illuminating reflections on universality and pluralism in "Our Culture, Their Culture," *New Republic* (1 April 1996), 27.

14. P. C. Chang, *China at the Crossroads: The Chinese Situation in Perspective* (London: Evans, 1936), 124–25.

HOW CAN THERE BE UNIVERSAL RIGHTS
IN DIVERSE CULTURES?

Let us now turn to a more sophisticated version of the cultural-relativism critique. Assume that the UNESCO philosophers were right that a few basic norms of decent human behavior are very widely shared. Even if that is so at a general level, different nations and cultures attach quite different weights to these norms. Moreover, different political and economic conditions affect each nation's ability to bring human rights principles to life. That being so, what sense does it make to speak of universality?

That version of the cultural-relativism critique rests on a false premise shared by many rights activists and rights skeptics alike. It is the assumption that universal principles must be implemented in the same way everywhere. The Declaration's framers, however, never envisioned that its "common standard of achievement" would or should produce completely uniform practices.[15] P. C. Chang stressed that point in his 9 December 1948 speech to the General Assembly urging adoption of the Declaration. He deplored the fact that colonial powers had tried to impose on other peoples a standardized way of thinking and a single way of life. That sort of uniformity could be achieved, he said, only by force or at the expense of truth. It could never last.[16] Chang and his colleagues on the Drafting Committee expected the Declaration's rights would be inculturated in various ways, and that over time the corpus of human rights would be enriched by these varied experiences.

The framers of the Universal Declaration also knew it was neither possible nor desirable for the Declaration to be frozen in time. They never claimed to have produced the last word on human rights. They expected that new rights would emerge in the future as they had in the past and that old rights might be reformulated. That did not mean, however, that interpretation was up for grabs. They tried to provide the Declaration with safe passage through such transitions by giving it an interpretive matrix: freedom and solidarity, linked to a thick concept of personhood, and grounded in dignity.

The framers' approach was remembered by at least one distinguished in-

---

15. Jacques Maritain, introduction to *Human Rights: Comments and Interpretations,* ed. UNESCO (New York: Wingate, 1949), 16.

16. P. C. Chang's speech may be found in U.N. General Assembly, 182d Plenary Session, December 10, 1948, Summary Records, p. 895.

ternational lawyer on the document's thirty-fifth anniversary in 1983. Philip Alston wrote on that occasion, "The Declaration does not purport to offer a single unified conception of the world as it should be nor does it purport to offer some sort of comprehensive recipe for the attainment of an ideal world. Its purpose is rather the more modest one of proclaiming a set of values which are capable of giving some guidance to modern society in choosing among a wide range of alternative policy options."[17] By the 1970s, however, the original understanding of the Declaration was largely forgotten. And what oblivion had not erased, opportunism was eroding. The abstentions by South Africa and Saudi Arabia from the final vote approving the Declaration had been early warnings of more trouble ahead. South Africa had objected, among other things, to the word "dignity," apparently fearing its implications for the apartheid system it was then constructing. And Saudi Arabia had claimed that some of the so-called universal rights, particularly the right to change one's religion, were really just "Western" ideas. In 1948, those were isolated claims. But no sooner was the Declaration adopted than the Cold War antagonists pulled apart and politicized its provisions. That set the stage for further mischief. In 1955, the charge that some rights represented "Western" neocolonialism resurfaced with particular vehemence at the Bandung conference, where the "nonaligned" nations found unity of a sort in shared resentment of a few rich and powerful countries' dominance in world affairs.

THE DECONSTRUCTION DERBY

Over the 1960s and 1970s, the Declaration's framers, one by one, were departing from the world stage. The United Nations grew into an elaborate bureaucracy with more than fifty thousand employees. Its specialized agencies become closely intertwined with the nongovernmental organizations that proliferated as the international human rights movement gained ground in the 1960s and 1970s. That movement in turn was deeply affected by the ideas about rights that predominated in the United States in those days.[18] The

---

17. Philip Alston, "The Universal Declaration at 35: Western and Passe or Alive and Universal?" *International Commission of Jurists Review* 30 (1983): 60, 69.

18. See generally Mary Ann Glendon, *Rights Talk: The Impoverishment of Political Discourse* (New York: Free Press, 1991) (especially chapter 6); Anthony Lester, "The Overseas Trade in the American Bill of Rights," *Columbia Law Review* 88 (1988): 537.

movement, like the Declaration itself, attracted many persons and groups who were more interested in harnessing its moral authority for their own ends than in furthering its original purposes.

Another important development, set in motion by the Cold War antagonists, was the nearly universal habit of reading the Declaration in the way that Americans read the Bill of Rights, that is, as a string of essentially separate guarantees. Its dignity-based language of rights began to be displaced by the more simplistic kinds of rights talk that were then making great inroads on political discourse in the United States. Several features of that new, hyper-individualistic dialect had the potential to wreak havoc with the Declaration: rights envisioned without individual or social responsibilities; one's favorite rights touted as absolute with others ignored; the rights-bearer imagined as radically autonomous and self-sufficient; the trivialization of core freedoms by special interests posing as new rights.[19]

Thus, ironically, the charge of cultural imperialism has more credibility than it had in 1948. The global spread of hyper-libertarian, radically individualistic, sound-bite rights ideas has rendered the contemporary international human rights project more vulnerable to the label of "Western" than the Declaration ever was. Launched as a commitment by the nations to compete in advancing human freedom and dignity, the Declaration is now in danger of becoming what its critics have always accused it of being—an instrument of neocolonialism!

For decades, the seamlessness of the Declaration has been ignored by its professed supporters as well as by its attackers. By isolating each part from its place in the overall design, the now common misreading of the Declaration promotes misunderstanding and facilitates misuse. Nations and interest groups ignore the provisions they find inconvenient and treat others as trumps. A major casualty has been the Declaration's insistence on the links between freedom and solidarity, just at a time when affluent nations seem increasingly to be washing their hands of poor countries and peoples.

For examples of deconstruction in operation, one could do no better than to eavesdrop on the rights babble of the big U.N. conferences of the 1990s. At first glance, the United Nations might seem to be an unlikely forum for the pursuit of law reform. But its agencies and conferences have attracted nu-

19. See generally Glendon, *Rights Talk.* On the need for care in accepting new rights, see Philip Alston, "Conjuring up New Rights: A Proposal for Quality Control," *American Journal of International Law* 78 (1984): 607.

merous special interest groups whose agendas have trouble passing muster in ordinary domestic political processes. Over the years, lobbyists of various sorts have acquired considerable influence in the U.N. bureaucracy, whose processes are even less transparent than those of U.S. administrative agencies.

Thus was the stage set for the United Nations and its conferences to become offshore manufacturing sites where the least popular (or least avowable) ideas of special interest groups could be converted into "international norms." These norms, though technically lacking the status of fundamental rights, could then be portrayed at home as universal standards, and imposed on poor countries as conditions for the receipt of aid.

At the United Nations' 1995 Women's Conference in Beijing, for example, strenuous efforts were made to advance a new human rights paradigm—mainly by representatives from affluent countries. In her speech to a plenary session on the second day of the conference, U.S. First Lady Hillary Rodham Clinton gave high visibility to a misleading slogan. "If there is one message that echoes forth from this conference," she asserted, "it is that human rights are women's rights, and women's rights are human rights."[20] The statement was half true, but only half true. Human rights do belong to everyone. But not every right that has been granted to women by a particular nation-state has gained the status of a human right. The slogan was mainly aimed at universalizing extreme, American-style abortion rights in a world where few countries, if any, go as far as the United States and China in permitting abortions of healthy, viable unborn children.

That there might be some such demolition derby in the Declaration's future was foreseen long ago by Richard McKeon. McKeon realized what every lawyer knows: practical agreements such as those reached by the U.N. member states in 1948 are achieved only at the price of a certain ambiguity. The framers knew that the same generality that made agreement possible rendered the document vulnerable to misunderstanding and manipulation. In his UNESCO report, McKeon pointed out that different understandings of the meanings of rights usually reflect divergent concepts of man and of society, which in turn cause the persons who hold those understandings to have different views of reality. Thus, he predicted that "difficulties will be discovered in the suspicions, suggested by these differences, concerning the tangential

20. Steven Mufson, "First Lady Critical of China, Others on Women's Rights," *Washington Post* (6 September 1995): A1.

uses that might be made of a declaration of human rights for the purpose of advancing special interests."[21] That was a philosopher's way of saying, "Watch out, this whole enterprise could be hijacked!"

In sum, the human rights project, launched as a multicultural commitment to compete in advancing freedom and dignity, is now in danger of becoming what its enemies and critics have always accused it of being—an instrument of "Western" cultural imperialism.

That irony did not escape the attention of Calcutta-born Cambridge economist Amartya Sen. In 1994, just before the United Nations' Cairo Conference on Population and Development, Sen warned in the *New York Review of Books* that the developed nations were exhibiting a dangerous tendency to approach population issues with a mentality that "treats the people involved not as reasonable beings, allies faced with a common problem, but as impulsive and uncontrolled sources of great social harm, in need of strong discipline."[22] Sen, who won the Nobel Prize for his works on inequality and world hunger, charged that international policymakers, by giving priority to "family planning arrangements in the Third World countries over other commitments such as education and health care, produce negative effects on people's well-being and reduce their freedoms."[23] In short, the whole range of human rights of poor people is at risk when special interests are dressed up as universal rights.

The good news is that as the United Nations enters a period of austerity, the era of big conferences such as Cairo and Beijing is probably drawing to a close. The bad news is that the same economic pressures that are putting a damper on huge international gatherings, however, may aggravate the danger of capture of U.N. agencies by well-financed special interests. A case in point is CNN founder Ted Turner's $1 billion "gift" to the United Nations announced in the fall of 1997. Many who look to the United Nations for leadership in humanitarian aid were overjoyed when Mr. Turner announced that his donation was to help "the poorest of the poor."[24] Paid out in installments

---

21. McKeon, "The Philosophic Bases and Material Circumstances of the Rights of Man," 35, 36.

22. Amartya Sen, "Population: Delusion and Reality," *New York Review of Books* (22 September 1994): 66.

23. See also Reed Boland, "The Environment, Population, and Women's Human Rights," *Environmental Law* 27 (1997): 1137.

24. Betsy Pisik, "Gift Keeps on Giving," *Washington Times* (19 January 1998): A1.

of $100 million a year for ten years, this infusion of funds would have ranked behind the annual contributions of only the U.S., Japan, and Germany.

The news seemed too good to be true. It was. It soon appeared that the United Nations would not have control over the funds. Rather, its agencies would be required to submit proposals, for approval, to a foundation headed by a man Mr. Turner chose because "he thinks as I do."[25] The man designated to have the chief say in allocating the Turner millions is former U.S. State Department official Timothy Wirth, who spearheaded the aggressive U.S. population control agenda at the 1994 Cairo conference. Wirth has been so zealous in advocating population control that he has even praised China, with its coercive one-child-per-family policy, for its "very, very effective high-investment family planning."[26] As for Mr. Turner, he told a California audience in 1998 that in the post–Cold War world, "The real threat is no longer an army marching on us, it's people infiltrating us, you know, people that are starving."[27]

As its details have unfolded, Mr. Turner's gesture looks less like a gift and more like a takeover bid aimed at U.N. agencies with privileged access to vulnerable populations. The next few years are thus likely to be a time of testing for the United Nations if its prestige and organizational resources are not to be, literally, for sale.

As memories fade about why the nations of the world determined after World War II to affirm certain basic rights as universal, efforts to deconstruct the Universal Declaration and remake it nearer to the heart's desire of this or that special interest group will continue. Whether the relatively rich and complex vision of human rights in the Universal Declaration can withstand the combined stresses of aggressive lobbying, heightened national and ethnic assertiveness, and the powerful, ambiguous forces of globalization, is impossible to foresee. Not only U.N. agencies, but the governments of several liberal democracies have become implicated in breaking down the connections among its indivisible rights and deconstructing its core principle, human dignity.

---

25. Barbara Crossette, "Turner Picks State Dept. Official to Allocate UN Fund," *International Herald Tribune* (21 November 1997): 4; Colin Woodard, "Ted Turner Gift Poised to Boost UN," *Christian Science Monitor* (22 April 1998): 1.

26. Quoted in Jeffrey Gedmin, "Clinton's Touchy-Feely Foreign Policy," *Weekly Standard* (13 May 1996): 19, 22.

27. Ann Bardach, "Turner in 2000?" *New Yorker* (23 November 1998): 36, 37.

THE CHALLENGE OF HUMAN RIGHTS

The contest for control of the meaning of the Declaration forcefully reminds us that the framers of the Universal Declaration left the human rights movement with a problem. As John Paul II put it in his Address to the Vatican Diplomatic Corps in January 1989, "[T]he 1948 Declaration does not contain the anthropological and moral bases for the human rights that it proclaims." How, then, can one handle the problem of reconciling tensions among the various rights, or the related problem of integrating new rights from time to time?

Those problems are serious, and have led some thoughtful persons to conclude that the Declaration is hopelessly incoherent. The late Michel Villey, for example, maintained that "[e]ach of the so-called human rights is the negation of other human rights, and when practiced separately generates injustices."[28] Alasdair MacIntyre argues that different rights, borrowed from different traditions, often rest on different, and incommensurable, moral premises.[29]

These problems were not overlooked by Maritain and his colleagues. Maritain noted that "[w]here difficulties and arguments begin is in the determination of the scale of values governing the exercise and concrete integration of these various rights."[30] The Declaration, he went on, would need some "ultimate value whereon those rights depend and in terms of which they are integrated by mutual limitations." That value, explicitly set forth in the Declaration, is human dignity. But as time went on, it has become painfully apparent that dignity possesses no more immunity to hijacking than any other concept. One need only think of current defenses of active euthanasia in terms of "the right to die with dignity." (There is no end, it seems, of pseudo-rights that the stronger are eager to confer upon the weaker whether the latter are willing or not.)

The shift from nature to dignity in modern thinking about the foundations of human rights thus entails a host of difficulties. The common secular understandings are that human beings have dignity because they are autonomous beings capable of making choices (Kant), or because of the sense

---

28. Michel Villey, *Le droit et les droits de l'homme* (Paris: Presses Universitaires de France, 1983), 13.

29. Alasdair MacIntyre, *After Virtue*, 2d ed. (Notre Dame, IN: University of Notre Dame Press, 1984).

30. Maritain, introduction to *Human Rights*, 9, 15–16.

of empathy that most human beings feel for other sentient creatures (Rousseau). But the former understanding has alarming implications for persons of diminished capacity, and the latter places all morality on the fragile basis of a transient feeling. Most believers, for their part, would say that dignity is grounded in the fact that human beings are made in the image and likeness of God, but that proposition is unintelligible to nonbelievers.

Moreover, the path from dignity to rights is not clear and straight, even for believers. Brian Benestad has pointed out that the term "dignity of the human person" has two different connotations in Christian teaching—"[it] is both a given and an achievement or an end to be gradually realized."[31] The Catholic Catechism, he notes, begins its discussion of morality with this quotation from Pope Leo the Great: "Christian, recognize your dignity, and now that you share in God's own nature, do not return by sin to your former base condition." But if dignity is a quality to be achieved by strenuous effort to overcome sin and practice virtue, then it is not altogether clear that the dignity of the rights claimant is an adequate basis for human rights. Not every rights claimant, obviously, has made strenuous effort to overcome sin. From a Christian point of view, the resolution of this dilemma may be that human rights are grounded in the obligation of everyone to perfect one's own dignity, which in turn obliges one to respect the "given" spark of dignity of others, whatever they may have done with it. In other words, it may be our own quest for dignity (individually and as a society) that requires us to refrain from inflicting cruel punishments on criminals, or from terminating the lives of the unborn and others whose faculties are undeveloped or dormant.

In that light, the drafters of the U.N. Charter were prudent to say that human rights rest upon a "faith" in human dignity. It would be a mistake, however, to leap from that proposition to the notion that this faith is merely an act of will, an arbitrary choice. All in all, one may say of "dignity" in the Universal Declaration what Abraham Lincoln once said about "equality" in the Declaration of Independence: it is a hard nut to crack. The framers of the Universal Declaration were far from naive about the difficulties that lay ahead. That is evident from many statements in which they acknowledged the priority of culture over law. Though Maritain was not, strictly speaking, a framer, he said it best. Whether the music played on the Declaration's thir-

---

31. Brian Benestad, "What Do Catholics Know about Catholic Social Thought?" in *Festschrift for George Kelly* (Christendom Press, forthcoming).

ty strings will be "in tune with, or harmful to, human dignity," he wrote, will depend primarily on the extent to which a "culture of human dignity develops."[32]

If Maritain, Eleanor Roosevelt, Charles Malik, Rene Cassin, and others who held this view were right, then a great challenge faces the world's religions, for religion is at the heart of culture. Ultimately it will be up to the religions to demonstrate whether they are capable of motivating their followers to fulfill their own calling to perfect their own dignity, and in so doing to respect the dignity of fellow members of the human family.

32. Maritain, introduction to *Human Rights,* 16.

AFTERWORD

Catholics and the Two Cultures

RUSSELL SHAW

Some people can tell you when their eyes were opened to the pleasures of good wine, religion, or the fiction of Henry James. I remember when I really began to understand the culture war. It happened like this.

One day in December in the early 1990s I found myself at the upscale headquarters of the Educational Testing Service in Princeton, New Jersey, attending a conference on religion and the media. Also there were some present or former staff members of such estimable publications as the *New York Times,* the *Washington Post,* the *Los Angeles Times,* and the *Philadelphia Inquirer,* together with people from the think-tank world.

By midafternoon I had grown weary of a conversation that avoided real issues. So I violated the etiquette of the occasion and said what I genuinely thought. Specifically, I questioned the fairness and even-handedness of the *New York Times* when it came to its treatment of the Catholic Church and some other religious bodies. By way of example, I cited the op-ed page of the *Times* and especially Anna Quindlen's column.

Anna Quindlen is what came before Maureen Dowd, very much as the Visigoths came before the Huns. She is a pro-choice Catholic feminist, and these days, I believe, she writes for *Newsweek.* Back then, she frequently used her column in the *Times* to savage Pope John Paul II and John Cardinal O'Connor for their views on abortion and sexual morality.

I didn't suggest that Quindlen should mend her ways or that the *Times* should drop her column. Neither thing seemed very likely. I merely made the point that, if the paper were truly committed to even-handedness, then as often as she used the column to attack the pope and the cardinal over abortion and sex, it would offer space to the cardinal or the pope—or anyway to someone who thought as they did—to make the case for the other side. Now, obviously the *Times* wasn't going to do that. And the fact that it not only wasn't but wouldn't even dream of it was symptomatic of the problem with the *New York Times*—an indicator that it wasn't nearly as fair and even-handed as it liked to think.

The journalists were very angry at me for saying this. As I later remarked, I felt like a man who'd told a dirty story at a tea party. Far and away the angriest was a woman who had worked for the *Times* and had recently quit to do freelancing. She said she'd been raised a Catholic but left the Church because of its injustices to women. She also identified herself as a friend of Anna Quindlen. Although she said a number of things to express her displeasure with me, her final comment was the most interesting. It was this:

"Our secular society has certain needs and imperatives of its own. And it will act on those imperatives and it will satisfy those needs. And if you [glaring at me] and people like you don't like it—that's your problem."

Well, yes.

Neither before that day nor since have I personally heard the reality of the two cultures stated quite so bluntly. "Our secular society"—her culture, the culture of the *New York Times,* and the secular culture as a whole—is fundamentally opposed to my culture and people like me. The *Times* is truly fair and even-handed in dealing with its own culture. As for me and mine: No quarter given.

Illustrations of the newspaper's bias in this area abound. Even the *Times*'s obligatory editorial on the occasion of Edward Cardinal Egan's receiving the red hat went out of its way to attack conscience clauses exempting Church hospitals and schools that object to providing contraceptive coverage—which often means abortifacient coverage—under employee insurance plans, and to instruct the cardinal to "take care to ensure" that government would not pay for religious aspects of faith-based initiatives under President Bush's plan for utilizing them to deliver social services.[1] In the cultural world inhabited by the *New York Times,* Catholics bear watching (as do Protestant evangelicals, but they aren't the subject here).

---

1. "New York's New Cardinal," *New York Times* (22 February 2001).

At times in recent years it was fashionable to say that the culture war had ended, and the reign of unconditional tolerance had begun. So, for instance, the sociologist Alan Wolfe argued that case in his interesting book *One Nation, After All*.[2] But the idea is wrong. The terms of the conflict no doubt have shifted now and then, but the underlying conflict has scarcely gone away. In fact, it may have intensified. Consider the controversy over federal judgeship nominations or the voting patterns in recent presidential elections. Does anyone seriously believe the country is not sharply divided along cultural, moral lines?

When we look at the demographics of voting, the divide between red states and blue, red counties and blue, we are looking at two cultures in conflict. Gertrude Himmelfarb, a sophisticated analyst of the two-cultures phenomenon, contends that the counterculture of the 1960s and the 1970s has become the dominant secular culture in the United States today, while people with traditional moral views and religious beliefs have become the "dissident culture"—the real counterculture now.[3]

About the only point on which I would seriously disagree with Himmelfarb concerns her statement that the moral-religious culture of traditional beliefs and values "coexists" with the dominant culture, albeit "somewhat uneasily." It is not the uneasiness but the coexistence that I doubt. On the contrary, the two cultures are engaged in constant hostilities—border raids and skirmishes, let us call them—which sometimes erupt into raging battles.

It is an interesting question whether we now are witnessing the inevitable working out of Enlightenment principles or their inevitable collapse. Whichever view you take, it is clear that the secular culture by and large no longer subscribes to central convictions of the Enlightenment ideal as described by Isaiah Berlin: a system in which it was assumed that there were

certain objectively recognizable human goals which all men . . . sought after, namely happiness, knowledge, justice, liberty, and what was somewhat vaguely described but well understood as virtue; that these goals were common to all men as such, were not unattainable, nor incompatible, that human misery, vice and folly were mainly due to ignorance either of what these goals consisted in or of the means of attaining them—ignorance due in turn to insufficient knowledge of the laws of nature . . . [and] that human nature was fundamentally the same in all times and places.[4]

2. *One Nation, After All* (New York: Viking Penguin, 1998).

3. *One Nation, Two Cultures* (New York: Random House Vintage Books, 2001), 124–125.

4. *Three Critics of the Enlightenment,* ed. Henry Hardy (Princeton: Princeton University Press, 2000), 277.

In the United States today, consensus about principles like these has diminished to the vanishing point.

Richard John Neuhaus suggests that the great change of the last several decades is the universal adoption of a fundamental principle of the '60s counterculture—"the personal is the political." Before the 1960s, Father Neuhaus says, politics was mainly about "great economic and military questions, issues of national security in the face of the Communist threat, and, for some years, racial desegregation and ending poverty." Now it is about "the proper roles of men and women, same-sex unions and divorce and having children and a host of other questions once thought not to be political, and all of them somehow entangled with and ever returning to the conflict created by . . . *Roe v. Wade.*"[5] The end of the Cold War did not halt this transformation. It simply gave us more leisure for battling over it.

Now, where do Catholics fit into this picture? To which culture do they belong? The answer is (and this is what makes Catholics such an interesting, frustrating group): both.

Obviously, any religious body of reasonable size and complexity is not totally homogeneous. There are deeply religious Orthodox Jews, whose views on many moral questions are very much like mine. I have seen some of them year after year at the March for Life here in Washington in January on the anniversary of *Roe v. Wade,* and I have been greatly edified by this testimony to the value of human life on the part of people who remember what the Holocaust was like. At the other extreme, one undoubtedly can find renegade Mormons who smoke and drink, support women's "right to choose," and believe in no-fault divorce. Still, people like these are exceptions to the rule of their own groups. The groups themselves are pretty much of a piece.

There was a time when it was like that with American Catholics. But not any more. Each of the two cultures contains a very large Catholic component. Catholics who go to Mass regularly are a significant component of the traditional-values counterculture; Catholics who seldom or never go to Mass belong to the secularized culture of libertarian "choice." Here, too, I grant the exceptions—pro-choice daily communicants, pro-life Catholics who have been away from the sacraments for years. But they *are* exceptions. The general pattern holds true.

5. "The Two Politics of Election 2000," *First Things* 110 (February 2001): 57–76.

※

There is absolutely no guarantee that the political ascendancy of religiously active Catholics, associated with the pontificates of John Paul II and Benedict XVI as well as the presidency of George W. Bush, will last. Many factors are working in a quite different direction. A few years ago, the Commonweal Foundation and the Faith and Reason Institute released results of a survey of Catholic opinion carried out for them by the Center for Applied Research in the Apostolate. Along with finding that only one American Catholic in three attended Mass weekly, the study showed: that Catholics are split down the middle on legalizing assisted suicide; that slightly more consider themselves than pro-choice than pro-life—49 percent to 45.7 percent; and that a large majority—62.1 percent—think abortion should be legal. About 40 percent admitted that in making political choices they draw on Catholic faith and values only "a little" or—somewhat more numerous—"not at all."[6] This was neither the first poll nor the last to produce results like these.

One of the people invited to respond to these findings at a press briefing was Mary McGrory, a longtime liberal Catholic political columnist of the *Washington Post*. Looking at these numbers, Ms. McGrory remarked, with apparent dismay, that many of her coreligionists had been "assimilated into the prevailing attitudes." So they have.

But the story of Catholic assimilation since World War II is hardly new. It has been told many times. Here I merely note an aspect of assimilation pointed out, among others, by Charles Morris, in his shrewd popular history *American Catholic*.[7] The argument is along the following lines. Sometime in the late 1950s, leaders in the American Catholic intellectual and academic communities decided that the Catholic subculture had outlived its usefulness and should be dismantled. And dismantle it they proceeded to do, via a kind of self-inflicted Catholic *Kulturkampf* extending through the 1960s and 1970s. Of this "fearsome exercise" Morris says: "It was nothing less than the dangerous and potentially catastrophic project of severing the connection

---

6. *The Political Preferences of American Catholics on the Eve of the 2000 Elections,* a report prepared by the Center for Applied Research in the Apostolate for the Commonweal Foundation and the Faith and Reason Institute as part of the "Faith in the Public Square" project, October 2000.

7. *American Catholic* (New York: Random House Times Books, 1997), 279–280. See also Joseph A. Varacalli, *Bright Promise, Failed Community: Catholics and the American Public Order* (Lanham, Md.: Lexington Books, 2000).

between the Catholic religion and the separatist American Catholic culture that had always been the source of its dynamism, its appeal, and its power."

❧

But what does all this have to do with Catholic perspectives on American law? It provides the cultural context for the effort to develop Catholic legal theory in the United States. The effort is taking place within a weakened Catholic subculture. This project is meant to apply Catholic perspectives to American law not just notionally and in the abstract, but, somewhere down the line, in actual, concrete fact. But that seems most unlikely to happen as matters now stand. Specifically, it will not happen until the Catholic subculture regains the critical mass to be a culture-forming agent in America.

As Charles Morris points out, there was a time when it was that—or, at least, was very close to becoming it. The brief moment came in the late '40s and early '50s, before the intellectuals launched the "dangerous and potentially catastrophic project"—the separation of religion from culture—of which Morris speaks. Once that project began, however, the opportunity was lost. Whether permanently or not, I cannot tell.

When I try to explain what I think American Catholics now ought to be doing, I sometimes say, "Back to the ghetto." Although I say it mainly to get people's attention, "Back to the ghetto" does point to an important truth. Unless believing, practicing Catholics re-create a viable subculture as the basis for their efforts to engage and, let us hope, reform the secular culture, there is little or no chance that a change for the better will occur. On the contrary, in that case it is likely that the Catholic Church in the United States will continue to decline in cultural relevance and, sooner or later, in numbers as well, while the culture will continue to slide into moral decadence marked by ongoing culture war.

As a result of immigration, the numerical decline in American Catholicism has not set in yet, except in certain categories, notably priests and religious women. But very large numbers have in fact quit the Church, without necessarily abandoning the name "Catholic." As for the Church's decline in cultural relevance, it has been underway for several decades and is now well advanced. Radical steps will be needed to turn that around.

In speaking of a ghetto, I do not mean something like the ghetto Catholicism of the good old/bad old days in the '30s and '40s. Along with its many strengths and virtues, that ghetto was intellectually shallow as well as triumphalistic and defensive to the point of paranoia. One of the symptoms of this was the compulsion of Catholics to out-patriot everybody else; and it is perhaps no coincidence that the heyday of the Catholic subculture coincided with Cold War, when hyper-patriotism was in vogue. I do not desire a return to *that*.

Instead, I mean the sort of healthy community, possessing a strong and self-confident sense of its identity, of which Avery Cardinal Dulles speaks: "Because the secular world is preponderantly antithetical to Christian revelation, faith requires for its growth an alternative environment, under the guidance of masters who are well grounded in Christian doctrine and exemplary in conduct."[8] An alternative environment or plausibility structure is necessary not only for the transmission of faith from generation to generation, but also for an evangelizing of culture that will include bringing Catholic perspectives to bear on the law.

I take it that, in one way or another, applying Catholic perspectives to the legal field will involve the recovery of the natural law tradition. Unfortunately, I have the impression that someone or other has been hard at work recovering the natural law tradition for as long as I can remember. Like one of those sunken treasure ships that resist salvaging, natural law is a treasure that no one has gotten back to the surface yet. One of these days, maybe. But not yet.

In the meantime, the dominant culture has no visible sympathy for the effort. When Clarence Thomas was undergoing the grilling that these days passes for a Senate confirmation process for Supreme Court nominees, one of the things held against him was that he had expressed a friendly interest in natural law. This was held by some to be prima facie proof of his unfitness, as if he had admitted that he found astrology helpful in settling hard cases. (As a matter of fact, I suspect that some critics would have taken a more favorable view of Thomas if he'd spoken well of astrology instead of natural law.)

More recently, the same mindset or something close to it was visible in the public debate that attended the nominations of John G. Roberts Jr. and Samuel A. Alito to serve on the court. In the minds of some commentators, it was clear, traditional views on law and, especially, on an issue such as abortion automatically place someone holding them outside the cited mainstream of acceptable American opinion as defined by those same commentators and

8. *The New World of Faith* (Huntington, IN: Our Sunday Visitor Publishing Division, 2000), 163.

their friends. It did not help, needless to say, that Roberts and Alito were Catholics and that their presence on the Court would raise the number of Catholic justices to an unprecedented five.

"Catholic perspectives" people have their work cut out for them, in regard to law and much else. Consider that the House of Delegates of the American Bar Association has for years voted overwhelmingly in support of legalized abortion and against amending the ABA constitution to declare defending the right to life of all innocent human beings, including all those unborn, a purpose of the association.[9]

Note, however, that the challenge for those seeking to effect a fundamental reorientation of American law comes not just from the secular culture but from culturally assimilated Catholics. Many educated Catholics today know next to nothing about natural law and care less. I suspect that includes many graduates of Catholic law schools, who to this layman appear to have been trained as technicians, with no informing philosophy or set of values to guide them—and certainly not one grounded in natural law.

In short, the first task for people seeking to apply Catholic perspectives to American law or anything else is to open the eyes of *Catholics* to those perspectives. If that were done, the result would be as startling an epiphany for some as my sudden plunge into the culture war was for me. And whether it is done or not, it is indispensable to reconstituting that alternative environment called the American Catholic subculture.

9. Interested parties will find extensive documentation on the ABA website.

EPILOGUE

✿

RANDY LEE

When the editors of this book allowed me to read it in advance of its publication and then invited me to write my thoughts on how Catholic lawyers and lawmakers might respond to it, I was both hesitant and humbled. With contributions from so many people whose insights, lives, and work I have so long respected, this book, I felt, needed no additional words from me. But when Michael Scaperlanda persisted that I might at least be able to offer some brief words about "where we go from here," I offered the matter up to prayer, and then, ultimately, began to think that perhaps that much I might be able to contribute.

To understand where one might go from here, however, one first must acknowledge where we, as a Church and also as a nation, come from, legally speaking. In their Introduction, the editors told the story of America's legal heritage.[1] Here, I will add to that a brief story of the Church's legal heritage. To understand that heritage, one must understand two stories from the Bible. One is the story of law in the hands of men and the other is the story of law in the hands of God. One is a very glorious, grace-filled story. The other is not. Yet, both are essential to addressing the question of how we may now best use the wisdom to be found in this book.

The glorious, grace-filled story is the story of law in the hands of God, and it begins shortly before God gave the first rules to Adam. Before God gave Adam rules such as "[b]e fruitful and multiply, fill the earth and subdue it,"[2] and "cultivate and care for [the garden],"[3] God created Adam into a com-

---

1. See Michael Scaperlanda and Teresa Collett, Introduction to this volume.
2. Genesis 1:28.   3. Ibid. at 2:15.

munity of love and placed him in the garden surrounding the tree of life.[4]
Among all the rules that God gave Adam in the garden, God never forbade
Adam to eat of the fruit of the tree of eternal life.[5] In fact, God gave Adam
that community, that home, and those rules in hopes that Adam would eat
the fruit of eternal life out of love so Adam could spend eternity with God.[6]
In fact, that hope of God's is the whole point of the story of Adam, God, and
rules.

It is not enough, then, to recognize that God gave Adam rules or even to
recognize what rules God gave Adam. To understand the story of law in the
hands of God, one must understand that God gave Adam law out of a community of love in the hope of eternal salvation. Even after Adam proved dis-
obedient to the laws of God and rebellious against God's community,[7] God
persisted in making laws for men in this spirit. In fact one can see this in
God's relationship with Adam's son Cain.

After Cain failed to heed God's warning but, instead, deceived and then
killed his brother Abel,[8] God confronted Cain. Although the popular my-
thology of this story is that God then condemned Cain, the truth is that God
used His judgment, His justice, and His mercy to save Cain. Although in
subsequent expressions of His law, God would invoke the death penalty for
the crime of Cain,[9] God limited the punishment of Cain to a banishment
from tilling the earth and a life of restless wandering.[10] Although the punishment is one Cain considered "too great to bear,"[11] it offered Cain time to turn
his heart to redemption. In fact, God guaranteed Cain that time by creating
His first expressed rule of this era of man's knowing good and bad. God de-
creed that "[i]f anyone kills Cain, Cain shall be avenged sevenfold," and God
"put a mark on Cain" so that all would be on notice of the rule.[12]

---

4. Ibid. at 2:8–9.

5. Ibid. at 2:16–17 ("You are free to eat from any of the trees of this garden except the tree
of knowledge of good and bad.").

6. The Bible culminates in God returning man to the tree of eternal life, where he is once
more free to eat of its fruit. Revelation 22:1–3.

7. Genesis 3 (In violation of God's rule, Adam and Eve eat of the fruit of the tree of knowledge of good and bad.).

8. Ibid. at 4:8.

9. See, e.g., Leviticus 24:17. For a discussion of what Jewish teachings can contribute to
the death penalty debate in America, see Samuel J. Levine, "Playing God: An Essay on Law,
Philosophy, and American Capital Punishment," *New Mexico Law Review* 31 (2001): 277.

10. Genesis 4:11–12.   11. Ibid. at 4:13.

12. Ibid. at 4:15.

The Bible does not say how Cain's heart responded to this opportunity. It does indicate, however, that the remainder of his days were not spent alone as a "restless wanderer" as Cain had anticipated.[13] Cain married,[14] the fate God had planned for man,[15] and Cain and his wife "produced a man with the help of the Lord."[16] Cain also founded the first city mentioned in the Bible,[17] and among his descendants were counted "all who play the lyre and the pipe"[18] and "all who forge instruments of bronze and iron."[19]

Later, God also gave law to the Jewish people as a community, but before God gave them the law as a nation, He called them to Himself out of Egypt,[20] gathered them together around Mount Sinai,[21] and promised His people that they would be His people forever.[22] Furthermore, the Jewish people have long understood that God gave them the law not to crush them beneath the weight of the stone tablets but to make their steps easier to God.[23] In fact, the Jewish people were so sensitive to God's purpose in the law that Scripture tells us the Jewish people were apt to weep at the recognition of God's love in the law.[24]

The story of law in the hands of God continues into the Gospels in this same spirit of love, community, and salvation. In fact, when the time came for God to send to us His only Son, God sent His only Son to all men "not to abolish the Law but to fulfill it."[25] Yet, even before God's Son could speak a word, God had already extended to both the great and the humble a promise of salvation through His infant Son and an invitation to come to community around the Child in a manger.[26] Jesus too gave to His Church law, a new law to love one another as He loved us.[27] But before He did so, He began His public ministry by calling twelve friends to Himself and dedicating the last three years of His earthly life to preparing those friends to bring others to Him for

13. Ibid. at 4:14.
14. Ibid. at 4:17.
15. Ibid. at 2:24.
16. Ibid. at 4:1, 4:17.
17. Ibid. at 4:17.
18. Ibid. at 4:21.
19. Ibid. at 4:22.
20. Exodus 12:37.
21. Ibid. at 19:1–3.
22. Ibid. at 19:5 ("If you hearken to my voice and keep my covenant, you shall be my special possession, dearer to me than all other people, though all the earth is mine.").
23. Rabbi Lawrence A. Hoffman, "Response to Joseph Allegretti: The Relevance of Religion to a Lawyer's Work," *Fordham Law Review* 66 (1998): 1157, 1162.
24. Nehemiah 8:9.
25. Matthew 5:17.
26. Luke 2:8–20; Matthew 2:1–12 (visit of the magi).
27. John 15:12.

eternity in Heaven. Thus, throughout the history of man, the story of law in the hands of God has been a story of love creating community and law arising out of that community to save and to preserve the community of love for eternity.

All of which brings us to the not so grace-filled story, which is the story of law in the hands of men. That story begins when Lamech, a great-great-great-grandson of Cain, produced the first human law. Inspired by God's rule that "Cain shall be avenged sevenfold,"[28] Lamech devised the rule that Lamech was entitled to be avenged "seventy-sevenfold" for an offense, and relying on this rule, Lamech subsequently "killed a man for wounding [him] and a boy for bruising [him]."[29]

Everything about Lamech's attempt at making law ran counter to the rule of God that had inspired Lamech's effort. While God's rule about Cain had been designed to protect Cain and offer him the opportunity for salvation, Lamech's rule was designed to justify condemnation for and harm to Lamech's enemies. While God's rule had postponed an ultimate judgment of Cain by God, Lamech's rule had invited an ultimate judgment of other people by Lamech. Finally, while God's rule arose out of an undeterrable love for Cain, Lamech's rule arose out of Lamech's thirst for vengeance and his selfish longing for laws that would serve Lamech to the detriment of others.

Unlike God, Lamech created his rule outside the context of a relationship of love. As a result, the consequences of Lamech's rulemaking proved the opposite of the consequences of God's. Although in the life of Cain, we see new life, creativity, and a return to God's plan emerging from obedience to God's rule, the consequence of obedience to Lamech's rule is the death of a man and a child.

Formalization of human lawmaking did little to improve its quality. When the people of Israel tired of being led by judges, they demanded a king.[30] It was a demand that God would grant[31] but only after providing the following warning about the inclinations of human government:

[Your king] will take your sons and assign them to his chariots and horses, and they will run before his chariot. He will also appoint from among them his commanders of groups of a thousand and of a hundred soldiers. He will set them to do his plowing and his harvesting, and to make his implements of war and the equipment of his chariots. He will use your daughters as ointment-makers, as cooks and as bakers. He will take

---

28. See supra text accompanying note 12.   29. Genesis 4:23–24.
30. 1 Samuel 8:4–5.   31. Ibid. at 8:22.

the best of your fields, vineyards, and olive groves, and give them to his officials. He will tithe your crops and your vineyards, and give the revenue to his eunuchs and slaves. He will take your female and male servants, as well as your best oxen and asses, and use them to do his work. He will tithe your flocks and you yourselves will become his slaves. When this takes place, you will complain against the king whom you have chosen, but on that day the lord will not answer you.[32]

Within the reign of the first king, the Nation of Israel was engaged in a sort of civil war.[33] By the reign of the fourth king, the nation had discovered the concepts of revolution and secession.[34]

Human efforts at law fared little better in the New Testament. The lawyers one meets in the Gospels are not, in fact, very nice people. They are people who seek power, people who seek wealth and status, people who press the burdens of the law on others without accepting those burdens themselves, people who judge and condemn, and people who try to use their cleverness to escape the commands of God. Readers of any of the Gospels are unavoidably familiar with them and their agendas: Look, Jesus, he didn't wash his hands;[35] Look, Jesus, he picked grain on the Sabbath;[36] Look, Jesus, we caught her in the very act of adultery;[37] But Jesus, who would my neighbor be?[38] Get him, Jesus; punish him, Jesus; kill her, Jesus. They are people who tempt us to think that even in God's realm, the only way to use law is the way they used it, as did Lamech, as an arbitrary use of power for force, for condemnation, and for their own advantage.

Ultimately the hearts of the lawyers of the Gospels drew down the just judgment of God. As His ministry on Earth was nearing its end, Jesus said to them,

"Woe also to you lawyers! You impose on people burdens hard to carry, but you yourselves do not lift one finger to touch them. Woe to you! You build the memorials of the prophets whom your ancestors killed. Consequently, you bear witness and give consent to the deeds of your ancestors, for they killed them and you do the building. . . . Woe to

32. Ibid. at 8:11–18.

33. Ibid. at 21–31 (Saul and his army pursue David and his army.).

34. 1 Kings 12:1–25 (the separation of Israel from Judah).

35. Luke 11:38 ("The Pharisee was amazed to see that Jesus did not observe the prescribed washing before the meal.").

36. See, e.g., Matthew 12:2.

37. John 8:4.

38. Luke 10:29 ("But because he wished to justify himself, he said to Jesus, 'And who is my neighbor?'").

you lawyers! You have taken away the key of knowledge. You yourselves did not enter and you stopped those trying to enter."[39]

And, of course, these lawmakers hated Him for His wisdom and for His honesty, and they sought to ensnare Him and to destroy Him.[40]

This story of law in the Church leads us, then, to much the same point as did the editors' story of law in America: to Russell Shaw's observation that Catholic law will not win American minds unless a healthy Catholic community wins human hearts.[41] One should take from Professors Scaperlanda and Collett's Introduction to this volume a calling to fight and win the battle for the American mind, but winning that battle will not bring to an end any war. "For Catholic perspectives on American law to gain traction,"[42] for them to alter lives in a meaningful way and win the war for America's soul, Catholics must win not only the battle for America's mind, but also the battle for America's heart.

Four hundred years ago, Saint Thomas More called for lawyers to seek to improve the quality of secular law,[43] and today the Church continues to echo his call.[44] In fact, Pope John Paul II designated Saint Thomas More the patron saint of lawmakers, at least on the political side.[45] This volume responds to this calling to law, and the efforts included here reflect insight and sensitivity with respect to the issues of the world as well as reflecting an attention to the teachings of the Church. Most certainly, the various articles here can help us make better the state of secular law in the United States. But we must remember that the end is not to perfect secular law. We must remember that even if we could perfect that law and somehow bring all Americans into obedience with it, that alone would not perfect God's plan for men. God has called lawyers not only to emulate His law but also to emulate His heart.

---

39. Luke 11:46–52.

40. Id. at 11:53–54.

41. Scaperlanda and Collett, Introduction to this volume.

42. Ibid.

43. Thomas More, *Utopia,* ed. George M. Logan and Robert M. Adams (Cambridge: Cambridge University Press, 1989), 36.

44. See, e.g., Pope John Paul II's statement on October 28, 2002, that lawyers "must always decline to use their professional skills for ends that are contrary to justice" (spoken in the context of Catholic lawyers participating in divorce actions).

45. Pope John Paul II, *Letter on Saint Thomas More* (Oct. 31, 2000) (declaring Saint Thomas More the patron saint of statesmen and politicians).

If law is not created out of a loving sense of community for the purpose of salvation, then it cannot reflect the wisdom of God.

As Professors Scaperlanda and Collett pointed out in the Introduction, from its inception, America had a right legal framework that could have guaranteed human dignity to African Americans. That framework, however, did little to help our African-American brothers and sisters until America began to acknowledge almost two hundred years later that it had a wrong heart. Similarly today, we may, someday within our lifetimes, again see American law mirror Catholic perspective on abortion. The depth of that victory will be reduced, however, to the degree that we do not seek healing for all those who have been scarred by abortion or that we harden our hearts and return to an age when pregnant girls were ostracized and single mothers and their children were forgotten.

In the end, as we seek to understand where we go from here, as we try to understand how to help Catholic perspectives flourish in American law, we must understand that we must aspire to the deeper victory rather than the shallow one. And to attain those deeper victories through the law, we masters of words need look no further than the "Word made flesh."[46]

When the Word "dwelt among us,"[47] the Word forgave, the Word healed, the Word educated, the Word transformed, the Word challenged, and the Word inspired, but the Word never condemned. God in His wisdom used His justice and His mercy for just one purpose, to save, "[f]or God so loved the world that He gave His only son so that he Who believes in Him might not perish but might have eternal life. For God did not send His son into the world to condemn the world, but that the world might be saved through him."[48] In fact, Jesus, the name divinely intended for the Word made flesh[49] means God saves. Motivated by love, God gave us His law, God gave us His wisdom, gave us His word, gave us His son, to save us, and we are called to "be like Him."[50]

As we have seen, many people in the Gospels who sought to use law for power or personal gain or to burden or condemn others called themselves lawyers. From a Catholic perspective, however, they were not lawyers, for in

46. John 1:14. 47. Ibid.

48. Ibid. at 3:16–17.

49. Matthew 1:21 (angel telling Joseph the Child is to be named "Jesus"); Luke 1:31 (Gabriel telling Mary the Child is to be named "Jesus").

50. 1 John 3:2.

the eyes of God, a lawyer is one who motivated by love uses the law and the wisdom of God to save.

I have a friend who is a judge in juvenile court. He works for legal reform in his writings and in his teachings, but he also must apply the law as it is now. As he does so, he agonizes over every child who comes through his court. He agonizes over how he can save them: what do they need; what can he do; what should he say; who can he involve; what services, punishments, resources should he access. And he struggles so much and he feels hurt so much because he loves so much and because he wants to use the law to save those kids so much. And sometimes he does save one.

We are called to take the wisdom in this book and do likewise. That is where we must go from here.

BIBLIOGRAPHY

Law Cases

Abrams v. U.S., 250 US 616 (1919).
American Home Improvement Co. v. MacIver, 201 A2d 886 (NH 1964).
Anderson v. Stream, 295 NW2d 595, 603 (Minn 1980).
Attwood v. Attwood, 633 SW2d 366 (Ark 1982).
Barker v. Lull Engineering Company, 575 P2d 443 (Colo App 1978).
Barnes v. Barnes, 603 NE2d 1337 (Ind 1992).
Bear Valley Church of Christ v. DeBose, 928 P2d 1315 (Colo 1996).
Biddle v. Perovich, 274 US 480 (1927).
Board of City Supervisors of Prince City, Virginia v. U.S., 48 F3d 520 (Fed Cir 1995).
Bowman v. Wathen. 1 How. 189 (1843).
Brady v. Brady, 64 NY2d 339 (1985).
Brewer v. Lewis, 989 F2d 1021 (9th Cir 1993).
Brewer v. Lewis, 997 F2d 550 (9th Cir 1993).
Byrd v. Faber, 565 NE2d 584 (Ohio 1991).
Calvary Baptist Church v. Joseph, 522 NE2d 371 (Ind 1988).
Catholic Charities v. Superior Court, 85 P3d 67 (Cal 2004).
Cepada v. Cumberland Engineering Company, 386 A2d 816 (NJ 1978).
Cox v. Thee Evergreen Church, 836 SW2d 167 (Tex 1992).
Destefano v. Grabrian, 763 P2d 275 (Colo 1988).
Drakes v. INS, 330 F3d 600 (3d Cir 2003).
EEOC v. Townley Engineering and Manufacturing Company, 859 F2d 610, 624 (9th Cir 1988).
Eisenstadt v. Baird, 405 US 438 (1972).
Employment Div. v. Smith, 494 US 872 (1990).
Erickson v. Christenson, 781 P2d 383 (Or 1989).
F.G. v. MacDonell, 696 A2d 697 (NJ 1997).
Faretta v. California, 422 US 806 (1975).
Frostifresh v. Reynoso, 274 NYS2d 757 (Sup Ct 1966).
Frostifresh v. Reynoso, 281 NYS2d 964 (App 1967).
Funkhouser v. Wilson, 950 P2d 501 (Wash Ct App 1998).
Furman v. Georgia, 408 US 238 (1972).
George v. International Society for Krishna Consciousness, 262 Cal Rptr 217 (Ct App 1989).
Gibson v. Gibson, 479 P2d 648 (Cal 1974).
Gilmore v. Utah, 429 US 1012 (1976).
Godinez v. Moran, 509 US 389 (1993).
Goldblatt v. Town of Hempstead, 369 US 590, 592 (1962).

Greenman v. Yuba Power Products, 59 Cal 2d 57 (1963).

Grimshaw v. Ford Motor Company, 119 Cal App 3d 757 (1981).

Griswold v. Connecticut, 381 US 479 (1965).

Guinn v. Collinsville Church of Christ. 775 P2d 766 (Okla 1989).

Hernandez-Mancilla v. INS, 246 F3d 1002 (7th Cir 2001).

Hewlett v. George, 9 So 885, 887 (Miss 1891).

Holodook v. Spencer, 324 NE2d 338, 346 (NY 1974).

Hope Clinic v. Ryan, 195 F3d 857 (1999).

Jacobson v. Massachusetts, 197 US 11 (1905).

Johnson v. M'Intosh. 21 US (8 Wheat) 572 (1823).

Jones v. Star Credit Corp., 298 NYS2d 264 (Sup Ct 1969).

Jordan v. Duff Phelps, Inc., 815 F2d 429 (7th Cir 1987).

Khalayleh v. INS, 287 F3d 978 (10th Cir 2002).

L.L.N. v. Clauder, 563 NW2d 434 (Wis 1997).

Lentz v. Baker, 792 SW2d 71 (Tenn 1989).

Lundman v. McKown, 530 NW2d 807 (Minn Ct App 1995).

MacDonald v. Maxwell, 655 NE2d 1249, 1250 (Ind 1995).

MacPherson v. Buick Motor Co., 217 NY 382 (1916).

Marshall v. International Longshoremen's and Warehousemen's Union, 371 P2d 987, 990 (Cal 1962).

Maynard v. Hill, 125 US 190 (1888).

Moses v. Diocese of Colorado, 863 P2d 310 (1998).

Mugalli v. Ashcroft, 258 F3d 52 (2d Cir 2001).

Municipal City of South Bend v. Kimsey, 781 NE2d 683 (Ind 2003).

Nally v. Grace Community Church, 763 P2d 948 (Cal 1988).

Palsgraf v. Long Island R.R. Co., 162 NE 99 (NY 1928).

Paris Adult Theatre v. Slaton, 413 US 49 (1973).

People v. Pozo, 746 P2d 523 (Col 1987).

Planned Parenthood of Southeastern Pennsylvania v. Casey, 505 US 833 (1992).

Prince v. Massachusetts, 321 US 158 (1944).

Pritzlaff v. Archdiocese of Milwaukee, 533 NW2d 780 (1995).

Renko v. McLean, 697 A2d 468 (Md 1997).

Roe v. Wade, 410 US 113 (1973).

Schmidt v. Bishop, 779 FSupp 321 (SDNY 1991).

Sinha v. Sinha, 515 Pa 14, 526 A2d 765 (1987).

Smith v. O'Connell, 986 FSupp 73 (DRI 1997).

Soule v. General Motors, 882 P2d 298 (Cal 1994).

State v. Brewer, 506 US 872 (1992).

State v. Brewer, 826 P2d 783, 788 (Ariz 1992).

Stenberg v. Carhart, 530 US 914 (2000).

Swanson v. Roman Catholic Bishop of Portland, 692 A2d 441 (Me 1997).

Tapia Garcia v. INS, 237 F3d 1216 (10th Cir 2001).

Thomas v. Winchester, 6 NY 397 (1852).

U.S. v. Couto, 311 F3d 179, 188 (2d Cir. 2002).

United States v. Fry, 322 F3d 1198 (9th Cir 2003).

Webster v. Reproductive Services, 492 US 490 (1989).

Whitmore v. Arkansas, 495 US 149 (1990).

Wollersheim v. Church of Scientology, 260 Cal Rptr 331 (Ct App 1989).
Zehner v. Wilkinson Memorial United Methodist Church, 581 A2d 1388 (Pa 1990).

Books and Articles

Abel, Richard L. "A Critique of Torts." *UCLA Law Review* 37 (1990): 785–831.
Ackerman, Bruce. *Social Justice in the Liberal State.* New Haven: Yale University Press, 1980.
Ackerman, Robert M. "Tort Law and Communitarianism: Where Rights Meet Responsibilities." *Wake Forest Law Review* 30 (1995): 649–690.
Acton, John Lord. "The Roman Question." *The Rambler* 2nd new series 2 (January 1860).
Adams, John. "Letter to Officers of the First Brigade, 11 October 1798." In *The Works of John Adams,* vol. 9. Boston: Little, Brown, 1854.
Adler, Mortimer J. *The Angels and Us.* New York: Macmillan, Collier Books, 1988.
———. *Freedom: A Study of the Development of the Concept in the English and American Traditions of Philosophy.* Albany, NY: Magi Books, 1968.
Aleinikoff, Thomas Alexander, et al. *Immigration and Citizenship: Process and Policy.* 4th ed. Eagan, MN: Thomson West, 1998.
Alexander, Larry. "Good God, Garvey! The Inevitability and Impossibility of a Religious Justification of Free Exemptions." *Drake Law Review* 47 (1998): 35–43.
Alston, Phillip. "Conjuring up New Rights: A Proposal for Quality Control." *American Journal of International Law* 78 (1984): 607–21.
———. "The Universal Declaration at 35: Western and Passe or Alive and Universal?" *International Commission of Jurists Review* 30 (1983): 60.
Althouse, Ann. "Standing in Fluffy Slippers." *Virginia Law Review* 77 (1991): 1177–1200.
Ambrosetti, Giovanni. "Diritto privato ed economia nella seconda scolastica." In *La seconda scolastica nella formazione del diritto privato moderno,* edited by P. Grossi. Milan: Giuffrè, 1973.
Anscombe, G. E. M. "Modern Moral Philosophy." *Philosophy* 33/34 (Jan. 1958): 1–19.
Apel, Karl Otto. "Types of Rationality Today: The Continuum of Reason between Science and Ethics." In *La Rationalité Aujourd'hui.* Ottawa: University of Ottawa Press, 1979.
Aquinas, Thomas [Saint]. *Commentary on Aristotle's De Anima.* Translated by Silvester Humphries. Notre Dame, IN: Dumb Ox Books, 1999.
———. *In decem libros ethicorum expositio.* Edited by A. Pirotta. Turin, 1934.
———. *Summa Theologica.* Translated by Fathers of the English Dominican Province. Allen, TX: Christian Classics, 1948.
Araujo, Robert J. "Justice as Right Relationship: A Philosophical and Theological Reflection on Affirmative Action." *Pepperdine Law Review* 27 (2000): 377–476.
Aristotle. *The Basic Works of Aristotle.* Edited by Richard McKeon. New York: Random House Books, 1941.
———. *The Complete Works of Aristotle: The Revised Oxford Translation.* Edited by Jonathan Barnes. Princeton: Princeton University Press, 1984.
———. *Introduction to Aristotle.* 2nd ed. Edited by Richard McKeon. Chicago: University of Chicago Press, 1974.
———. *Nicomachean Ethics.* Princeton: Princeton University Press, 1984.
———. *Politics.* Book I. Translated by Benjamin Jowett. Oxford: Clarendon Press, 1926.
Arredondo, Caesar A. "Help the Poor Now: A Practical Plan." *Catholicism in Crisis* (February 1985): 14.

Ashley, Benedict M. *Choosing a Worldview and Value System: An Ecumenical Apologetics.* Staten Island, NY: Alba House, 2000.

———. "Truth and Technology." *American Catholic Philosophical Association Proceedings, The Importance of Truth* 68 (1993): 27–40.

Ashley, Benedict M., and Albert Moraczewski. "Cloning, Aquinas, and the Embryonic Person." *National Catholic Bioethics Quarterly* 1 (2001): 189–202.

Ashley, Benedict M., and Kevin D. O'Rourke, O.P. *Health Care Ethics: A Theological Analysis.* 4th ed., rev. Washington, DC: Georgetown University Press, 1997.

Augustine [Saint]. *The City of God.* Translated by Philip Levine. Cambridge: Harvard University Press, 1966.

———. *The City of God.* Translated by Henry Bettenson. New York: Penguin Books, 2003.

———. *Confessions.* Translated by Henry Chadwick. Oxford: Oxford University Press, 1998.

Austin, John. *Lectures on Jurisprudence, or the Philosophy of Positive Law.* Lecture 6. Revised 5th ed. Edited by Robert Campbell. London: J. Murray, 1885.

Bainbridge, Stephen M. "Corporate Decisionmaking and the Moral Rights of Employees: Participatory Management and Natural Law." *Villanova Law Review* 43 (1998): 741–828.

Bandow, Doug. *Beyond Good Intentions: A Biblical View of Politics.* Westchester, IL: Crossway Books, 1988.

———. *The Politics of Envy: Statism as Theology.* New Brunswick: Transaction Publishers, 1994.

Bandow, Doug, and David L. Schindler. *Wealth, Poverty and Human Destiny.* Wilmington, DE: ISI Books, 2003.

Barber, Benjamin R. *Strong Democracy: Participatory Politics for a New Age.* Berkeley: University of California Press, 1984.

Bardach, Ann. "Turner in 2000?" *New Yorker* (23 November 1998): 36.

Barfield, Daniel A. "Better to Give than to Receive: Should Nonprofit Corporations and Charities Pay Punitive Damages?" *Valparaiso University Law Review* 29 (1995): 1193–1250.

Barry, Brian. "How Not to Defend Liberal Institutions." In *Liberalism and the Good,* edited by R. Bruce Douglass, Gerald R. Mara, and Henry S. Richardson. New York: Routledge, 1990.

Baudouin-Croix, Marie. *Leonie Martin: A Difficult Life.* Translated by Mary Frances Mooney. Dublin: Veritas Publications, 1993.

Baum, Gregory. "An Ethical Critique of Capitalism: Contribution of Modern Catholic Social Teaching." In *Religion and Economic Justice,* edited by Michael Zweig. Philadelphia: Temple University Press, 1991.

Belfiore, Elizabeth S. *Murder among Friends: Violation of Philia in Greek Tragedy.* New York: Oxford University Press, 2000.

Bellah, Robert. *Habits of the Heart.* Berkeley: University of California Press, 1996.

Benedict XVI (Pope). Encyclical Letter, 25 December 2005. *Deus caritas est.* http://www.vatican.va/holy_father/benedict_xvi/encyclicals.

Benestad, J. Brian. "Virtue in Catholic Social Teaching." In *Private Virtue and Public Policy: Catholic Thought and National Life.* New Brunswick: Transaction Publishers, 1990.

———. "What Do Catholics Know about Catholic Social Thought?" In *Festschrift for George Kelly*. Christendom Press, forthcoming.

Bennett, William. *The Index of Leading Cultural Indicators: Facts and Figures on the State of American Society*. New York: Simon and Schuster, 1994.

Benson, Lenni. "Back to the Future: Congress Attacks the Right to Judicial Review of Immigration Proceedings." *Connecticut Law Review* 29 (1997): 1411–94.

Berger, Brigitte, and Peter L. Berger. *The War over the Family: Capturing the Middle Ground*. Garden City, NY: 1983.

Berger, Lawrence. "An Analysis of the Doctrine That 'First in Time Is First in Right.'" *Nebraska Law Review* 64 (1985): 349–88.

Berger, Peter L., and Richard John Neuhaus. *To Empower People: From State to Civil Society*. Washington, DC: American Enterprise Institute, 1977.

Berkowitz, Peter. "Liberalism, Postmodernism, and Public Philosophy." In *Public Morality, Civic Virtue, and the Problem of Modern Liberalism*, edited by T. William Boxx and Gary M. Quinlivan. Grand Rapids, MI: Eerdmans, 2000.

Berlin, Isaiah. *Three Critics of the Enlightenment*. Edited by Henry Hardy. Princeton: Princeton University Press, 2000.

———. "Two Concepts of Liberty." In *Five Essays on Liberty*. Oxford: Oxford University Press, 2002.

Berman, Harold J. *Law and Revolution: The Formation of the Western Legal Tradition*. Cambridge: Harvard University Press, 1983.

Bernardin, Joseph Cardinal. "The Dark Side of the Legal Profession: Have Lawyers Lost the Noble Cause?" *Human Rights* 14 (Spring 1987): 20–23.

Bernat, James L. "A Defense of the Whole-Brained Concept of Death." *Hastings Center Report* 28, no. 2 (1998): 14–26.

Black's Law Dictionary. 7th ed. Edited by Bryan A. Garner and Henry Cambell Black. St. Paul, MN: West, 1999.

Blackburn, Simon, *Oxford Dictionary of Philosophy*. Oxford: Oxford University Press, 1996.

Blackstone, William. *Commentaries on the Laws of England*. Vol. 1. 1765. New York: Garland Publishing, 1978.

———. *Commentaries on the Laws of England*. Facsimile. Chicago: University of Chicago Press, 1979.

Blackwell, Richard J. "The Structure of Wolffian Philosophy." *Modern Schoolman* 38 (1960): 203–18.

Block, Walter. *The U.S. Bishops and Their Critics: An Economic and Ethical Perspective*. Vancouver, BC: Fraser Institute, 1986.

Board of Professional Responsibility of the Superior Court of Tennessee. Formal Opinion 96-F-140 (1996).

Boland, Reed. "The Environment, Population, and Women's Human Rights." *Environmental Law* 27 (1997): 1137–67.

Bolick, Clint. "Subverting the American Dream: Government Dictated 'Smart Growth' Is Unwise and Unconstitutional." *University of Pennsylvania Law Review* 148 (2000): 859–72.

Bonnie, Richard J. "The Dignity of the Condemned." *Virginia Law Review* 74 (1988): 1363–91.

Bosniak, Linda. "Exclusion and Membership: The Dual Identity of the Undocumented Worker under United States Law." *Wisconsin Law Review* (1988): 955–1042.

———. "Membership, Equality, and the Difference That Membership Makes." *New York University Law Review* 69 (1994): 1047–1149.

Brewbaker, William. "Who Cares? Why Bother? What Jeff Powell and Mark Tushnet Have to Say to Each Other." *Oklahoma Law Review* 55 (2002): 533–57.

Briffault, Richard. "The Local Government Boundary Problem in Metropolitan Areas." *Stanford Law Review* 48 (1996): 1115–71.

Brugger, E. Christian. *Capital Punishment and the Roman Catholic Moral Tradition.* Notre Dame, IN: University of Notre Dame Press, 2003.

Bruni, Luigino. "Toward an Economic Rationality 'Capable of Communion.'" In *The Economy of Communion: Toward a Multi-Dimensional Economic Culture.* Edited by Luigino Bruni; translated by Lorna Gold. New York: New City Press, 2002.

Bryk, Anthony, Valerie Lee, and Peter Holland. *Catholic Schools and the Common Good.* Cambridge: Harvard University Press, 1993.

Bush, George W. "Inaugural Address of 20 January 2001." http://www.whitehouse.gov/news/inaugural-address.html.

Bush, Robert A. "Between Two Worlds: The Shift from Individual to Group Responsibility in the Law of Causation of Injury." *UCLA Law Review* 33 (1986): 1473–1563.

Buttiglione, Rocco. *Karol Wojtyla: The Thought of the Man Who Became Pope John Paul II.* Translated by Paolo Guietti and Francesca Murphy. Grand Rapids, MI: Eerdmans, 1997.

Calabresi, Guido. *Ideals, Beliefs, Attitudes, and the Law.* Syracuse, NY: Syracuse University Press, 1985.

Calabresi, Guido, and Philip Bobbit. *Tragic Choices.* New York: W. W. Norton , 1978.

Cambon. *Trinità Modello Sociale* (The Trinity as a Social Model). Rome: Città Nuova, 1999.

Carens, Joseph H. "Aliens and Citizens: The Case for Open Borders." *Review of Politics* 49 (1987): 251–73.

———. *Culture, Citizenship and Community: A Contextual Exploration of Justice as Evenhandedness.* Oxford: Oxford University Press, 2000.

———. "Migration and Morality: A Liberal Egalitarian Perspective." In *Free Movement: Ethical Issues in the Transnational Movement of People and of Money,* edited by Brian Barry and Robert Goodin. University Park: Pennsylvania State University Press, 1992.

Cashin, Sheryll D. "Localism, Self-Interest, and the Tyranny of the Favored Quarter: Addressing the Barriers to New Regionalism." *Georgetown Law Journal* 88 (2000): 1985–2048.

Catechism of the Catholic Church. New York: Bantam, Doubleday, Dell Publishing Group, 1995.

Catechism of the Catholic Church. 2d ed. Vatican: Libreria Editrice, 1997.

Catechism of the Catholic Church. 2nd ed. San Francisco: Ignatius Press, 1997.

Catholic Charities of Oklahoma. *Family Support Services.* http://www.catholiccharitiesok.org/family_support.html.

Cessario, Romanus. *Introduction of Moral Theology.* Washington, DC: The Catholic University of America Press, 2001.

Chandler, Christy. "Voluntary Executions." *Standford Law Review* 50 (1998): 1897–1927.

Chang, Howard F. "The Immigration Paradox: Poverty, Distributive Justice, and Liberal Egalitarianism." *DePaul Law Review* 52 (2003): 759–76.

———. "Immigration Policy, Liberal Principles, and the Republican Tradition." *Georgetown Law Journal* 85 (1997): 2105–2119.

Chang, P. C. *China at the Crossroads: The Chinese Situation in Perspective.* London: Evans, 1936.

Charles, Roger, and Drosten MacLaren. *The Social Teaching of Vatican II, Its Origin and Development.* San Francisco: Ignatius Press, 1982.

Chesterton, G. K. *Saint Thomas Aquinas.* San Francisco: Ignatius Press, 1986.

Chin, Gabriel. "Segregation's Last Stronghold: Discrimination and the Constitutional Law of Immigration." *UCLA Law Review* 46 (1998): 1–74.

Chin, Gabriel, and Richard Holmes. "Effective Assistance of Counsel and the Consequences of Guilty Pleas." *Cornell Law Review* 87 (2002): 697–742.

Chroust, Anton-Hermann. "Hugo Grotius and the Scholastic Natural Law Tradition." *New Scholasticism* 17 (1943): 101–33.

Cicero, Marcus T. *De Re Publica, De Legibus.* Translated by Clinton Walker Keyes. Cambridge: Harvard University Press, 1928.

Clark, Brietta. "When Free Exercise Exemptions Undermine Religious Liberty and the Liberty of Conscience: A Case Study of the Catholic Hospital Conflict." *Oregon Law Review* 82 (2003): 625–93.

Clark, Robert C. *Corporate Law.* Boston: Little, Brown, 1986.

Cochran, Robert F., Jr. "Tort Law and Intermediate Communities: Calvinist and Catholic Insights." In *Christian Perspectives on Legal Thought,* edited by Michael McConnell, Robert F. Cochran, Jr., and Angela C. Carmella. New Haven: Yale University Press, 2001.

Code of Canon Law (1989).

Coleman, John A. *One Hundred Years of Catholic Social Thought.* Maryknoll, NY: Orbis Books, 1991.

———. "Pluralism and the Retrieval of a Catholic Sense of the Common Good." Speech at Loyola Marymount University, Los Angeles, May 12–14, 2000, Commonweal Symposium.

Collett, Teresa Stanton. "Professional versus Moral Duty: Accepting Appointments in Unjust Civil Cases." *Wake Forest Law Review* 32 (1997): 635–70.

Congregation for the Doctrine of the Faith. *Instruction on Christian Freedom and Liberation* (1986). http://www.vatican.va/roman_curia/congregations/cfaith/documents/rc_con_cfaith_doc_19860322_freedom-liberation_en.html, 1986.

Cook, Douglas H. "Negligence or Strict Liability? A Study in Biblical Tort Law." *Whittier Law Review* 13 (1992): 1–15.

Cooper, John M. "Aristotle on the Forms of Friendship." *Review of Metaphysics* 30 (1977): 619.

Copleston, Frederick. *A History of Philosophy.* Vol. 1. New York: Doubleday, 1993.

Cornell, Drucilla. "Fatherhood and Its Discontents: Men, Patriarchy and Freedom." In *Lost Fathers: The Politics of Fatherlessness in America,* edited by Cynthia R. Daniels. New York: St. Martin's Press, 1998.

Coughlin, John J. "Canonical Equity." *Studia Canonica* 30 (1996): 403–35.

———. "Law and Theology: Reflections on What It Means to Be Human from a Franciscan Perspective." *St. John's Law Review* 74 (2000): 609–28.

Coulanges, Fustel des. *The Ancient City.* Baltimore: Johns Hopkins University Press, 1980.

Cover, Robert. "Nomos and Narrative." In *Narrative, Violence, and the Law,* edited by

Martha Minow, Michael Ryan, and Austin Sarat. Ann Arbor: University of Michigan Press, 1995.

Cover, Robert, Judith Resnik, and Owen M. Fiss. *Procedure.* New York: Foundation Press, 1988.

Cronin, John F. *Catholic Social Principles.* Milwaukee: Bruce, 1950.

Crossette, Barbara. "Turner Picks State Department Official to Allocate UN Fund." *International Herald Tribune* (21 November 1997): 4.

Curran, Charles E. *Directions in Catholic Social Ethics.* Notre Dame, IN: University of Notre Dame Press, 1985.

Dalberg-Acton, John E. E. *Essays in Religion, Politics, and Morality.* Indianapolis: Liberty Classics, 1988.

Dalton, Clare, and Elizabeth M. Schneider. *Battered Women and the Law.* New York: Foundation Press, 2001.

Dangerfield, George. *The Strange Death of Liberal England.* New York: Capricorn Books, 1935.

Demsetz, Harold. "Toward a Theory of Property Rights." *American Economic Review* 57 (1967): 347–59.

Dickinson, John. *Administrative Justice and the Supremacy of Law.* Cambridge: Harvard University Press, 1959.

Dieter, Richard C. "Ethical Choices for Attorneys Whose Clients Elect Execution." *Georgetown Journal of Legal Ethics* 3 (1990): 799–820.

Dukeminier, Jesse, and James E. Krier. *Property.* 5th ed. New York: Aspen, 2002.

Dulles, Avery. *The New World of Faith.* Huntington, IN: Our Sunday Visitor Publishing Division, 2000.

Duncan, Kyle. "Secularism's Laws: State Blaine Amendments and Religious Persecution." *Fordham Law Review* 72 (2003): 493–593.

Dutile, Ferdinand N. "A Catholic University Maybe, but a Catholic Law School?" In *The Challenge and the Promise of a Catholic University,* edited by Theodore M. Hesburgh. Notre Dame, IN: University of Notre Dame Press, 1994.

Dworkin, Ronald. *A Matter of Principle.* Cambridge: Harvard University Press, 1985.

Dwyer, James G. *Religious Schools v. Children's Rights.* Ithaca, NY: Cornell University Press, 1998.

———. "School Vouchers: Inviting the Public into the Religious Square." *William and Mary Law Review* 42 (2001): 963–1006.

———. *Vouchers within Reason: A Child-Centered Approach to Education Reform.* Ithaca, NY: Cornell University Press, 2001.

Dwyer, Jim, Barry Scheck, and Peter Neufeld. *Actual Innocence: Five Days to Execution and Other Dispatches from the Wrongly Convicted.* New York: Doubleday, 2000.

Easterbrook, Frank H., and Daniel R. Fischel. "Contract and Fiduciary Duty." *Journal of Law and Economics* 36 (1993): 425–46.

———. *The Economic Structure of Corporate Law.* Cambridge: Harvard University Press, 1991.

Easterbrook, Gregg. "The Case for Sprawl." *New Republic* (15 March 1999): 18–21.

Elshtain, Jean B. "The Dignity of the Human Person and the Idea of Human Rights: Four Inquiries." *Journal of Law and Religion* 14 (1999/2000): 53–65.

———. "Catholic Social Thought, the City, and Liberal America." In *Catholicism, Liberalism, and Communitarianism: The Catholic Intellectual Tradition and the Moral*

Foundations of Democracy, edited by Kenneth L. Grasso, Gerard V. Bradley, and Robert P. Hunt. New York: Rowan and Littlefield, 1995.

Ely, John H. *Democracy and Distrust: A Theory of Judicial Review*. Cambridge: Harvard University Press, 1980.

Epstein, Richard A. "In Defense of the Contract at Will." *University of Chicago Law Review* 51 (1984): 947–82.

———. "Possession as the Root of Title." *Georgia Law Review* 13 (1979): 1221–43.

———. "A Theory of Strict Liability." *Journal of Legal Studies* 2 (1973): 151–204.

Ewing, Reid, et al. Smart Growth America. *Measuring Sprawl and Its Impact* (2002). http://www.smartgrowthamerica.org/sprawlindex/MeasuringSprawl.PDF.

Farand, Max. *The Records of the Federal Convention of 1787.* Vol. 1. New Haven: Yale University Press, 1966.

Farnsworth, E. A. *Contracts*. 3rd ed. New York: Aspen Publishers, 1999.

Fejfar, Anthony J. "In Search of Reality: A Critical Realist Critique of John Rawls' *A Theory of Justice*." *St. Louis University Public Law Review* 9 (1990): 227–310.

Finnis, John. *Aquinas: Moral, Political, and Legal Theory*. Oxford: Oxford University Press, 1998.

———. *Moral Absolutes*. Washington, DC: Catholic University of America Press, 1991.

———. *Natural Law and Natural Rights*. Oxford: Clarendon Press, 1980.

FitzGibbon, Scott. "The Failure of the Freedom-Based and Utilitarian Arguments for Assisted Suicide." *American Journal of Jurisprudence* 42 (1997): 211–61.

———. "Fiduciary Relationships Are Not Contracts." *Marquette Law Review* 82 (1999): 303–53.

Flanagan, Owen. *Varieties of Moral Personality*. Cambridge: Harvard University Press, 1991.

Fleming, Thomas. *The Politics of Human Nature*. New Brunswick: Transaction Publishers, 1988.

Foot, Philippa. "Utilitarianism and the Virtues." In *Consequentialism and Its Critics*, edited by Samuel Scheffler. Oxford: Oxford University Press, 1988.

Ford, Henry. *My Life and Work*. Kila, MT: Kessinger, 1922.

Fortin, Earnest. *Human Rights, Virtue, and the Common Good*. Edited by J. Brian Benestad. Lanham, MD: Rowman and Littlefield, 1996.

Foster, Dave Ruel. "The Implications of *Fides et Ratio* for Catholic Universities." In *The Two Wings of Catholic Thought: Essays on Fides et Ratio*, edited by Dave R. Foster and Joseph W. Koterski. Washington, DC: The Catholic University of America Press, 2003.

Fox-Genovese, Elizabeth. "Thoughts on the History of the Family." In *The Family, Civil Society, and the State*, edited by Christopher Wolfe. Lanham, MD: Rowman and Littlefield, 1998.

Frankena, William F. *Ethics*. Englewood Cliffs, NJ: Prentice-Hall, 1973.

Frankfurt, Harry. "Freedom of the Will and the Concept of a Person." *Journal of Philosophy* 68 (1971): 5–20.

Frey, William H. *Melting Pot Suburbs: A Census 2000 Study of Suburban Diversity*. Washington, DC: Brookings Institution, 2001.

Fried, Charles. "The Value of Life." *Harvard Law Review* 82 (1969): 1415–37.

Frug, Gerald E. *City Making: Building Communities without Building Walls*. Princeton: Princeton University Press, 1999.

Fuller, Lon L. *The Morality of Law*. New Haven, CT: Yale University Press, 1964.

———. "Reply to Critics." In *The Morality of Law*. 2nd ed. New Haven, CT: Yale University Press, 1969.

Gamwell, Franklin I. *The Meaning of Religious Freedom*. Albany: State University of New York Press, 1995.

Gardels, Nathan. "An Interview with Czeslaw Milosz." *N.Y. Review of Books* (20 February 1986): 34.

Garnett, Richard W. "Sectarian Reflections on Lawyers' Ethics and Death Row Volunteers." *Notre Dame Law Review* 77 (2002): 795–829.

———. "Taking Pierce Seriously: The Family, Religious Education, and Harm to Children." *Notre Dame Law Review* 76 (2000): 109–46.

Garvey, George. "A Catholic Social Teaching Critique of Law and Economics." In *Christian Perspectives on Legal Thought*, edited by Michael McConnell, Robert F. Cochran Jr., and Angela Carmella. New Haven: Yale University Press, 2001.

Gautier, Mary L. "Church Attendance and Religious Belief in Postcommunist Societies." *Journal for the Scientific Study of Religion* 36 (1977): 289–96.

Geertz, Clifford. "The Struggle for the Real." In *Islam Observed: Religious Development in Morocco and Indonesia*. Chicago: University of Chicago Press, 2004.

George, Robert P. *In Defense of Natural Law*. Oxford: Clarendon Press, 1999.

———. *Making Men Moral: Civil Liberties and Public Morality*. Oxford: Clarendon Press, 1993.

———. "Natural Law Ethics." In *A Companion to Philosophy of Religion*, edited by Philip L. Quinn and Charles Taliaferro. Oxford: Blackwell Publishers, 1997.

Gilles, Stephen G. "The Invisible Hand Formula." *Virginia Law Review* 80 (1994): 1015–54.

Gilson, Etienne. *The Spirit of Medieval Philosophy*. New York: Charles Scribner's Sons, 1991.

Giussani, Luigi. *The Religious Sense*. Montreal: McGill-Queens University Press, 1997.

Glendon, Mary A. *Abortion and Divorce in Western Law: American Failures, European Challenges*. Cambridge: Harvard University Press, 1987.

———. *The New Family and the New Property*. Toronto: Butterworth's, 1981.

———. *Rights Talk: The Impoverishment of Political Discourse*. New York: Free Press, 1991.

———. *The Transformation of Family Law, State Law, and Family in the United States and Western Europe*. Chicago: University of Chicago Press, 1989.

———. *A World Made New: Eleanor Roosevelt and the Universal Declaration of Human Rights*. New York: Random House, 2001.

Glendon, Mary A., Michael Gordon, and Christopher Osakwe. *Comparative Legal Traditions*. 2nd ed. St. Paul, MN: West, 1994.

Goldstein, Joseph. "For Harold Lasswell: Some Reflections on Human Dignity, Entrapment, Informed Consent, and the Plea Bargain." *Yale Law Journal* 84 (1975): 683–95.

Gordley, James. "Contract Law in the Aristotelian Tradition." In *The Theory of Contract Law: New Essays*, edited by P. Benson. Cambridge: Cambridge University Press, 2001.

———. "Equality in Exchange." *California Law Review* 69 (1981): 1587–1656.

———. "Myths of the French Civil Code." *American Journal of Comparative Law* 42 (1994): 459–505.

———. *The Philosophical Origins of Modern Contract Doctrine*. Oxford: Clarendon Press, 1991.

Gordon, Peter, and Harry Richardson. "Critiquing Sprawl's Critics." *Cato Institute.* 20 June 2003. http://www.cato.org/pubs/pas/pa-365es.html.

———. "Defending Urban Sprawl." *Public Interest* 139 (Spring 2000): 65–73.

Gray, John. *Liberalism.* 2d ed. Minneapolis: University of Minnesota Press, 1995.

Green, Michael D. "The Place of Workers in Corporate Law." *Boston College Law Review* 39 (1998): 283–327.

———. "The Schizophrenia of Risk-Benefit Analysis in Design Defect Litigation." *Vanderbilt Law Review* 48 (1995): 609–29.

Greenfield, Kent. "Using Behavioral Economics to Show the Power and Efficiency of Corporate Law as a Regulatory Tool." Boston College of Law and Economics Working Paper No. 01-02. 8 July 2001. http://papers.ssrn.com/sol3/papers.cfm?abstract_id=276168 (17 June 2003).

Gregory of Nyssa. *De Hominis Opificio.*

Griffith, Elwin. "The Road between the Section 212(c) Waiver and Cancellation of Removal under 240A of the Immigration and Nationality Act—The Impact of the 1996 Reform Legislation." *Georgetown Immigration Law Journal* 12 (1997): 65–124.

Grisez, Germain. "Moral Absolutes: A Critique of the View of Josef Fuchs, S.J." *Anthropos* 176 (1985): 155–201.

———. "Practical Principles, Moral Truth, and Ultimate Ends." *American Journal of Jurisprudence* 32 (1987): 99.

———. *The Way of the Lord Jesus.* Vol. 1: *Christian Moral Principles.* Chicago: Franciscan Herald Press, 1983.

———. *The Way of the Lord Jesus.* Vol. 3: *Difficult Moral Questions.* Chicago: Franciscan Press, 1997.

Grisez, Germain, Joseph M. Boyle Jr., and Olaf Tollefsen. *Free Choice: A Self-Referential Argument.* South Bend, IN: University of Notre Dame Press, 1976.

Grisham, John. *The Chamber.* New York: Island Books, 1994.

Grotius, Hugo. *De iure belli ac pacis libri tres.* Edited by B. J. A. de Kanter-van Ketting Tromp. Leiden, 1939.

Gunn, Giles. *Beyond Solidarity: Pragmatism and Difference in a Globalized World.* Chicago: University of Chicago Press, 2001.

Hamburger, Philip. *Separation of Church and State.* Cambridge: Harvard University Press, 2002.

Hamilton, Alexander, James Madison, and John Jay. *The Federalist Papers.* Edited by Clinton Rossiter. New York: New American Library, 1961.

Harnsberger, Caroline T., ed. *A Treasury of Presidential Quotations.* Chicago: Follett, 1964.

Harrington, C. L. "A Community Divided: Defense Attorneys and the Ethics of Death-Row Volunteering." *Law and Social Inquiry* 25 (2000): 849–81.

Harsanyi, John. "Rule Utilitarianism and Decision Theory." *Erkenntnis* 11 (1977): 25–53.

Hart, H. L. A. *The Concept of Law.* Oxford: Clarendon Press, 1961.

———. *Essays on Bentham.* Oxford: Clarendon Press, 1983.

———. "Murder and the Principles of Punishment." In *Punishment and Responsibility: Essays in the Philosophy of Law.* Oxford: Oxford University Press, 1968.

———. "Review of *The Morality of Law,* by Lon L. Fuller." *Harvard Law Review* 78 (1965): 1281–96.

Harvey, James S. "Owner as Manager, Extended Horizons and the Family Firm." *International Journal of Economics of Business* 6 (1999): 41–55.

Harvey, John F. *The Truth about Homosexuality.* San Francisco: Ignatius Press, 1996.

Hasson, Kevin. *God and Man at the Supreme Court: Rethinking Religion in Public Life.* http://www.leaderu.com/socialsciences/hasson.html.

Havel, Václav. *Living in Truth.* London: Faber and Faber, 1987.

Hayek, F. A. *Capitalism and the Historians.* Chicago: University of Chicago Press, 1974.

———. *The Fatal Conceit: The Errors of Socialism.* Chicago: University of Chicago, 1988.

———. "The Uses of Knowledge in Society." In *Individualism and the Economic Order.* Chicago: Gateway, 1972.

Hazlitt, Henry. *The Conquest of Poverty.* New Rochelle, NY: Arlington House, 1973.

Henderson, James A. "Judicial Review of Manufacturers' Conscious Design Choices: The Limits of Adjudication." *Columbia Law Review* 73 (1973): 1531–78.

Henderson, James A., and Aaron D. Twerski. "Achieving Consensus on Defective Product Design." *Cornell Law Review* 83 (1998): 867–920.

———. "Intuition and Technology in Product Design Litigation: An Essay on Proximate Causation." *Georgia Law Journal* 88 (2000): 659–89.

Henkin, Louis. "Human Rights: Ideology and Aspiration, Reality and Prospect." In *Realizing Human Rights,* edited by S. Power and G. Allison. New York: St. Martin's Press, 2000.

Hepple, Bob, ed. *The Making of Labour Law in Europe: A Comparative Study of Nine Countries up to 1945.* London: Mansell, 1986.

Higgins, George G. *Voluntarism in Organized Labor in the United States, 1930–1940.* N.p.: Arno, 1960.

Himmelfarb, Gertrude. *Lord Acton: A Study in Conscience and Politics.* Chicago: University of Chicago Press, 1952.

———. *One Nation, Two Cultures.* New York: Random House Vintage Books, 2001.

History of Political Philosophy. 3rd ed. Edited by Leo Strauss and Joseph Cropsey. Chicago: University of Chicago Press, 1987.

Hittinger, Russell. *The First Grace: Rediscovering the Natural Law in a Post-Christian World.* Wilmington, DE: ISI Books, 2003.

Hoagland, Victor, C.P. *The Book of Saints.* Farmingdale, NY: Reginia Press, 1986.

Hobbes, Thomas. *Leviathan.* Edited by Michael Oakeshott. Oxford: Blackwell, 1957.

———. *Leviathan.* Edited by C. B. MacPherson. New York: Penguin Books, 1981.

Hobhouse, L. T. *Liberalism.* London: Williams and Norgate, 1911.

Hoffman, Lawrence. "Response to Joseph Allegretti: The Relevance of Religion to a Lawyer's Work." *Fordham Law Review* 66 (1998): 1157–65.

Hollenbach, David. *The Common Good and Christian Ethics.* Cambridge: Cambridge University Press, 2002.

Hollis, Martin, and Robert Sugden. "Rationality in Action." *Mind* 102 (1993): 1–28.

Holmes, Oliver W., Jr. *The Common Law.* Cambridge: Belknap Press of Harvard University Press, 1951."The Path of the Law."

———. *Harvard Law Review* 10 (1897): 457–78.

Horwitz, Morton J. *The Transformation of American Law 1790–1860.* Cambridge: Harvard University Press, 1977.

Hume, David. *A Treatise on Human Nature.* Edited by David Fate Norton and Mary J. Norton. Oxford: Oxford University Press, 2000.

In re Luis Manuel Ramos, I and N 23 (Dec. 2002): 336.

International Theological Commission. "The Use of Force in the Service of Truth." In

Memory and Reconciliation: The Church and the Faults of the Past. http://www.vatican. va/roman_curia/congregations/cfaith/cti_documents/rc_con_cfaith_doc_20000307_ memory-reconc-itc_en.html, 1999.

Jacobs, Antoine. "Collective Self-Regulation." In *The Making of Labour Law in Europe: A Comparative Study of Nine Countries,* edited by Bob Hepple. London: Mansell, 1986.

Jahsmann, Allan H., and Martin P. Simon. *More Little Visits with God.* St. Louis: Concordia Publishing House, 1961.

Jay, John, James Madison, and Alexander Hamilton. *The Federalist Papers.* Edited by Clinton Rossiter. New York: New American Library, 1961.

Jefferson, Thomas. "A Bill for Establishing Religious Freedom." In *The Portable Thomas Jefferson,* edited by Merrill D. Peterson. New York: Viking Press, 1975.

———. "Notes on the State of Virginia." 1787. http://xroads.virginia.edu/~hyper/ jefferson/ch18.html.

John XXIII (Pope). *Mater et magistra.* Encyclical Letter, 15 May 1961. http://www.vatican. va/holy_father/john_xxiii/encyclicals/documents/hf_j-xxiii_enc_15051961_mater_ en.html, 1961.

———. *Pacem in terris.* Encyclical Letter, 11 April 1963. http://www.vatican.va/holy_ father/john_xxiii/encyclicals/documents/hf_j-xxiii_enc_11041963_pacem_en.html, 1963.

John Paul II (Pope). "Address of John Paul II to H.E. Mrs. Corine (Lindy) Claiborne Boggs: New Ambassador of the United States of America to the Holy See—16 December 1997." http://www.vatican.va/holy_father/john_paul_ii/speeches/1997/ december/documents/hf_jp-ii_spe_19971216_ambassador-usa_en.html, 1997.

———. Ad Limina Address to the Bishops of Texas, Oklahoma, and Arkansas. 06 June 1998. http://www.cin.org/jp2/jp980606.html, 1998.

———. *Centesimus annus.* Encyclical Letter, 01 May 1991. http://www.vatican.va/ holy_father/john_paul_ii/encyclicals/documents/hf_jp-ii_enc_01051991_centesimus- annus_en.html.

———. [*Centesimus annus*] *On the Hundredth Anniversary of Rerum Novarum.* Boston: Pauline Books and Media, 1991.

———. "Departing Remarks from Detroit—September 19, 1987." 16 June 2003. http:// www.priestsforlife.org/magisterium/87-09-19popejohnpaulusa.htm (16 June 2003).

———. "Departing Remarks from New York Visit—8 October 1995." http://www. catholic-forum.com/saints/pope0264iw.htm (16 June 2003).

———. *Ecclesia in America.* Post-Synodal Exhortation, 22 January 1999. http://www. vatican.va/holy_father/john_paul_ii/apost_exhortations/documents/hf_jpii_exh_ 22011999_ecclesia-in-america_en.html, 1999.

———. *The Encyclicals of John Paul II.* Edited by J. Michael Miller. Huntington, IN: Our Sunday Visitor, 1996.

———. *Evangelium vitae.* Encyclical Letter, 25 March 1995. http://www.vatican.va/ holy_father/john_paul_ii/encyclicals/documents/hf_jp-ii_enc_25031995_evangelium- vitae_en.html.

———. *Ex corde ecclesiae.* Apostolic Constitution, 15 August 1990. http://www.vatican. va/holy_father/john_paul_ii/apost_constitutions/documents/hf_jp-ii_apc_15081990_ ex-corde-ecclesiae_en.html.

———. [*Ex corde ecclesiae*] *On Catholic Universities.* Washington, DC: United States Catholic Conference, 1990.

———. *Fides et ratio.* Encyclical Letter, 14 September 1998. http://www.vatican.va/ holy_father/john_paul_ii/encyclicals/documents/hf_jp-ii_enc_15101998_fides-et-ratio_en.html.

———. [*Fides et ratio*] *On the Relationship between Faith and Reason.* Boston: Pauline Books and Media, 1998.

———. *Homily for the Day of Pardon.* 12 March 2000. http://www.vatican.va/holy_ father/john_paul_ii/homilies/documents/hf_jp-ii_hom_20000312_pardon_en.html, 2000.

———. "John Paul II on the American Experiment." *First Things* 82 (1998): 36–37.

———. *Laborem exercens.* Encyclical Letter, 14 September 1981. http://www.vatican.va/ edocs/ENG0217/_INDEX.HTM.

———. *Letter of the Holy Father to Women in Advance of the United Nations Conference on Women.* Beijing, 1995.

———. *Novo millennio ineunte.* Apostolic Letter, 6 January 2001. http://www.vatican. va/holy_father/john_paul_ii/apost_letters/documents/hf_jp-ii_apl_20010106_novo-millennio-ineunte_en.html.

———. *Redemptor hominis.* Encyclical Letter, 4 March 1979. http://www.vatican.va/ holy_father/john_paul_ii/encyclicals/documents/hf_jp-ii_enc_04031979_redemptor-hominis_en.html.

———. *Sollicitudo rei socialis.* Encyclical Letter, 30 December 1987. http://www. vatican.va/holy_father/john_paul_ii/encyclicals/documents/hf_jp-ii_enc_30121987_ sollicitudo-rei-socialis_en.html.

———. [*Sollicitudo rei socialis*] "Litterae Encylicae *Sollicitudo rei socialis,* 32 (die 30 m. decembris a. 1987)." *Acta Apostolicae Sedis* 80 (1988): 545.

———. *The Theology of the Body: Human Love in the Divine Plan.* Boston: Pauline Books and Media, 1997.

———. *Veritatis splendor.* Encyclical Letter, 6 August 1993. http://www.vatican.va/ holy_father/john_paul_ii/encyclicals/documents/hf_jp-ii_enc_06081993_veritatis-splendor_en.html.

———. *Veritatis splendor. Acta Apostolicae Sedis* 85 (1993): 1133–1228.

———. [*Veritatis Splendor*] *The Splendor of Truth.* Boston: Pauline Books and Media, 1993.

Johnson, Kevin. "Los Olvidados: Images of the Immigrant, Political Power of Noncitizens, and Immigration Law and Enforcement." *Brigham Young University Law Review* (1993): 1139–1241.

———. "Open Borders." *UCLA Law Review* 51 (2003): 193–265.

Johnson, Phillip. *A Reason in the Balance.* Downers Grove, IL: InterVarsity Press 1995.

Jolls, Christine. "A Behavioral Approach to Law and Economics." *Stanford Law Review* 50 (1998): 1471–1550.

Keating, Gregory C. "Pressing Precaution beyond the Point of Cost-Justification." *Vanderbilt Law Review* 56 (2003): 653–748.

Keeton, G., and L. Sheridan. *Equity.* 3rd ed. N.p.: 1987.

Kekes, John. *Against Liberalism.* Ithaca, NY: Cornell University Press, 1997.

Kelly, Alicia B. "The Marital Partnership Pretense and Career Assets: The Ascendancy of Self over the Marital Community." *Boston University Law Review* 81 (2001): 59–125.

Kelsen, Hans. *General Theory of Law and State.* Translated by Anders Wedberg. New York: Russell and Russell, 1961.

———. "The Pure Theory of Law and Analytical Jurisprudence." *Harvard Law Review* 55 (1941): 44–70.

Kohler, Thomas. "Models of Worker Participation: The Uncertain Significance of Section 8(a)(2)." *Boston College Law Review* 27 (1986): 499–551.

———. "The Notion of Solidarity and the Secret History of American Labor Law." *Buffalo Law Review* 53 (2005): 883.

Komonchak, Joseph A. "Subsidiarity in the Church: The State of the Question." *Jurist* 48 (1988): 298–344.

Koniak, Susan P. "The Law between the Bar and the State." *North Carolina Law Review* 70 (1992): 1389–1487.

Kraynak, Robert. *Christian Faith and Modern Democracy*. Notre Dame, IN: University of Notre Dame Press, 2001.

Kressel, Kenneth, et al. "A Provisional Typology of Lawyer Attitudes towards Divorce Practice: Gladiators, Advocates, Counselors and Journeyman." In *Readings in Family Law*, edited by Frederica K. Lombard. New York: Foundation Press, 1990.

Kuhn, Thomas S. *The Structure of Scientific Revolutions*. 2nd ed. Chicago: University of Chicago Press, 1970.

Kuyper, Abraham. *Lectures on Calvinism*. Grand Rapids, MI: Eerdmans, 1943.

———. "Sphere Sovereignty." Translated by George Kamp. In *Abraham Kuyper: A Centennial Reader*, edited by James D. Bratt. Grand Rapids, MI: Eerdmans, 1998.

Kysar, Douglas A. "The Expectations of Consumers." *Columbia Law Review* 103 (2003): 1700, 1700–1790.

Lacey, Robert. *Ford: The Men and the Machine*. Boston: Little Brown, 1986.

Langbein, John H. "The Contractarian Basis of the Law of Trusts." *Yale Law Journal* 105 (1995): 630–75.

Langevoort, Donald C. "Behavioral Theories of Judgment and Decision Making in Legal Scholarship: A Literature Review." *Vanderbilt Law Review* 51 (1998): 1499–1540.

Lasch, Christopher. *The Revolt of the Elites*. New York: W. W. Norton, 1995.

Lee, Kevin. "The Collapse of the Fact/Value Dichotomy: A Brief for Catholic Legal Scholars." *Journal of Catholic Social Thought* 1 (2004): 685–706.

Lee, Randy. "Faith through Lawyering: Finding and Doing What Is Mine to Do." *Regent Law Review* 11 (1998–99): 71–135.

———. "Lawyers and the Uncommon Good: Navigating and Transcending the Gray." *South Texas Law Review* 40 (1999): 207–26.

———. "A Look at God, Feminism, and Tort Law." *Marquette Law Review* 75 (1992): 369–408.

———. "Reflections on a Rose in Its Sixth Season: A Review of H. Jefferson Powell's *The Moral Tradition of American Constitutionalism*." *Creighton Law Review* 32 (1999): 1205–62.

Leff, Arthur. "Unspeakable Ethics, Unnatural Law." *Duke Law Journal* (1979): 1229–49.

Leo XIII (Pope). *Libertas praestantissimum*. Encyclical Letter, 20 June 1888. http://www.vatican.va/holy_father/leo_xiii/encyclicals/documents/hf_l-xiii_enc_20061888_libertas_en.html, 1888.

———. "Of New Things." In *The Papal Encyclicals in Their Historical Context*, edited and reprinted by Anne Fremantle. New York: New American Library/Mentor, 1956.

———. *Rerum novarum*. Encyclical Letter, 15 May 1891. http://www.vatican.va/holy_father/leo_xiii/encyclicals/documents/hf_l-xiii_enc_15051891_rerum-novarum_en.html, 1891.

Lessius, Leonardus. *De iustitia et iure, ceterique virtutibus cardinalis libri quatuor.* Paris, 1628.

Lester, Anthony. "The Overseas Trade in the American Bill of Rights." *Columbia Law Review* 88 (1988): 537–61.

Levine, Samuel. "Playing God: An Essay on, Law, Philosophy, and American Capital Punishment." *New Mexico Law Review* 31 (2001): 277–97.

Levinson, Meira. *The Demands of Liberal Education.* Oxford: Oxford University Press, 1999.

Lewis, C. S. *The Weight of Glory.* 2nd rev. ed. New York: MacMillan, 1980.

Lewontin, Timothy. *Parsons' Mill.* Hanover, NH: University Press of New England, 1989.

Lincoln, Abraham. *The Collected Works of Abraham Lincoln.* Vol. 2. Edited by Roy P. Basler. New Brunswick: Rutgers University Press, 1953.

Lisska, Anthony. *Aquinas's Theory of Natural Law: An Analytic Reconstruction.* Oxford: Oxford University Press, 1996.

Locke, John. "Second Treatise on Government." In *An Essay Concerning the True, Original, and End of Civil Government.* Edited by Peter Laslett. Cambridge: Cambridge University Press, 1988.

———. *Two Treatises of Government and a Letter Concerning Toleration.* New Haven: Yale University Press, 2003.

Luban, David. *Lawyers and Justice: An Ethical Study.* Princeton: Princeton University Press, 1988.

———. "The Social Responsibilities of Lawyers: A Green Perspective." *George Washington Law Review* 63 (1995): 955–83.

Lubich, Chiara. *Essential Writings.* Hyde Park, N.Y.: New City Press, 2007.

———. "Spiritualità dell'unità e vita trinitaria" [The Sprituality of Unity and Trinitarian Life]. *Nuova Umanità* 26 (2004).

———. "Toward a Theology and Philosophy of Unity." In *An Introduction to the Abba School: Conversations from the Focolare's Interdisciplinary Study Center.* Hyde Park, NY: New City Press, 2002.

MacCormick, Neil. "Natural Law and the Separation of Law and Morals." In *Natural Law Theory: Contemporary Essays,* edited by Robert P. George. Oxford: Clarendon Press, 1992.

MacIntyre, Alasdair. *After Virtue: A Study in Moral Theory.* 2d ed. Notre Dame, IN: University of Notre Dame Press, 1984.

———. *Dependent Rational Animals: Why Human Beings Need the Virtues.* Chicago: Open Court, 2001.

———. "How We Can Learn What 'Veritatis Splendor' Has to Teach." In *Veritatis Splendor and the Renewal of Moral Theology,* edited by J. A. DiNoia, O.P. and Romanus Cesario, O.P. Chicago: Midwest Theological Forum, 1999.

Madison, James. "Memorial and Remonstrance against Religious Assessments." 1785. http://www.law.ou.edu/hist/remon.html.

———. "Speech of June 20, 1788." In *The Debates in the Several State Conventions,* edited by Jonathan Elliott. Vol. 3. Philadelphia: Lippincott, 1836.

Madison, James, Alexander Hamilton, and John Jay. *The Federalist Papers.* Edited by Clinton Rossiter. New York: New American Library, 1961.

Mailer, Norman. *The Executioner's Song.* Boston: Little, Brown, 1979.

Maitland, F. *Equity.* 2nd ed. N.p.: 1936.

Malik, Charles. "Introduction." In O. Frederick Nolde, *Free and Equal: Human Rights in Ecumenical Perspective*. Geneva: World Council of Churches, 1968.

———. "The More Important Speeches and Interventions of Charles Malik." Papers of Charles Malik, Library of Congress, Manuscript Division.

Maritain, Jacques. *Christianity and Democracy*. San Francisco: Ignatius Press, 1944.

———. "Introduction." In *Human Rights: Comments and Interpretation*. Edited by UNESCO. New York: Wingate, 1949.

———. *The Person and the Common Good*. Translated by John Fitzgerald. Notre Dame, IN: Notre Dame University Press, 1966.

Marsden, George M. *The Outrageous Idea of Christian Scholarship*. Oxford: Oxford University Press, 1998.

Marshall, Bruce D. *Trinity and Truth*. Edited by Bruce D. Marshall and Daniel W. Hardy. Cambridge: Cambridge University Press, 2003.

McClay, Wilfred M. "The Continuing Irony of American History." *First Things* 120 (February 2002): 20–25.

McConnell, Michael, Robert Cochran Jr., and Angela Carmella, eds. *Christian Perspectives on Legal Thought*. New Haven, CT: Yale University Press, 2001.

McKeon, Richard, ed. *The Basic Works of Aristotle*. New York: Random House Books, 1941.

———. "The Philosophic Bases and Material Circumstances of the Rights of Man." In *Human Rights: Comments and Interpretations*. New York: Columbia University Press, 1949.

Meilaender, Gilbert. "Still Waiting for Benedict." *First Things* 96 (October 1999): 48–55.

Melina, Livio. "Desire for Happiness and the Commandments in the First Chapter of 'Veritatis Splendor.'" In *Veritatis Splendor and the Renewal of Moral Theology,* edited by J. A. DiNoia, O.P., and Romanus Cesario, O.P. Chicago: Midwest Theological Forum, 1999.

Mello, Michael. "A Letter on a Lawyer's Life of Death." *South Texas Law Review* 38 (1997): 121–224.

———. *The United State v. Theodore John Kaczinski: Ethics, Power, and the Invention of the Unabomber*. New York: Context Books, 1999.

Mello, Michael. "The Non-Trial of the Century: Representation of the Unabomber." *Vermont Law Review* 24 (2000): 417–535.

Messner, Johannes. *Social Ethics*. St. Louis: B. Herder, 1958.

Mill, John S. *Utilitarianism*. Edited by Samuel Gorovitz. Indianapolis, IN: Bobbs-Merrill, 1971.

Milosz, Czeslaw. "The Religious Imagination at 2000." *New Perspectives Quarterly* (Fall 1997): 32–37.

Minow, Martha. "All in the Family and in All Families: Membership, Loving and Owing." *West Virginia Law Review* 95 (winter 1992/1993): 275–332.

———. "Children's Studies: A Proposal." *Ohio State Law Journal* 57 (1996): 511–18.

———. "Learning from Experience: The Impact of Research about Family Support Programs on Public Policy." *University of Pennsylvania Law Review* 143 (1994): 221–52.

———. "The Welfare of Single Mothers and Their Children." *Connecticut Law Review* 26 (1994): 817–42.

Mises, Ludwig von. *Money, Method, and the Market Process*. Boston: Kluwer, 1990.

Mishel, Lawrence, and Jared Bernstein. *The State of Working America 1994-1995*. Armonk, NY: M. E. Sharpe, 1995.

Mitchell, Lawrence. "Death of Fiduciary Duty in Close Corporations." *University of Pennsylvania Law Review* 138 (1990): 1675–1731.

Molina, Ludovicus. *De iustitia et iure tractatus.* Venice, 1613.

Monsma, Stephen V. *Pursuing Justice in a Sinful World.* Grand Rapids, MI: Eerdmans, 1984.

More, Thomas. *Utopia.* Edited by George M. Logan and Robert M. Adams. New York: Cambridge University Press, 1989.

Morris, Aldon D. *The Origins of the Civil Rights Movement: Black Communities Organizing for Change.* New York: Free Press, 1984.

Morris, Charles R. *American Catholic: The Saints and Sinners Who Built America's Most Powerful Church.* New York: Random House Times Books, 1997.

Morsink, Johannes. *The Universal Declaration of Human Rights: Origins, Drafting, and Intent.* Philadelphia: University of Pennsylvania Press, 1999.

Mother Teresa. *One Heart Full of Love.* Edited by Jose L. Gonzalez-Balado. Ann Arbor, MI: Servant Publications, 1989.

———. *Words to Love by.* Edited by Frank J. Cunningham. Notre Dame, IN: Ave Maria Press, 1983.

Mueller, Franz H. *The Church and the Social Question.* Washington, DC: American Enterprise Institute, 1984.

Murray, John C. *We Hold These Truths: Catholic Reflections on the American Proposition.* New York: Sheed and Ward, 1960.

Neuhaus, Richard J. *Doing Well and Doing Good.* New York: Doubleday, 1992.

———. "The Liberalism of Pope John Paul II." *First Things* 73 (May 1997): 16–21.

———. "Proposing Democracy Anew." *First Things* 98 (December 1999): 68–88.

———. "The Two Politics of Election 2000." *First Things* 110 (February 2001): 57–76.

Neuman, Gerald. "Habeas Corpus, Executive Detention, and the Removal of Aliens." 98 *Columbia Law Review* 98 (1998): 961–1067.

Newcombe, Brent. (Comment) "Immigration Law and the Criminal Alien: A Comparison of Policies for Arbitrary Deportations of Legal Permanent Residents Convicted of Aggravated Felonies." *Oklahoma Law Review* 51 (1998): 697–725.

Newman, John H. *Grammar of Assent.* Garden City: Doubleday Image, 1955.

———. "Letter to the Duke of Norfolk." In *Newman and Gladstone: The Vatican Decrees,* edited by Alvan S. Ryan. Notre Dame, IN: University of Notre Dame Press, 1962.

Nisbet, Robert. *The Resent Age: Progress and Anarchy in Modern America.* New York, NY: Harper and Row, 1988.

Noonan, John T., Jr. "A Catholic Law School." *Notre Dame Law Review* 67 (1992): 1037–48.

———. *Contraception: A History of Its Treatment by the Catholic Theologians and Canonists.* Cambridge: Harvard University Press, 1965.

———. *Persons and Masks of the Law: Cardozo, Holmes, Jefferson and Wythe as Makers of the Masks.* New York: Farrar, Straus and Giroux, 1976.

———. *The Scholastic Analysis of Usury.* Cambridge: Harvard University Press, 1957.

Novak, Michael. "The Bishops and the Poor." *Commentary* (May 1985).

———. *Free Persons and the Common Good.* Lanham, MD: Madison Books, 1989.

———. *The Spirit of Democratic Capitalism.* Washington, DC: American Enterprise Institute, 1982.

Nozick, Robert. *Anarchy, State, and Utopia.* New York: Basic Books, 1974.

———. *Philosophical Explanations.* Cambridge: Belknap Press of Harvard University Press, 1981.

Nussbaum, C. "Flawed Foundations: The Philosophical Critique of a Particular Type of Economics." *University of Chicago Law Review* 64 (1997): 1197–1214.

Oakeshott, Michael. *Rationalism in Politics and Other Essays.* Indianapolis: LibertyPress, 1991.

O'Brien, David, and Thomas Shannon, eds. *Catholic Social Thought: The Documentary Heritage.* Maryknoll, NY: Orbis Books, 1995.

Olasky, Marvin. *The Tragedy of American Compassion.* Washington, DC: Regnery Gateway, 1992.

O'Neal, F., and R. Thompson. *Oppression of Minority Shareholders.* 2d ed. Eagan, MN: West Group, 1985.

Otis, James. "The Rights of the British Colonies." In *American Legal History: Cases and Materials,* edited by Kermit L. Hall, William M. Wiecek, and Paul Finkelman. Oxford: Oxford University Press, 1991.

Owen, David G. "The Moral Foundations of Products Liability Law: Toward First Principles." *Notre Dame Law Review* 68 (1993): 427–506.

Passerin d'Entrèves, Alexander. *Natural Law: An Introduction to Legal Philosophy.* New Brunswick, NJ: Transaction Publishers, 1994.

Paton, George W. *A Text-Book of Jurisprudence.* 4th ed. Edited by G. W. Patton and David P. Derham. Oxford: Oxford University Press, 1972.

Patrick, Michael. "Tell It to the Judge—Judicial Review of Immigration Decisions." *Immigration Briefings* 88-10 (Oct. 1988).

Paul VI (Pope). *Humanae vitae.* Encyclical Letter, 25 July 1968. http://www.vatican. va/holy_father/paul_vi/encyclicals/documents/hf_p-vi_enc_25071968_humanae-vitae_en.html, 1968.

———. "Litterae Encyclicae *Humane vitae,* 12 (die 25 m. iullius a. 1968)." *Acta Apostolicae Sedis* 60 (1968): 481–503.

———. *Octogesima adveniens.* Encyclical Letter, 14 May 1971. http://www.vatican. va/holy_father/paul_vi/apost_letters/documents/hf_p-vi_apl_19710514_octogesima-adveniens_en.html, 1971.

———. *Populorum progressio.* Encyclical Letter, 26 March 1967. http://www.vatican. va/holy_father/paul_vi/encyclicals/documents/hf_p-vi_enc_26031967_populorum_en.html, 1967.

Penrose, Roger. *The Emperor's New Mind: Concerning Computers, Minds, and the Laws of Physics.* New York: Viking-Penguin, 1990.

Pepper, Stephen. "The Lawyer's Amoral Ethical Role: A Defense, a Problem, and Some Possibilities." *American Bar Foundation Research Journal* (1986): 613–35.

Pieper, Josef. *In Defense of Philosophy.* San Francisco: Ignatius Press, 1995.

Pinckaers, Servais. *The Sources of Christian Ethics.* Washington, DC: The Catholic University of America Press, 1993.

Pius XI (Pope). *Quadragesimo anno.* Encyclical Letter, 15 May 1931. http://www.vatican. va/holy_father/pius_xi/encyclicals/documents/hf_p-xi_enc_19310515_quadragesimo-anno_en.html, 1931.

Pius XII (Pope). "1942 Christmas Address of Pope Pius XII." In *Principles for Peace—Selection from Papal Documents: Leo XIII to Pius XII,* edited by Harry Koenig. Washington, DC: National Catholic Welfare Conference, 1943.

———. *Summi pontificatus.* Encyclical Letter, 20 October 1939. http://www.vatican. va/holy_father/pius_xii/encyclicals/documents/hf_p-xii_enc_20101939_summi-pontificatus_en.html, 1939.

Plato. *Complete Works*. Edited by John M. Cooper. Indianapolis, IN: Hackett, 1997.

Polanyi, Michael. *Personal Knowledge*. New York: Harper Torchbooks, 1964.

Pontifical Council for Justice and Peace. *Compendium of the Social Doctrine of the Church*. Vatican: Libreria Editrice Vaticana, 2004.

Pontifical Council for the Family. *The Family and Human Rights*. Vatican: Pontifical Council for the Family, 1999.

Porter, Jean. *The Recovery of Virtue: The Relevance of Aquinas for Christian Ethics*. Louisville, KY: Westminster John Knox, 1990.

Posner, Richard A. *Economic Analysis of Law*. 4th ed. Boston: Little, Brown , 1992.

———. *Economic Analysis of Law*. 6th ed. New York: Aspen, 2003.

———. "Gratuitous Promises in Economics and Law." *Journal of Legal Studies* 6 (1977): 411–26.

———. *The Problematics of Moral and Legal Theory*. Cambridge: Harvard University Press, 1999.

———. *Sex and Reason*. Cambridge: Harvard University Press, 1992.

———. "A Theory of Negligence." *Journal of Legal Studies* 1 (1972): 29–96.

———. "Utilitarianism, Economics and Legal Theory." *Journal of Legal Studies* 9 (1979): 103–40.

Poticha, Shelley B. "Foreword to the Charter of the New Urbanism." In *The Charter of the New Urbanism*, edited by Michael Leccese and Kathleen McCormick. New York: McGraw-Hill Professional, 2000.

Pound, Roscoe. *The Lawyer from Antiquity to Modern Times*. St. Paul, MN: West, 1953.

Powell, H. J. *The Moral Tradition of American Constitutionalism: A Theological Interpretation*. Durham, NC: Duke University Press, 1993.

Price, A. W. *Price, Love and Friendship in Plato and Aristotle*. Oxford: Clarendon Press, 1989.

Prosser, William, W. Page Keeton, and Dan B. Dobbs. *Prosser and Keeton on the Law of Torts*. 5th ed. Eagan, MN: West Wadsworth, 1984.

Pufendorf, Samuel. *De iure naturae et gentium libri octo*. Amsterdam, 1688.

Putnam, Robert D. *Bowling Alone: The Collapse and Revival of American Community*. New York: Simon and Schuster, 2000.

Quinn, Kevin. "Viewing Health Care as a Common Good: Looking Beyond Political Liberalism." *Southern California Law Review* 73 (2000): 277–375.

Radin, Margaret J. *Contested Commodities: The Trouble with Trade in Sex, Children, Body Parts and Other Things*. Cambridge: Harvard University Press, 1996.

———. *Reinterpreting Property*. Chicago: University of Chicago Press, 1993.

Rahner, Karl. *The Trinity*. New York: Herder and Herder, 1970.

Ranouil, Valérie. *L'Autonomie de la volonté: naissance et évolution d'un concept*. Paris: Presses Universitaires de France, 1980.

Ratzinger, Joseph. "Some Reflections on Subjectivity, Christology, and the Church." In *Proclaiming the Truth of Jesus Christ, Papers from the Vallonbrosa Meeting*. Washington, DC: United States Catholic Conference, 2000.

Rausher, A. "Institutions of Social Organization: Family, Private Property, State." In *Principles of Catholic Social Teaching*, edited by David A. Boileau. Milwaukee, WI: Marquette University Press, 1998.

Rawls, John. *Political Liberalism*. New York: Columbia University Press, 1992.

———. *A Theory of Justice*. Cambridge: Belknap Press of Harvard University Press, 1971.

Raz, Joseph. *The Morality of Freedom*. Oxford: Oxford University Press, 1986.

———. "The Rule of Law and Its Virtue." *Law Quarterly Review* 93 (1977): 195–211.

Reich, Charles A. "The New Property." *Yale Law Journal* 73 (1964): 733–87.

———. "Property Law and the Economic Order: A Betrayal of Middle Americans and the Poor." *Chicago-Kent Law Review* 71 (1996): 817–23.

Richardson, James D. *A Compilation of the Messages and Papers of the Presidents 1789–1908.* New York: Bureau of National Literature, 1908.

Ritchie, David G. *Natural Rights: A Criticism of Some Political and Ethical Conceptions.* London: Allen and Unwin, 1895.

Robinson, Daniel N. *Philosophy of Psychology.* New York: Columbia University Press, 1985.

Rodgers, Charles, S.J. *Christian Social Witness and Teaching: The Catholic Tradition from Genesis to Centisimus Annus.* Vol. 2. Leominster, England: Gracewing/Folwer Wright Books, 1998.

Romero, Victor. "Proxies for Loyalty in Constitutional Immigration Law: Citizenship and Race after September 11." *DePaul Law Review* 52 (2003): 871–91.

Rommen, H. A. *The State in Catholic Thought: A Treatise in Political Philosophy.* St. Louis: B. Herder, 1945.

Rommen, Heinrich. *The Natural Law: A Study in Legal and Social History and Philosophy.* Translated by Thomas R. Hanley and Russell Hittinger. Indianapolis: Liberty Fund, 1998.

Roover, Raymond de. "The Concept of the Just Price and Economic Policy." *Journal of Economic History* 18 (1958): 418–34.

Ropke, Wilhelm. *The Social Crisis of Our Time.* New Brunswick: Transaction Press, 1992.

Rorty, Richard. *Contingency, Irony, and Solidarity.* Cambridge: Cambridge University Press, 1989.

Rousseau, Jean-Jacques. *On the Social Contract or Principles of Political Right.* Edited by Roger D. Masters, translated by Judith R. Masters. New York: St. Martins Press, 1978.

———. *The Social Contract and Discourses.* Translated by G. D. H. Cole. New York: E. P. Dutton, 1950.

Rowland, Tracey. *Culture and the Thomist Tradition.* New York: Routledge Press, 2003.

Sabine, George H. *A History of Political Theory.* New York: H. Holt, 1950.

Sandel, Michael. *Democracy's Discontent.* Cambridge: Harvard University Press, 1996.

Scaperlanda, Anthony E. "John Paul II's Vision of the Role of Multinational Enterprise Expansion in Building the Social Economy." *International Journal of Social Economics* (1998): 1764–75.

Scaperlanda, Michael. "Partial Membership: Aliens and the Constitutional Community." *Iowa Law Review* 81 (1996): 707–73.

———. "Producing Trousered Apes in Dwyer's Totalitarian State." Review of *Vouchers within Reason: A Child-Centered Approach to Education Reform,* by James G. Dwyer. *Texas Review of Law and Politics* 7 (2002): 175–221.

———. "Realism, Freedom, and the Integral Development of the Human Person: A Catholic View of Education." *Journal of Catholic Legal Studies* 44 (2005): 65–97.

———. "Who Is My Neighbor? An Essay on Immigrants, Welfare Reform, and the Constitution." *Connecticut Law Review* 29 (1997): 1587–1625.

Schindler, David. *Heart of the World, Center of the Church.* Grand Rapids, MI: Eerdmans, 1996.

———. "A Modernity, Postmodernity, and the Problem of Atheism." *Communio* 27 (1997): 563–67.

Schlossberg, Herbert. *Idols for Destruction: Christian Faith and Its Confrontation with American Society.* Nashville: Nelson, 1983.

Schuck, Peter H. "Rethinking Informed Consent." *Yale Law Journal* 103 (1994): 899–959.

———. "The Transformation of Immigration Law." *Columbia Law Review* 84 (1984): 1–90.

———. "When Exception Becomes the Rule: Regulatory Equity and the Formulation of Regulatory Policy through an Exceptions Process." *Duke Law Journal* 1984 (1984): 163–300.

Schwartz, Gary T. "The Myth of the Ford Pinto Case." *Rutgers Law Review* 43 (1991): 1013–68.

Schwartz, Rebecca J. "Public Gated Communities: The Rosemont, Illinois, Approach and Its Constitutional Implications." *Urban Law* 29 (1997): 123–43.

Scott, L. W. "Liability of Parents for Conduct of Their Child under Section 33.01 of the Texas Family Code: Defining the Requisite Standards of 'Culpability.'" *St. Mary's Law Journal* 20 (1988): 69–87.

Sebeok, Thomas A., and Robert Rosenthal. *The Clever Hans Phenomenon: Communication with Horses, Whales, Apes, and People.* New York: New York Academy of Sciences, 1981.

Second Vatican Ecumenical Council. *Dignitatis humanae.* 7 December 1965. http://www.vatican.va/archive/hist_councils/ii_vatican_council/documents/vat-ii_decl_19651207_dignitatis-humanae_en.html, 1965.

———. *Gaudium et spes.* 07 December 1965. http://www.vatican.va/archive/hist_councils/ii_vatican_council/documents/vat-ii_cons_19651207_gaudium-et-spes_en.html, 1965.

———. *Gaudium et spes.* In *Vatican Council II: The Conciliar and Post Conciliar Documents,* edited by Austin Flannery. Northport, NY: Costello Publishing Co., 1975.

———. [*Gaudium et spes*]"Constitutio pastoralis de ecclesia in mundo huius temporis, *Gaudium et spes,* 51 (die 7 m. decembris a. 1965)." *Acta Apostolicae Sedis* 58 (1966): 1025.

Sen, Amartya. "The Formulation of Rational Choice." *American Economic Review* 84 (1994): 385–90.

———. *On Ethics and Economics.* Oxford: Blackwell Publishers, Ltd., 1987.

———. "Our Culture, Their Culture." *New Republic* (1 April 1996): 27.

———. "Population: Delusion and Reality." *New York Review of Books* (22 September 1994): 62–71.

Shaffer, Thomas L. "How I Changed My Mind." *Journal of Law and Religion* 10 (1993/1994): 291–301.

———. "Human Nature and Moral Responsibility in Lawyer-Client Relationships." *American Journal of Jurisprudence* 40 (1995): 1–25.

———. "The Legal Ethics of Radical Individualism." *Texas Law Review* 65 (1987): 963–91.

———. "Should a Christian Lawyer Serve the Guilty?" *Georgia Law Review* 23 (1989): 1021–34.

Shaffer, Thomas L., and Robert F. Cochran, Jr. "Lawyers as Strangers and Friends: A Reply to Professor Sammons." *University of Arkansas Little Rock Law Journal* 18 (1995): 69–84.

Simon, William H. "Lawyer Advice and Client Autonomy: Mrs. Jones's Case." *Maryland Law Review* 50 (1991): 213–26.

Simon, Yves. *The Philosophy of Democratic Government.* Chicago: University of Chicago Press, 1951.

Simpson, A. W. B. "Innovation in Nineteenth Century Contract Law." *Law Quarterly Review* 91 (1975): 247–78.

Skillen, James W. "Toward a Contemporary Christian Democratic Politics in the U.S." In *Christianity and Democracy in Global Context,* edited by John Witte, Jr. Boulder, CO: Harper-Westview, 1993.

Slater, Thomas. *A Manual of Moral Theology for English-Speaking Countries.* Vol. 1. New York: Benziger Brothers, 1925.

Smith, Adam. *An Inquiry into the Nature and Causes of the Wealth of Nations.* 1776. Vol. 1. Edited by R. H. Campell and A. S. Skinner. Indianapolis: Liberty Classics, 1981.

———. *An Inquiry into the Nature and Causes of the Wealth of Nations.* 2d ed. N.p.: 1778.

Smith, Steven D. "The Restoration of Tolerance." *California Law Review* 73 (1990): 305–56.

Song, Robert. *Christianity and Liberal Society.* Oxford: Clarendon Press, 1997.

Soto, Domenicus. *De iustitia et iure libri decem.* Salamanca, 1556.

Stern-Gillet, Suzanne. *Aristotle's Philosophy of Friendship.* Albany: State University of New York Press, 1995.

Story, Joseph. *Commentaries on Equity Jurisprudence as Administered in England and America.* 14th ed. Vol. 1. Boston: Little, Brown, 1918.

———. *Equity Jurisprudence as Administered in England and America.* Vol. 1. Frederick, MD: Beard Books, 2000.

Strier, Franklin. "The Educated Jury: A Proposal for Complex Litigation." *DePaul Law Review* 47 (1997): 49–83.

Stuntz, William J. "Christian Legal Theory." *Harvard Law Review* 116 (2003): 1707–49.

Sunstein, Cass R. "Incommensurability and Valuation in Law." *Michigan Law Review* 92 (1994): 779–861.

Supreme Court of Tennessee. Board of Prof'l Responsibility Formal Opinion 96-F-140 (1996).

"Symposium: La Trinità-Esperienza di Dio (The Trinity: Experience of God)." *Nuova Umanità* 24 (2002): 127–390.

Tanner, Michael. *The End of Welfare: Fighting Poverty in the Civil Society.* Washington, DC: Cato Institute, 1996.

Teubner, Gunther. "Substantive and Reflexive Elements in Modern Law." *Law and Society Review* 17 (1983): 229, 254–55.

Thomas, Clarence. "Be Not Afraid." Lecture, Francis Boyer Lecture, American Enterprise Institute for Public Policy Research, Washington, D.C., 13 Feb. 2001. http://www.aei. org/boyer/thomas.htm.

Thomas à Kempis. *The Imitation of Christ.* 1530. Translated by Richard Whitford. N.p.: n.d.

Tocqueville, Alexis de. *Democracy in America.* Vol. 1. New York: A. A. Knopf, 1945.

———. *Democracy in America.* Edited by J. P. Meyer, translated by George Lawrence. Garden City: Anchor Books, Doubleday, 1969.

———. *Democracy in America.* Vol. 1. New York: A. A. Knopf, 1991.

———. *Democracy in America.* Edited and translated by Harvey C. Mansfield and Delba Winthrop. Chicago: University of Chicago Press, 2000.

Trebilcock, Michael. *The Limits of Freedom of Contract.* Cambridge: Harvard University Press, 1993.

Tushnet, Mark. "Immigration Policy in Liberal Political Theory." In *Justice in Immigration,* edited by Warren A. Schwartz. Cambridge: Cambridge University Press, 1995.

Twerski, Aaron D. "From Risk-Utility to Consumer Expectation: Enhancing the Role of Judicial Screening in Product Liability Litigation." *Hofstra Law Review* 11 (1983): 861–935.

Unger, Roberto M. *Knowledge and Politics.* New York: Free Press, 1975.

United States Catholic Conference. *Sharing Catholic Social Teaching: Challenges and Directions.* Washington, DC: United States Catholic Conference, 1998.

United States Department of Homeland Security. *Immigration Information.* "2001 Statistical Yearbook of the Immigration and Naturalization Service."

Unsecular America: Essays by Paul Johnson. Edited by Richard John Neuhaus. Grand Rapids, MI: Eerdmans, 1996.

"U.S. Bishops' Pastoral Letter on Catholic Social Teaching and the U.S. Economy." *Origins* 14, no. 22/23 (1984).

Vandal, Frank J., and Joshua F. Vandal. "A Call for an Accurate Restatement (Third) of Torts: Design Defect." *University of Memphis Law Review* 33 (2003): 909–44.

Varacalli, Joseph A. *Bright Promise, Failed Community: Catholics and the American Public Order.* Lanham, MD: Lexington Books, 2000.

Vasoli, Robert H. *What God Has Joined Together: The Annulment Crisis in American Catholicism.* New York: Oxford University Press, 1998.

Vatican Council II. *The Conciliar and Post Conciliar Documents.* Edited by Austin Flannery. North Port, NY: Costello, 1975.

Vedder, Richard, and Lowell E. Gallaway. *Out of Work: Unemployment and Government in Twentieth-Century America.* New York: Holmes and Meier, 1993.

Verstraeten, Johann. "Solidarity and Subsidiarity." In *Principles of Catholic Teaching,* edited by David A. Boileau. Milwaukee, WI: Marquette University Press, 1998.

Villey, Michel. *Le droit et les droits de l'homme.* Paris: Presses Universitaires de France, 1983.

———. *La formation de la pensee juridique moderne.* 4th ed. Paris: Montchrestien, 1975.

Vischer, Robert K. "Subsidiarity as a Principle of Governance: Beyond Devolution." *Indiana Law Review* 35 (2001): 103–42.

Wade, John W. "On the Nature of Strict Tort Liability for Products." *Mississippi Law Journal* 44 (1973): 825–51.

Waite, Linda J., and Maggie Gallagher. *The Case for Marriage: Why Married People Are Happier, Healthier, and Better Off Financially.* New York: Doubleday, 2000.

Waldron, Jeremy. *Liberal Rights.* Cambridge: Cambridge University Press, 1993.

Wallerstein, Judith S., Julia M. Lewis, and Sandra Blakeslee. *The Unexpected Legacy of Divorce: A 25 Year Landmark Study.* New York: Hyperion, 2000.

Walzer, Michael. *Spheres of Justice: A Defense of Pluralism and Equality.* New York: Basic Books, 1983.

Washington, George. "Farewell Address (Sept. 17, 1796)." In *The Writings of George Washington from the Original Manuscript Sources* (1745–1789), vol. 35, edited by John C. Fitzpatrick. Washington, D.C.: Government Printing Office, 1940.

Wasserstrom, Richard. "Roles and Morality." In *The Good Lawyer: Lawyers' Roles and Lawyers' Ethics,* edited by David Luban. Totowa, NJ: Rowman and Allanheld, 1983.

Webb, Sidney, and Beatrice Webb. *The History of Trade Unionism.* Revised Edition, Extended to 1920. New York: Longmans Green, 1935.

Weber, Max. *The Protestant Ethic and the Spirit of Capitalism.* Translated by Talcott Parsons. London: Unwin, 1948.

Weigel, George. *The Cube and the Cathedral: Europe, America, and Politics without God.* New York: Basic Books, 2005.

———. *Witness to Hope.* New York: Harper Collins, 1999.

Weik, Jesse. *Herndon's Life of Lincoln: The History and Personal Recollections of Abraham Lincoln, as Originally Written by William F. Herndon and Jesse W. Weik.* New York: DeCapo Press, 1983.

Weinreb, Lloyd L. *Natural Law and Justice.* Cambridge: Harvard University Press, 1987.

Weisberg, Richard. *The Failure of the World.* New Haven: Yale University Press, 1984.

Wells, Michael. "Scientific Policymaking and the Torts Revolution: The Revenge of the Ordinary Observer." *Georgia Law Review* 26 (1992): 725–56.

West, Thomas. "Vindicating John Locke: How a Seventeenth Century Liberal Was Really a Social Conservative." *Witherspoon Lecture for the Family Research Council.* 2001. http://www.frc.org/get.cfm?i=WT01F1.

White, James B. *Justice as Translation.* Chicago: University of Chicago Press, 1990.

———. *The Legal Imagination.* Boston: Little, Brown, 1973.

White, Welsh S. "Defendants Who Elect Execution." *University of Pittsburgh Law Review* 48 (1987): 853–78.

Williams, Joan. *Unbending Gender: Why Family and Work Conflict and What to Do about It.* Oxford: Oxford University Press, 2001.

Williams, Thomas, L.C. "Capital Punishment and the Just Society." *Catholic Dossier* (Sept.–Oct. 1998): 30.

Wilson, James. *The Works of James Wilson.* Edited by Robert G. McCloskey. 2 vols. Cambridge: Belknap Press of Harvard University Press, 1967.

Wilson, R. J. *In Quest of Community: Social Philosophy in the United States 1860–1920.* New York: John Wiley and Sons, 1968.

Wilson, Robin F. "Children at Risk: The Sexual Exploitation of Female Children after Divorce." *Cornell Law Review* 86 (2001): 251–327.

Witte, John, Jr. "Between Sanctity and Dignity: Human Dignity in Protestant Perspective." In *In Defense of Human Dignity: Essays for Our Times,* edited by Robert P. Kraynak and Glenn Tinder. Notre Dame, IN: University of Notre Dame Press, 2003.

———. *From Sacrament to Contract: Marriage, Religion and Law in the Western Tradition.* Louisville, KY: Westminster/John Knox Press, 1997.

Wojtyla, Karol. *The Acting Person.* Translated by Anna-Teresa Tymieniecka. N.p.: Kluwer Academic Publishers Group, 1979.

———. *The Acting Person.* Dordrecht, Holland: D. Reidel, 1979.

———. "Intervention of September 25, 1964." In *Acta synodalia Concilii Vaticani II, Period III,* vol. 2.

———. *Love and Responsibility.* Translated by H. T. Willetts. Fort Collins, CO: Ignatius Press, 1981.

———. *Person and Community: Selected Essays.* Edited by Theresa Sandok, O.S.M. New York: P. Lang, 1993.

———. "Vatican Council II: Light for the Church and for the Modern World." *Jubilaeum A.D. 2000.* http://www.vatican.va/jubilee_2000/magazine/documents/ju_mag_01051997_p-21_en.html.

Wolfe, Alan. *One Nation, After All.* New York: Viking Penguin, 1998.

Wolfe, Christopher. *Liberalism at the Crossroads.* Edited by Alan Wolfe and Russell Hittinger. Lanham, MD: Rowman and Littlefield, 1994.

———. "The Marriage of Your Choice." *First Things* 50 (February 1995): 37–41.

———. "Natural Law and Judicial Review." In *Natural Law and Contemporary Public Policy,* edited by David Forte. Washington, DC: Georgetown University Press, 1998.

———. *Natural Law Liberalism.* Cambridge: Cambridge University Press, 2006.

———. "Subsidiarity: The 'Other' Ground for Limited Government." In *Liberalism, and Communitarianism: Essays on the Catholic Intellectual Tradition and the Moral Foundations of Democracy,* edited by Kenneth L. Grasso, Gerard V. Bradley, and Robert P. Hunt. Lanham, MD: Rowman and Littlefield, 1995.

———. "Tocqueville and the Religious Revival." *This World* 1 (Winter/Spring 1982): 85–96.

Woodson, Robert L., Sr. *One Nation, Two Cultures.* New York: Random House Vintage Books, 2001.

Wright, Robert R., and Morton Gitelman. *Land Use: Cases and Materials.* 4th ed. Eagan, MN: West, 1991.

Yorio, Edward. "A Defense of Equitable Defenses." *Ohio State Law Journal* 51 (1990): 1201–41.

Zagzebski, Linda T. *Virtues of the Mind: An Inquiry into the Nature of Virtue and the Ethical Foundations of Knowledge.* Cambridge: Cambridge University Press, 1996.

Zamagni, Stefano. "On the Foundation and Meaning of the 'Economy of Communion Experience.'" In *Economy of Communion toward a Multi-Dimensional Economic Culture,* translated by Lorna Gold. New York: New City Press, 2002.

Zimmerman, Michael E. *Heidegger's Confrontation with Modernity: Technology, Politics, Art.* Bloomington: Indiana University Press, 1990.

CONTRIBUTORS

Lorenzo Albacete

Monsignor Albacete is the Responsible in North America of the Fraternity of Communion and Liberation. He has been visiting professor at St. Joseph's Seminary in New York, president of the Pontifical Catholic University of Puerto Rico, and professor of the John Paul II Institute for Studies on Marriage and Family. His most recent book is *God at the Ritz* (Crossroads, 2002).

Robert John Araujo, S.J.

Robert John Araujo, S.J., is professor of ethics and international relations at the Pontifical Gregorian University and the Robert Bellarmine University Professor of Public and International Law at Gonzaga University. He also serves as an adviser to the Holy See. He is coauthor of a book series on papal diplomacy and has published articles that address issues dealing with public international law, constitutional law, and law and religion.

Benedict M. Ashley, O.P.

Benedict M. Ashley, O.P., is a priest of the Dominican Order, Chicago Province. He is a graduate of the University of Chicago and the University of Notre Dame and has doctorates in philosophy and political science, and the postdoctoral degree of master of sacred theology conferred by an international committee of the Order of Preachers. He was formerly president of Aquinas Institute of Theology, St. Louis; professor of theology at the Institute of Religion and Human Development, Houston, Texas; professor of theology at the Pontifical John Paul II Institute for Studies on Marriage and Family, Washington, D.C.; and visiting lecturer in humanities at the University of Chicago (1999). He has been honored with the medal Pro Ecclesia et Pontifice conferred by John Paul II and the Thomas Linacre Award from the National Federation of Catholic Physicians' Guilds.

Teresa Stanton Collett

Teresa Stanton Collett, professor of law at the University of St. Thomas School of Law (Minnesota), graduated with honors from the University of Oklahoma College of Law. She has also held a faculty appointment at South Texas College of Law and visiting faculty appointments at University of Oklahoma College of Law, the University of Texas School of Law, the University of Houston Law Center, Washington University (St. Louis) School of Law, and Notre Dame Law School. Professor Collett is a nationally prominent speaker and scholar on issues related to the integration of faith into professional life, and she has been active in attempts to rebuild the Culture of Life and protect the institutions of marriage and family. She is an elected member of the American Law Institute and has testified before committees of the United States House of Representatives and before legislative committees in six states. Professor Collett has published over forty legal articles and is the coauthor of a law casebook on professional responsibility.

John J. Coughlin, O.F.M.

Rev. John J. Coughlin, O.F.M., has been a Franciscan priest since 1983 and currently serves as professor of law, University of Notre Dame. He holds a B.A., Niagara University; M.A., Columbia University; Th.M., Princeton Seminary; J.D., Harvard Law School; J.C.L., J.C.D., Gregorian University, Rome. Previously, he has taught at St. Bonaventure University, St. Joseph's Seminary of the Archdiocese of New York, and St. John's University School of Law.

Avery Cardinal Dulles, S.J.

Avery Cardinal Dulles, S.J., is currently the Laurence J. McGinley Professor of Religion and Society at Fordham University, a position he has held since 1988. He was created a cardinal of the Catholic Church in Rome on February 21, 2001, by Pope John Paul II, the first American-born theologian who was not a bishop to receive this honor. Cardinal Dulles served on the faculty of Woodstock College from 1960 to 1974 and that of the Catholic University of America from 1974 to 1988. He has been a visiting professor at several universities, including the Gregorian University (Rome), Weston School of Theology, Princeton Theological Seminary, Boston College, Campion Hall (Oxford University), the University of Notre Dame, the Catholic University at Leuven, and Yale University. The author of more than 750 articles on theological topics, Cardinal Dulles has published twenty-two books, including *The Splendor of Faith: The Theological Vision of Pope John Paul II* (1999; revised in 2003 for the twenty-fifth anniversary of the papal election), *The New*

World of Faith (2000), *Newman* (2002). The fiftieth anniversary edition of his book *A Testimonial to Grace,* the account of his conversion to Catholicism, was republished in 1996 by the original publishers, Sheed and Ward, with an afterword containing his reflections on the fifty years since he became a Catholic.

Richard W. Garnett

Richard W. Garnett is the Lilly Endowment Associate Professor of Law at Notre Dame Law School, where he teaches and writes about criminal law, constitutional law, capital punishment, religious freedom, and the freedom of speech. He received his B.A. in philosophy summa cum laude from Duke University in 1990, and his J.D. from Yale Law School in 1995. At Yale, he served as senior editor of the *Yale Law Journal* and as editor of the *Yale Journal of Law and the Humanities.* Professor Garnett also spent a year in the Jesuit Volunteer Corps, working on juvenile justice and prison reform issues in San Francisco, California. Before coming to Notre Dame, he served as law clerk to Chief Justice Rehnquist during October Term 1996 and to then Chief Judge Richard S. Arnold of the United States Court of Appeals for the Eighth Circuit. He practiced law at the Washington, D.C., law firm of Miller, Cassidy, Larroca and Lewin, specializing in criminal defense, religious liberty, and education reform matters. He lives in South Bend, Indiana, with his wife, Professor Nicole Stelle Garnett, and three children, Margaret, Thomas, and Elizabeth.

Robert P. George

Robert P. George is McCormick professor of jurisprudence and director of the James Madison Program in American Ideals and Institutions at Princeton University. In addition, he is a member of the President's Council on Bioethics. He has served as a presidential appointee to the United States Commission on Civil Rights (1993–98), and a judicial fellow at the Supreme Court of the United States (1989–90), where he received the Justice Tom C. Clark Award. A graduate of Swarthmore College, where he was elected to Phi Beta Kappa, Professor George holds an M.T.S. and a J.D. from Harvard University, and a D. Phil. in philosophy of law from Oxford University, as well as several honorary doctorates. He is the author of *Making Men Moral: Civil Liberties and Public Morality* (Oxford University Press), *In Defense of Natural Law* (Oxford University Press), and *The Clash of Orthodoxies: Law, Morality, and Religion in Crisis* (ISI Books). He is a member of the Council on Foreign Relations. In 2005, he received a Bradley Prize for Intellectual and Civic Achievement and the Philip Merrill Award for Outstanding Contributions to the Liberal Arts of the American Council of Trustees and Alumni.

Mary Ann Glendon

Mary Ann Glendon is the Learned Hand Professor of Law at Harvard University and president of the Pontifical Academy of Social Sciences. She has authored several books and articles on comparative law and human rights, including *A World Made New: Eleanor Roosevelt and the Universal Declaration of Human Rights,* which was described by the *New York Times* reviewer as the definitive study of the framing of the UDHR. In 2005, she was awarded the National Humanities Medal by President George W. Bush.

James Gordley

James Gordley received a B.A degree (1967) and an M.B.A degree (1968) from the University of Chicago. He received a J.D. degree (1970) from Harvard Law School. He became an acting professor at the School of Law of the University of California at Berkeley in 1978, a full professor in 1981, and Shannon Cecil Turner Professor of Jurisprudence in 1996. He has been a Guggenheim fellow, a Fulbright fellow, a Senior NATO fellow, a fellow of the Deutscheforschungsgemeinschaft, a fellow of the Medieval Institute of Canon Law, and an Ezra Ripley Thayer fellow at Harvard Law School. He is Co-Editor in Chief of the *American Journal of Comparative Law.* He has been elected a fellow of the American Academy of Arts and Sciences and a membre titulaire of the Académie internationale du droit comparé. He has been a visiting professor at the Universities of Trent, Regensburg, Fribourg, Milan, and Munich, and a visiting scholar at the Max Planck Institut für ausländisches und internationales Privatrecht, the European University Institute in Fiesole, and the University of Cologne. His publications include *An Introduction to the Comparative Study of Private Law* (2006) (with Arthur von Mehren), *Foundations of Private Law* (2006), *The Enforceability of Promises in European Contract Law* (2001), and *The Philosophical Origins of Modern Contract Doctrine* (1991).

Thomas C. Kohler

Thomas C. Kohler is concurrent professor of law and philosophy at Boston College. An internationally recognized authority in the areas of comparative and domestic labor, employment, and employment discrimination law, he has published and lectured widely on these themes in the United States, Europe, and Asia. A member of the American Law Institute, he also serves on the Advisory Board of the *Restatement of European Labour Law* and is a member of the Executive Board of the International Society for Labor and Social Security Law. He has been a Bradley fellow, a Fulbright fellow, and a German-Marshall Fund fellow. Professor Kohler has held visiting appointments at the Graduate School of Business, Columbia University; the Law Faculty of the University of Frankfurt (Germany); and the University of Texas School of Law.

Kevin P. Lee

Kevin P. Lee is associate professor of law at Campbell University, Norman A. Wiggins School of Law. His publications include "Insights and Hindsights from Seeking a Global Ethic," in *Natural Law and the Possibility of a Global Ethics,* ed. Mark J. Cherry (Kluwer Publishers, 2003), coauthored with Phillip Thompson, and "Inherit the Myth: How William Jennings Bryan's Struggle with Social Darwinism and Legal Formalism Demythologize the Scopes Monkey Trial," *Capital University Law Review* 33 (2004): 347–82. He is a Ph.D. candidate in the field of social and political ethics at the Divinity School of the University of Chicago.

Randy Lee

Randy Lee is a professor at Widener University School of Law's Harrisburg campus, where he has been recognized by both students and alumni with outstanding teaching awards. He advocates for the rights of people who are deaf or hard of hearing and is a former chair of the Professional Responsibility Section of the Association of American Law Schools. He has published articles on torts, constitutional law, ethics, legal writing, law and literature, and the intersection of law and religion.

Vincent D. Rougeau

Professor Vincent D. Rougeau has been a member of the law faculty at Notre Dame since 1998. He teaches courses in contract and real estate law, as well as a seminar on law, public policy, and Catholic social teaching. Professor Rougeau's most recent writing and research have considered how American understandings of the free market and the role of the individual in society diverge from Catholic social teaching and the philosophical and theological ideas that inform it, creating a legal and political culture in the United States that tends to promote individual autonomy and material well-being over community cohesion. Professor Rougeau is currently working on a book for Oxford University Press entitled *Christians in the American Empire: Faith and Citizenship in the New World Order,* which will examine the effects of this phenomenon in various areas of American law and will consider how this culture might affect Christian participation in the ongoing American economic and political dominance of world affairs.

Michael A. Scaperlanda

Michael Scaperlanda is the Gene and Elaine Edwards Family Chair in Law at the University of Oklahoma College of Law, where he also serves as associate dean for research. In addition to OU, where he has taught since 1989, Scaperlanda has been a visiting professor at the University of Texas, an adjunct professor at the University of Oklahoma Department of Political Science, and an affiliate faculty member in the University of Oklahoma's Religious Studies Program. He is the author of numerous scholarly articles and two books: *The Journey: A Guide for the Modern Pilgrim* (with María Ruiz Scaperlanda) and *Immigration and the Constitution* (coedited with Gabriel Chin and Victor Romero). Scaperlanda also frequently speaks to and writes articles for the general public on immigration issues, the role of the judiciary in shaping our constitutional community, and the place of religion in the public square. Before joining the OU faculty, he practiced law with Hughes and Luce and with Hogan and Hartson. He has been married to María Ruiz Scaperlanda since 1981. They have four children.

Russell Shaw

Russell Shaw, a writer and journalist in Washington, D.C., is the author or co-author of eighteen books and has published numerous articles, reviews, and columns. Shaw was information director of the Catholic bishops' conference of the United States from 1969 to 1987 and of the Knights of Columbus from 1987 to 1997. He is a contributing editor of *Crisis* magazine and *Our Sunday Visitor* newspaper, and is a lecturer at the Pontifical University of the Holy Cross, Rome. He is serving his third term as a consultor of the Pontifical Council for Social Communications. Shaw is married and has five children and ten grandchildren.

Amelia J. Uelmen

Amelia J. Uelmen is the director of the Institute on Religion, Law and Lawyer's Work at Fordham University School of Law, where she teaches a seminar on Catholic Social Thought and the Law. She is a member of the editorial board of the *Journal of Law and Religion* and has authored several articles on how religious values and Catholic spirituality may be integrated into various areas of legal practice. Throughout her career she has worked closely with the Focolare Movement in planning interfaith conferences and programs. She is a graduate of Georgetown University's College and Law School.

Robert K. Vischer

Robert K. Vischer is associate professor at the University of St. Thomas School of Law in Minneapolis. He received his B.A. degree, summa cum laude, from the University of New Orleans, and his J.D., cum laude, from Harvard, where he was an editor of the *Harvard Law Review*. His scholarship focuses on the intersection of law, religion, and public policy, with a particular emphasis on the integration of faith with professional identity.

Christopher Wolfe

Christopher Wolfe is professor of political science at Marquette University, president of the American Public Philosophy Institute, and co-director of the Ralph McInerny Center for Thomistic Studies. He received his B.A. from the University of Notre Dame in 1971 and his Ph.D. from Boston College in 1978. He is the author of *The Rise of Modern Judicial Review* (1986), *Judicial Activism* (1990), *How To Read the Constitution* (1996), and *Natural Law Liberalism* (2006).

INDEX

Abel, 342

Abortion, 89, 92, 109–10, 116, 120, 124, 126, 132, 276n7, 284n49, 327, 333–34, 337, 339–40, 347; live-birth, 115; partial-birth, 105, 112–14, 116; rights, 114–15, 327

Abraham, 30n70

Abrams v. U.S., 147n23

Abuse of power, 270

Ackerman, Bruce, 294n4, 295–96, 298–301, 305, 307

Acton, John, 69, 73, 82

Acts, Book of, 41n2

Adam, 42n3, 46, 341–42

Adams, John, 3, 83

Adler, Mortimer, 65n18, 69

Adultery, 48, 277n10, 279, 345

Affirmative action, 121n73, 183

Age Discrimination in Employment Act (1967), 183

Aggravated felonies, 293, 313–16

Agnosticism, 81, 299

Albacete, Lorenzo, 9

Aleinikoff, Thomas Alexander, 312n79

Alexander, Larry, 305n55

Alienation, 48, 285n53, 286; alienated, 10, 229; alienating, 10, 229

Alito, Samuel A., 339–40

Allegemeinen Deutschen Arbeiterverein, 167

Allegretti, Joseph, 343n23

Alston, Philip, 320n9, 325, 326n19

Alternative design requirement. *See* Products liability

Althouse, Ann, 261

Ambrosetti, Giovanni, 199n14

American Bar Association, 340

American Civil Liberties Union, 260–62

American Enterprise Institute, 39

American experiment, 80, 82

American Federation of Labor, 166–67

American Home Improvement Co. v. MacIver, 200n19

American life: privatization of, 208; modern, 88

American Revolution, 279

Americans with Disabilities Act, 183

Ancien regime, 149

Anscombe, G. E. M., 32n85

Anselm, 61n12

Anthropological assumptions, 86, 266, 271–73; autonomy centered, 271, 308n63; flawed, 87; theologically informed, 94

Anthropology, 184, 190, 207, 330: adequate, 43–48, 50; *Casey*-based and autonomy-centered, 271–72; Catholic, xii, 11, 174n19, 257; Christian, xi, 10, 86, 234, 236; derivative of Christology, 42–43; human experience as basis, 43–44; Jewish, 174n19; of John Paul II, 40, 42; liberal, 169–70; metaphysical, 43; moral, 86, 256–57, 270; nuptial meaning of the body as basis, 46; philosophical, 42–43; psychological, 42; secular, 330; sociological, 42; theological, 42–43, 48; traditional, 305n56; Trinitarian, 235

Anti-Drug Abuse Act (1988), 313

Anti-Terrorism and Effective Death Penalty Act, 314

Apartheid, 156, 325

Apel, Karl Otto, 20n33

Apostolic Constitution on Higher Education, 17

Aquinas, Thomas, 29–32, 55–57, 61n12, 63–64, 80, 118, 135–36, 141, 152, 160n17, 185, 191, 193, 196–203, 283–84, 287–88

Araujo, Robert John, 11, 121

Aristocracy, 149, 196

Aristotle, 2, 29, 56n7, 57n8, 64n17, 106–7, 110,

Recovering Self-Evident Truths: Catholic Perspectives on American Law was designed and typeset in Minion by Kachergis Book Design of Pittsboro, North Carolina. It was printed on 60-pound EB Natural and bound by Edwards Brothers of Lillington, North Carolina.